A

HISTORY OF THE HUGUENOTS.

BY

(W.) CARLOS MARTYN,

AUTHOR OF "THE LIFE AND TIMES OF JOHN MILTON," AND "THE LIFE AND TIMES OF MARTIN LUTHER."

AMERICAN TRACT SOCIETY,
150 NASSAU-STREET, NEW YORK.

CONTENTS.

CHAPTER I.

CHAPTER II.

CHAPTER III.

CHAPTER IV.

CHAPTER V.

CHAPTER VI.

CHAPTER VII.

CHAPTER VIII.

CHAPTER IX.

CHAPTER X.

CHAPTER XI.

CHAPTER XII.

CHAPTER XIII.

CHAPTER XIV.

CHAPTER XV.

CHAPTER XVI.

CHAPTER XVII.

CHAPTER XVIII.

CHAPTER XIX.

CHAPTER XX.

CHAPTER XXI.

CHAPTER XXII.

CHAPTER XXIII.

CHAPTER XXIV.

CHAPTER XXV.

CHAPTER XXVI.

CHAPTER XXVII.

CHAPTER XXVIII.

CHAPTER XXIX.

CHAPTER XXX.

CHAPTER XXXI.

CHAPTER XXXII.

CHAPTER XXXIII.

CHAPTER XXXIV.

CHAPTER XXXV.

CHAPTER XXXVI.

PREFACE.

THERE is no page of history which is at once so fascinating in the dramatic interest of its scenes, and so momentous as that which records the story of the Huguenots—none more worthy of the careful study of thoughtful men. Whether judged by its motive, its influence, or its episodes, it is equally grand. Sublimer than any epic, it depicts a struggle to renovate the individual, the church, and society at large.

Isolated phases of the history of the Huguenots have been often and vividly portrayed in our English letters: poets have celebrated many thrilling episodes; romancists have given full play to the imagination; biographers have recited the lives of many illustrious men; historians have dwelt upon numerous stirring scenes: but these are the mosaics of history—broken voices, telling half the tale.

Nearly all of the English histories which bear upon this subject, deal with particular periods—with the epoch of the Vaudois, with the age of Calvin, with the era of Coligny, with the times of Henri Quatre, and with collateral reformatory movements. This volume covers five of the most eventful centuries since Christ: it traces the story up through the ages from the first murmur of dissent from Rome to the revocation of the edict of Nantes; and the sketch of the Vaudois, those early but much neglected teachers, is especially full. The story of the sixteenth century, distinctively the era of the Reformation, is not as minute in this volume as in some others, but an effort has been made to give an authoritative and succinct detail of all essential incidents.

The materials for the compilation of such a work are vast, but ill-digested; to collect and glean them has been no slight task. Most of the standard authorities have been consulted, and in addition to these, a thousand pages of subsidiary matter, personal narratives, diaries, memoirs, from the graphic pens of contemporaneous actors in the drama, have been liberally used. It is not necessary to recapitulate their titles, these will be found scattered through the body of the book; and numerous notes have been added, where they seemed likely to enhance the interest or to elucidate the text.

The series of which this volume is one has not been written for the instruction of mere scholars; no effort is made to pour light culled from pedantic lore upon mooted and nice points of history; they are plain tales of momentous eras. They are sketched for the edification of the masses; written with attempted care and accuracy, but compiled from every available and authoritative source, and with no especial claim to originality. Whatever seemed vivid and important and interesting, where-ever it rested, has been seized and grouped into this picture of "times that tried men's souls."

Of course a volume which covers so broad a field must be, in some sense, a summary of events, and the problem which the historian has to solve is this: How shall an epitome be made graphic, be vivified, be made to speak—to tell its own story? How shall this summary be made to reflect an accurate likeness of the past, and appear not to be a summary? "The reproduction of contemporary documents," remarks a writer whose pages have become classic, "is not the only business of the historian. He must do more than exhume from the sepulchre in which they are sleeping, the relics of men and things of times past, that he may exhibit them in the light of day. Men value highly such a work, and those who perform it, for it is a necessary one; yet it is not sufficient. Dry bones do not faithfully represent the men of other days. They did not live as skeletons, but as beings full of life and activity. The historian is not simply a resurrectionist; he needs—strange but necessary ambition—a power that can restore the dead to life.

"When a historian comes across a speech of one of the actors in the great drama of human affairs, he ought to lay hold of it as a pearl; he should weave it into his tapestry in order to relieve the duller colors, and give more solidity and brilliancy. Whether the speech be met with in the writings of the actor himself, or in those of the chroniclers, is a matter of no importance; he should take it wherever he finds it. The history which exhibits men thinking, feeling, and acting as they did in their lifetime, is of far higher value than those purely intellectual compositions in which the actors are deprived of speech and even of life."

It is a favorite sophism of the Romanist philosophers, that Protestantism is a mushroom growth—an upstart of yesterday, without antiquity or patristical authority. But epigrammatic sneers do not overthrow plain historic facts. The lineage of Christian dissent from the tenets of the papacy is as venerable and as well ascertained as that of the Roman hierarchy. This antique dissent is essentially that form of belief which is now denominated Protestantism.

"Nothing," says Brook, "has so much obstructed the progress of Christianity in the world as the absurd and selfish doctrines, the superstitious and slavish practices, which have been blended with it by the wicked wit of man. As the religion of Jesus Christ was for many centuries almost buried under so great a mass of rubbish that it could scarcely be distinguished from the foulest paganism; so to free Christianity from these heterogeneous mixtures, and to fix it on its only foundation—faith in Christ—unclouded and unencumbered by human appendages, is the noblest work of man, and the greatest benefit to society."

This was the effort of the Huguenots. They found the Bible silent, covered with the dust of ancient libraries, in some places secured by an iron chain—a sad image of the interdict under which it was placed in the Christian world. The Reformation was an enfranchisement; these words of Christ were its motto: "THE TRUTH SHALL MAKE YOU FREE."

One of the chief lessons of the history of the Huguenots, is the sinfulness and the uselessness of persecution for religious opinion. It inculcates with persuasive eloquence the sacredness of conscience; it is at once an inspiration and an admonition; descanting upon the virtuous actions of the heroes of the past who fought the "good fight" for God and liberty, it repeats the scriptural command, "Go thou and do likewise;" depicting the vicious diplomacy of the Vatican, whose motto was then, as it is now, "*The end justifies the means,*" and that other twin maxim, that "*no faith is to be kept with heretics,*" it warns the present and the future to shun the vices of Babylonish Rome; as Seneca has hymned it:

> "Consulere patriæ; parcere afflictis; ferâ
> Cæde abstinere; tempus atque iræ dare;
> Orbi quietem; sæculo pacem suo:
> Hæc summa virtus; petitur hâc cœlum viâ."

Liberty of thought, liberty of faith, liberty of worship—this was the aspiration of the Huguenots. It is singular what an inevitable tendency there was in the movement towards republicanism—as if the democracy of Christianity necessitated the democracy of politics. But the Christ they taught was not simply the apostle of political liberty. "The greatest and most dangerous of despotisms," says D'Aubigné, "is that beneath which the depraved inclination of human nature, the deadly influence of the world, sin, miserably subjects the human conscience. In order to become free outwardly, men must first succeed in being free inwardly. In the human heart there is a vast country to be delivered from slavery—abysses which man cannot cross alone, heights which he cannot climb unaided, fortresses he cannot take, armies he cannot put to flight. In order to conquer in this moral battle, man must unite with One stronger than himself—the Son of God."

THE HUGUENOTS.

CHAPTER I.

THE VAUDOIS.

THE venerable muse of history recites many lessons which are full of tears, but upon no occasion does her voice sink into deeper pathos than when she relates the story of French Protestantism. From its inception in the grey dawn of the Christian era, down through the dismal centuries to the crowning disaster of the revocation of the edict of Nantes, it is one prolonged tragedy. The night of persecution is only illuminated by the marvellous constancy, the patient meekness, the Christian heroism, and the deep devotion of these earliest Protestants, who were called the VAUDOIS at the outset, and afterwards the HUGUENOTS.

God seems to have designed their moving story to be the convincing proof not only of the vitality of Christianity, but also of the woful cost at which it has been planted and preserved. Such a consideration adds new grandeur to a chapter of history which is indeed intrinsically momentous, and makes it still more worthy of the attentive study of thoughtful minds.

History attests that the sixteenth century was the epoch of the Reformation. But revolutions are not made—they grow. "First the blade, then the ear, then the full corn in the ear."* The Reformation had its forerunner in the wilderness—its John the Baptist. It is not an isolated fact, a picture standing out upon the historic canvas without a background. There were preceding intellectual insurrections, which, however unhappy in their separate denouement, yet led inevitably to that triumphant movement which finally, by the aid of Faust's type and Luther's luminous eloquence, enfranchised Christendom.

Anterior to Luther, anterior to that Bradwardine who, in the cloister of the Oxford University, taught Wickliffe ethics,† apostles were found who held tenaciously, and who zealously inculcated, both by their precepts and by their blameless lives, the essential tenets of the Reformation. And though the feudal system, which banished uniformity of laws and customs, and made each petty lord a despot in his own pocket-handkerchief territory, the obstacles to free intercourse between the nations, the prevailing ignorance, the absence of those mighty magicians, steam and the printing-press, which have conjured modern civilization into existence, and above all, the fanaticism of a priestly oligarchy, united their powerful hands to throttle the infant reform of these early teachers, we ought not

* St. Mark 4:28.

† D'Aubigné's Hist. of Ref. in Eng., p. 84.

for these reasons to withhold our grateful recognition of their faithful service and martyrdom; nor ought we to remain in ignorance of the momentous influence which these voices, raised in the dim twilight of Christianity, exerted upon mediæval life and thought, long before Europe was animated by a murmur from the grave of Wickliffe, from the ashes of Huss, or from the vigils of Calvin.

In the fourth century,* after enduring a persecution of remorseless severity with that patient, unfaltering heroism which is one of its most marked characteristics, Christianity, in the person of that Constantine who fought under the "flaming cross" which his heated imagination had descried in the heavens beneath the sun, with the inscription, "*In hoc signo vinces*"—By this sign thou shalt conquer †—ascended the Roman throne, and thenceforward, covered by the imperial purple, secured protection and controlled the government; so that the successive bishops of that feeble church which St. Paul had planted under the shadow of the throne of the Cæsars, gradually arrogated to themselves the supreme authority both in spiritual and in temporal affairs. Under Constantine, and indeed so late as Charlemagne, these bishops or popes were elected by the priests, nobles, and people of Rome, and this election could be voided by the veto of the emperor.‡ But

* Gibbon's Decline and Fall of the Roman Empire, chap. XX. Mosheim's Eccl. Hist., (Murdock's translation,) etc.

† Eusebius' "Vita Constantini," Lib. L., chap. XXVIII. Waddington's Hist. of the Chh., Pt. II., p. 82. Gibbon, chap. XX.

‡ Waddington's Hist. of the Chh., p. 205.

the death of Charlemagne was the signal for the most determined and unscrupulous effort on the part of the Roman bishops, not only to free themselves from the imperial trammels by securing the independence of papal election, but also to usurp dominion over the Western empire, and to subdue to unquestioning vassalage the entire ecclesiastical and lay bodies.* Unhappily this utter departure from the primitive simplicity and humility was acquiesced in very generally, until, under Hildebrand in the eleventh century, the stupendous structure of the papal despotism gloomed upon the misty horizon, awful and irresistible.

Then for five centuries the most atrocious vices, the most unchecked wickedness, the most unbridled sacerdotal ambition, and the most meaningless ceremonies corrupted and disgraced religion. It was the *saturnalia* of the church. Nominal Christianity ruled Europe and some portions of the African territory which fringed the Mediterranean sea, but vital piety lay torpid; *stat nominis umbrâ.* A priest-caste anchored itself in the prejudices and superstitions of the people; an oligarchy was built up, whose right hand was usurped authority linked with spiritual pride, and whose left hand was dogmatism and bigotry fiercer than the pagan.

Then a few true hearts revolted;† they yearned to reinaugurate the primitive practice of apostolic days, and this was the first dissent. But from the

* Waddington's Ch. Hist., Pt. III., p. 205.

† Bossuét's Histoire des Variations.

germ of that feeble protest has grown the full flower of modern civilization and Christianity.

It was not until the eleventh century that Rome fully awoke to the danger which menaced her unity from the new "heresy,"* though from the fourth century she had persecuted those isolated individuals who, through rashness or regardless zeal, had overstepped that prudence which necessitated secrecy, and ventured openly to proclaim the apostolic tenets.† But now acting with her accustomed energy, and greatly startled by the spread of the dissent, and by the increasing boldness of its advocates, she summoned those mailed crusaders whom she had just hurled upon the Saracen, and bade them tread out the reform under their iron heels.

The whole south of Europe was more or less infected with the dissenting tenets, but their chief seat was in Southern France, that beautiful country which extends around the mouth of the Rhone, and stretches westward to the city of Toulouse, and southward to the Pyrenees—a territory which comprised the old governments of Avignon, Provence, and Languedoc."‡

Christian liberty is indebted to a sect of eastern extraction, called, from their professed imitation of St. Paul, the *Paulicians*,§ for the impulse given in these early centuries to religious inquiry. By the

* Introduc. to the Eng. trans. of Sismondi's Hist. of the Crusades against the Albigenses, p. 1. † Ibid.

‡ Bossuét's Histoire des Variations, Liv. IX.

§ Sismondi's Hist. of the Crus. against the Albig., p. 23. Gibbon's Decline and Fall of the R. Empire, Chap. LIV.

various chances of war, of trade, of persecution, and of missionary enterprise—for they were indefatigable proselyters—the Paulicians spread from their Asiatic cradle throughout Southern Europe with singular rapidity; and the suddenness with which they sprang into existence, their simultaneous appearance in widely separated sections, and the secrecy with which they taught, gave them an imposing air of mystery, while it magnified their power and resources in the popular estimation.

Though the Paulicians were certainly, notwithstanding their vehement disclaimers, somewhat tainted with the Manichean* errors, and with the principles of Gnosticism,† and though they held

* The MANICHEES were an ancient Persian sect who held to the tenets of Zoroaster, a man of whom little is known outside of his theological code, whose age is problematical, though he flourished many centuries before the Christian era, and whose history is shrouded in the most misty tradition. The leading idea of his creed was, that the world derived its present form from two primary principles, the one good, the other evil. The former was described as the parent of light, and of our rational nature; the latter as the parent of darkness, and of the material system. These rival powers were viewed as not only the creators, but the governors of this mixed order of affairs. Hence the perpetual conflict between good and evil in the natural and moral worlds. But above these two powers sat enthroned a supreme deity, Mithra, whose emblem was the sun, or in its absence the sacred fire which was never extinguished. The heavenly bodies, matter, the souls of men—all things were possessed of a species of intelligence, and were happy in proportion to their closeness to Mithra, who was eventually to refine and restore all intelligences to the great source from which they were said to have proceeded. See Vaughan's "Causes of the Corruption of Christianity," Lec. V., p. 170.

† The extravagant theory which, in the age of the apostles or soon afterwards, became known under the designation of GNOS-

some doctrines which could not but render them odious to the apostolic church: as that all matter was intrinsically depraved and the source of moral evil; that the universe was shaped from chaos by a secondary being, by whom the Mosaic dispensation was given, and by whom the Old Testament was inspired; and that the body in which Christ appeared upon earth, and his crucifixion, were apparent, not real;* yet they had not been debauched by the enormous corruptions of the Roman see, and they abhorred and incessantly inveighed against the worship of saints, the use of images, relics, pompous ceremonies, and ecclesiastical domination.†

In different countries the Paulicians were known by different names. When they crossed the channel

TICISM, and which played an important part in the early history of Christianity, was derived in part from the cabalistic dogmas of the Alexandrian Jews, in part from the leading doctrines of Platonism, but still more from the Oriental or Manichean theology. GNOSTICISM is chiefly distinguished from the Oriental doctrines by its adoption of the fanciful conceits of Plato, by its more visionary details with regard to celestial bodies, and by its admission of many of the gospel articles of belief. The "Christian Gnostics," as they were called, not only held to the two principles of good and evil described by Zoroaster, but they thought that Mithra, or Bythus, the supreme deity, had dispatched Christ to the earth as his instrument, that he might remedy the evil inflicted on the souls of men by Demiurgos, the former of the material world, and deliver mankind from their connection with matter, while at the same time he procured for them the gift of perfection in divine knowledge. From the assumption that the path in which they trod could alone lead to this valuable possession, these errorists were named Gnostics, which signifies the *knowing*, the *enlightened*. See Vaughan, Lecture V., p. 204.

* Intro. to Eng. trans. of Sismondi.

† Matter's "Histoire du Gnosticisme."

into England they were called *Publicans*, a probable corruption of the original designation. In Germany they were termed, from the blamelessness of their lives, *Cathari*, or the Pure. In France they were named *Bos Homos*, good men; while in Italy, and on the Alpine frontier, they were styled *Paterins*.*

The mission of the Paulicians appears to have been to awaken a spirit of inquiry, to accustom men to hear the haughty and fraudulent pretensions of the Roman diocese denied, and thus to prepare the way for a higher and holier ecclesiastical development. Meantime upon these bold dissenters was launched the awful malediction of the church of Rome. Nor did that merciless hierarchy content itself with simply placing them under the ban; it used every weapon which wit could suggest or which a Satanic ingenuity could devise to exterminate the heresy.

While the din of this ecclesiastical strife still resounded throughout Europe, in the middle of the twelfth century a sect which wrapped itself in the apostolic mantle, which carried in its hand the primitive taper, and which is venerated by the later Protestants, and respected even by the Romanists, reared its head and began to teach with authoritative mildness. The Vaudois† commenced to prop-

* Gibbon, chap. 54.

† Authorities differ concerning the origin of the names *Vaudois*, *Waldenses*, and *Albigenses*, for by all three of them were these reformers indiscriminately called. Perhaps the most competent writers have decided that *Vaudois* was derived from those

agate their tenets in the territories of the Aragonese and in Southern France.*

Standing midway between two mighty revolutions, the epoch of the Vaudois stretches forth a hand to both. It leans upon the period of the establishment of Christianity as its precursor, and brings forward the Reformation of the sixteenth century as its direct descendant. What then were its salient characteristics? Of what a warp and what a woof was the garment of its Christianity woven?

Piedmontese valleys whence the sect received their creed, and which were called in the Piedmontese *patois*, *Vaux;* that *Waldense* is a derivitive of *Waldo*, the name of a famous teacher among the Vaudois; and that *Albigense* is derived from the ancient duchy of *Alby*, where large numbers of the Vaudois resided. See Venema, Sismondi, and others.

* Bossuét, Hist. des Variations.

CHAPTER II.

THE PROVENÇALS.

France during the feudal period did not form a united monarchy. It was ruled by four independent kings; so that the north of France was Walloon, a name afterwards confined to the French Flemings, and which was then given to the language spoken by Philip Augustus; towards the west was an English France; to the east a German France; and in the south a Spanish or Aragonese France.*

Spain also was somewhat similarly divided. The Moors, an exotic race, held most of the peninsula; Castile and Aragon were still separate and often inimical kingdoms.† Although Catalonia, Provence, and Languedoc had originally formed portions of the swollen and clumsy empire of Charlemagne, yet when, no longer shaped by his plastic hand, the heterogeneous mass crumbled to pieces, these territories more or less completely allied themselves to the Aragonese throne; so that it was with difficulty that even the powerful Count of Toulouse, the hereditary lord of Provence and of Forcalquier, surrounded as he was by a brilliant retinue of vassals and loyal states, could maintain his independence of the Spanish king.‡

* Sismondi, Histoire des Français, p. 28.

† Prescott, Ferdinand and Isabella, Vol. I., passim.

‡ Sismondi, Hist. des Français, p. 30.

These territories were then the garden of the world, bright and sunny as that Goshen of old.* They were the home of the exiled arts, of poetry, of painting, of music, of sculpture. The Provençal slopes bore up an industrious and intellectual race, who, more familiar with the Greek text than with the Greek phalanx, abjured war, garnered wealth in commerce, and found culture in study. The whole Pyrenean country offered the strongest contrast to the rest of Europe, which was wrapped in a darkness to be felt and seen, like that of Egypt.

During the feudal ages, the whole intellectual horizon of northern Europe was singularly clouded. Poetry was unknown. Philosophy was proscribed, as a rebellion against religion. A barbarous jargon of provincial dialects had supplanted that sounding Latin which had preserved so many trophies of thought and taste. Commerce was unknown. A library of a hundred manuscript volumes was esteemed a magnificent endowment for the wealthiest monastery. "Not a priest south of the Thames," in king Alfred's phrase, "could translate Latin or Greek into his mother-tongue."† Not a philosopher could be met with in Italy, according to Tiriboschi. Europe was

"rent asunder—
The rich men despots, and the poor banditti;
Sloth in the mart, and schism within the temple;
Brawls festering to rebellion; and weak laws
Rotting away with rust in antique sheaths."‡

* Genesis, chaps. 45-47, passim.

† Hallam, Hist. of the Middle Ages.

‡ Bulwer Lytton's "Richelieu."

But these dismal shadows grow fainter and fainter as we advance towards the south, until, in Languedoc, in Provence, in Catalonia, the twilight reddened and broadened into day. "Knowledge," said Lord Bacon, "is spread over the surface of a country in proportion to the facilities of education, to the free circulation of books, to the endowments and distinctions which literary attainments are found to produce, and above all, to the reward which they meet in the general respect and approbation of society."* The Provençals understood this law which the great Englishman so finely states. The corner-stone of their prosperity was laid in fostered letters. "From Ganges to the Icebergs" there could be found no more civilized society.

> "The arts
> Quit for their schools, the old Hesperides,
> The golden Italy! while throughout the veins
> Of their whole empire flowed in strengthening tides
> Trade, the calm health of nations; and from the ashes
> Of the old feudal and decrepit carcass,
> Civilization, on her luminous wings,
> Soared, phœnix-like, to heaven."†

This singular people had elaborated a language of remarkable beauty from the old French patois. It was distinguished from all the mediæval dialects by its rich vocabulary, its picturesque phrases, and its flexibility.‡

The Provençal tongue, studied by all the genius of the age, consecrated to the innumerable songs

* Bacon's Advancement of Learning.

† Bulwer Lytton's "Richelieu."

‡ Sism. Hist. des Français, p. 30.

of love and war, and to the stirring psalms of praise, appeared certain to become the most elegant of modern languages.

The various courts of the smaller princes among whom these arcadian provinces were divided, aspired to be models of taste, politeness, and purity. Like all commercial communities, the Provençals were more addicted to the arts of peace than to the stern science of war. Their cities were numerous and flourishing, their governments were framed on the ancient democratic models, and consuls, chosen by a popular vote, possessed the privilege of forming communes, as did those Italian republics, Venice, Genoa, Florence, with which they traded.*

To the south of the Provençals lay the dominions of the Spanish Moors, a remarkably refined and civilized people. They were already masters of a great portion of the east, of the country of the Magi and the Chaldeans, whence the first light of knowledge had shone upon the world; of that fertile Egypt, the storehouse of human science; of Asia Minor, the smiling land where poetry and the fine arts had their birth; and of burning Africa, the country of impetuous eloquence and subtle intellect. Yet, pushed by a territorial greed which knows no parallel, the Moriscoes had recently, by a series of victories as brilliant as the Arabian conquests of Syria and Egypt, added the Spanish peninsula to their enormous eastern domain. They had even attempted to carry the fiery creed of their

* Sism. Hist. des Français, p. 31.

prophet from the Levant by way of the Danube to the Arctic ocean upon one side, and from the rock of Gibraltar to the English channel upon the other. Confined, however, within the limits of the Pyrenees by the prowess of Charles Martel at Tours, the Moors gave up the Mahommedan principle of conquest, and sought, by planting numerous schools and by patronizing learning, to conquer Europe by the Oriental philosophy, if they could not by Mahomet's sword; at the same time, by an admirable code of liberal laws, they strove to establish a peaceful and permanent dominion in the Spanish peninsula.*

An active and profitable commercial intercourse with these polished infidels, and also with the Jews, had enlarged the capacity of the Provençals, and convinced them of the folly of the prevalent bigotry. Thus their land became the asylum of all dissenters from Rome. They respected the sacred rights of conscience at a time when the peoples to the north of the Loire not only rattled their secular chains, but when they lay lassoed at the feet of their priests, under the complete dominion of fanaticism.

At this period, the Spaniards also, afterwards the most bigoted of modern races, the unhesitating butchers of the Inquisition, the volunteer executers of the wildest caprices of the papacy, emulated the toleration of their Provençal cousins, for they still remembered the time when they had themselves been compelled to sue for religious freedom under

* Prescott's Ferdinand and Isabella, Vol. I,, passim.

the Moorish yoke. Indeed, a century before the Sicilian Vespers, the kings of Aragon were the declared protectors of all who were persecuted by the papal despotism. In imitation of the Castilian sovereigns, they were upon one occasion the mediators for the Vaudois at the court of Rome, and upon another, their mailed defenders in the field.*

Even before the first mutter of the Vaudois dissent, the arrogant pretensions of the papal see had not imposed upon the enlightened Provençals, who despised the licentiousness of the priesthood, the credulity of the Romish believers, and the pompous ceremonies of the church.†

The Troubadours, as those minstrel-poets were called who were formed in the Moorish schools of Grenada, Cordova, and Seville, and who went from castle to castle keeping aglow the embers of literature by reciting their tales and chanting their madrigals, had very early launched their satirical verses at the abuses of the papacy.

One of the most celebrated of the troubadours, Pierre Cardinal, who sang in the twelfth century, levelled this *sirvente*‡ at the Roman vices:

"Indulgences and pardons, God and the devil, the priests put them all in requisition. Upon these they bestow paradise by their pardons; upon those, perdition by their excommunications. They inflict blows which cannot be parried. No one is so skil-

* Sism., Literature of the South of Europe, Vol. I., p. 115.

† Lampe, Eccles. Hist.

‡ *Sirvente* is the provençal French for the English word, *satire*

ful in imposition, that they cannot impose upon him. There are no crimes for which the monks cannot give absolution. To live at ease, to buy the whitest bread, the best fish, the finest wine—this is their object the whole year round. God willing, I too would be of this same order, if I but thought that I could purchase my salvation at that price."*

It will be seen from this recital how well the Catalonians and the Provençals were prepared by their simplicity of manners, by their tolerant principles, by their studious habits, by their active intelligence, by their commercial customs, and by their preëxisting prejudice against the Roman usurpations, for the reception of that mild and primitive Christianity which was about to flood their valleys with its light.

Towards the middle of the fourth century, while the newly converted emperor, Constantine, was inscribing the bastard legends of a paganized Christianity upon those banners which had before been surmounted by the hungry eagles of the early empire, and cementing the foundations of the papacy, a few sincere Italian ecclesiastics of Milan, dissatisfied with the increasing corruptions of the grandly simple faith which they so dearly loved, withdrew from Italy, and erected their Ebenezer in the beautiful, secluded, and labyrinthine valleys of Piedmont.†

* Sism., Literature of Southern Europe, Vol. I., p. 103.

† D. Vaissete, Hist. de Languedoc, Vol. III., p. 129. Browning, Hist. of the Huguenots, p. 14. Huguenots in France and America, Intro. chap., p. 18.

Here, kneeling at their primitive altars, and shut out as well from the temptations of the world as from its honors, the simple invocation, "Our Father, who art in heaven," diffused light, liberty, and happiness around them, as it did around those first Christians, who were ever found, in mountain desert and in the open air, in dungeons and in fetters, yes, even in the awful Golgotha of the catacombs, with the same sublime prayer upon their lips. Though these inoffensive pilgrims were taunted by their enemies with the epithet, Manicheans, yet it has been conclusively shown, by unimpeachable historians, that their confession of faith, like that of their disciples, the Vaudois, was pure Protestantism, and would have obtained the approbation of Calvin or of Beza.*

In 1124, three men, whose names ecclesiastical history loves to take upon its lips, Peter of Bruys, Henry, and Arnold of Brescia, and who are doubly dear on account of the martyrdom which they suffered for their sacred cause, lighted their torches at the pure altar of the Piedmontese, and carried the light of reformation from those obscure vales into the Provençal territories.†

The first discovery of a congregation of this kind was at Orleans, in France, where several of the regular clergy, and numbers of the most re-

* Browning, Hist. of the Huguenots, p. 14. Lampe, Hist. Eccl., p. 246–249.

† D. Vaissette, Hist. de Languedoc, Vol. II., p. 98. **Huguenots** in France and America, Intro. chap., p. 18.

spectable citizens were open adherents of the Piedmontese tenets.* A council was immediately convened, which, after laboring in vain to reclaim the "Protestants," had recourse to the final argument of the Roman church, and burned them all at the stake.†

Some time after this event, the conversion of Peter Waldo, one of the finest names in history, and the chief promoter of the Vaudois, as the dissenters were now called,‡ occurred.

This mediæval teacher was, in 1150, a wealthy citizen-merchant of Lyons.§ Amid the toils and bustle of mercantile life, he had found leisure to study the *belles-lettres* of the epoch; he had also looked into the Scriptures.

While engaged in consultation with several other of the principal citizens, Waldo beheld one of the group stricken with sudden death. This occurrence is said to have so impressed him with a sense of human frailty and of the divine wrath, that he renounced all worldly pursuits, and ever after devoted his immense riches, as well as his rare eloquence, to the promulgation of the gospel.‖

He began with his own family; and then, as his fame spread, he admitted to his hearthstone and instruction a few others, until, by the year 1165, he

* Sismondi, Hist. des Français. Mosheim, Ins. of Eccl. Hist. Waddington's Hist. of the Church.

† Intro. to Eng. trans. of Sism. Hist. of the Albigenses, p. 23.

‡ Chap. I., p. 32.

§ D. Vaissette, Hist. Languedoc, Vol. II., p. 54.

‖ Venema, Eccl. Hist., t. VI., p. 115, 116.

had quitted his elegant home, and fully embarked upon an active apostolic career.*

The Roman clergy, not only of Lyons, but of the whole neighborhood, set themselves to choke Waldo's expositions of primitive Christianity, and they even opposed and prohibited his domestic instructions, but without avail; for the resolute reformer was led, by the obstacles which priestly malice threw in his path, to examine the more diligently into the opinions of the clergy, into the rites and customs of the papal *régime;* and then, since in his case as in that of the latter reformers examination meant emancipation from the thraldom of Rome, to oppose their antichristian usurpations the more decidedly.

That Peter Waldo was not destitute of erudition, Flacius Illyricus proves from evidence derived from the ancient writings;† and perceiving, as Wickliffe did in England not many years later, and as Luther did four centuries afterwards, that since the luminous tenets of his dissent from Rome were based upon the Scriptures, it was momentously important to unlock the treasure-house of biblical knowledge to the comprehension of the provençal people, and to prove his doctrine from the inspired pages, he translated the Latin Bible into the vernacular language of Gaul.‡

The irreconcilable difference between primitive Christianity, with its later manifestations, called

* Venema, Eccl. Hist., t. VI., pp. 115, 116.

† Ibid., p. 115. ‡ Ibid.

Protestantism, and the Roman heresy—for Rome is indeed the crowned and ermined heresiarch of the ages—is in no one instance more grandly shown than in the treatment of the Bible by the respective advocates of the two systems. The priests, like the juggling augurs of pagan Rome, and like their prototypes, the mutterers of the heathen legends of Egyptian Isis and Osiris, made a mystery of their religion, carefully concealed the sources of their divinity, padlocked that Bible which the apostle commanded mankind to search,* and then, having hidden the evidences of their faith, preached a bastard Christianity of forms, of images, and of human merit and omnipotence.

Protestantism, on the contrary, has nothing to hide; believes in the popularization of knowledge; is democratic in its creed; knows no *caste;* asks nothing but, with the ancient cynic, that inimical systems "get out of its sunlight;" makes no secret of its tenets; proclaims the worthlessness of human merit; preaches the sole reliance of the human race,

"By one man's disobedience lost,"†

upon the gracious mercy of "Christ crucified" for a "recovered paradise;" and teaches justification by faith alone:‡ and since it culls these precious truths from the sacred oracles, it marches down through the centuries with faith aglow in its heart, and an open Bible in its hands. This was why

* St. John 5:39.

† Milton's Paradise Regained, (Mitford's ed.,) p. 1.

‡ St. Paul's Epistle to the Romans, 3:28; Heb. 10:38.

Luther in Germany, Wickliffe in England, and, earliest of all, Waldo of Languedoc, translated the gospels into their respective mother-tongues.

It is interesting to notice how singularly this venerable Vaudois creed agrees with the essential articles of that Protestantism which we of to-day bury in our heart of hearts.

These were the chief articles of their faith, as recited by competent historians, both friendly and inimical:

I. The Vaudois held the holy Scriptures to be the source of faith and religion, without regard to the authority of the fathers or to tradition; and though they principally used the New Testament, yet, as Usher proves from Reinier and others, they regarded the Old also as canonical scripture. From their greater use of the New Testament, their adversaries charged them however with despising the Old Testament.*

II. They held the entire faith according to all the articles of the apostles' creed.†

III. They rejected all the external rites of the dominant church, excepting baptism and the sacrament of the Lord's supper, as, for instance, temples, vestures, images, crosses, pilgrimages, the religious worship of the holy relics, and the rest of the Roman sacraments; these they considered as

* Venema, quoted in the Appen. of Sism. Hist. of Albig., Eng. trans.

† Ibid. Perrin, b. I., chap. XII. Blair, Hist. Waldenses, vol. I., pp. 503, 505.

inventions of Satan and of the flesh, full of superstition.*

IV. They rejected the papal doctrine of purgatory, with masses, or prayers for the dead, acknowledging only two terminations of the earthly state—heaven and hell.†

V. They admitted no indulgences nor confessions of sin, with any of their consequences, excepting mutual confessions of the faithful for instruction and consolation.‡

VI. They held the sacraments of baptism and of the eucharist to be only symbols, denying the real presence of Christ in the bread and wine, as we find in the authoritative book of the sect concerning antichrist, and as Ebrard de Bethunia accuses them in his book *Antihœresios*.§

VII. They held only three ecclesiastical orders: bishops, priests, and deacons; other systems they esteemed mere human figments; that monasticism, then in great vogue, was a putrid carcass, and vows the invention of men; and that the marriage of the clergy was lawful and necessary.‖

VIII. Finally, they denounced Rome as the whore of Babylon, denied obedience to the papal

* Lampe, Hist. Eccles., pp. 246–249.

† Venema.

‡ Venema. This confession of faith is also borne out by a singular theological poem which was written in the early part of the twelfth century, and called "The Noble Lesson." In this, not only great purity of faith is claimed for the Vaudois, but great antiquity, even an apostolic descent. Blair, vol. I., pp. 473, 484, gives the poem entire.

§ Venema.

‖ Ibid.

domination, and vehemently repudiated the notions that the pope had any authority over other churches, and that he had the power either of the civil or the ecclesiastical sword.*

Such was the remarkably enlightened and pure Protestantism of these early teachers; such were the tenets proclaimed by Waldo and the Vaudois, in the middle of the twelfth century, upon the rich provençal plains, and upon the listening and willing slopes of the French and Spanish Pyrenees.

Is it strange that when an abused and neglected populace, disgusted by the palpable avarice, despotism, and mummery of the Roman see, beheld a brotherhood of Christians enthusiastic in their religion, blameless in their lives,† humble in their demeanor, honest in their dealings, and disclaiming all tyranny over the consciences of men, propagating their tenets by the eloquence of their actions, many were won to embrace the salvation so sweetly taught, and that all generous souls were stirred at least to admire, if not to sympathize with a religion dear to God, but which Rome's unhallowed bulls denominated "heresy?"

* Venema.

† "That their morals were good, we have the unwilling testimony of Gretzer, a Jesuit, who laments that the regular clergy should give such examples of pride, avarice, incontinence, anger, envy, and drunkenness, because it made the Vaudois place more faith in their heresiarchs, who gave them good examples of humility, charity, chastity, sobriety, peace, brotherly love, and other virtues." Lampe, quoted in Browning's "History of the Huguenots," p. 14.

CHAPTER III.

THE PREACHING OF THE CRUSADE.

AT length Rome began to move. Innocent III., who in 1198 ascended the pontifical throne in the vigor of his life, was the first who appeared to be fully impressed with the importance of crushing remorselessly that independent and inquiring spirit which was rapidly assuming the character of a universal revolt from the Roman communion.

His predecessors, engaged in a tedious and perilous struggle with the secular power, with the two Henrys, and with Frederick Barbarossa, thought their entire force not too great to defend them against the emperors; and in those times they had themselves accepted the name of the *paterins*, or sufferers.*

But Innocent III., one of the haughtiest and most flagitious of the pontiffs, whose genius aspired to govern the universe, was as incapable of temporizing as he was of feeling pity. At the same time that he destroyed the political balance of Italy and Germany; that he menaced by turns the kings of Spain, France, and England; that he affected the tone of a master to the sovereigns of Bohemia, Hungary, Bulgaria, Norway, and Armenia; in a word, that he directed or repressed at his

* Sism. Hist. des Francais, p. 36.

will the crusaders who were occupied in overturning the Greek empire, and in establishing the Latin rule and the Roman theology at Constantinople—Innocent III., as if he had no other occupation, searched for, attacked, and punished all opinions different from his own, all independence of mind, every exercise of the faculty of thinking in the august domain of religion.

Though it was in the countries where the provençal language was spoken, and especially in Languedoc, that the Vaudois reformation counted the majority of its disciples, yet it had also spread into other portions of Christendom, into Italy, into Flanders, into Germany, and into Spain.*

Innocent III., both from character and policy, judged that the church ought to keep no faith with heretics. He thought that if it did not annihilate them, if it did not, in his phrase, "exterminate the whole pestilential race," and strike Christendom with horror, their example would be speedily followed, and that the fermentation of mind would be productive of a consuming conflagration throughout the Roman world.

Instead therefore of making converts, he charged his satellites to burn the chiefs of the Vaudois, to disperse their flocks, to confiscate their property, and to consign to perdition every soul who ventured to think otherwise than as he directed.†

* Calmet, Hist. de Lorraine, tom. II., liv. XXII., ch. CXXIV., p. 199. Hist. de Languedoc, liv. XXI., p. 130.

† Sism., Hist. des Français, p. 31.

At first the wily priest required those provinces where the Reformation had made but small progress to set the example of persecution, thus feeling his way gradually towards a wider cruelty. In this way many leaders of the reformed church perished in the flames at Nevers, in 1198, and in the succeeding years.*

Innocent next requested Otho IV., his imperial puppet, who danced as his master pulled the strings, to grant him an edict for the destruction of the Italian Vaudois, who were also called *Gazari.*†

The Roman vulture then paused a moment and plumed his wings for a higher flight. Innocent determined that the lovely provençal territory should be delivered over in the midst of its growing prosperity to the fury of countless hordes of armed fanatics, its cities razed, its population butchered, its commerce destroyed, its arts thrown back into barbarism, and its dialect degraded from the rank of a poetic language to the condition of a vulgar jargon.‡

There were a number of lords and high barons in Southern France who had themselves adopted the reformed opinions, and who, instead of persecuting, protected the Vaudois. Others saw in them only enlightened and industrious vassals, whom they could not destroy without affecting prejudi-

* Hist. de Languedoc.

† Edictum Ferrariæ promulgatum, 1210; Apud Muratorii Antiq. Ital., dissert. LX., pp. 89, 90.

‡ Sism., Hist. of Crusades against the Albigenses, p. 31.

cially their own revenues and military strength. But when did Rome permit her cherished plans to be baffled by the intervention of human rights or weighty obstacles? Innocent instantly armed a present interest and a brutal avarice against the calculating economy of the barons. He abandoned to them the confiscated property of all heretics, exhorting them to take possession of it, after banishing or murdering those whom they had plundered. At the same time this flagitious pontiff anathematized all who refused to seize upon the estates thus confiscated by his usurped power, and placed their dominions under an interdict.*

In 1198, Innocent had dispatched two legates, monks of Citeaux, brother Guy and brother Regnier, into Languedoc, and the other heretical districts; but rather, as it should seem, for the purpose of exploring and menacing than actually to commence the contest.† These legates were armed with full power, and it was enjoined upon the faithful to execute scrupulously their orders. Regnier having fallen sick, Innocent joined with him Pierre de Castelnovo, whose zeal, more furious than that of any of his predecessors, is worthy of those sentiments which the very name of the Inquisition inspires.‡

Presently afterwards a more numerous commission, the advance of the martial array, invaded the

* Sism., Hist. of Crusades against the Albigenses, p. 38. Innocentii III. Epistolæ, lib. I., epist. 81, 82, etc.

† Waddington, Hist. Chh., p. 292.

‡ Hist. Gen. de Languedoc, IV., XXI., p. 131.

haunts of heresy, and brought the subtleties of the schools to the support of intimidation. This body received great additional efficiency from the accession of a young Spanish monk named Dominic, the founder of the most bigoted and servile of ecclesiastical orders, and who was afterwards canonized as a reward for his diabolical cruelty in the ensuing Vaudois crusades. These itinerant spiritual missionaries were generally known by the title of Inquisitors, a name not indeed honorable or innocent even in its origin, but not then associated with horror and infamy.*

These inquisitors were at the outset empowered by the pope to discover, to convert, or to arraign before the ecclesiastical courts all guilty or suspected of heresy. But this was the limit of their commission. They did not at first constitute an independent, irresponsible tribunal, nor were they clothed with any judicial power. The process was still carried on according to the practice then prevailing, before the bishop of the diocese, and the secular arm was invited when necessary to enforce the sentence.†

But this form of procedure was not found to be sufficiently rapid or arbitrary to satisfy the eagerness of the pope and his missionaries. The work of extirpation was sometimes retarded by the compunctions of a merciful prelate, sometimes by the reluctance of the civil authorities to execute a bar-

* Waddington, Hist. Chh., p. 292.
† Limboch, Hist. of the Inquisition, Lib. I., Cap. XVI.

barous or an unpopular sentence. In order to remove these impediments to the free course of destruction, there was no recourse but to institute in the infected provinces, with the direct coöperation of the ruling powers, a separate, independent tribunal for the trial of heresy.* This was rendered more easy by the spread of the Franciscan and Dominican orders. As they were the faithful, unquestioning myrmidons of the Roman see, more devoted in their allegiance than either the secular or the regular clergy, they were invested with the separate jurisdiction.†

Such was the origin in the gloomy and heated brain of a fanatic pope of that ghastly court of inquisition, whose mere remembrance causes civilization to shudder.

Innocent's Languedocian inquisitors speedily offended all classes of society by their arrogance. Some bishops they accused of simony, others of negligence in the fulfilment of their duties. Under such pretences they deposed the archbishop of Narbonne, and the bishops of Toulouse and Viviers.‡ Indeed they branded most of the regular clergy as heretics, and at the same time tormented the count of Toulouse and all the lords of the country by accusations continually renewed. Thus they deprived themselves of the means of kindling so many fires as they could have desired. However, to gain a

* Limboch, Hist. of the Inquisition.

† Waddington, Hist. Chh., p. 358.

‡ Sism,. Hist. Albigenses, p. 41.

little popularity, they took the utmost pains to confound the heretics with the *routiers*, or hireling soldiers, afterwards so celebrated throughout Europe as the "Free Lances."

The companies of these, generally composed in great measure of strangers, were still known in the south by the name of *Catalans*, as they were in the north by that of *Brabançons*.* The routiers were lawless banditti, who pillaged the churches and the priests for purposes of plunder, but having no connection with the Vaudois, nor indeed taking any interest in theological paradoxes and doctrinal disputations. This ruse of the legates did not meet with much success. The result was, that the Catalans also were offended at the denunciations levelled at them, and in their turn they avenged themselves by plundering the ecclesiastics with heartier zest.†

At the commencement of the thirteenth century, Raymond VI., count of Toulouse, was the sovereign of Languedoc and Provence, though his rule seems to have been shared to some degree by his nephew Raymond Roger, viscount of Alby, Beziers, Carcassonne, and Limoux, in Rasiz. Although Raymond of Toulouse, of whose history before the crusade little is known, had won some fame as a soldier, he was possessed of but little strength of intellect or vigor of purpose. He had succeeded to his father, Raymond V., in 1194, in the thirty-eighth year of his age, and had already, at the head of the

* Sism., Hist. Albigenses.

† Hist. Gen. de Languedoc, LIV., LXXI., p. 138.

routiers, of whom he had made himself captain, made war upon many of his neighbors.*

He had disputed with some of the barons of Baux, and with the lords of Languedoc and Provence, his own vassals. This was apparently the reason why he had sought the alliance of Peter II. of Aragon, while his ancestors had constantly endeavored to repress the encroaching ambition of that house. Raymond VI. married his fourth wife, Eleanor, sister of the Aragonese king, in the year 1200; and five years later he promised his son, afterwards Raymond VII., to Sancha, the infant daughter of this same sovereign.†

The Viscount of Alby, Count Raymond's nephew, was made of sterner stuff. Now in his twenty-fifth year, generous, lofty, and enthusiastic, this prince was not of a temper to submit tamely to insult, nor would he stand quietly by and see his states mercilessly harried. He had like his uncle succeeded to his father in 1194, and during his minority his dominions had been governed by guardians inclined to the Vaudois doctrines.‡

In the spring of 1207 these two princes were upon the borders of the Rhone, busied in quelling an insurrection of the barons of Baux, when the papal legate, Pierre de Castelnovo, ordered them to furl their banners and declare peace with the insurgents.

The legate had first visited the barons and ob-

* Sism., Hist. of the Albigenses, pp. 41, 42.

† Ibid., p. 43.

‡ Ibid., p. 51.

tained from them a promise that, if Count Raymond would acquiesce in their pretensions, they would employ their united forces in the extermination of heresy—in Castelnovo's mind, "a consummation devoutly to be wished." After agreeing with them upon the form of the treaty, the legate returned to the count of Toulouse, and required him to sign it.*

But Raymond was nowise inclined to purchase, by the renunciation of his rights, the entrance into his states of a hostile army who were to pillage and kill those of his subjects whom the priests should indicate. He therefore refused his signature. Pierre de Castelnovo, in his wrath, excommunicated him, laid his country under an interdict, and wrote a hot letter to the pope, to obtain the pontifical confirmation of his sentence.†

Audacious as was the conduct of his legate, Innocent III. meant to uphold him. He sought for an opportunity to commence hostilities. He was desirous to adjourn the contest from the arena of argument, where his success was worse than dubious, to the arbitrament of arms. Tired of the subtleties of the schools, he invoked the subtleties of war. He was persuaded that, after the progress which it had made in public opinion, the heresy could only be destroyed by the swords of his crusaders. Accordingly he made no effort to medicine the wound, but, like a bungling surgeon, he applied an irritant.

* Petri Vallis Cernai, Hist. Albigens., cap. III., p. 559. Innocentii III., lib. X., ep. LXIX. Hist. de Languedoc, LIV., XXI ch. XXVII, p. 150.

† Ibid.

On the 29th of May, 1207, he wrote personally to Count Raymond a letter confirming the interdiction, and beginning thus: "If we could open your heart, we should find, and would point out to you, the detestable abominations that you have committed; but as it is harder than the rock, it is in vain tc strike it with the words of salvation; we cannot penetrate it. Pestilential man, what pride has seized your heart, and what is your folly, to refuse peace with your neighbors, and to brave the divine laws by protecting the enemies of the faith? If you do not fear eternal flames, ought you not to dread the temporal chastisements which you have merited by your so many crimes?"*

So insulting a letter addressed to a sovereign prince must have been revolting to his pride. Nevertheless, the monk Pierre de Vaux Cernai informs us that "the wars which the barons of Baux, and others of the faithful, carried on against him through the industry of that man of God, Pierre de Castelnovo, together with the excommunication which he published in every place against the count, compelled him, at last, to accept the original terms of peace, and to engage himself by oath to their observance; but as often as he swore to observe them, so often he perjured himself."†

The legate soon judged that the count did not proceed with adequate zeal. He sought Raymond,

* Innocentii III., lib. X., ep. LXIX. Hist. Gen. de Lang., LIV., XXI., ch. XXXIII., p. 150.

† Petri Vallis Cernai, Hist. Albig., LIV., III., p. 159.

reproached him to his face with his tolerance, which he termed baseness, treated him as perjured, and again let fall upon him the bolt of excommunication. This violent scene occurred in January, 1208, at St. Gilles, where Count Raymond had granted De Castelnovo an interview.*

The count of Toulouse was naturally very much provoked at the insolence of this upstart churchman, and he uttered some vague threats. The legate, disregarding his words, quitted the Provençal court without a reconciliation, and came to sleep, on the night of the 14th of January, 1208, in a little inn on the banks of the Rhone, which river he intended to cross on the morrow.

Meantime one of the count's gentlemen chanced to meet him there, or perhaps had followed him. In the morning this gentleman entered into a dispute with Castelnovo respecting heresy and its punishment. The legate had never spared the most insulting epithets to the advocates of toleration; and at length the noble, already heated by the Roman's insolence to his sovereign, now feeling himself personally insulted, drew his poignard, and striking Castelnovo in the side, killed him.†

This unhappy event furnished Innocent with the desired pretext for instant war. Although Raymond VI. had by no means so direct a part in Castelnovo's death as Henry II. of England had in Thomas à Becket's, his punishment was far more

* Sismondi, History of the Albigenses, p. 46.

† Ibid, p. 46.

terrible; for Innocent III. was more haughty and implacable than Alexander III.

Neither knowing nor desiring any better preachers of his creed than war, murder, fire, and incest, the excited pontiff began to preach a crusade against the Vaudois. In the commencement of 1208, Innocent addressed a bull to all the counts, barons, knights, and yeomen of Southern Gaul, in which he affirmed that it was Satan who had instigated his prime minister, Raymond of Toulouse, against the sacred person of his legate. He laid under an interdict all places which should afford a refuge to the slayer of De Castelnovo; and demanded that the count of Toulouse should be publicly anathematized in all the churches. This furious bull closed with this remarkable declaration:

"As, following the canonical sanctions of the holy fathers, we must not observe faith towards those who do not keep faith towards God, *or who are separated from the communion of the faithful*, we discharge, by apostolic authority, all those who believe themselves bound towards this count by any oath either of alliance or of fidelity. We permit any man to pursue his person, to occupy and to retain his territories."*

From this it should seem that the famous Jesuit phrase, "No faith is to be kept with heretics," though often attributed, with similar enormities, to Ignatius Loyola, is of far older origin. The fanatic Spaniard

* Petri Vallis Cernai, Cap. VIII., p. 564. Sism., Hist. Albig., pp. 46, 47.

merely stole the atrocious sentiment from the decretals of Pope Innocent III., when he incorporated it in the constitution of his protean propaganda.

Having now reduced these dissenting Christians of Southern France to the same level, in a religious estimation, with the Turk and the Saracen, Innocent next let loose an infuriated multitude of fanatics against them; and the word "crusade," which had hitherto signified only religious madness, was extended to the more deliberate atrocity of sectarian persecution.

CHAPTER IV.

PREPARATIONS FOR THE "SACRED WAR."

INNOCENT III. had in November, 1207, exhorted Philip Augustus, the duke of Burgundy, the counts of Bar, of Nevers, of Dreux, and others of the old crusaders who had fleshed their swords on the plains of Palestine, and gathered barren laurels on the Syrian shore, to marshal their hosts against the Vaudois.*

But early in 1208 the flames of his hatred were fanned into increased fury by the bloody catastrophe of Castelnovo's death. The pontiff fulminated a series of epistles from the Vatican, which summoned all the faithful to the holocaust in Languedoc.†

Galono, cardinal deacon of *San Maria dello Portico*, was dispatched into France by the crafty pontiff with these letters. He did not receive much consideration from Philip Augustus, who was now more occupied by his rivalry with the English king and with Otho of Germany than with obtaining the barren honor of heading another crusade in a sacred war.‡ But notwithstanding the king's polite indifference, the monks of Citeaux,§ who had received full powers from Rome, began to preach the cru-

* Innocentii III. Epistolæ, lib. X., ep. CXLIX.

† Ibid.

‡ Sism., Hist. Albig., p. 47.

§ Chap. III., p. 51

sade among the nobility and the yeomen of France with a perseverance and enthusiasm which had not been surpassed by Fouldques de Neuilly, or by the fanatical eloquence of Peter the Hermit.*

Innocent III. offered to those who should take the cross against the Vaudois the utmost extent of indulgence which his predecessors had ever granted to those who fought for the deliverance of the Holy Land and the sepulchre of Christ. As soon as these new crusaders had assumed the sacred sign of the cross—which, to distinguish themselves from those of the East, they wore on the breast, instead of upon the shoulder—they were instantly placed under the protection of the holy see, freed from the payment of the interest of their debts, and exempted from the jurisdiction of all the tribunals; while the war which they were to wage at their doors, almost without danger or expense, was to expiate all the vices of a whole life—was warranted, by the impious usurper of the apostolic name at Rome, to efface the crimes of threescore years and ten from the heavenly records.†

The belief in the efficacy of these indulgences, which in the sunlight of the nineteenth century we can scarcely comprehend, was then in its full flush. The barons of the feudal ages never doubted that, while fighting in the Holy Land, they had the full assurance of paradise.

But those distant expeditions had been attended with so many disasters; so many hundreds of thou-

* Sism., Hist. Albig., p. 48. † Ibid.

sands had perished on the scorching sands of Asia, succumbing either to the heat or to the Saracenic scimitars, or else had fallen by the way from hunger, misery, sickness, "and the thousand ills that flesh is heir to," that the boldest and most knightly hearts now wanted courage to essay the fight.

It was then with transports of joy that the faithful received these indulgences. War was their passion. The discipline of the holy wars was much less severe than that of the political, while the fruits of victory were much more alluring. In them they might without remorse, since *no faith was to be kept with heretics*, and without restraint from their officers, pillage and appropriate all the property, violate the women, and massacre the men of the interdicted territories.

The crusaders of the East well knew that the distance was so great as to afford them but small chance of bringing home the booty gained by their swords. But now, instead of riches which were to be sought at a distance amid great perils, and which must be torn from the resolute grasp of barbarians whose language they could not understand, the French knights were exhorted, nay, commanded, by an authoritative voice from the shekinah at Rome, to reap the bloody harvest of a neighboring field, to appropriate the spoils of a house which they might hope to carry to their own, while captives were abandoned to their desires who spoke the same language with themselves.*

* Sism., Hist. Albig., p. 49.

Never therefore had the cross been assumed amid greater enthusiasm or with a more unanimous consent. The first to engage in this atrocious harry, which was baptized with the name of a *sacred war*, were Eudes III., duke of Burgundy, Simon de Montfort, count of Leicester—a bloody monster who glooms yet upon the historic horizon, pilloried to the scornful horror of the ages—and the counts of Nevers, of St. Paul, of Auxerre, of Genéve, and of Foréz.*

Meantime, though the crusaders were not ready to march in 1208, the din of their immense preparations resounded through Europe, and filled Languedoc with terror. Count Raymond, learning that Arnold, abbot of Citeaux, leader of the crusade, had been appointed by the pope his legate in those provinces from which he designed to eradicate heresy, and that Arnold had convened a council of the chiefs of the sacred war at Aubenaz, in the Vivarais,

> "To advise how war may best upheld
> More by her two main nerves, iron and gold,
> In all her equipage,"†

repaired thither in company with his nephew, to see if haply the storm might be averted.

The legate received them with great haughtiness; and though they both protested that they

* Rigordus de Gestis Philippi Augusti, p. 62 et finis. Historia de las Grans Faicts d'Armas, p. 4. Hist. Gen. de Languedoc, liv. XXI., chap. XLI., p. 156.

† Milton's "Sonnet on Sir Henry Vane the Younger." Mitford's ed., vol. II., p. 356.

were personally strangers to the heresy, that they were innocent of the death of Pierre de Castelnovo, and that they ought not to be judged and condemned unheard, yet the insolent prelate upbraided them with stinging emphasis, declared that he could do nothing for them, and informing them that if they wished to obtain any mitigation of the measures adopted against them, they must apply to the pope, he motioned them from the council-chamber.*

Then the differing characters of uncle and nephew were fully developed. Count Raymond, overwhelmed with terror, declared himself ready to submit to any terms, even to be himself the executer of the unhallowed violence of the ecclesiastics upon his best subjects, whose sole offence was their heroic devotion to primitive Christianity. The craven noble even stooped so low as to affirm his readiness to make war upon his own family, if thereby he might obtain the pontifical absolution.†

Not so the heroic nephew, noblest of a noble band of martyrs. Perceiving from the legate's language that nothing was to be expected from negotiation, and determined never peacefully to admit the crusaders into his states to ravage his clients, he boldly urged upon his uncle to place strong garrisons in the larger towns, to prepare valiantly for the defence of their country, and to take the initiative by at once commencing the campaign before

* Sismondi's History of the Albigenses, p. 51.

† Ibid, pp. 51, 52.

the invading host could don its mail or draw its sword.*

But the two relatives were unable to agree upon their policy, and they separated with reproaches and menaces.

Raymond VI., after assembling his most faithful servants at Arles, engaged the archbishop of Auch, the abbot of Condom, the prior of the Hospitallers of St. Gilles, and Bernard, lord of Rabasteens in Bigorre, to proceed to Rouen, in order to offer his complete submission to Innocent III., and to receive his indulgence.†

The frightened count at the same time applied to his cousin, Philip Augustus king of France, and to Otho of Germany, for their protection. Philip at the outset received him with fair words, but afterwards refused him all assistance, on the pretext of his solicitations to his rival Otho.‡ The German emperor did not deign even to notice his prayer.

The ambassadors of Raymond to the pontiff were, on the contrary, received with apparent cordiality. But it was required of them that their master should make common cause with the crusaders; that he should personally assist them in exterminating his subjects and in desolating his own territories; and that he should surrender seven

* Sismondi's History of the Albigenses, p. 52.

† Petri Vallis Cern. Hist. Albig., ch. IX., p. 566.

‡ Hist. de las Armas, pp. 4–6. Hist. de Lang., liv. XXI., ch. XLII., p. 157.

of his best castles in the heart of his dominions, as a pledge of his fidelity. Upon these conditions, Innocent bade Raymond *hope* that he might *eventually* absolve him for the heinous crime of respecting the rights of conscience, and attempting to protect his subjects from slaughter.*

But notwithstanding Raymond's servile submission and his own fair words, the implacable pontiff was far from having forgiven him in the bottom of his heart. His assurances of favor were, *vox et preterea nihil*—went no lower than his throat. For while he was amusing the count's ambassadors with pacific declarations and paternal mandates, he wrote this real *exposé* of his sentiments to the bishops of Riez and Cansevans and to the abbot of Citeaux: "We counsel you, with the apostle Paul, to employ guile with regard to this same count; for in this case it ought to be called prudence. We attack separately those who are separated from our unity. Leave then the count of Toulouse for a time, employing towards him a wise dissimulation, that thus the other heretics may be more easily defeated, and that afterwards we may crush him when he shall be left alone."†

Such was the equivocating morality, such the perfidious policy of a pontiff who claimed *to sit as God, in the temple of God.*

* Historïa de las Faicts d'Armas, p. 6. Cernai, Hist. Albig., chap. XI., p. 567.

‡ Innocentii III. Epist., lib. XI., ep. 232. Hist. Gen. de Languedoc. liv. XXI., p. 160.

"We cannot but remark," says Sismondi, "that whenever ambitious and perfidious priests had any disgraceful orders to communicate, they never failed to pervert for this purpose some passage of the holy Scriptures. One would say that they had only studied the Bible to make sacrilegious applications of it."*

Meantime the gallant young viscount of Alby, undeceived by the cunning politics of the Roman count, able

"To unfold
The drift of hollow states, hard to be spelled,"

preserving his honor and his governmental oath untarnished, retired to his states, labored like a Hercules to put them in a defensive condition, and at length, having done all that enthusiasm and devotion could do to protect his territories and to save the "lives, the fortunes, and the sacred honor" of a people in whose faith he did not share, the noble prince threw himself into the city of Beziers with a body of his armed retainers, and announced his purpose to hold it to the last for "Christ and liberty."†

In the spring of 1209, the swarms of fanatics whom the harangues of the monks of Citeaux and the pope's indulgence letters had persuaded to devote themselves to the sacred war, began to move.‡

Different historians have variously estimated

* Sism., Hist. of Albig., p. 53.

† Historia de las Faicts d'Armas de Tolosa, p. 7. Hist. Languedoc, liv. XXI., ch. XLII., p. 157.

‡ Hist. de las Faicts d'Armas de Tolosa, p. 10.

the numbers of these crusaders. They have been computed to have been three, and even five hundred thousand strong.* But a very competent authority reckons but fifty thousand in this first campaign.†

This calculation, however, did not include the ignorant and infuriated multitude which, following each preacher, armed with scythes and clubs, and sweeping through the country with a more desolating tread than the crusaders themselves, though in no condition to combat the chivalrous knights of Languedoc, undertook at least to murder the women and children of the heretics.‡

Several places had been assigned for the rendezvous of these demoniac hosts. Arnold Amalric, abbot of Citeaux, legate of the pope, and chief director of the crusade, collected the greater number of combatants, principally those who had taken arms in the kingdom of Arles, and who were vassals of Otho IV., at Lyons: the archbishop of Bordeaux had assembled a second body in the Agenois; these were the subjects of the king of England: the bishop of Puy commanded a third body in the Valai, who were the subjects of Philip Augustus.§

When Count Raymond learned that these terrible bands were about to be let loose, the naked sword in one hand and the blazing torch in the

* Hist. de las Faicts d'Armas de Tolosa, p. 10.

† Petri Vallis Cernai, Hist. Albigens., cap. XXII., p. 584.

‡ Sism., Hist. Albig., p. 54.

§ Petri Vallis Cernai, Hist. Albigens., cap. XVI., p. 571. Hist. Gen. de Languedoc, liv. XXI., ch. LIII., pp. 167, 168.

other, upon his beautiful states and those of his nephew, he represented to the pope that the legate Arnold, who conducted them, was his personal enemy. "It would be unjust," said he, "to profit by my submission, to deliver me up to the mercy of a man who would listen only to his resentment against me."

Then occurred another notable instance of the profound duplicity of the sovereign pontiff. In order, *in appearance*, to take from the count of Toulouse this motive for complaint, Innocent III. named a new legate, his secretary Milon. But far from endeavoring to alleviate the woes of the Provençals by this means, or to restrain the hatred of the abbot of Citeaux, we are assured by the monkish historian Vaux Cernai, that the only aim was to deceive the count. He adds exultingly, "For the lord pope expressly said to this new legate, 'Let the abbot of Citeaux do every thing, and be only his organ; for in fact, the count of Toulouse has suspicions concerning him, while he does not suspect thee.' "*

The nearer the crusaders approached, the more the count of Toulouse gave himself up to terror. On the one hand, he endeavored to gain the affections of his subjects by granting new privileges to some, and pardoning the offences of others who had incurred his resentment;† on the other hand, he consented to purchase his absolution by the most

* Petri Vallis Cernai, cap. X., p. 566.

† Remissio Consulibus et Habilatoribus Nemonsi; Preuves de Languedoc, p. 211.

humiliating concessions. He consigned to the pontifical notary seven of his finest castles. He permitted the consuls of his best cities to engage themselves to abandon him if he should depart from the conditions imposed upon him. He submitted beforehand to any sentence which the legate should be pleased to pronounce upon fifteen unproved accusations laid against him by the inquisitors; and to crown all, he suffered himself, on the 18th of June, 1209, to be conducted into the church of St. Gilles with a cord about his neck; and there he received the discipline before the altar upon his naked shoulders. He was then, upon promising to become the guide of the invaders, allowed to take the cross against his own subjects, and against that gallant nephew who stood tranquilly awaiting the assault.*

* Acta inter Innocentii Epistolas, tom. II., p. 347, et seq. Cern. Hist. des Albigeois, cap. XII., p. 568.

CHAPTER V.

THE COMMENCEMENT OF THE TRAGEDY.

THE jubilant host of the crusaders, in the summer of 1209, wound slowly down into the smiling valley of the Rhone, through the friendly cities of Lyons, Valence, Montelimart, and Avignon, afterwards so celebrated as the seat of one of the two pontiffs between whom the immaculate and *seamless* robe of Roman *unity* was *divided*. The entrapped count of Toulouse repaired to Valence to meet these ferocious forces; from which city he conducted them to Montpellier, where they rested for several days.*

The viscount of Alby, though hopeless of success, still determined to make one more effort to still the tempest conjured up against his innocent subjects by the cruel necromancy of the arch-juggler at Rome. To this end he went to Montpellier, and seeking the legate, told him, according to the ancient chronicle of Toulouse, that "he had done the church no wrong; that he but walked in the well-defined footsteps of his ancestors in granting toleration in his states; that as for himself he was a servant of the church, wishing to live and die so."†

But the legate was imperturbable. Taking his cue from the master-priest of the holy see, he told

* Hist. Gen. de Languedoc, liv. 21, p. 175.

† Historia de las Faicts d'Armas de Tolosa, p. 7.

young Raymond Roger that what he had to do was to defend himself as best he might, for he should show him no mercy.*

The viscount quitted the ancient walls of Montpellier sad but resolute. He had done his utmost—stepped to the verge of honor to avert the impending avalanche by diplomacy. Now nothing remained but to draw the sword and fling away the scabbard.

He immediately summoned to him all his vassals, friends, and allies; laid before them the representations which he had made to the legate; informed them of the manner in which he had been received; and upon calling on them for advice, found the whole body of his retainers as resolutely determined to defend their hearth-stones as he was himself.†

Nor were all those who took arms with him heretics.‡ Let it be written for the honor of human nature, that even in that sullen and ferocious age, there were not wanting gallant spirits ready and eager to die for the toleration of a creed in whose tenets they did not share.

The knightly gentlemen of those days resided in castles which were more or less strongly fortified, while their vassals lived in little cots scattered over the estates at various distances from the fortilace. Languedoc was spotted with these *chateaus;* and now, upon the approach of the crusaders, the yeo-

* Historia de las Faicts d'Armas de Tolosa, p. 7. † Ibid., p. 8
‡ Ibid. Sism., Hist. Albig., (Eng. trans.,) p. 57.

men rushed in vast numbers to the protection of these fortified walls; while the nobles, provisioning their larders for a siege, shut themselves up in their keeps with that *nonchalance* which is the offspring of long habit and danger often braved.

Some castles, as Servian and Puy-la-rouque, were abandoned ere the Roman *banditti* reached them. Others, among which the old historians mention Caussadi and St. Antonia, where it was not supposed that any heretics lurked, ransomed themselves by heavy contributions. Still others nobly met a sterner fate. Villeum was burned. Chasseneuil, after a vigorous defence, capitulated. The garrison, who were *routiers*, or "free lances," obtained permission to retire with what they could carry; but the inhabitants, who were Vaudois, were abandoned to the mercy of the legate. The ghastly carnival now began. The town was fired; men, women, and children were precipitated into the hungry flames, amid the acclamations of their fiendish conquerors, and night only closed the frightful orgies.*

From this sad opening scene even the pages of the monkish historians of the foray are blotted with pitying tears. The crusaders, rendered still more ferocious by this taste of blood, pressed fiercely on towards the viscount's capital, Beziers, leaving, as was charged upon that Attilla of old, no blade of grass nor any living thing behind them."†

* Hist. Gen. de Languedoc, liv. XXI., p. 168. Hist. de las Faicts, etc., p. 18.

† Ibid.

In July, 1209,* they arrived under the walls of Beziers, and formally summoned it to surrender. Raymond Roger had chiefly calculated upon the defence of his two great cities, Beziers and Carcassonne. He had divided between them his most valiant knights, and the *routiers* who were attached to his fortune. He had at first thrown himself into Beziers; but after assuring himself that the city was provided with every thing in his power to bestow, he quitted its walls for those of Carcassonne, a town built upon a rock, partly surrounded by a river, the Aude, and whose suburbs were environed by walls and ditches.†

The citizens of Beziers felt themselves intimidated, when they knew that their young lord had left them for the stronger protection of Carcassonne, and their inquietude was redoubled when they beheld the three grand divisions of the Roman army, under the legate, the archbishop of Bourdeaux, and the bishop of Puy,‡ arrive and unite before their city.

Just before the crusaders reached Beziers, they had been visited by the bishop of that city, Reginald de Montpeyroux, who delivered to the legate a list of those in the city who were accounted Vaudois, and whom he desired to see thrown into the flames. He then returned to Beziers, assembled the inhabitants in the cathedral of St. Nicaise, and after representing to them with vivid eloquence the

* Fleury, Hist. Eccles., liv. LXXVI.

† Hist. de las Faicts, etc., p. 19. ‡ Chap. IV., p. 69.

vast numbers of the crusaders, and the impossibility of resisting their onset, exhorted them not to draw down upon themselves, their wives, and their children the wrath of heaven and of the church by protecting their Vaudois fellow-townsmen, but to yield them up to the avengers of the faith.

"Tell the legate," replied the citizens, "that our city is good and strong, that our dear Lord God will not fail to succor us in great necessities, and that rather than commit the baseness demanded of us, we will eat our own children."*

But though equal in courage and infinitely superior in generosity and Christian purpose to their savage foes, the unhappy citizens of Beziers were not equal to them in military skill or in the discipline of trained arms.

While the crusaders were occupied in tracing their camp, the citizens made a sortie, hoping thus to take their enemies by surprise. But instantly the united battalions of the besiegers precipitated themselves upon the disconcerted trainbands of the city, and forcing them to retire, pursued them so hotly that both parties entered the open gates together, and Beziers was captured before the crusaders had even formed their plan of attack.†

Then the bloody orgies of Chasseneuil were reenacted on a broader theatre. Arnold Amalric,

* Hist. de las Faicts, etc., p. 20. Petri Vall. Cern., Hist. Albig., cap. XV., p. 570.

† Raynaldi, Annal Eccles., 1209, sec. XXII., p. 186. Hist. de Lang., liv. XXI., ch. LVII., p. 169. De Thou, liv. VI.

abbot of Citeaux, upon learning that he had triumphed almost without a struggle, and determined not to be baulked of the expected feast of blood, upon being asked by some of his companions in arms how the Romanist citizens were to be distinguished from the Vaudois, made that famous reply, worthy of Nero or Caligula: "KILL THEM ALL; GOD WILL WELL KNOW HIS OWN!"*

The fixed population of Beziers did not perhaps exceed fifteen thousand persons; but all the inhabitants of the country, of the open villages, of the plains, and of the castles which had not been judged capable of safe defence, had taken refuge in Beziers, which was regarded as exceedingly strong. Even those who had remained to guard the strong *chateaus*, had, for the most part, sent their wives, their children, and their helpless ones to the city.

At the moment when the crusaders became masters of the gates, the whole multitude thronged to the churches. The great cathedral of Nicaise contained the larger number. The canons, clothed in their choral habits, surrounded the altar and sounded the bells, as if to express their prayers to their furious assailants. But these supplications of brass were as little heeded as were those of the human voice. Still the bells ceased not to sound until, of that immense multitude, not one remained alive. The massacre spread equally to the other churches; seven thousand dead bodies were counted in that

* Cæsar Heister bachiensis, lib. V., cap. XXI. Sism., Liter. of South of Europe, vol. I., p. 116, note. Sism., Hist. Albig., p. 60.

of Magdalene alone. Thus even the benefit of sanctuary, respected at that period for the vilest malefactors, was not awarded to the Vaudois.*

An old Provençal historian has, by the simplicity of his language, augmented the terrors of this scene: "They entered the city of Beziers, where they murdered more people than was ever before known in the world; for they spared neither young nor old, nor infants at the breast. They killed and murdered them all, which being seen by the said people of the city, they that were able did retreat into the great church of St. Nazarius, both men and women. The chaplains thereof, when they had so retreated, caused the bells to be rung until everybody was dead. But neither the sound of the bells, nor the chaplains in their priestly habits, nor the clerks, could hinder them from being put to the sword. One only escaped, for all the rest were slain and died. Nothing so pitiable was ever heard of or done before."†

When the crusaders had completely pillaged it, and massacred every living creature, the city was fired in every part at once, and reduced to a vast funeral pile.‡

Historians differ as to the number of victims sacrificed on this awful occasion to the greed of the insatiable demon of persecution. The abbot of

* Sism., Hist. Albigen., pp. 60, 61.

† Preuves de l'Histoire de Languedoc, tom. III., p. 2; also quoted in Sism., Lit. of the South of Europe, at p. 117, vol. I

‡ Ibid.

Citeaux, feeling some shame for the butchery which he had ordered, in the account which he transmitted to Innocent III., reduces the number to fifteen thousand. Other and more reliable contemporary chroniclers reckon it at from forty to sixty thousand.*

Having "supped full of horrors" at Beziers, yet without being satiated, the crusaders pressed on through a deserted country—for the inhabitants preferred taking refuge in caves, woods, mountains, to waiting for such enemies within the enclosure of walls which might serve as a prison—towards Carcassonne. They reached this Vaudois citadel on the 1st of August, 1209, and pitching their tents, invested it in due form.†

Although the generous heart of Raymond Roger had been terribly wrung by the massacre of his loyal subjects of Beziers, and by the destruction of his capital, he "bated no jot of heart or hope;" while the brave inhabitants of Carcassonne renewed their oath of allegiance to him, and of fidelity to each other.‡

Carcassonne was accounted almost impregnable. Built upon one side of the river Aude, in whose waters it bathed upon the right, it had been strongly fortified by the skill of the young viscount upon

* Bernard Ilier of Limages, a contemporary, makes the number slain 38,000; Abberic, a monk, 60,000. See Sism., Hist. Albig., p. 61, note.

† Hist. Albig., p. 62.

‡ Sism., Liter. of South. Europe, vol. I., p. 117.

the more exposed angles. It was besides defended by a numerous and devoted garrison.

The attack commenced upon one of the suburbs without the city walls. Here the combat raged fiercely for two hours, during which time Raymond Roger on one side, and Simon de Montfort upon the other, gave evidence of extraordinary personal prowess. Eventually the suburb was taken by mere stress of numbers. The besieged retreated into the second suburb, which the assailants pressed on to attack. For eight days the viscount defended this redoubt with success, but on the ninth day he evacuated it, and, having fired it, retired slowly and sullenly into the city, clanging the ponderous gates in the faces of the outwitted foe.*

Meantime Raymond Roger had found means to communicate with his uncle, Don Pedro II. king of Aragon. The Aragonese sovereign had witnessed the oppression and outrage inflicted upon his relative with chagrin. He therefore quitted his kingdom, and hastening to the camp of the crusaders endeavored to negotiate a peace.†

Having obtained permission of the legate to visit his nephew, the king entered Carcassonne to confer with the viscount. "My dear uncle," said the frank young soldier, "if you wish to arrange for me any honorable adjustment, I freely leave with you its form and manner, and I will ratify it without hesitation; for I see clearly that we cannot long maintain ourselves here, owing to the multitude of

* Hist. de las Faicts de Tolosa, p. 12 † Ibid.

countrymen, women, and children who have taken refuge with us. We cannot reckon them, but they die, alas, in great numbers every day. But were there only myself and my soldiers here, I swear to you that I would rather die of that ghastly famine which now stares us in the face than surrender to this same cruel legate."*

The king of Aragon very injudiciously related this discourse to the wily legate, who, thus familiar with the precise condition of the viscount, was thereby enabled to offer, with some assurance of success, propositions much less generous than he would otherwise have ventured to make; for be it remembered, it was no part of this atrocious monk's purpose to accommodate affairs. He wished to glut the vengeance of a cruel faith. Still he did not dare absolutely to repel such a mediator as the king of Aragon. But knowing well the high and chivalric character of the viscount, he achieved his object by proposing terms which it would be impossible for a gallant and knightly spirit to accept.

"Tell your nephew, sire," said the abbot of Citeaux, "that he himself, with any twelve others whom he may choose, may freely quit the city. But the remainder of the citizens and soldiers must be abandoned to our good pleasure." The king carried the message. "Now, out upon the priestly catiff," was the noble reply: "rather than submit to

* Hist. de las Faicts, p. 13. Hist. de Languedoc, liv. XXI., ch. LXXIX., p. 171. Petri Vallis Ceınai, Hist. Albig., cap. XVI., p. 571.

these disgraceful terms, I would suffer myself to be flayed alive. No, he shall not have the meanest of my people at his mercy; for it is on my account that they are now in danger."*

The chivalric king approved the generous purpose of his nephew, and turning towards the assembled citizens and knights of Carcassonne, he informed them of the legate's conditions, and added, "You now know what you have to expect; mind and defend yourselves well, for he who acts the part of a brave man always finds good mercy at last."†

Don Pedro of Aragon with his retinue had scarcely quitted the city ere the impatient crusaders hurled themselves upon its walls, but in vain; the gallant viscount fought as nobly as he talked. Streams of boiling water, blazing oil, immense stones, projectiles of every kind then known to the cruel skill of war—all were put in requisition; and at length, maimed, bleeding, and balked, the crusaders fell back within the entrenchments of their camp.

The greater part of the crusaders had taken the cross but for forty days. The time now approached for their service to end. General and sullen discontent reigned in the pontifical camp. The soldiers had been promised the intervention of a miracle in their favor. Yet after two prolonged and bloody assaults, they still stood without the walls of Carcassonne, while

> "Many a corpse lay ghastly pale beneath the setting sun."

* Hist. de las Faicts, etc., p. 15.

† Ibid.

The legate remarking these symptoms of demoralization, and true to the perfidious maxims of the church whose livery he wore, now determined to have recourse to stratagem, if haply he might accomplish by his arts what had been denied his sword.

Accordingly he renewed the negotiations. The viscount, ignorant of what was passing in the camp of the crusaders, and profoundly anxious for an honorable accommodation, received the legate's messenger with the utmost cordiality. Fully conscious of the rectitude of his own intentions and proceedings, he could not but believe that, when the injustice of which his country had been the victim should be known, it would excite the commiseration of the great barons and ecclesiastics arrayed against him, and stay the devastation. Filled with this Quixotic idea, and as incapable of suspecting deliberate treachery in others as he was of himself performing a perfidious deed, young Raymond offered to accompany the envoy to the camp of the crusaders, for the purpose of having a personal interview with the chiefs of the sacred war, provided his personal safety and return should be solemnly guaranteed.*

The envoy flew to acquaint the legate with this offer. Arnold Amalric rubbed his hands gleefully when he heard this recital, and though he deliberately perjured himself by doing so, for he had instantly decided upon the confiding viscount's arrest,

* Historia de las Faicts d'Armas de Tolosa, p. 18.

he yet sent the desired safe-conduct, to which he attached the seal of Rome.

The viscount soon made his appearance, accompanied by three hundred of his choicest chivalry. Repairing to the legate's tent, where the chiefs of the crusade were assembled, he nobly and powerfully vindicated his conduct and the policy of his ancestors, and again affirmed, that though the fast friend of religious toleration, he was still a true servant of the Roman church.*

Then Rome gave another proof of the pitiless, unhallowed, and abandoned wickedness of her politics. Not only the legate, but the great lords who accompanied him, were penetrated with the diabolical maxim of Innocent III.: "*To keep faith with heretics is an offence against the faith.*" Accordingly watching for a propitious moment, the crusaders threw themselves upon the surprised and insignificant retinue of the Provençal prince, all of whom, after a brief struggle, were disarmed, and together with their young lord consigned to the care of Simon de Montfort.†

* Sism., Hist. Albig., Eng. transl., p. 65.

† Petri Vall. Cern., Hist. Albigens., cap. XXI., p. 571. Hist. de Lang., liv. XXI., ch. LVIII., p. 160. Sism., Hist. Albig., pp. 65, 66.

CHAPTER VI.

THE REIGN OF TERROR.

THE crusaders thought that the flagitious perfidy exhibited by their chiefs towards the beloved prince of Alby would strike terror, like a dagger, into the hearts of the inhabitants of Carcassonne. It did indeed chill them with horror, but it also withdrew the entire population from the clutches of these bloodhounds of the Roman church.*

There was an immense cavern, dark, freezing, and awful, which yawned in the bowels of the earth, and stretched away from the river-gate of Carcassonne three leagues, to the towers of Cabardes. To the protection of this gloomy sanctuary—for to their despair it was indeed a temple—the citizens rushed; and on, on, through the ooze of the dreadful cavern, which in happier times the boldest had shrunk from approaching, esteeming it haunted by hobgoblins, they tramped, willing to face the spirits of the yawning depth, if only they might escape the fiends who raged before their city walls.

Meantime, when the curtain of the night was lifted, and the light of day began to dazzle in the grey eastern horizon, the crusaders were astonished at not beholding the accustomed Vaudois sentries

* Historia de las Faicts d'Armas de Tolosa, p. 21. Sism., Hist. Albig., p. 66.

pacing the city walls. "Conscience does make cowards of us all," and remembering their own treachery of the day before, they feared that some stupendous mischief underlay the silence and desertion; for those of them who had grown greyest in the wars had never before seen a large population melt into nothing in a night.

At length however they entered Carcassonne, and the legate took possession of the spoil in the name of the church, excommunicating those of the crusaders who should have appropriated any part of it. But it long remained a mystery what had become of the teeming population which had vanished under cover of that August night.*

The abbot of Citeaux thought himself obliged to dissemble the villany to which he had had recourse, and which had succeeded so badly. Accordingly on the 15th of August, 1209, the day of the occupation of the city, he issued a proclamation, in which he unblushingly announced that he had signed a capitulation by which he had permitted all the citizens to quit Carcassonne with their lives only.† And then, deeming it essential to the honor of the holy church that all the heretics should not escape him, he caused a number of Vaudois whom he had picked up upon his march, together with the knights who had accompanied the viscount of Alby and Beziers to his camp, to be collected in a group four hundred and fifty large. Then this wanton butcher

* Sismondi, Hist. Crusades against the Albigenses, p. 66.

† Ibid.

selected out of that number fifty to be hanged, and the remaining four hundred were burned alive, to propitiate the malignant fury of his vengeful church.*

All was now esteemed to have been accomplished. The count of Toulouse had submitted to the most degrading conditions ever before offered to or accepted by a sovereign prince. The beautiful and virgin Provençal plains had been rudely violated and soaked in blood. The gallant viscount of Alby and Beziers was a hopeless prisoner in the iron grasp of Montfort. The other Provençal nobles had published in their jurisdictions laws against the Vaudois even more severe, if that were possible, than Rome demanded.

The French lords who, to gain the indulgence of the church, had marched to the crusade, thought that they had done enough to effect the salvation of their souls; and weary of blood and ashamed of the violation of their plighted faith, they chafed to return to their castles.

All seemed satisfied, save the monks—save Dominic Guzman, and Francis d'Assise his companion in infamy, the founder of the despicable order of St. Francis, and at their head the abbot of Citeaux. The Vaudois were frozen with terror, but these fanatics thirsted for their blood. The heretics, leaving their homes to the pillage of the avaricious and to the incendiary torch of the marauder, had hidden in the mountains, and were outwardly silent;

* Sismondi, Hist. Crusades against the Albigenses, p. 66.

but these bigots knew that inwardly they prayed to that dear Jesus who for them had been nailed upon the tree, that the torch of primitive Christianity still smoked, if it did not blaze, and this thought would not let them rest.

The Vaudois were not exterminated. Their opinions would still secretly circulate. Resentment for outrages already suffered would alienate them yet more irreconcilably from the Roman communion. Their suffering would attach them still more devotedly to the tenets of their dissent, and the reformation would break out afresh. "To turn back the march of civilization, to obliterate the traces of a mighty progress of the human mind, to efface the foot-prints of the primitive and pure apostolic faith, it was not sufficient to sacrifice, as an example, hecatombs of victims; *the nation must be destroyed.* All who had participated in this grand development of evangelical knowledge, of Christian thought, of luminous science, must perish. None must be spared, save the most boorish rustics, whose intelligence was scarcely superior to the beasts whose labor they shared."*

Such was the flagitious *rationale* of the Roman see—such the avowed policy of the abbot of Citeaux, and his twin jackals, Dominic and Francis d'Assise.

At the conclusion of the first crusade, just before the great lords separated, the legate assembled a council, and desired them to award the states of Raymond Roger, forfeit to the church, to some

* Sism., Hist. of the Albig., Eng. transl., p. 68.

lord who would engage to extirpate the remnant of the Vaudois. The conquered territories were first offered to Eudes III., duke of Burgundy; but he refused them, saying that "he had plenty of domains and lordships without taking that, to disinherit this unhappy viscount; and that it appeared to him that they had done him evil enough, without despoiling him of his ancestral states."*

This refusal, couched in such words, touched the honor of all the barons; and the counts of Nevers and of St. Paul, to each of whom the proffer was made, held the same language. Then the sovereignties were offered to Simon de Montfort, the most greedy and ferocious of the vengeful band. This infamous noble, then lord of but a single castle, Montfort Amaury, situated some ten leagues from Paris, though he was of an illustrious house, said to have been descended from king Robert by a natural son,† after some feigned reluctance, finally accepted the bloody and usurped gift, thus by his ambition raising himself to the rank of the grand feudatories.

De Montfort had held the rightful sovereign of the states of which he had just taken possession a close prisoner in his donjon-keep ever since his capture. It now became necessary to sweep this

* Sism., Hist. of the Albig., Eng. transl., p. 68.

† Præfatio Camaratii Tricassini in Petrum Vallis Cernai. This historian of the crusade, so often quoted in these pages, was a Bernardin monk; his convent was situated near Montfort Amaury; and he was a vassal of Simon de Montfort, whom he followed to the war.

obstacle completely from his path; for even in chains the young viscount haunted him, presaging evil to himself and to his house. Raymond Roger was a rare character. His neighbors loved him. His people idolized him, and prayed for him daily. The Vaudois especially enshrined him in their heart of hearts. Possibly his powerful and kingly relative of Aragon would be disposed to throw his royal ermine over his hapless nephew's defenceless form. Clearly it was Montfort's policy to get rid of his prisoner, too strong even in irons. With this ferocious and sullen fanatic, to decide was to act. Accordingly Montfort gave the necessary order for his death, at the same time spreading a report that the viscount had died of dysentery. But the fraud was too transparent. The public voice and conscience openly accused De Montfort of having poisoned his princely captive; and even Innocent III. acknowledged that the viscount perished by violence.*

Thus, in the flower of his age, ended the mortal career of Raymond Roger, viscount Alby and Beziers, chivalric as any Paladin of them all; a knight, like Bayard, *sans peur et sans réproche*, worthy to be a martyr in the grandest of all causes; a heroic soldier in the "good fight" which Bunyan has described; another victim added to the swollen catalogue of Roman intolerance and depravity. History takes his name from the Roman rubric of heretical malefactors, and placing it among her jewels, writes

* Hist. de las Faicts, etc., p. 20. Innocentii III. Epist., lib. XV., ep. 212.

proudly, RAYMOND ROGER, THE DEFENDER OF THE VAUDOIS.

Upon the conclusion of the campaign of 1209, Count Raymond of Toulouse, having submitted in every thing to the pontifical requisition, thought himself sure of reconciliation with the church; but he was surrounded by men whose interest it was to prolong his punishment, if not to perpetuate it. The bishop of Toulouse, a recreant troubadour, Foulquét de Marseille, who had in other days gained some fame by his amatory verses, but who, disgusted with the world, had retired to a cloister, where he had fostered the passions of fanaticism and persecution,* was Count Raymond's open foe. The two jackal inquisitors, Dominic and Francis, hated him because he had once tolerated the Vaudois. The abbot of Citeaux was his declared enemy; while Simon de Montfort, looking from his usurped viscountal palace at Carcassonne across upon Raymond's contiguous territories, thought how goodly his heritage would be if only the countship of Toulouse could be added to it. He was urged on therefore by the double motive of religious fanaticism and political ambition. These worthies, working tirelessly and secretly, defeated every measure which Raymond of Toulouse could elaborate for the procuration of his pardon. In the early part of 1210, the count had visited Rome, and in an interview with Innocent, had learned that the consideration of his case had been confided to an

* Sism., Literature of the South of Europe, vol. I., p. 115.

ecclesiastical council about to be convened at St. Gilles.*

Raymond hastened home to meet the council. Meantime the abbot of Citeaux had harangued its members, and so prejudiced them against the count, that, without granting him an opportunity to clear himself of the charges laid against him, the council again fulminated an excommunication against him in the name of the church.†

Simon de Montfort, with a powerful army—for though most of the great barons had retired, many, influenced either by that fanaticism which led them to take the cross, by the hope of securing a permanent establishment in a conquered country, or by the promise of plunder and adventure, still adhered to the banner of the crusade which the new viscount carried—had now the desired pretext for entering and ravaging Count Raymond's dominions. At the same time crowds of monks headed by Guy and Arnold Amalric of Citeaux, issued from their convents, and recommenced preaching the crusade. Gathering about them troops of ferocious and superstitious warriors, they proclaimed that there was no vice so deeply rooted, no crime so black, that a gala campaign of forty days in the south of France would not obliterate. Paradise with all its glories was opened to them, without the necessity of the slightest reformation of their conduct.‡

* Innocentii III. Epistolæ, lib. XII., pp. 159, 169.

† Petri Vall. Cern., cap. XXXIX., p. 586, Hist. Albig.

‡ Sism., Hist. of the Albig., p. 83.

Accustomed to confide their consciences to their priests, to listen to the voice of Rome as to the thunders of the dread God of Sinai, never to submit what appertained to the faith to the arbitrament of reason, these besotted crowds really regarded those beloved children of God's right hand, the Vaudois, as a nest of heretics who bred contagion.

So the roads were once more blocked with the advancing enthusiasts. Alice of Montmorency, De Montfort's wife, assumed the control of the forces raised by the exhortations of the monks.*

At the commencement of Lent, 1210, her husband came to meet her at Pezenas. He no sooner found himself at the head of a large and well-appointed army, than he gave full sway to his evil passions.

A few lords still ventured to defend either the independence of their jurisdiction, or that of their conscience. De Montfort now essayed to crush this opposition by new judicial massacres. His fresh horde of fanatics swept through the country with desolating fury. The feudal state of independence had multiplied the isolated fortresses which served at once for residences and strong-holds. The smallest provinces were covered with citadels. These castles then received De Montfort's first attention. Many of them were abandoned on his approach. Others which ventured to resist, were razed, while their heroic defenders were either hanged upon gibbets, or roasted alive for the honor of the mother church. The castle of Brom being cap-

* Hist. de Languedoc., liv. XXI., p. 197. Fleury, Hist. Eccles.

tured by the crusaders on the third day of the siege, De Montfort selected a hundred of its wretched inhabitants, Vaudois who had been denounced by the priestly spies who sped before the men-at-arms to procure lists of heretics, and having torn out their eyes and cut off their noses, sent them in this state, under the guidance of a one-eyed man, to the neighboring Vaudois castle of Cabaret, to announce to that garrison the fate which awaited them.*

When De Montfort found the citadels deserted, not being able to reach human beings, he wreaked his vengeance upon the twining vines, the olive-trees, and the blooming gardens which lent rare beauty to the landscape, and made Provence the queen of nations, the idyl of territories.†

The pen of history falters when it follows this rude butcher upon his devastating marauds, nor is it necessary to detail with absolute minuteness the harrowing scenes of this frightful war, which yet possesses strange interest.

The siege of the castle of Minerva was one of the most remarkable of the war, and is detailed at length by the ancient chroniclers. This citadel was built upon a steep and almost inaccessible rock, surrounded by precipices, and was regarded as one of the most impregnable strong-holds in the Gauls. It belonged to Guiraud de Minerva, a Vaudois nobleman, and one of the best knights in Southern

* Histoire de Languedoc, liv. XXI., ch. LXXXIX., p. 191.

† Petri Val. Cer., Hist. Albig., cap. XXXIV. ét V., pp. 581, 582.

France. The crusaders brought against it their finest men-at-arms, De Montfort and the abbot of Citeaux being present in person.*

The Vaudois defended themselves for seven weeks with a valor which extorted the admiration even of De Montfort. But when, on account of the heat of summer—it was under the fierce sun of July—the water in their wells and cisterns failed, they demanded a capitulation. Terms were finally agreed upon; but when they were read in the council of war, one article, which provided that those Vaudois who were converted to the Roman faith might quit the castle alive, was violently opposed. "Robert de Mauvoisin," says the monk Vaux Cernai, "a nobleman entirely devoted to the papal see, cried that 'the pilgrims would never submit to this; since it was not to convert heretics, or to show mercy to them, but to kill them, that they had taken the cross.' The abbot Arnold, better acquainted with the obstinate devotion of the heretics, replied, 'Fear not, for I believe that very few will be converted.'"†

Shortly after, the crusaders entered the castle chanting the *Te Deum*, and preceded by the cross and by the standards of Montfort.

God's children had assembled in two Vaudois churches, the men in one, the women in the other, and while the fanatical bands of Rome began to sing the *Te Deum*, they calmly responded by chanting one of their simple hymns of praise, pausing be-

* Petri Vall. Cern., Hist. Albig., cap. XXXV., p. 586.

† Ibid. p. 588.

tween each sob of the music to encourage each other by a mute caress, or to seek new strength in fervent prayer. Not one flinched; not one made the slightest effort to escape the awful doom which each knew awaited him. The honor of becoming a martyr for the holy cause of that sweet Jesus who was himself a man of sorrow, gave unwonted dignity to the rudest carriage. It was the ecstacy of religious faith, one of the grandest sermons to which that brutal band of heated zealots, smeared with martyr-blood, ever listened.

The abbot, Guy de Vaux Cernai, to fulfil the articles of capitulation, came to these Vaudois, and began to preach the Roman faith to them. He was instantly interrupted. "Sir priest," was the unanimous cry, "we want not your exhortations. We have renounced the church of Rome; we have become the children of a purer light; we draw our consolation from a higher source, even from our Lord and Saviour Jesus Christ, to whom be glory for evermore, Amen. Your labor is vain; desist. For neither life nor death can make us renounce that precious Bible whose truths we have embraced."*

The abbot, surprised and strangely moved, next visited the assembly of Vaudois women. He found them as resolute, and still more enthusiastic in their declarations.†

The ferocious De Montfort, in his turn, visited the Vaudois. Already he had piled up enormous

* Petri Vall. Cern., Hist. Albig., cap. XXXVII., p. 583.

† Ibid.

masses of dry wood. The executioners, in their black gowns, stood ready. The impatient soldiery clamored hoarsely for the *fête* to begin. "*Be converted to the Roman faith,*" said the ruthless crusader, "*or ascend this pile.*" None were shaken. The wood was fired; the whole square was enveloped in a tremendous conflagration. The greedy tongues of the lurid flame licked the crackling wood as if hungry and impatient for their human prey. The Vaudois were conducted to their funeral pyre, but no violence was necessary to compel them to enter the blazing, torturing fire; they voluntarily precipitated themselves into it, their sweet Provençal hymns quivering upon their lips, or else repeating that grandest of the beatitudes: "*Blessed are ye when men shall revile you, and persecute you, and shall say all manner of evil against you falsely, for my sake. Rejoice, and be exceeding glad: for great is your reward in heaven; for so persecuted they the prophets which were before you.*"* High above the fierce crackling of the flames, high above the hoarse roar of the fanatic multitude, rose the pathetic wail of the Vaudois supplication, until God came to their deliverance, and through the open and thrice welcome door of death their unfettered souls winged

* St. Matthew 5:11, 12. Petri Cern., cap. XXXVII., p. 584. We are indebted to this monk, the panegyrist both of his abbot Guy de Vaux Cernai and Simon de Montfort, a bigoted Romanist, who narrates gleefully the most hideous details of the Vaudois persecution, for the account given above of the conduct of the Minerva "heretics." His account is more summarily confirmed by the "Historia de las Faicts de Tolosa."

their way to that bourne where "the wicked cease from troubling, and the weary be at rest."

The capture of Minerva was quickly followed by the siege of Termes, a strong castle upon the borders of Roussilon, which was commanded by its lord, a valiant captain named Raymond of Termes. This gallant soldier made a grand defence for "Christ and liberty." The patience of the crusaders was sorely tried, and De Montfort beheld his army terribly thinned by sickness and the Vaudois sword. He made a fresh appeal to the fanaticism of the French provinces, each of which, in response, dispatched in its turn a numerous contingent to his camp. Meantime, after four weary months of incessant combat, gaunt famine stared the Vaudois in the face, and thirst parched their throats. An attempt was made to escape from the castle into the surrounding mountains.

The Vaudois did indeed pass the first line of De Montfort's intrenchments, and dispersing in the shadowy recesses of the country, shaped their flight towards Catalonia. But soon their escape became known in the camp of the crusaders. The knights mounted in hot haste and scoured the roads; the men-at-arms, impressing peasants to guide them, searched the innermost recesses of the mountains. Each one exhorted the other not to let those who had cost the host so much sweat and blood escape their vengeance.

The unhappy Vaudois, encumbered by aged men by women, by children, were speedily overtaken ar remorselessly slaughtered where they stood. A few were conducted alive to the presence of Simon de Montfort, among the number the gallant Raymond of Termes. These, with the exception of their lord, were publicly burned alive for the edification of the crusaders. But De Montfort reserved Raymond of Termes for a more hapless lot. He confined him at the bottom of a tower in Carcassonne, in a damp dungeon whose walls were coated with ice, where, with exquisite cruelty, he suffered him to languish for many years,* a prototype of the wretched prisoners of the Inquisition, or perhaps of that mysterious "iron mask," whose lineage is enshrouded with such gloomy interest in French history.

The miserable inhabitants of this unhappiest of countries found no asylum which could protect them. Neither woodland dell nor mountain cavern could screen them from the keen sight of the hunters of the Romish Babylon. Provence shivered in mute sympathy with the agony of her children. The pagan cruelty of the most monstrous of the Roman emperors was white when set against the blackness of De Montfort's infamy. Torquemada himself might have learned from him new lessons in the cruel skill of torture. Horror was heaped upon horror, until the benumbed and decimated Vaudois began to creep with languid footsteps across the borders of a territory surrendered to the ravage of demoniacs into happier lands.

* Petri Vall. Cern., Hist. Albig., cap. XLII., p. 592. Hist. de las Faicts, etc., p. 29. Ber. Guidonis, Vita Innocentii III., p. 482.

CHAPTER VII.

THE REVOLT.

At length even the timid patience of Count Raymond of Toulouse was exhausted. He had surrendered every thing, promised every thing, submitted to every thing, in his efforts to court a reconciliation with the church. But cozened and maltreated by the perfidious minions of the pontifical see, he was now goaded to desperation, and like the hunted stag, turned at bay. Well would it have been for his knightly fame and for his Christian honor if, instead of faltering so long, he had at the outset united with his nephew in the defence of their mutual states.

He now formed a close alliance with the counts of Comiges and of Foix, with Gaston, viscount of Béarn, Savary de Mauléon, seneschal of Aquitaine, and the other lords of those provinces who were accused of heresy or of tolerance, and whose interests were united with his own.*

Count Raymond also negotiated a treaty of offence and defence with Don Pedro of Aragon; and gathering his forces well in hand, dashed with gallant purpose against the invaders of his country.†

* Sism., Hist. of Albig., p. 95.

† Ibid.

De Montfort also was at the head of a fine army, inured to danger, well disciplined, and accustomed to victory.

He first advanced to Lavaur, a strong castle five leagues distant from Toulouse. This stronghold, afterwards raised to the rank of an episcopal see, was then the property of a widow named Guiraude, whom her brother Aimery de Montreal had recently joined, with eighty other knights like himself despoiled by the crusaders of their fiefs. Aimery, Guiraude, and most of their defenders, were all open believers in the Vaudois creed. They had opened an asylum to those of the reformed who were persecuted in the various adjacent villages; so that their fortress, which was kept well stored and well manned, and which was surrounded with strong walls and girded with deep ditches, was esteemed one of the principal seats of the heresy.*

The defence of Lavaur was long and stubborn. But at length the fanaticism, the numbers, and the pernicious skill of the crusaders triumphed; the city was taken by assault, and De Montfort, beholding his too ardent soldiers already busied in the work of indiscriminate massacre, besought them rather to make prisoners, that the priests of the living God might not be deprived of their promised joys.† "Very soon"—we here quote from the narrative of the monk of Vaux Cernai, himself an eyewitness of the scene—"they dragged out of the

* Petri Vall. Cern., Hist. Albigens, cap. XLIX., p. 596.
† Ibid.

castle Aimery de Montreal and other knights to the number of eighty. The noble count of Montfort immediately ordered these to be hanged; but as Aimery, the stoutest of them, was strung up, the gallows fell, for in their haste the executioners had not well fixed it in the ground. The count, seeing that this would cause great delay, ordered the rest to be massacred; and the pilgrims receiving the command with the greatest avidity, very soon slew them on the spot. The lady of the castle, who was a sister of Aimery and an execrable heretic, was, by the count's order, thrown alive into a pit, which was slowly filled up with stones. Afterwards our pilgrims collected the innumerable heretics who had fled to this citadel, and burned them alive with the utmost joy."*

Such is the gloating recital of an unblushing monk who was at once the witness and the panegyrist of these freezing horrors.

The crusaders quitted the ruins of Lavaur to hasten forward to the siege of Toulouse, Count Raymond's capital.

"This city," says Sismondi, "was far from having been completely converted to the reformation of the Vaudois; the Romanists still composed the greater number of the inhabitants, though the Vaudois were numerous and counted their disciples

* Petri Vall. Cern., Hist. Albigens, cap. LIII., pp. 598, 599. This account is confirmed by Bernardi Guidonis in the Vita Innocenti III., p. 482, where we are informed that four hundred of the Vaudois were burned at Lavaur.

among the most enlightened citizens. The magistrates, when asked why they did not drive out the heretics, replied, 'We cannot; we have been brought up among them, we have relations among them, and we daily witness the goodness of their lives.' The Romanism of Toulouse was therefore very different from that of Northern France. The proverbial imprecation, '*I would rather be a priest, than have done such a thing*,' was as common in Roman as in Vaudois mouths. Indeed the Romanism of Toulouse was so unnaturally liberal, owing to the leaven of the Reformation, as quite to justify the indignant affirmation of the most ancient historian of the crusade, that Toulouse ought rather to be called *Tota dolosa*."*

Still the bishop Fouquét had imbued a number of the most ignorant citizens with his own fanaticism. These formed themselves into a society called *The White Company*, five thousand of whom had joined De Montfort beneath the walls of Lavaur.† This society had erected a tribunal by its own authority, before which it dragged those who were accused by its spies of being Vaudois. The partisans of the Reformation, reinforced by the friends of toleration, formed a counter association called *The Black Company*, whose object it was to resist and punish the lawless outrages of the fanatics. These two troops met often in the streets, armed, and with ensigns displayed; and many

* Sismondi, History of the Albigenses, p. 99.

† Ibid.

towns, which belonged to one side or the other, were alternately besieged.* "Thus," says William Puy Laurens, a contemporaneous chronicler, "did our Lord, by the ministry of his servant the bishop, instead of a bad peace, excite among them a good war."†

But while Fouquét was striving to kindle a war among his flock, Count Raymond was busied in restoring peace among his subjects. He succeeded so well that, when De Montfort appeared before the city and summoned it to surrender, the united voice of the city spoke in the tone of the consul, who said that Toulouse refused either to renounce its fidelity to its count, notwithstanding his excommunication, or to deliver up to punishment those of its citizens who were suspected of cherishing the Vaudois tenets.‡

Fouquét, bitterly angered at this refusal, instantly called in his priests, assembled them in a body at the cathedral, excommunicated all the Toulousians, and then quitted the city barefoot at the head of his monks, who carried the holy sacrament in the procession and chanted litanies as they marched.§

However, Toulouse did not suffer the fate to which its charitable bishop had deserted it. On

* Guill. de Podie Laur., cap. XV., p. 675.

† Ibid, p. 675

‡ Sism., Hist. Albigen., p. 100. Fleury, Hist. Eccles. de las Faicts de Tolosa, p. 30.

§ Petri Vall. Cern., cap. LV., p. 600.

the contrary, Count Raymond, assisted by the counts of Foix and of Comiges, so pressed De Montfort, that he was not only compelled to raise the siege of Toulouse, but to retreat in his turn before the victorious Provençal squadrons to the shelter of one of his strong-holds, Castelnaudory.*

But De Montfort's cry for aid soon brought another swarm of fanatics to his assistance. Count Raymond was repulsed. The country which, in his hour of misfortune, had vented its hate against him by rising in universal insurrection and spewing forth his garrisons, was again furiously harried; while Count Raymond retired into Aragon to recruit his forces and to form a junction with his royal ally and kinsman.†

Marked by these and similar vicissitudes, several years passed sadly by. In the autumn of 1213 the disastrous battle of Murét was fought, in which king Pedro of Aragon, who had generously advanced to reinstate his brother in his dignities, lost his life,‡ and Count Raymond's star, with that of religious toleration, seemed for ever sunk below the angry horizon.

The ferocious activity of De Montfort was not decreased by the victory of Murét, or by the voluntary exile of Count Raymond in the Aragonese ter-

* Petri Vall. Cern., cap. 55, p. 601.

† Preuves de l'Histoire de Languedoc, p. 232. Hist. de las Faicts, etc., p. 38. Lettre des Habitants de Toulouse á Pierre, Roi d'Aragon.

‡ Raynaldi, Annal. Eccl., 1213, p. 249. Joan Marianæ, Hist. Hisp., cap. 2, p. 558.

ritories. Entering upon that unhappy nobleman's vacant countship, he ravaged it for the third time from corner to corner, and himself assuming the reins of government, with the congenial Fouquét as his adviser, gave full sway to his bigotry and insatiable ambition.

In 1216, Pope Innocent III. died.* His pontificate had been one of the most stormy and arbitrary in the papal annals. Possessed of remarkable executive talent, and of an ambition as far reaching as that of Lucifer, no one of the popes, excepting perhaps Hildebrand, had done so much to consolidate the Roman despotism. He was merciless in the execution of his ecclesiastical projects, steeled against the presumptuous wretch who ventured to reject his creed, impious in his profanation of God's name and of the cross of Christ, and his memory is burdened with the inception of the Inquisition, with the incorporation of the most perfidious maxims into the canons of his church, and with the curses of those innocent children of the Most High, the Vaudois, whom his stentorian voice, echoing over Europe, first taught the nations to persecute.

Meantime Count Raymond was not idle. Secretly informed of all that was passing in Provence, he learned with joy that the barbarous and iron rule of Simon de Montfort was felt to be intolerable by the most tolerant people on the face of the globe. The inhabitants of Toulouse dispatched an embassy to invite him to return to them, and pledg-

* Bernardi Guidonis, Vita Innocentii III.

ing themselves to support him with the heartiest and most loving zeal.*

Encouraged by these attestations of attachment, the count raised an army in Aragon and Catalonia, at the head of which, after some reverses, he finally marched, in 1217, into Provence, entering once more his ancient capital amid the joyous acclamations of the populace.†

De Montfort's mingled fanaticism and ambition made him equal to the occasion. Instantly dispatching Fouquét, bishop of Toulouse, with James de Vitry, the historian of the last combats of the Holy Land, into France, to preach a new crusade, he summoned his brother Guy de Montfort and his son Amaury to his side, and hastening towards Toulouse, hoped to attack it before the citizens could rebuild their levelled walls, and while, haunted by the memory of former chastisements, they yet hesitated between affection and fear.‡

Appearing before the capital early in September, the crusaders at once made a vigorous assault. They were as vigorously hurled back into the surrounding ditches; while Simon's brother Guy, together with his nephew the count of Bigorre, fell dangerously wounded.

De Montfort then commenced a regular siege, at the same time sending his wife Alice of Montmorency to the court of Philip Augustus, to solicit

* Histoire de las Faicts de Tolosa, p. 45.

† Hist. Albigenses, cap. LXXXIV., LXXXV., p. 662. Sism , Hist. Albig., p. 143.

‡ Fleury, Hist. Eccles.

his aid.* Meantime the siege proved tedious. Prolonged through the winter, it dragged ineffectually into the ensuing spring and summer. Daily darting from their citadels, the Toulousians stung their besiegers with constantly increasing venom.

At length, on the 25th of June, 1218, Count Raymond made a sally, and pushing resolutely towards one of De Montfort's most destructive engines, called a "cat," because with its ponderous paw it beat breaches in the wall, captured it.

The butcher of the Vaudois was at mass when the news of the sortie was brought to him. Instantly arming himself, he headed his men-at-arms, and charged fiercely to the rescue of his favorite engine. He was successful. The Vaudois were repulsed. But while De Montfort stood with his battalion before the unwieldy paw of his strange machine, an enormous stone, cast with Titanic power and with vengeful certainty from a catapulta upon the city walls, struck the redoubted monster full upon the head, and hurled him maimed and lifeless to the ground, while his countenance was still distorted with a grin of sardonic satisfaction on account of his latest and last success.†

Amaury de Montfort, the dead fanatic's son and heir, collected his scattered and affrighted soldiers,

* Hist. de las Faicts d'Armas de Tolosa, p. 93.

† Petri Valli Cernai, Hist. Albigen., cap. LXXXVI., p. 664. Guil. de Podie, cap. XXX., p. 684. Hist. de las Faicts de Tolosa, p. 94. Hist. de Languedoc, liv. XXIII., chap. XXVIII., p. 303. Sism., Hist. Albigenses, p. 150.

and receiving their homage and oath of fidelity as his father's successor in the usurped countship of Toulouse, for a little longer persisted in the siege of the jubilant city.

But in vain. In the latter days of July, 1218, he retired with his shattered cohorts into Carcassonne, where De Montfort was buried with great pomp.*

* Petri Vallis Cern., Hist. Albig., cap. XXXVI., p. 664. Guil. de Podie, cap. XXX., p. 684. Hist. de las Faicts de Tolosa, p. 94. Hist. de Languedoc, liv. XXIII., ch. XXVIII., p. 303. Sismondi, Hist. Albig., p. 150.

CHAPTER VIII.

THE FINAL MASSACRE.

For a few brief years Provence enjoyed comparative repose. Its singular fertility, which the Vandal hoof of war was unable to tread out, soon made Languedoc begin once more to smile. After De Montfort's death, the demon of fanaticism fled with a shriek. Count Raymond, old and broken, delegated his government to his son Raymond VII., already rendered illustrious by high exploits, and who, possessed of a more experienced constancy and of a loftier character, seemed destined for a happier reign.*

Rome, torn by internecine broils, and ruled by the irresolute sceptre of Honorius III., who had succeeded the grasping Innocent, appeared to relax its vigilance. Northern Europe, engaged in preparing for another crusade against the Saracens, was for a moment oblivious of Provence, where her knights considered that they had drowned the Vaudois church in the blood of its martyrs. Philip Augustus, busied in the west in wrenching English France from the craven grasp of king John, was inclined to temporize with the Provençals. The Vaudois nobles had united and driven out Amaury de Montfort from the viscounty of Alby and Be-

* Sism., Hist. Crusade against the Albigenses, p. 144.

ziers, installing the son and heir of the murdered prince, Raymond Roger, in his rightful states. The horizon was lit up with a deceptive brilliancy—too soon, alas, followed by the devastating storm—and the Vaudois church, rising from the sea of gore, enjoyed an apparent resurrection, and with unshaken constancy relumed the lamp of the ancient faith.*

After the extinction of a fire, some sparks will still lie concealed under the ashes. These, fanned by the gale, may kindle a new flame, which, after devouring all the combustible matter within its reach, will in its turn be quenched. So the momentary toleration in Provence recalled the preachers of the crusades, reattracted the attention of Europe, reawoke the napping fanaticism of the faithful, and launched a new horde of brutal enthusiasts upon the Vaudois, so that those of them who had escaped the first massacre were mostly involved in the searching destruction of the second.

In 1222, while the gathering tempest soughed ominously in the scowling heavens, but before the fell fury of the storm burst, Raymond VI. died suddenly at Toulouse.† Though this prince had shown neither distinguished talents nor force of character; though he had been early induced to assent to what he disapproved, and to inscribe his name among

* On the renewed progress of the Vaudois, not only in Provence, but in Leon and Galicia, see Jo. Mariana de rebus Hispan., lib. II., cap. V., p. 556.

† Sismondi's History of the Albigenses, p. 165.

those who came to ravish his country, and who cherished the secret purpose of depriving him of his heritage; though he had submitted with patient feebleness to all the ecclesiastical censures, to all the personal outrages which the legates, the pope, and the council of the Lateran could heap upon him, yet he died regretted and loved by his Vaudois subjects, who did not forget that he had incurred all this contumely by his indulgence towards them; that he had abhorred the bloodshed and racking tortures inflicted upon his states by the crusaders; and that, spite of the persuasion with which the crusaders had succeeded in inspiring him, that his religious duty as well as his temporal interest demanded these persecutions, he had always done his utmost to check the barbarous zeal of the executioners.

His administration had been gentle. Public liberty in the cities, commerce, manufactures, science, poetry—all had made rapid progress under his fostering care. But he was accused of feeling compassion for heretics. For this reason he was not only persecuted through life, but the spiteful vengeance of Rome followed him even for ages after death. His son could never obtain the honors of sepulture for his body. His coffin was deposited near the burial-ground of St. John of Toulouse, waiting the permission of the holy see for its interment. It was still there in the middle of the fourteenth century; but as it was only of wood, and as no one took care for its preservation, it was broken, and his bones were dispersed in the sixteenth century. The skull alone of the hapless count was long preserved in the *chateau* of the Hospitallers of St. John of Toulouse, to which order Raymond VI. had once belonged.*

In the year following the death of the count of Toulouse, 1223, Philip Augustus breathed his last.† One of the ablest kings since the weighty sceptre of Charlemagne swayed Europe, he aspired to consolidate an empire as vast as that of his great predecessor. He did indeed add materially to the grandeur of mediæval France, leaving to his successor an enlarged kingdom whose resources were carefully husbanded.

The ferocious bishop Fouquét, who was at Rheims on the accession of Louis VIII., better known in history as Saint Louis, eagerly seized that opportunity to enlist the superstitious young king in a new crusade against the Vaudois. Louis listened approvingly to the seductive eloquence of the renegade troubadour, ordered the sacred war to be preached throughout France, persuaded Honorius III. to kindle the zeal of Europe at large, and then, arming with avidity, swept like a vulture to the banquet of blood.‡

Then the cruelties of De Montfort's *régime* were

* Sism., Hist. Albigenses, Eng. transl., p. 166.

† Chronique St. Denys, p. 416. Raynaldi, Annal. Eccles. Fleury, Hist. Eccles.

‡ Preuves de l'Hist. de Languedoc. Bernardi Guidonis, Vita Honorii III., p. 570. Matthew of Paris, p. 267, et Hist. de France, p. 758.

reënacted. The crusaders had returned with seven other devils worse than the first. Hell was once more in full chorus, while all good Romanists joined in the tune. Monks marched from city to city preaching ferocity, and then facilitating by perfidy the execution of their counsels. The fanatics pillaged towns and villages and castles; outraged women, and even little girls; and then forming in circles around the blazing stakes at which the Vaudois were burning, with an impious affectation of devotion, chanted in unison the hymn *Veni Creator*, while the wail of their tortured victims ascended to the pitying heavens.*

No human calculation can ascertain with any precision the dissipation of wealth, or the wanton destruction of innocent life, which were the consequences of these crusades against a people whose only crime was that their lives bloomed with the beatitudes. Scarcely a peasant but reckoned some member of his family cut short in the flower of his days by fanatical violence; not one but had repeatedly seen his property ravaged and his household insulted by the crusaders. More than three quarters of the knights and landed proprietors of the proscribed territories had been despoiled of their fiefs.†

Yet the sanguinary fury of fanaticism was not glutted. In 1229, the council of Toulouse established the Inquisition in Provence as a permanent

* Sismondi, History of the Albigenses, p. 129.

† Ibid., p. 145.

institution.* The military power was reinforced by the subtlety of the monks. A code of procedure, framed for the express purpose of entrapping over-cautious heretics into unsafe admissions, was publicly circulated among the inquisitors.†

The Vaudois supported their doctrines by the authority of the holy Scriptures—the most unlearned among them could repeat large portions of the Bible by heart. Therefore the first indication of heresy was considered to be the citation either of the epistles or of the gospels; the second was any exhortation against the vices of the day, or any assertion of the necessity of a change of spirit in order to be saved; and the third was to show any compassion to the prisoners of the Inquisition.‡

The Council of Toulouse decided that the reading of the sacred Scriptures should not be permitted. "We prohibit," says the fourth canon of that memorable council, "the laity from having the books of the Old and New Testaments, unless it be, at the most, that any one wishes to have, from devotion, a psalter, a breviary, or the hours of the blessed Mary; but we forbid them, even then, to have these translated into the vulgar tongue."§

Another article read thus: "We command that whosoever shall be accused of the Vaudois heresy, or be noted with suspicion, shall be deprived in

* Lambock, Hist. Inqui. Matthew of Paris, etc.

† Hist. de Languedoc. Sism., pp. 233–235. ‡ Ibid.

§ Labbei, Concil. Tolosau, l. 11, p. 427, et seq. Fleury, Hist. Eccles., liv. 79, p. 58.

sickness of the assistance of a physician. Likewise, when a sick person shall have received the holy communion of his priest, it is our will that he be watched with the greatest care to the day of death or convalescence, that no heretic, nor any one suspected of heresy, may have access to such a one."*

A little later, when executions became less frequent because it was more difficult to procure Vaudois for their *autos da fé*, it was decreed, that the scent of the human hounds might be rendered keener by a bribe, that the confiscated property of a heretic should be shared between the spy who denounced and the judge who condemned him.†

The philosophy of Rome in these measures is evident. The reform had arisen from the first advancement in literature, and from the application of judicious reason to religious instruction. By thickening the darkness, by striking the developing mind and conscience of Christendom with a blight, this fermentation could be arrested, and mankind would bow once more in blind submission to their hereditary belief. "I can never admit," wrote Pasquier to the Dominican president, Brulart, "that the material arms of De Montfort would have overcome the Vaudois without the holy exhortations and the inquisitorial compulsions of St. Dominic and St. Francis."‡

* Labbei, Concil. Tolosau, l. 11, p. 427, et seq. Fleury, Hist. Eccles., liv. 79, p. 58.

† Raynaldi, Annal. Eccles., A. 1231, 16 et 17.

‡ Quoted in Browning, Hist. Huguenots, p. 17

The Vaudois met their fate with the meek heroism of the earliest Christians. Very few renounced their faith.* Blood never ceased to flow, nor the flames to devour their victims in these provinces, now completely abandoned to the dark fanaticism of the inquisitors. Tranquillity was never restored, persecution was never suspended, even by the death of its victims. The Provençals lived in a protracted agony.

Still the war raged. The French king had another motive besides the extirpation of heresy for its prosecution. The struggle had a political phase. The French court desired to round the empire into symmetrical form by adding to it these provinces, which bathed their feet in the blue waters of the Mediterranean.† As this object was not definitively accomplished until the year 1243,‡ the "sacred war" continued to devastate those fields which should have been covered by the richest harvests of the south, those cities which had been animated by commerce, industry, and intelligence, and to butcher that noble population whose devotion to their faith is the grandest legacy which the history of that time has bequeathed to posterity.

Beneath the accumulated tortures to which they were subjected the Vaudois melted slowly away. Their opinions ceased to influence society. The Provençal faith was no longer moulded on the primitive apostolic model. By the middle of the

* Fleury, Hist. Eccles.

† Sism., Hist. Albigen., p. 242.

‡ Ibid., pp. 226, 272.

thirteenth century the Vaudois had apparently disappeared. Terror was still extreme, suspicion universal. Though the teaching of the proscribed doctrine had seemingly ceased, yet the sight of a book caused a shudder, and ignorance was a salutary guarantee of safety.*

The Vaudois died as grandly as they lived. No refinement of torture could rack from their suffering lips a disavowal of their belief. Often they scorned to stoop even to concealment. Entering voluntarily the lurid fires of the Inquisition, they showed how martyrs could die for "Christ and liberty." Gaining strength from the devotional rapture of St. Paul, they earned a right to repeat with him,

"What shall we then say to these things? If God be for us, who can be against us? He that spared not his own Son, but delivered him up for us all, how shall he not with him also freely give us all things?

"Who shall lay any thing to the charge of God's elect? It is God that justifieth. Who is he that condemneth? It is Christ that died, yea rather, that is risen again, who is even at the right hand of God, who also maketh intercession for us. Who shall separate us from the love of Christ? shall tribulation, or distress, or persecution, or famine, or nakedness, or peril, or sword? As it is written, For thy sake we are killed all the day long; we are accounted as sheep for the slaughter. Nay, in all

* Sism., Hist. Albigenses, p. 238.

these things we are more than conquerors, through him that loved us.

"For I am persuaded, that neither death, nor life, nor angels, nor principalities, nor powers, nor things present, nor things to come, nor height, nor depth, nor any other creature, shall be able to separate us from the love of God which is in Christ Jesus our Lord."*

* Romans 8 : 31–39.

CHAPTER IX.

THE INTERREGNUM.

THE crime against the Vaudois was not the separate wickedness of a single nation. It was a mosaic of infamy, the legitimate, inevitable offspring of an ecclesiasticism which had employed every art to pervert the understanding and to corrupt the heart.

The Italian, Innocent III., first gave the signal for this outrage upon human nature; and he also bestowed the recompense. He continually sharpened the swords of the murderers, blunted in slaughter. When the fanaticism of Europe drooped, weary in its madness, he aroused it once more to raving fury by his clamorous appeals.

The two Spaniards, the bishop of Ozma and St. Dominic, the founders of the Inquisition, first taught the perfidious art of seeking out in the villages those whom the priests were afterwards to tie to their stakes. The Germans, invited by their monks, flocked from the extremities of Austria to glut their faith in massacre. And the English Matthew Paris renders zealous testimony to the activity of his countrymen in the same abandoned cause, and to their triumphant joy at the miracle—

for so he called the treachery of Beziers*—which had avenged the Lord.†

But the crime from which individual nationalities are to be absolved, is to be laid upon the conscience of Europe at large, and especially upon the pernicious counsels of the Roman church, which incited it, and juggled mankind into believing that the elect could be saved by a baptism of innocent and Christian blood.

Thus the reformation, of which the church had so much need, the light which was to illuminate the mind, to restore to morals their purity, to reason its empire, and to religion its pristine flavor and omnipotence, was repelled for three whole centuries, and even much longer with regard to those Italian and Spanish provinces which spoke the Romanesque languages.

The Vaudois taught too soon. Spreading their pure instructions through all the countries of the western empire in the superstitious infancy of Europe; called to combat with an established and arrogant ecclesiasticism—while the intellect of the Sclavonic, the Latin, the Anglo-Saxon, and the Germanic nations was not yet sufficiently awake to perceive the light, but saw men as trees walking—they had no fulcrum upon which to rest their lever. Their truth was throttled by the mailed hand of Rome.

As in the impious days of the crucifixion, "from

* See Chapter 5, p. 75, and onwards.

† Matthew of Paris, London edition, p. 203.

the sixth hour there was darkness over all the land unto the ninth hour,"* so now, when Christ was crucified again in the person of his gospel, an awful darkness intervened. A frightful interregnum yawned through three hundred years.

The Vatican smiled happily. It flattered itself that it had for ever fettered the human mind, that it had for ever choked the wail of outraged conscience, that it had for ever crushed the insurrection of the soul. The Vatican was mistaken. The interregnum meant *postponement*, not conquest. For two hundred years the fires had been kindled, yet still at intervals Romanists abandoned the faith of their fathers to embrace that which must lead them to the flames. In vain did the Inquisition essay to compel the unfetterable mind to submission, and to establish an invariable rule of faith. It saw in the midst of the darkness which it had created some luminous points loom up on the horizon. It saw those sparks which it thought that it had for ever quenched, but *scattered* by its folly, to light the universe once more. It had no sooner conquered, than it was obliged to renew the combat.

The Vaudois were not exterminated, they were only dispersed. Proscribed, far from their country, now no more theirs, alas, they wandered from the shores of the Mediterranean to the borders of the frozen sea, from the Carpathian mountains to the Orkney islands. Many also found their way

* St. Matthew 27 : 45.

into those obscure Piedmontese valleys which had been the cradle of their reform.*

Finding an asylum in the cottages of the peasants or poor artisans, whose labors they shared in profound secrecy, they taught their hosts to read the gospel in common, to pray in their native tongue without the ministry of priests, while they themselves continued to praise God and to submit gratefully to the chastisements which his hand had inflicted as the means of their sanctification.

The sufferings which they had endured for their sake made them cherish their tenets with the most reverential awe, and hand them down from generation to generation unaltered, uncorrupted, embalmed in the traditions of the Languedocian massacre.

Unable under the jealous eye of Rome to enjoy the external consolations of religion, they were shut up still more to internal communion. They ceased to care for the visible world. They placed their hands in God's, and sobbed their griefs away upon His heart who is the great Consoler. They believed that heaven was the substantial world, that its joys were the real joys, even for the body and the sense, and that there was no delight except as it flowed from God into heaven, and as it descended from heaven into time.

Though robed in rags, they esteemed themselves clothed more richly than the earth is when she makes herself gay with flowers for her summer

* Sism., Hist. Albig. Bossuet, Hist. des Variations. Calvin's Letters, etc.

bridegroom; more richly than the firmament is when it wraps round itself the jewelled mantle of the stars, puts constellations beneath its feet and sunlight galaxies upon its head. For the joy of God is woven into garments more splendid than those which wrap the flaming spheres.

The truths of salvation which Christ had taught, which he had embalmed for ever by his sacred sufferings, by the bloody sweat, and by the death on Calvary, were to them august beyond all pictured magnificence, radiant beyond all starry and all solar splendors, sweeter than the embodied essences of all odors which the spring pours in her jewelled cup before God, more musical than the harmonies that swell in grand cathedrals, that echo from hill and vale in summer woods, that come borne in soft sweetness in the happy talk of lovers, in the song of storied saints, in voices of rapture pulsing by moonlight over time's dim sea. Before the supernal vision of God's judgment they could only kneel in speechless adoration; if they tried to sing, the hymn wailed out but brokenly through the imperfect human instrument.

After their dispersion, the Vaudois seemed to vanish from the sullen history of the time. Seeking safety in obscurity, they no longer, to the superficial observer, appeared to impress their creed upon the human mind. Yet a deeper view discloses that they were the scatterers of God's seed in the furrows of these centuries, that they carried the unflickering taper of the gospel from which the later reformers were enabled to light their torches. They were the bridge which spanned the black abyss which yawned between the overthrow of the Vaudois church in Languedoc and the birth of Luther.

Though it is not clear that any of the Provençal Christians established themselves in England, it can hardly be doubted that Wickliffe acquired his first evangelical conceptions from their preachers. Wickliffe was a profound politician before he became a luminous teacher of divinity. A favorite at the court of St. James, he was dispatched in early life by Edward III. on several diplomatic missions to the popes at Rome and Avignon. Travelling therefore through the south of France at a time when the Vaudois were hunted and burned with patient vindictiveness, his acute and inquiring mind could not but occupy itself with investigating the grounds of their dissent.* A little later, Wickliffe held and publicly taught precisely the same tenets which he had seen men roasted alive for holding in Provence.

It may therefore be legitimately concluded that the Vaudois convinced the great Englishman that the church of Rome itself was wallowing in heresy.

Many of the Vaudois took refuge in Germany and in Bohemia, where Peter Waldo, their most celebrated teacher, had found an asylum when driven by priestly spite from his native Lyons, from

* Browning, Hist. Huguenots, p. 16. Life of Wickliffe, London, 1783, p. 63.

Dauphiny, from Picardy, from Saxony; and where he had died surrounded by the Bohemian mountaineers, the ancestors of Huss and Jerome.* Thus it was that God inoculated Bohemia with the truths of primitive Christianity. When Wickliffe's writings became known, the Bohemian Vaudois rallied, and resumed existence as an independent evangelical church.†

An interesting historical episode proves that there were still some Vaudois remaining in Southern France in the middle of the fifteenth century. It is recorded that the Vaudois of the towns of Cabriéres and Merindole, upon being menaced by the inquisitors—always busy, always ubiquitous through these sad years—dispatched deputies to Louis XII. to plead their cause before that able and just king. Although the priests strove to prevent it, they secured an audience. The Vaudois ambassadors declared that they received and taught the plenary inspiration of the holy Scriptures, the apostles' creed, the decalogue, and the Christian sacraments; but that they did not acknowledge the authority of the pope, nor adopt the antichristian dogmas of the Romish Babylon. Louis, surprised at the intelligence, moderation, and Christian appearance of the deputies, sent an envoy to inquire on the spot if their assertions were indeed correct. The commissioner, on his return, reported "that in those parts

* Waddington, Hist. Chh. previous to the Reformation, p. 292.

† L'Enfant, Hist. de la Guerre des Hussites, et du Concile de Bâle.

baptism was administered; that the articles of faith and the ten commandments were taught; that the Sabbath was solemnly observed; that the word of God was intelligently expounded, while portions of it were familiar to the most unlettered rustics; and that as to the fornications and poisonings of which they were accused, no instance of either could be found." "Wonderful!" ejaculated Louis; "these people are much better Christians than myself and all the rest of my orthodox subjects; let them remain undisturbed." And this *fiat* of the king was respected scrupulously throughout his life.*

For some generations the Piedmontese Vaudois, although known to exist, were suffered to remain in despised security.† But this may have been owing to the fact that the latter part of the thirteenth century and the commencement of the fourteenth were occupied with the fierce struggles between the rival factions in Italy of the Guelphs and Ghibelines. It is also possible that the preaching of another crusade in the East,‡ Europe's last mighty effort to wring the Holy Sepulchre from the Saracen, left their persecution to abate.

But the Vaudois barely sufficed to keep aglow the sinking embers of the gospel in these dismal ages. Huss with his Bohemians, Wickliffe with his Lollards, were in too fearful a minority to inaugurate any thing but feeble local reforms, trodden

* Lampe, Hist. Eccl., p. 291. Browning, Hist. Huguenots, p. 16. Turretin, Hist. Eccl. † Waddington, Hist. Chh., p. 292.

‡ Hallam, Hist. Middle Ages.

down, with those who launched them, as soon as the Roman sentinels descried them from the Vatican. They were powerless to reshape the character of their epoch; their opinions did not mould society at large. They could only wait and suffer and pray, floating down the centuries faith personified.

As proverbially it is darkest just before the morning smiles, so now the gloom wrapped the universe, thick, impenetrable, ominous. Then came those days never to be remembered without a blush, the age of dwarfish virtues and gigantic vices; the epoch of unreasoning superstition and unbridled wrong; the paradise of bigots. Swarms of licentious priests swept through Europe, sparing neither man in their wrath nor woman in their lust. The misshapen carcass of nominal Christianity lay huge and drunken across Christendom. Grown lazy with wicked prosperity, Rome was almost too indolent to persecute.

Decked out in her gaudy rags, gay with silk and velvet and satin, the gilded and painted strumpet of the papacy thought only of *fêtes*, of feasts, of dances, of pantomimes; the very services of the altar were turned into a carouse.* The church traded, like a Jewish huckster, in the relics of saints, and bartered her usurped rights for gold with which to fill her coffers, emptied in debauchery.† Pontiffs, like Alexander VI., bloated with wine, with murder, with adultery, with incest, *sat as God, in*

* D'Aubigné, Hist. Ref., vol. 1, passim.

† Michelét, Life of Martin Luther, p. 20.

the temple of God, with horrible profanity cursing the saints, and bestowing the apostolic benediction upon sinners with drunken gravity.* Indecent orgies were daily held in the Vatican, which were openly attended by the pontifical mistresses. Europe was surrendered to the domination of demons, while pandemonium held wild jubilee.

> "Thus all did turn degenerate, all depraved,
> Justice and temperance, truth and faith forgot."†

But God had long been preparing the way to a glorious reformation by a baptism of suffering. This reformation was to be the result of two distinct forces, the revival of learning and the resurrection of the gospel. The latter was the great motor power, but the former was necessary as a means.‡ The ignorance of Europe had enabled Rome to stifle the cry of the Vaudois preachers. There was no public opinion to which they could appeal. There existed but two classes in society, lawless despots and breadless serfs.

The invention of printing insured the triumph of nascent Protestantism. By emancipating Europe from the thraldom of ignorance, it secured its deliverance from the harder slavery of Roman ecclesiasticism. Faust, under God, dug Christendom out of mediæval Jesuitism. Henceforth truth could not be throttled. Its voice animated ten thousand

* Ranke, Hist. of the Popes—Alexander VI.

† Paradise Lost, book 11, p. 34, Mitford's edition.

‡ D'Aubigné, Hist. Ref. in Eng., p. 113.

never-weary witnesses. It spoke trumpet-toned and everlasting through the press.

Then came Luther. He set before mankind

> "The paths of righteousness, hcw much more safe
> And full of peace, denouncing wrath to come
> On their impenitence."

Thus Vaudoisism and learning, the study of the classics, of Greek, of Hebrew, the dawn of an eager and discriminating intelligence through the cultivation of letters, were the two laboratories of reform. A few earnest souls had discovered the light in lowly valleys; mankind were soon to discern it upon the lofty mountain tops.

CHAPTER X.

THE RESURRECTION OF REFORM.

The sixteenth century witnessed the resurrection of reform. The infant form of civil and religious liberty had been rocked in the cradle of an earlier epoch, only to die in its bright youth. Now the veil of the tomb was rent, and it came forth armed with new strength. That era, like a first conqueror, founded a new realm, the realm of opinion. Instantly the customary, the mediæval, received a check. The scholastic methods of the universities began to recede before the progressive spirit of emancipated philosophy. The further usurpations of paganized Christianity were vetoed by the authoritative voice of primitive faith.

The new instinct was so full and active, that it bubbled over into secondary spheres. It showed itself even in architecture; and the Gothic towers of the old royal keeps were replaced by creations formed on the models of chaste ancient art. It showed itself in war, and the mailed, mounted chivalry went down before the infantry and the artillery of innovating science.

Moral and political Europe, equally rotten, began to be revolutionized. Now, as always before, Rome set herself to subdue the rebellion against her theology and her politics, using her old weapons, thumb-screws, racks, unearthly dungeons, and slow fires, invoking the grim horrors of the Inquisition to aid her in chilling the rising lava-like enthusiasm for the truth.

But God was not mocked. He sat serenely in the blue heavens, making the wrath of man to praise him. It had been decreed in His councils who is from everlasting to everlasting, that the spiteful drama in which Rome played the part of Sir Omnipotent should not be lengthened into further acts without a vigorous and successful protest.

When the pontiffs condescended to recite the articles of their belief to mediæval Europe, the Amen of Christendom was fiercely fervent. But at length Leo X. stepped out upon the balcony of the Vatican, and commenced to intone his creed: We believe in the observance of the minutest trifles of the ceremonial law;* we believe that human nature is neither hereditarily corrupt nor intrinsically depraved;† we believe that the saints and martyrs had a superfluity of merit, which they delegated to the church, and which, placed in the huge tureen of Rome, may be ladled out to those hungry souls who are willing to buy heaven with a price;‡ we believe in the theoretical celibacy of the clergy;§ we believe in the dogma of monachism;|| we believe that there exists in the priesthood of the holy see a me-

* Fleury, Eccl. Hist.

† Pelagius, in Aug. de Gratia Dei, cap. 4.

‡ Waddington, Hist. Chh.

§ Ibid., Pontificate of Hildebrand.

|| Ibid., p. 297.

diatorial caste between God and man;* we believe that the pope, *sitting as God, in the temple of God*, cannot err;† we believe that salvation is to be obtained by good works, by *ave Marias*, by penances, and by gold.‡

And when the courtly Medici's last cadence died quite away, as he ended his impious recital, while Europe stood ominously silent, a clear, resonant voice, echoing from the heights of the obscure town of Wittemberg, in semi-barbarous Germany, replied, "Oh nations, ye have listened to Pope Leo's Babylonian heresies: hark ye now to the Christian truth; for thus saith the Lord God: 'By one man sin entered into the world, and death by sin; and so death passed upon all men, for that all

* Bossuet, Institutes.

† D'Aubigné, Hist. Ref., vol. I., p. 50. ‡ Ibid.

The ludicrous yet heated assertion of the papal infallibility, made by all the Roman philosophers and polemics, cannot but excite a smile from the historical student. If it be true, the doctrine covers and makes right the lechery and the murders of Alexander VI., the martial madness of Julius II., and the palpable errors of Leo X. It is also difficult to reconcile this claim with the fact that for seventy-one years, from 1305 until 1376, there were *two infallible* heads of the Roman church, one at Rome, the other at Avignon, each hating the other with mortal hatred, fulminating decrees of excommunication against each other, and filling the universe with the noise of their dissensions. Pray, which of these popes uttered the voice of God? which breathed forth idle wind?

Pope John XXII. was formally impeached in the early part of the fourteenth century, by order of two faithful emperors, backed by several prelates, before an ecclesiastical council held at Milan; and his accusers endeavored to convict this infallible pontiff, this vicar of Christ, of heretical depravity. And John was forced to make a lame apology. Not only the *heel*, but the *whole body* of this Achilles is vulnerable. See Waddington, Hist. Chh., p. 386.

have sinned. But not as the offence, so also is the free gift. For if by one man's offence death reigned by one; much more they which receive abundance of *grace* and of the gift of righteousness shall reign in life by one, Jesus Christ.' "*

By these words Luther launched the Reformation, whose soul was, *salvation by faith* in Jesus Christ.

Then the mutterers of the mass and the children of the Bible joined battle to decide which should shape the future.

That struggle was the epic of the sixteenth century. The Roman publicists have affirmed, and certain rationalistic philosophers on both sides of the water have claimed, that it meant emancipation from the dominion of the religious principle—that it meant, not a *reformation*, but an *abolition* of Christianity.

But the choral song of the Reformation was not materialism. The movement which Luther inaugurated, and which Calvin organized, did indeed clasp hands with liberty and strike off chains; but only as a logical *result*, not as its chief *purpose*. The *object* of the Reformation was, to reopen the path by which God and man unite. This path, which Christ had opened, had been blocked up in ages of superstition by the worship paid the Virgin, the saints, the host, by meritorious, magical, supererogatory works, by ecclesiastical formalities.† Men

* Romans 5, passim.

† D'Aubigné, Ref. in the time of Calvin, vol. 1, p. 318.

awoke to protest; Protestantism arose from the inner impulses of European life.

Religion was long the terror of the world. It was attempted to dissipate it by amusing nations, or to pile it over with strata of society—a layer of soldiers, over that a layer of lords, and a king on top, with clamps of priests and hoops of castles. But the religious sentiment would penetrate this motley mountain which lay piled huge and unshapely upon the human conscience; it would burst the hoops, and rive the earthy matter laid on top of it.

> "The ethereal mould,
> Incapable of stain, would soon expel
> Her mischief, and purge off the baser fire,
> Victorious."*

The reformers recognized the cheat, believed in a real unity, heard the cry of smothered conscience beneath the mountain of priest-caste which Rome had reared with the patient labor of ages, invoked God's earthquake to topple it over; and as layer after layer fell, while society grouped itself on the level of faith in God, not in men, the angels themselves sang pæans. The overthrow of an ecclesiastical oligarchy, God and man brought face to face through faith in Christ, this was the *grand work* of the Reformation, whatever other beneficent *results* might follow in its train.

So far was Protestantism from involving a principle contradictory to religion: it simply sought to comprehend it, and to secure to mankind the lib-

* Paradise Lost, book 2.

erty to understand it, in a more spiritual and unselfish disposition, in opposition to a worldly priesthood;* it called on man to ground his faith, not on the word of a priest, but on the infallible word of God.

In 1519, two years after Luther had openly denied the infallibility of the church of Rome, the college of the Sorbonne, the most famous in mediæval Europe, where Reuchlin had studied, where Erasmus had been graduated, but always the champion of Latin orthodoxy, denounced the new opinions. Twenty-four months later, the Parisian faculty of theology published their memorable condemnation of the Lutheran heresy.†

At the same time Leo X. was launching the thunderbolts of the Vatican upon the Reformation in Germany. Attracted by the universal hubbub, scholars paused in the first flush of their enthusiasm for resuscitated learning, to look up from their Greek text and inquire into the meaning of the din. The fascination of ancient letters was forgotten for a moment. Persons of the highest stations and of the lowest became curious to examine and weigh the merits of a controversy to which so much importance seemed attached. France especially was in a fever of excitement. Authentic records show that so early as 1523 there were in several of the provinces of that realm, and particularly in Southern France, Languedoc, Provence, the ancient seats

* Ranke's Civil Wars and Monarchy in France, p. 131.

† Duncan, Religious Wars of France, Introduction.

of the Vaudois creed, great numbers both of the gentry and the commons who had embraced the reformed tenets; and even some of the episcopal order were tainted with Lutheranism.*

In 1519, two of Luther's ablest and most eloquent disciples, Martin Bucer, all fire and energy, and Melancthon, the personification of calm, persuasive Christian philosophy, had visited France and created a desire for reform.†

At the outset, the omens were favorable to the reception of the new theology in France. As the abuses of Rome were wide-spread, ripe, and pregnant, the dissenters made many and rapid converts. Francis I., who ruled the realm at the commencement of the Reformation, was the puppet of his own vanity, inordinately fond of gayety, pomp, and dissipation. Without fixed principles of religion, he regarded questions of faith with indifference, so long as they did not trench upon the domain of policy. The historical rival of Charles V. of Spain, when that cunning emperor temporized with the German dissenters, he also tolerated their brothers in France.

Thus it was that the Reformation secured time to ground itself in that kingdom; and this comparative immunity from persecution, this portentous stillness which ushered in a frightful storm, was so

* Mosheim, Eccl. Hist., vol. 4, p. 87.

† Brantome, Vie de Margaret, vol. 1, p. 384. Maimbourg, Hist du Calvinisme, liv. 1, p. 10. Maimbourg complains of the liberty which these insolent doctors took in venturing to interpret the Bible differently from Rome.

well employed that when the trial hour came, it was found that half of France, headed by some of the most historic names in her annals, were the devoted disciples of the reformed theology.*

The numbers and influence of these disciples of a pure faith soon made them loom up into importance. It began to be thought that they might subvert the established religion. Influenced by this fear, and pushed on by the incessant solicitation of the churchmen resident at his court, as well as by the active example of Charles V. in the Netherlands, Francis I. was persuaded to persecute the reformers, timidly at first, but finally with Titanic energy.†

The French prelates, though immersed in the lewd pleasures of the court, were too clear-sighted not to see with alarm the precipice upon which their order stood. They had sanctioned the aid furnished by Francis to foment the rebellion of the German Protestants, in order that internecine broils might weaken and perplex the political power of Charles V. But they were not disposed to tolerate the new opinions in France, lest their ascendency should despoil them of their revenues, as it had already despoiled the Germanic bishops. It was the dread of pecuniary loss, rather than care for religious unity, that urged these worldly and foppish prelates, lapped in luxury, bloated with pride, and swollen with license, to desert for an instant

* Davilla, Hist. des Guerres Civiles de la France, p. 20, folio edition.

† Duncan, Religious Wars of France, Introduc.

the arms of their mistresses, to button-hole the king, and insist upon the adoption of sanguinary measures for the extirpation of heresy; it was this which impelled them to admonish Francis that the maintenance of the old faith in its integrity would be a full atonement for all the sins he had committed or might commit—would be a passport to paradise.

The effects of this policy of the courtier prelates were soon experienced. On the 9th of June, 1523, a severe edict against the heretics was published.* Then, in the autumn of the middle ages, the reapers of intolerant Rome went out into the field to glean once more a bloody harvest.

The first step of the victorious priests, under the king's decree, was to disperse an influential and numerous congregation of reformers at Meaux.† This city was in the episcopal see of William Briçonnét, an earnest and devout churchman, who had studied the canons of the Scripture as well as the canons of the church, and who, animated by the words of Luther, had himself ascended the pulpit, proclaimed the doctrine of salvation by faith, and conducted himself as a bishop should, by striving to instruct his flock, by identifying his interests with theirs, instead of neglecting them to immerse himself, as most of his order did, in the unhallowed dissipations of the gayest capital in Christendom.‡

* Maimbourg, Hist. du Calvinisme, liv. 1. Browning, Hist. Huguenots, p. 21.

† Davilla.

‡ Ranke, Civil Wars and Monarchy in France, pp. 133, 134.

But the platforms of the Sorbonne echoed with denunciation. The "novelties" of Briçonnét were placed under the ban, as the deviations of Wickliffe, of Huss, of Jerome, of Luther, had already been, and the good bishop's instructive eloquence died away in a stifled groan.*

Lefèvre of Estaples was the friend and mentor of Briçonnét. This patriarch of the Reformation had ventured to study the original records of the faith, while Europe yet shivered in the chilly gloom of superstition. He drew from the Pauline epistles certain maxims concerning justification and faith, which a little later formed the soul of the reformed theology; and this indefatigable student, at the advanced age of eighty, preserving his vivacity and intellectual strength untouched by time, commenced a translation of the Bible, which forms the basis of the French version of the Scriptures.†

For a time Francis I. wavered in his determination. The fickle monarch, influenced by Erasmus, then the learned idol of lettered Europe, befriended Lefèvre, and even established a college for the cultivation of the ancient languages, in opposition to the Sorbonne.‡ The deep religious spirit of the age touched for a moment the callous, selfish heart of the knight-errant king. With his mother and sister he frequently read the Scriptures, and they were heard to remark that the divine truth—which seemed to them to be there—ought not to be de-

* Ranke, Civil Wars, etc., p. 133, 134.

† Ibid., pp. 132, 133.

‡ Ibid., 137.

nominated heresy. Luther was frequently lauded at the court, while the Sorbonne sullenly lamented that the persecution of the followers of the heretic and the destruction of his writings, despite the king's decree of the 9th of June, met with obstructions from the Louvre.

But Francis remained for a little under the influence of his sister and the scholars of the empire. He even spoke of nullifying his edict, and was heard to regret the dispersion of the Meaux assembly;* affirming at the same time that he saw no reason why Roussel and Aranda—two celebrated orators of the Reformation—should not preach at the court.†

The shuttlecock king soon had a relapse. When Erasmus nudged his elbow, he was tolerant; when the prelates pointed to the rising tide of the reform, and bade him beware lest it swamp his throne, he grew alarmed.

The first symptom of the change was an *auto da fé.*

In the initial days of the Reformation, Louis de Berquin, one of the earliest opponents of the Sorbonne, an eminent scholar, an enthusiastic Christian, enjoyed the special favor of Francis, who, like all pedants, loved to surround himself with *literati*, with artists, with sculptors, and who petted Leonardo da Vinci with one hand, while he patted French scholarship upon the shoulder with the other.

* Davilla. † Ranke, Civil Wars, etc., p. 136.

Berquin's boldness soon impelled him to cross swords with the Sorbonne. The consequence was, that while his royal master, captured by Charles V. at Pavia, languished in a Spanish prison, he lay in the dungeons of the Inquisition. Francis, on his return to France, liberated the incarcerated scholar, who was no sooner out however, than, making it a point of honor not to retire before his persecutors, he recommenced the combat, undertaking to convict Beda, the syndic of the Sorbonne, of himself holding heretical opinions.*

Berquin relied upon the monarch's support. But meantime Francis, who had hurled himself upon Italy like an avalanche, was once more foiled by the calm tactics of the wily emperor, and returned into his kingdom with shattered health, a decimated army, and weakened authority; for, as Erasmus remarked in a warning to Berquin, the king's defeat had weakened his domestic power.

The Sorbonne saw the opportunity, seized it, actually secured the consent of the king to their programme of procedure, and taking Berquin, in 1529, publicly burned him on the Place de Gréve. The Parisian populace, over whom the preachers of the Sorbonne exercised unlimited influence, are said to have shown less sympathy for this hapless victim than they ordinarily exhibited for the most abandoned criminals.†

* Erasmus ad Carolum Ulenhofium; cal. Jul., 1529.

† Ibid. "Sic omnium animos in illum excitârunt qui . . . . . nihil non possunt apud simplices et imperitos." Benoit, Hist. de l'Edit de Nantes, vol. 1, p. 8.

Francis I. never afterwards paused. The demon of persecution took full possession of him. To the end of his life he continued to slaughter his subjects with an indiscriminate malignity which bordered on frenzy.

To this chapter of persecution, the Jesuit Fleury refers with an unfeeling jeer: "From time to time some false prophet appeared upon the scene, to publish his fanaticism or to sound the disposition of the court. But repression was prompt: it cost dear to one Berquin of Arras, to Jean Leclerc, a wool-carder of Meaux, and to Jaques Parané, a clothier of Boulogne. They were all burned alive, and a dread of the fire silenced the spirit of several oracles. History doubtless mentions these despicable names to perpetuate the reproach of their birth or their impiety, rather than to celebrate these vile founders of the Calvinistic church."*

Rail on, proud mocker, at God's lowly poor. But these despised and scattered members of a torn body were made one again in Jesus Christ; while from their ashes they spoke with grander, more persuasive eloquence than that with which antique art endowed him who

> "Fulmined over Greece
> To Macedon, and Artaxerxes' throne."

* Hist. du Cardinal de Tournon, par le P. Charles Fleury, de la Compagnie de Jesus, p. 215; Paris, 1728. This violent writer must not be confounded with Claude Fleury, author of the Hist. Eccles.

CHAPTER XI.

THE COURT OF FRANCIS I.

THE opening phases of the Reformation bear the impress of two illustrious women.

The first of these was Renée, duchess of Ferrara, and daughter of Louis XII. This lady had been early won to adopt the resurrected tenets of the gospel. Under the beautiful sky of fatal Italy she listened to the hurried words of the flitting reformers who ventured to mutter their opinions in an undertone even beneath the very throne of Leo X. The situation of her husband's estates in the near vicinity of Rome, made him fearful of exciting either the temporal or spiritual wrath of the pontiff, lest that arbiter both of this world and the next should pounce upon him and despoil him of his heritage.

Therefore Renée concealed her sentiments during the duke of Ferrara's life. But a little later, become a widow, she quitted the stifling atmosphere of Italy, and taking possession of the castle of Montargis, an hour's ride from Paris, openly avowed her adherence to the reformed theology, and gave the warmest of welcomes to the evangelical preachers, besides offering to the persecuted the safest of asylums.*

* Brantome, vol. 1, page 328. Gibbon, Antiquities of the

The other of these ladies was Margaret de Valois, queen of Navarre, the daughter, the sister, the wife, the mother of kings, the greatest woman of her age.

Margaret, like Renée, had given her cordial assent to the teachings of the "evangelicals,"* as the French reformers were sometimes called.

The sister of Francis I. lived much at the court, figured in state ceremonies and in the councils at the Louvre, at St. Germaine, at Fontainebleau; yet she preserved her sweet simplicity, her religious zeal, her calm faith, amid the wicked fascinations of her brother's court, giving her heart to the three things she loved best—the king, France, and the gospel of her Christ.†

Margaret went wrapped in the respectful veneration of Europe. The scholars of Christendom were especially proud of one who had devoted her May of life to literature and divinity, who wrote and spoke with equal grace and eloquence, who was familiar with Latin, with Greek, with Hebrew;‡ they enthroned her as their princess, they hailed her as their Mæcenas.

She had also been early initiated into politics. The diplomats counted her one of the best heads in Europe; and Dandolo, the Venetian am-

House of Brunswick. Browning, History of the Huguenots, p. 20.

* D'Aubigné, History of the Reformation in the time of Calvin, vol. 1, book 2, passim † Ibid., p. 326.

‡ Ibid.

bassador, affirmed her to be the ablest politician in France.*

Margaret is said to have been beautiful and stately in her person;† and thus accomplished, influential, politic, and courageous in her Christian belief, she walked through the kingdom binding up the wounds of the hunted dissenters, succoring the needy, befriending the outlawed professors of the hated truth, earning the benediction of the sixth beatitude: "Blessed are the pure in heart; for they shall see God."‡

"A perfect woman, nobly planned
To warn, to comfort, and command;
And yet a spirit pure and bright,
With something of an angel's light."§

After Francis had decided to fight heresy under the banners of the Sorbonne, Brantome relates that the constable, Anne of Montmorenci, when conversing with him upon the most effectual mode of extirpating heresy, did not scruple to say that "his majesty should begin with his court and his own relations," naming Margaret as one of the most dangerous of the heretics. Francis replied, "Nay, speak no more of her; she loves me too well not to believe what I believe,"‖ with which equivocating phrase he turned off his overzealous counsellor.

* Questa credo sii la piu sana, non dico delle donne de Franza ma forse anche delli huomini, etc. Dandolo, 1542.

† Brantome, Vie de Margaret. ‡ St. Matthew 5:8.

§ Wordsworth, Lines on his Wife.

‖ Brantome, Vie de Margaret.

Margaret has been finely called the mother of French reform. She did indeed by her life, by her precepts, by her station, by her enthusiasm, attract many to the gospel. Her influence in the upper tiers of society was especially marked. But there is always danger when princes turn missionaries. When the Bible spoke through the eloquent lips of the most beautiful woman of the day, there were some who yielded an apparent assent, not because they were penetrated by the truth, but because they were fascinated by the bewitching speaker; for when Margaret exhorted, who so stout as not to bow his head, and at least simulate conviction? But such Christianity was of course but superficial at the best; and when danger lowered, these fair-weather disciples skulked away. Others yielded an intellectual assent to the truths of Protestantism, but preserved the heart icy and untouched—a sad error, decomposing to the religious life of a church, destructive of the existence of nationalities.

Thus from one cause or another it chanced that there were many enlightened consciences in the upper ranks of French society, but there were few consciences which were *smitten* by the word of God. This weakened even the apparent strength of the Reformation in Latin Europe. For as Merle D'Aubigné has well said, "Conscience is the palladium of Protestantism, far more than the statue of Pallas was the pledge of the preservation of Troy in the heroic fable of the Odyssy."

When, a little later, Margaret, who had been

already wed to the duke of Alençon—a prince of the blood, but a man without courage, amiability, or understanding, chief cause of the disaster at Pavia, from which field he had fled in disgrace, and eventually died of shame—married again Henry d'Albrét, king of Navarre, the companion in arms of Francis, a prince brave, gay, accomplished, handsome, witty, learned, and eloquent, the young queen wrote religious toleration upon the first line of the first page of her code of laws, and opened an asylum for the persecuted "evangelicals," which even kings long hesitated to violate.*

Meantime the persecution continued with increased severity. The reform saw her children around her, some already dead, some in chains, all threatened with a fatal blow. Martyrdom followed martyrdom. Such havoc was made among the "evangelicals," that an annual procession was instituted to render thanks to the Almighty that they had been permitted to spill so much heretical blood.† When Dymond Leroy, with five others, suffered in 1528, Francis went personally to witness the execution, and stood bareheaded while the fires were kindled. When the *fête* was over, the monarch marched away from the scene at the head of a procession of monks and priests.‡

Of course the encouragement thus given by the king's personal attendance at an *auto da fé* could

* Brantome, Vie de Margaret. Crespin, *Martyrologue.*
† Browning, Hist. Huguenots, p. 21.
‡ Maimbourg, Hist de Calvanismo, liv. 1.

not but be productive of increased enthusiasm in persecution. France bled from every pore. To record these sufferings would convert these pages into a martyrology.

Francois, archbishop of Lyons and cardinal of Tournon, was the chief instigator of these massacres. This haughty and intolerant prelate was the representative of an ancient family. He had entered the church at an early age, and had risen rapidly through the various ecclesiastical grades—monk, abbé, bishop, archbishop—until, in 1530, in his forty-second year, he received the red hat of a cardinal.*

Tournon was celebrated as a negotiator and as a statesman, but it is as a persecutor that he achieved his widest fame.† To use his panegyrist's expression, "He made it as dangerous to converse in secret as to discuss in public. Nothing escaped this great man, who seemed to multiply himself in order to discover artifice or punish temerity; so that foreign princes were accustomed to say that he alone was equal to an inquisition in France."‡

The overweening pride and bigotry of this inflated prelate had been sharply curbed by Margaret while she resided at the court. But upon her departure for her kingdom of Navarre, the emancipated cardinal became the confidant and adviser of the king. He was thus enabled to give loose rein to his atrocities.

* Hist. du Cardinal de Tournon, par Charles Fleury.

† Fleury, ut antea. ‡ Ibid., p. 214.

Under the iron hand of Tournon, the vacillating monarch was kept sternly immovable in the policy of blood. On one occasion when Margaret had persuaded her brother to listen to a sermon by one of her favorite preachers, Lecoq, curate of St. Eustache, who ventured "to preach the doctrines of Zwingle," as we are assured by Maimbourg, "though the king could not at first discern the venom concealed under his fine phrases," the cardinal compelled Lecoq publicly to retract, and imposed a penance on Francis for listening to his sermon.*

At another time the queen of Navarre so highly extolled the piety and genius of Melancthon, that Francis consented to invite him to a conference with the French divines upon the best means of restoring harmony to the divided church.

The clergy were in consternation. The prospect of contending with the learned and eloquent St. John of the Reformation alarmed them as greatly as it elated the evangelicals. Francis had already dispatched the invitation; but Tournon undertook even at the last moment to prevent the visit. His scheme for changing the king's opinion is described by Maimbourg as worthy of immortality.

He entered the royal apartment apparently absorbed in the pages of a book which he held in his hand. Francis, noticing his abstraction, inquired the name of the volume which interested him so deeply. The prelate paused in his measured walk,

* Maimbourg, Hist. du Calvinisme, liv. 1, p. 26.

looked up with a well-affected start, and replied, "Sire, it is a work by St. Irenæus." He then instantly directed the monarch's attention to a passage where Irenæus had given full scope to his feelings against heretics, showing that the apostles would not even frequent any public place where they were admitted. The wily cardinal then expressed his grief that, with such examples before him, the eldest son of the church should have sent for a heresiarch who was the most subtle and celebrated of Luther's disciples. Francis, surprised and shocked, instantly sent to revoke his invitation, protested by all the saints in the calendar that he would never renounce his hereditary faith, and, to give emphasis to the declaration, issued orders for the persecution of the heretics with additional vigor. "This sudden and *generous* resolution," moralizes the Jesuit who chronicles the episode, "fell like a thunderbolt upon the Protestants, who felt secure from such a reverse under the protection of the queen of Navarre."*

The prospects of reform grew gloomier every day. The provinces were abandoned to the cruelty of the prelates. The capital was governed by the court. The court was controlled by two harlots.

It was during the reign of Francis I. that women acquired that ascendency at court which enabled them, under the two or three succeeding sovereigns, to nominate and to depose ministers, marshals, and

* Maimbourg, Hist. du Calvinisme, liv. 1, p. 29.

judges—to dictate the policy of France. Francis, fond of gallantry and intrigue, thought that the charms of the softer sex would smooth the rough manners of his courtiers into becoming gentleness. From that idea sprang the new *régime.* The age of iron was succeeded by the age of debauchery. Ladies flocked to the court, each anxious to secure credit and influence, and careless of the means by which that object was gained. Chastity soon ceased to be a virtue—it became *prudery;* female honor was bartered for the privilege of bestowing pensions, or for the *éclat* of station. The authority of the ministers was merely nominal; the wives and daughters of the nobles swayed the sceptre, each one retaining it so long as her beauty, talents, and intrigues enabled her to command an ascendency.*

Hence originated the excessive luxury, the super-refinement, the loose morality of the higher circles of French society. Men of letters, wits, poets, flitted through the galleries of the Louvre, each one attracted thither by avarice, by pleasure, by ambition, or by all.

The servility of these mocking letters increased the corruption of the age. The wits and poets who thronged the halls of the palace lowered the moral tone of the court circles by their nauseating flatteries, by their unchaste songs, by their profane epigrams.

They soon made themselves of use to the ladies by chanting hymns to the beauty of some favorite,

* Miss Pardoe, Court of Francis I.

and by satirizing her rivals. They held their talents to be a marketable commodity, to be knocked down to the highest bidder. Their verses conferred taste and genius upon their patrons, though nature might have denied them common-sense.

This mixture of lewd women, atheistic bishops, servile wits, and scheming courtiers, formed what was deemed a brilliant and gallant court.

The courtiers were divided into two rival factions, each of which obeyed one or the other of two beautiful but abandoned women, the Duchess d'Estampes, mistress of Francis I., and the famous Diana of Poitiers, mistress of the king's eldest son Henry, the dauphin.*

Atheism might be bred by such an atmosphere; bigotry might be made to grow in such a soil; persecution might thrive in such ground; but the austere precepts of the Reformation were too rare an exotic to be fostered there. The self-denial, the pure morality, the indifference to unlawful worldly pleasure, which characterized the "evangelicals," awoke no responsive chord in the breast of a court surrendered to dissolute levities. Nay, the courtiers soon came to hate their reproving Nathan. "We are weary," pouted Diana of Poitiers, "of the declamation of the reformed preachers against the vices of the court and of the church."†

And so the guilty court spun out its wild dance, unmindful, as it quaffed its brimming bowl, as it

* Duncan, Religious Wars in France, pp. 4, 5.

† Miss Pardoe, Court of Francis I.

reeled and joked and laughed, of the earthquake which growled beneath its feet.

But the orgies at the capital did not stay the devastating tread of persecution. The inquisitors walked across France, from the English channel to the Pyrenees, hunting heretics and kindling *autos da fé*, until, to borrow the striking expression of a writer who has painted that epoch for the instruction of shuddering Christendom, "France scented burning bodies in every breeze."*

* Crespin, Martyrologue, folio p. 138.

CHAPTER XII.

THE APOSTLES OF THE FAITH.

Reference has been already made to several of the worthies who aided in the resurrection of the gospel in France—to Renée of Ferrara, to the beautiful Margaret of Navarre, to Lefèvre, to that Berquin who suffered in the Place de Gréve, and who, with his Testament in hand, had traversed the neighborhood of Abbeville, the banks of the Somme, the towns, manors, and fields of Artois and Picardy, filling them with love for the word of God.

But there were other apostles of the faith besides these.

A nobleman of the German city of Strasburg, Count Sigismund of Haute-Flamme, a friend and ally of queen Margaret, who called him her good cousin, had been touched by Luther's heroism and the preaching of Zell. His conscience once aroused, he endeavored to live according to the will of God. Sigismund was not one of those nobles, rather numerous then, who spoke in secret of the Saviour, but before the world seemed not to know him. The reformers all bore loving testimony to his frankness and courage.*

Although a dignitary of the church, and dean of

* "Videmus quosdam tui ordinis, qui abscondite Christo adherunt, publice autem negant." Lambert to Hohenlohe.

a celebrated theological chapter, the count labored to spread the evangelical truth around him; and one day, while busied in revolving the best means of doing so, he conceived a grand idea.

Finding himself placed between Germany and France, and himself speaking fluently the languages of both, he resolved to undertake the task of leavening France with the precepts of Christ.

He instantly commenced his self-imposed labor. As soon as he received any new work from Luther, he had it translated into French and forwarded to Margaret.*

He did more. Esteeming the queen of Navarre to be the door through which the principles of the Reformation were to enter France, he wrote Luther, urging him to pen a letter to Margaret, or to compose some pamphlet calculated to encourage her in her zealous labors.†

Count Sigismund's labors with the priests and nobles who surrounded him were not crowned with success. Some few gentlemen indeed spoke brave words, but they were only lip deep. But the monks looked at him with genuine amazement. Their dreams were disturbed, their licentiousness was reproached, the *dolce far niente* of their lives was to be broken up. "Ah ha! the Reformation then means that we must change our easy life, give up our naps, quit our cloisters, surrender our illicit amours;" 'twas thus they reasoned. The keen eye

* D'Aubigné, Hist. Ref. in the time of Calvin, vol. 1, p. 340.

† Ibid.

of Lambert of Avignon, one of the ablest of the reformers, detected this commotion in the monkish dove-cotes, and turning to the count, he said with a smile, "You will not succeed here; these folks are afraid of damaging their wallets, their kitchens, their stables, and their bellies."*

Sigismund succeeded better with Margaret. Soon after the defeat at Pavia, he wrote her a sympathetic letter; and again, when her sisterly affection drove her to seek Francis, when he languished in his Spanish prison, Margaret was strengthened and comforted by her *good cousin's* kind words.†

Pierre Toussaint, prebendary of Metz, Roussel, one of queen Margaret's favorite preachers, and Farel, were also active servants in the vineyard during these initial years. They all endured great sufferings for the sake of that gospel which they loved. Still, nothing could shake their faith. They continued to tune their voices into harmony with the celestial chorus.

On one occasion, when Toussaint chanced to pass through the diocese of the abbot of St. Antoine, that violent and merciless priest seized the young evangelist, and despite his candor, sweetness, and the broken health under which he rested, plunged his fragile victim into a frightful dungeon full of stagnant water and other filth.‡ Toussaint

* D'Aubigné, p. 340.

† Letters de la Reine de Navarre, 1, p. 211. Boston city Library.

‡ "In carcere pleno aqua et sordibus." Herzog Œcolampade, Piéces Justificatives.

could hardly stand erect in this hideous den. With his back against the wall, and his feet on the only spot which the water did not reach, stifled by the poisonous vapors emitted around him, the young preacher recalled the cheerful house of his uncle the dean of Metz, and the magnificent palace of the cardinal of Lorraine, where he had been so kindly received ere he became a heretic. What a contrast! His health declined, his mind sank, his tottering limbs could scarcely support him.*

Meantime poor Toussaint's friends had acquainted Margaret with his condition, and the indignant queen hastened by post to Paris, threw herself at the feet of her brother, and finally rescued this lamb from the fangs of the wild beast.

When the young evangelist came out of this fearful den, he was thin, weak, and pale as a faded flower. He stood bewildered. No one offered to receive this heretic who had just cheated the scaffold. But at length he went boldly to Paris, sought Margaret, and found an asylum with her.†

Toussaint found the young queen surrounded by distinguished personages, all eager to present their homage. "Side by side with nobles and ambassadors dressed in the most costly garments, and soldiers with their glittering arms, were cardinals robed in scarlet and ermine, bishops with their satin copes, ecclesiastics of every order with long gowns and tonsured heads."‡ These, desirous of

* D'Aubigné, p. 359. † Ibid., p. 364.

‡ Toussanus Œcolampadio. Quoted in D'Aubig., vol. 1, p. 366.

enlisting the influence of Margaret in their favor, spoke to her of the gospel and of reform. Toussaint, a stranger to the chicaneries of politics, listened with profound astonishment to this strange court language. At the outset he was deceived, and took the religious prattle of this troop of flatterers for sound piety. It was not long, however, before his eyes were opened. When he saw the drift of their artful harangues, he burned to expose them.

Learning that Lefèvre and Roussel had arrived in Paris from Blois, Toussaint, full of respect for them, hastened to their apartments, and with impetuous eloquence urged them to assist him in unmasking the hypocrites, and in boldly preaching the whole gospel in the midst of the giddy court.

"Patience, Toussaint," replied the two scholars, both timid by nature, and whom the debilitating air of the court had perhaps still further weakened; "patience; do n't spoil every thing; the time is not yet come."* Then Toussaint, ardent, generous, upright, burst into tears. "Yes," he said, "be wise after your fashion; wait, put off, dissemble: you will acknowledge however at last that it is impossible to preach the gospel without bearing the cross. The banner of divine mercy is now raised; the gate of the kingdom of heaven stands wide open. God calls us. He does not mean us to receive his summons with supineness. We must hasten, lest the opportunity should escape us, and the door be closed."†

* Toussanus Œcolampadio.

† Ibid.

But the timid scholars could not be moved. Then he wrote Œcolampadius, "Roussel is weak; Lefèvre lacks courage; God strengthen and support them."

For himself, he was stifled at the court; the air was closer to him than in the den of the abbot of St. Antoine. Disgusted by the lewd revels of the capital, he resolved to quit it. "Farewell to the court," said he; "it is the most dangerous and seductive of harlots."*

Then the young Metzer, putting behind his back certain "magnificent offers" which had been made to him if he would stay and connect himself with the mystical and timidly progressive wing of the Roman church, which Briçonnét then represented, quitted the kingdom. But foreseeing that a terrible struggle was approaching, he left with a prayer that God would enable France to show herself worthy of the Reformation.†

William Farel, another of those men upon whom God set the seal of his apostleship, was one whose simple, serious, earnest tones carry away the masses. "His voice of thunder made his hearers tremble. The strength of his convictions created faith in their souls; the fervor of his prayers raised them to heaven. When they listened to him, 'they felt,' as Calvin once said, 'not merely a few light pricks and stings, but were wounded to the heart, *pierced* with the truth; hypocrisy was dragged from those

"Aula, meretrix periculosissima." Touss. Œcolampadio.

† Neufchatel MS., cited by D'Aubigné, vol. 1, p. 368.

wonderful and more than tortuous hiding-places which lie deep in the heart of man.'

"He pulled down and built up with equal energy. Even his life, an apostleship full of self-sacrifice and danger and triumph, was as effectual as his sermons. He was not only a minister, he was a bishop. He was able to discern the young men best fitted to wield the weapons of the gospel, and to direct them in the great war of the age; for Farel never attacked a place, however difficult of access, which he did not take."*

Farel's native place was Gap, a little village in Dauphiny.† Desirous of preaching the gospel to his relatives there, on one occasion he took up his quarters in a corn-mill hard by the gates of the hamlet, where he explained a French Bible to the villagers who crowded about him.

Ere long he ventured to preach in the very heart of Gap; "desecrating," as the Capuchins phrased it, "a chapel dedicated to St. Colombe." "The magistrate forbade his preaching, and the parliament of Grenoble desired to have him burned;" so runs the record of the monks.

Farel replied by a formal refusal of obedience; upon which Benedict Olier, a zealous papist, and vice-bailiff, escorted by a *posse comitatus*, marched to St. Colombe. The doors were shut, and double-barred. The officers knocked. All were silent.

* D'Aubigné, vol. 1, pp. 374, 375.

† Charronnét, Les Guerres de la Religion dans les Hautes Alpes, Gap, 1861, p. 17.

They broke in. A large audience were assembled, but not a head was turned; all were drinking in greedily the eloquent words of the dauntless preacher. The officers went to the pulpit, seized Farel, and "with the crime in his hand," as the forcible expression of the Capuchins put it, referring to the Bible which he held, he was led through the crowd and imprisoned.

But the followers of the new doctrine were already to be found in every class—in the workman's garret, in the tradesman's shop, in the fortified chateau of the noble, and sometimes even in the bishop's palace. During the night the reformers rallied, and either by force or stratagem took the brave old man from prison, hurried him to the ramparts, let him down into the plain in a basket, and "accomplices" who awaited him sped with him to a place of safety.*

Although the larger part of Farel's apostleship was spent in foreign countries, for he was an exile from his dear France, yet he exercised a very marked influence upon the formation of the Gallican church.†

Under the distant inspiration of Luther's eloquence, under the zealous labors of Toussaint, Sigismond, Farel, and Margaret, supported by an active host of less distinguished representatives, the reform continued to spread, despite Tournon's exertions‡ and the denunciations of the Sorbonne. But

* Charronnét, ut antea. † Bossuét, Hist. des Variations.

‡ "Notwithstanding Tournon's ubiquity, the heresy spread rapidly." Fleury, Hist. du Cardinal de Tournon.

the dissenters were scattered, often ill-informed on vital points of faith, and lacked *uniformity* of effort and belief. Who shall organize the Reformation? Who shall mould this heterogeneous mass of dissent into a grand unit? This loose-jointed body of reform, whose plastic hand shall reshape it into strength and symmetry? Such were the questions which Farel, Œcolampadius, Sigismond, and the other chiefs of Latin reform began to put to each other with anxious emphasis.

Then the brain of French Protestantism began its work: John Calvin appeared.

CHAPTER XIII.

JOHN CALVIN.

John Calvin was born on the 10th of July, 1509, at Noyon, in Picardy,* which was also Lefèvre's native province.† He was emphatically a man of the people. His family was not one of marked importance. His grandfather was a cooper at Pont l'Evèque; his father was secretary to a bishop, and in the days of his greatest prosperity, apprenticed his brother Antony Calvin to a bookbinder. Simple, frugal, poor, intelligent, such were John Calvin's immediate progenitors.

His father valued letters, and he determined that his son should be liberally educated. The boy was therefore sent in his fifteenth year to the college of La Marche, at Paris.

There, pale, diffident to a painful degree, but with a look of striking intelligence, the bashful and studious boy of Noyon speedily shot to the head of his class. It was at the university that the famous friendship between Calvin and Mathurin Cordier began. Cordier, in 1523, when Calvin came to town, was a professor at La Marche. One of those men

* Beza, Life of Calvin.

† Ranke, Civil Wars and Monarchy in France, p. 147.

of ancient mould, who prefer the public good to their own advancement, he had neglected a brilliant career which had opened its alluring arms to welcome him, and devoted himself to the instruction of children.* The professor was instantly attracted towards his singular pupil. Calvin's purity, his quickness, his thoroughness, his genius captivated him, and he lavished his instructions upon the thoughtful boy with unstinted hand. He taught him Latin and Greek and Hebrew. He initiated him into the temple of mediæval culture. He imparted to him a certain knowledge of antiquity and of ancient chivalry. Indeed he inspired his pupil with his own ardor, and walked with him, arm in arm, in the "true path" of science.

In after years, when both master and scholar had been driven from France, and had taken up their abode in that little city at the foot of the Swiss Alps, whose mouth was to *speak great things*,† Calvin, then expanded into the most celebrated doctor in Europe, loved to recall these days of his student life, and publicly announcing his indebtedness to Cordier, he said, "Oh, Master Mathurin, Oh man gifted with learning and great fear of God, when my father sent me to Paris, while still a child and possessing only a few rudiments of the Latin language, it was God's will that I should have you for my teacher, in order that I might be directed in the true path and right mode of learning; and having first commenced the course of study under your

* D'Aubigné, vol. 1, p. 382.

† Daniel 7:8.

guidance, I have advanced so far that I can now in some degree profit the church of God."*

But in those days both Cordier and Calvin were strangers to the evangelical doctrine, and devoutly followed the papal ritual.

"Calvin," says one of his biographers and disciples, "was at first a strict observer of the practices of the church. He never missed a fast, a retreat, a mass, or a procession."† "It is a long time since Sorbonne or Montaigne had so pious a seminarist," was the common expression.

Thus Calvin, like Luther, while in the papal church, belonged to its strictest sect. "The austere exercises of a devotee's life were the schoolmaster that brought these men to Christ."

His application surprised his tutors. Absorbed in his books, he often forgot the hours for his meals, and even for sleep.‡ The people who resided in the neighborhood were accustomed to point out to each other as they returned home late at night, a tiny, solitary gleam, a window lit up till the starry tapers of the sky were quenched in the grey of the morning. There sat John Calvin, elaborating in his august reveries thoughts which a little later were to convulse the universe.

Calvin's father, familiar with his son's genius, had marked out for him a brilliant ecclesiastical career: an abbot's mitre, a bishop's cope, the red

* A Mathurin Cordier, Dédicace du Commentaire de la 1re Ep. aux Thess., par Calvin.

† Beza, Vita Calvini.

‡ D'Aubigné, vol. 1, p. 386.

hat and the scarlet gown of a cardinal glittered before his eyes. Therefore when he heard from time to time of young Calvin's rapid advancement in grammar, in philosophy, in scholastic theology, he would smooth his beard and say, "Ah ha! we shall see brave things yet."

In 1527, two years after leaving home, he went back to Noyon at vacation time, and "although he had not yet taken orders, he delivered several sermons before the people."* At eighteen he had a parish.†

Then it was that a new light, which had but little resemblance to the false radiance of scholasticism, began to shine around him. At that time there was a breath of the gospel in the murky air, and the reviving breeze reached the scholar within the walls of his college, the priest in the recesses of his convent; no one was protected from its influence. Calvin heard people talk about the Bible, Luther, Lefèvre, Melancthon, Farel, and of what was passing in Germany.

When the rays of the sun rise in the Alps, it is the highest peaks that catch them first. In the sunrise of the Reformation, the most eminent minds were first enlightened. In the colleges there were sharp and frequent altercations. Calvin was at first among the most inflexible opponents of the evangelical doctrine; but soon he was won to study. Thoroughness was his mania. With him, as with so many others, examination meant emancipation.

* Beza, Life of Calvin. † Ibid.

And at length, after a terrible struggle, he experienced that "joy and peace in believing" which had solaced Luther's torn soul in the Erfurth cloister. His conversion was hastened by witnessing several martyrdoms.* He opened his Bible. Everywhere he found Christ. Instantly the scales fell from his eyes. "Oh Father," he cried, "His sacrifice has appeased thy wrath; his blood has washed away my impurities; his cross has borne my curse; his death has atoned for me. We had devised for ourselves many useless follies, but thou hast placed thy word before me like a torch, and thou hast touched my heart, in order that I may hold in abomination all other merits save those of Jesus."†

Calvin then, at nineteen, broke with Rome, and quitting Paris repaired to Orleans, and later to Bourges, where he "wonderfully advanced the kingdom of God."‡

After a life of vicissitudes, extending from the year 1527 until 1535, frequently smitten by the bolts of excommunication, a fugitive at Angouleme, at Nevac, at Poitiers,§ yet preaching at Paris,‖ and haunting the scenes of his greatest danger, Calvin repaired to Geneva *en route* to Germany, where, unexpectedly to himself, his journey was summarily arrested; while his name became ever after united with that of the brave Alpine city which,

* D'Aubigné, vol. 1, pp. 393, 394.

† "Ut pro merito abominarer, animam meam pupugisti." Calvini Opusc. Latin, p. 123.

‡ Beza, Hist. des Egl. Ref., pp. 6, 7.

§ Ibid., p. 98.

‖ D'Aubigné.

under his sway became the Rome of the Reformation.

And here, at the name of Geneva, it becomes not only interesting and instructive, but germain to this history, to sketch the more salient outlines of the gallant and romantic story of that immortal city, as magnificent in the beauty of its landscape, clasped to the snowy bosom of the Alps, bathing its feet in the waters of lake Leman, as in the grandeur of its moving history.

Geneva was at first simply a rural township, and as a part of Gaul it became an appendage of the Roman empire when the emperors leashed the European provinces to their car of conquest. In the fourth century, under Honorius, it became a city, receiving this title after Caracalla had extended the franchise of citizenship to all the Gauls.*

From the earliest times, either before or after Charlemagne, Geneva possessed rights and liberties which guaranteed the citizens against the despotism of their feudal lords. The Genevese claimed to have been free so long that *the memory of man runneth not to the contrary*;† and it is certain that the precise date of the birth of their freedom is shrouded in the mist of remote antiquity.

The Genevese soil was composed of three *strata:* the political lords, the counts of Geneva, who even so early as the eleventh century had extended their rule over an immense and magnificent territory;

* Mem. d'Archéologie; quoted in D'Aubigné, vol. 1, p. 11.

† Ibid.

the bishops, who, gifted with superior intelligence, respected by the barbarians as the high-priests of Rome, and knowing how to acquire vast possessions by slow degrees, finally confiscated for a time the independence of the citizens without much ceremony, and united the quality of prince with that of bishop;* and the burghers, not very numerous, but always intelligent, and resolute to maintain their parchment guarantees.

When the counts of Geneva had been hoodwinked by the cunning of the bishops into ceding the city to them, they had reserved the old palace, and part of the criminal jurisprudence, and continued to hold the secondary towns and the rural district of their countship.†

But in process of time dissensions arose. The conflicting jurisdictions of the bishop-princes and the counts clashed.

Prelates who had already turned their croziers into swords, their flocks into serfs, and their pastoral dwellings into fortified castles, hungered for more power. The battered walls of Geneva yet bear the marks of the fierce struggle which ensued, and which continued through the thirteenth, fourteenth, and fifteenth centuries.

In the middle of the thirteenth century, Pierre de Savoy, a soldier and a politician, made a herculean effort to recover the city of his ancestors. The conflict lasted long; but eventually he was obliged to surrender his claims. Disgusted with his failure,

* D'Aubigné, vol. 1, p. 13.

† Ibid.

and exhausted by his unceasing activity, Pierre finally retired to his castle of Chillon, where every day he used to sail upon the beautiful lake, luxuriously enjoying the charms of nature lavished around; while the melodious voice of his minstrel, mingling with the rippling of the waters, celebrated the lofty deeds of this illustrious paladin.*

In the fifteenth century the counts of Savoy, having added several other provinces to Genevois, and become dukes, more eagerly desired the acquisition of Geneva than ever. They changed their tactics. Sheathing the ineffectual sword, they resorted to wily diplomacy. The new campaign was opened with spirit, and pope Martin V. was petitioned to confer upon the dukes of Savoy the full secular authority in Geneva.

But the citizens, who in the lapse of ages had engrossed the civil government of the city, became alarmed at the news of this manœuvre; and knowing that "Rome ought not to *lay its paw* upon kingdoms," good papists as they then were, they determined to resist the pope himself, if necessary, in the defence of their liberties. Placing their hands upon the gospels, they exclaimed, "No alienation of the city or of its territory; this we swear."†

The sovereign of Savoy, balked in his best scheme, withdrew his petition. But Martin V., while staying three months at Geneva, on his return in 1418 from the Council of Constance, ran a muck

* Monumenta Hist. Patriæ, vol. 3, p. 74.

† D'Aubigné, vol. 1, p. 18.

with the ancient city. There was something in the pontiff which told him that liberty did not accord with the papal rule. He was alarmed at witnessing the franchises of the Genevese. "He feared those general councils that spoil every thing," says a manuscript chronicle in the Turin library;* "he felt uneasy about those turbulent folk, imbued with the ideas of the Swiss, who were always whispering in the ears of the Genevese the *license of popular government.*"

"The pope," says D'Aubigné, "resolved to remedy this, but not in the way the dukes of Savoy proposed. These princes desired to secure Geneva in order to increase their own power. Martin thought it better to confiscate it to his benefit. At the Council of Constance it had just been decreed that episcopal elections should take place according to the canonical laws, by the *chapter*, unless for some *reasonable* and *manifest* cause the pontiff should think fit to name a person more useful to the church. Martin thought that the necessity of curbing republicanism was a *reasonable* motive; and accordingly, as soon as he reached Turin, he translated the bishop of Geneva to the archiepiscopal see of the Tarentoise, and heedless alike of the anger of the Savoy dukes, and of the rights of the canons and the citizens, he nominated Jean de Rochetaillée, patriarch *in partibus* of Constantinople, bishop and prince of Geneva."†

* D'Aubigné, vol. 1, p. 19, 20.

† D'Aubigné, Ref. in Calvin's Time, vol. 1, p. 20.

The Genevese, surprised and overawed, acquiesced in sullen discontent. Seventy odd years rolled away, and still the faithful citizens remembered their broken charters, and hugged the memory of their ancient franchises. At the commencement of the sixteenth century, driven to desperation by the tyranny of their bishop-prince, they determined to revolt, and turning towards Switzerland, whose

> "Hills, rock-ribbed, and ancient as the sun,"

had always borne up a hardy race of freemen, they invited the powerful Helvetic confederacy to assist them in expelling the usurper.*

In its earlier stages the contest was a political one, but ere long it assumed a religious phase. The Reformation was preached. Its spirit took invincible hold of German Switzerland. The towns of the Helvetic confederacy had often come into collision with the grasping dukes of Savoy. Cherishing republicanism as their palladium of safety, they also hated the bishop-prince of Geneva, who had despoiled their Genevese cousins of their birthright, besides planting an inimical state upon their borders. Switzerland therefore lent a willing ear to the Genevan ambassadors, who came to solicit the assistance of the confederation. And when, a little later, the Helvetic cities had the additional motive of wishing to clutch Geneva as a trophy won to the reformed faith which they professed, they threw themselves into the contest with re-

* Bonivard, Chroniq., 2, p. 290.

doubled ardor. Precisely as the house of Savoy, backed by the pope, wished to extend its limits in a monarchical and Romanist sense, Switzerland desired to extend hers in a popular and Protestant sense.*

The Genevese did not at once accept the Reformation. Numberless fierce quarrels followed its entrance within their walls.† But gradually the citizens, remembering the tyranny under which they had groaned when the bishop-prince swayed the sceptre of Geneva, recalling the mischief which pope Martin had worked them, and perceiving that the liberality of the reform contrasted strongly with the intolerant despotism of Latin orthodoxy, came over and ranged themselves under the Protestant banners, adjudging their franchises safer under the Reformation than under Rome.

William Farel of Gap had joined the Protestant missionaries when they undertook to extend their creed into the Romanic border lands,‡ and by his boldness, eloquence, and unceasing energy, he gave brave help in proselyting Geneva. Instigated by him, the city council had publicly proclaimed that Geneva adhered to the Reformation; and so wonderful was the spell of his preaching, that priests were seen to throw off their vestments before the altar, and confess the Protestant creed.§

Such was the posture of affairs when John Calvin entered Geneva in the year 1535. His inten-

* Ranke, Civil Wars and Monarchy in France, p. 142.

† Ibid., p. 144. ‡ Ibid., p. 142. § Ibid., p. 145.

tion was merely to visit Farel for a few days, and then seek in Germany an asylum where he might devote himself to tranquil meditation.* Farel, however, perceiving his vast ability, was resolved not to permit him to depart; and when Calvin refused to remain in Geneva, he announced the wrath of Almighty God upon him should he shirk his duty, for heaven, he said, would make the quietness of study a curse to him.†

Calvin afterwards said that it appeared to him as if he had seen the hand of God stretched forth from above to hold him back; he dared not resist it.‡

Calvin and Farel clasped hands, and immediately began to preach.

It seems that there were in Geneva certain persons who had adopted the reformed faith because they thought that it would bring them increased personal license. These latitudinarians were soon offended at the strict discipline which the two orators of the Reformation proclaimed. They intrigued so effectually that Farel and Calvin were exiled.§

Calvin was far from caring too anxiously for his person. He had been obliged to endure opposition, combined with agony of conscience, which he declared were more bitter than death—the mere remembrance of which made him tremble. He began now again to wander and to learn; in particular he commenced a correspondence with the

* Beza, Vita Calvini.
† Ranke, p. 147.
‡ Calvini, Opusc., Latin.
§ Ranke, p. 148.

German reformers, with Melancthon, with Bucer, with Capito, and formed a closer acquaintance with them at the Diet.*

It soon appeared that he could not be dispensed with at Geneva. The independence of the city was menaced in two directions: one party, which was inclined to the Vatican, were disposed to reinaugurate the old *régime;* the other showed a spirit of compliance with foreign dictation which imperilled the freedom of the town.

Both these factions were subdued, after long and sanguinary domestic contests, and those remained triumphant who regarded the maintenance of the strict Protestant discipline as the salvation of the city.

Deeply penetrated with this conviction, they looked upon all they had suffered as a punishment for the expulsion of their preachers. It was resolved to recall them. Although Calvin was extremely reluctant to return, yet Farel's solemn adjurations impelled him to accede to the call; and while Farel departed for Neufchatel, whither he had engaged to go, the great French divine reëntered Geneva as a conqueror in 1541.†

The condition of his return, though not distinctly stated, was still tacitly understood to be the adoption of his system of ecclesiastical discipline.‡

Calvin instantly went to work. He planted

* Ranke, pp. 148, 149. † Ibid., p. 149.
‡ Ibid.

education as the basis of his state.* He new-modelled the civil code, and shaped it to strict republicanism, sealing his renovation with these words of Christ: "THE TRUTH SHALL MAKE YOU FREE."† He next *organized* the Reformation. The Genevese reformers shaped their divinity on the model of his "Christian Institutes," which were written in 1536, and dedicated to Francis I., before the final return to Geneva.‡ Ere long this work was scattered broadcast through Latin Europe. The Reformation lost its heterogeneous character. The conflicting sects were melted into unity, and France at last accepted the essential tenets of the despised VAUDOIS when she permitted the plastic hand of her great Genevan doctor to mould her into PROTESTANTISM.

The abbé Anquétil, an old chronicler whose words at one time were in wide favor with the papists, considers the "Christian Institutes" to have been the chief support of the "heresy;" "for they systematized the Protestant doctrines, and enabled their assemblies to keep together even when their ministers were torn from them."§

God, by giving in the sixteenth century a man who to the lively faith of Luther and the scriptural understanding of Zwingle joined an organizing faculty and a creative mind of rare genius, furnished the complete reformer. If Luther laid the founda-

* Calvini, Opusc. † St. John 8:32.

‡ Duncan, Religious Wars of France, p. 8.

§ Anquétil, Esprit. de la Ligue.

tion, if Zwingle and others built the walls, Calvin completed the temple of God.*

Then Geneva became the school of the Latin and Anglo-Saxon, as Wittemberg was of the German and Sclavonic Reformation.

As soon as Guy de Brés and many other fiery scholars returned from Geneva to the Low Countries, the momentous contest between the rights of the people and the revolutionary and bloody despotism of Philip II. of Spain began; heroic struggles took place, and the creation of the republic of the United Netherlands was their glorious termination.

John Knox returned to his native Scotland from Geneva, where he studied several years; then popery, arbitrary power, and the exotic immorality of the French court, imported by queen Mary Stuart, made way on the north of the Tweed for the pure enthusiasm which bred Christian liberty and civilization.

Those Englishmen who sought an asylum in Geneva during the bitter persecutions of "Bloody Mary," imbibed there a love of the gospel and of civil liberty; and when they returned to Great Britain, these fountains gushed out beneath their footsteps.

Numberless disciples of Calvin carried with them every year into France the august principles of the Genevese school.†

Even the Pilgrim Fathers of New England,

* D'Aubigné, vol. I., p. 321. † Ibid., pp. 4, 5.

who, quitting their inhospitable country in the reign of that royal pedant James I., planted on this continent their populous and mighty colonies, may in no improper sense claim Geneva as their mother. Calvin, looming through the centuries, may stretch his hand across the water from Mont Blanc, and placing it upon the head of the American Republic, murmur a proud benediction, and say, "You too are mine; I created you."

CHAPTER XIV.

THE VALLEY OF THE SHADOW OF DEATH.

It will be remembered that the French king's first edict against heresy had been issued on the 9th of June, 1523.* Nearly three years later, February 5, 1526, government issued another fiat. In those days all proclamations were made by a herald who travelled from city to city, trumpet in hand, and sounding his trumpet in the public squares to collect an audience, cried out his message in a loud voice.

On the morning of the 5th of February there was an unwonted stir in the streets of Paris. Crowds of excited people thronged the pavements, and with vehement gesticulation and voluble tongue harangued one another upon some question of exciting import. The great rush was towards the Louvre. There, at ten in the morning, a herald took his stand upon the palace steps, and after the customary flourish of the trumpet, cried, by order of Parliament, "All persons are forbidden to put up to sale, or translate from the Latin into French, the epistles of St. Paul, the Apocalypse, and *other books*. Henceforward no printer shall print any of the writings of Luther. No one shall speak of the ordinances of the church or of images otherwise than as holy church ordains. All books of the

* See Chapter 10, p. 139.

Holy Bible, translated into French, shall be given up by those who possess them, and carried within a week to the clerks of the court. All prelates, priests, and their curates, shall forbid their parishioners to have the *least doubt* of the Romish faith."*

When the herald paused, the vast crowd began to disperse. The comments were various. "Heresy should be choked in blood," said some. "The Sorbonne fear Faust's type," said others. The majority turned away with the peculiar French shrug, and said quietly, "Patience; we shall see."

The prior of the Carthusians, the abbot of the Celestines, monks of all colors, "imps of antichrist," says an old chronicler, openly rejoiced in this brilliant triumph over heresy. "They gave help to the band of the Sorbonne," and cried, Amen, at the end of every sentence of the proclamation.

A little later the new edict was cried in Sens, Orleans, Meaux, and "in all the bailiwicks, seneschallies, provostries, viscounties, and estates of the realm."† And now Cardinal Tournon's inquisitors, taking one edict in the right hand and the other in the left, walked on their mission of destruction hedged about with the sanctity of public law.

France bled at every pore.

History teaches best by individual instances. Descriptions of collective cruelties lose their graphic power through the breadth of the delineation.

* Journal d'un Bourgeois de Paris sous Francois I., p. 276. Quoted in D'Aubigné, vol. 1, p. 342.

† Ibid.

There was a young man about twenty-eight years of age, a licentiate of laws, William Joubert, who had been sent by his father, king's advocate at La Rochelle, to Paris to study the practice of the metropolitan courts. Notwithstanding the prohibition of the Parliament, young Joubert, who was of a thoughtful disposition, ventured to inquire into the validity of the papal faith. Conceiving doubts, he said in the presence of some friends, that "not Genevieve nor even Mary could save him, but the Son of God alone."

For these words the unhappy licentiate was thrown into prison under the proclamation. His frightened father hastened to Paris by post; his son, his hope, a heretic, and on the point of being burned!

He gave himself no rest. Never before had he so exerted himself to save a client. He went to the Sorbonne; he visited the court; he besieged the Parliament. "Ask what you please," said the miserable father; "I am ready to give any sum to save my boy's life."

Vainly did the tireless advocate struggle. On Saturday, February 17, 1526, the inquisitor came for young Joubert, helped him into the tumbril, and carried him to the front of Notre Dame: "Beg our Lady's pardon for your infidelity," he said. Joubert was silent. He drove on to the front of St. Genevieve's church: "Ask pardon of St. Genevieve." The Rocheller was firm in his new faith.

He was then taken to the Place Maubert, where

the people, seeing his youth and handsome appearance, deeply commiserated his fate. "Do not pity him," said the inquisitorial guard; "he has spoken ill of our Lady and of the saints in paradise; he holds to the doctrine of Luther." The executioner then approached Joubert, pierced his tongue with a red-hot iron, strangled him, and then burned the body.*

A young student who already held a living faith, though not yet in priest's orders, had boldly declared that there was no other Saviour but Jesus Christ, and that the Virgin Mary had no more power than the other saints. This youthful cleric of Théronanne, in Picardy, had been imprisoned in 1525, the year preceding the last edict. Terrified by that punishment, he went on Christmas eve, with a lighted torch in his hand, and stripped to his shirt, and "asked pardon of God and of Mary" before the church of Notre Dame. In consideration of this "very great penitence," it was thought sufficient to confine him for seven years on bread and water in the prison of St. Martin-des-Champs!

Alone in his dungeon, the recusant scholar heard once more the voice of God in the depths of his heart; his conscience beat loud beneath the silent porch of his prison. He began to weep hot tears at the remembrance of his denial of the faith; "and forthwith," says the chronicler, "he returned to his folly." Whenever a monk entered his cell, the young cleric proclaimed the gospel to him. The

* Journal d'un Bourgeois, p. 251.

monks were astonished; the convent was in a ferment. Merlin, the grand penitentiary, went to him, and advised and entreated and stormed and menaced, all without effect. Finally, by order of the court, he was taken into the Place de Gréve, where poor Berquin suffered, and burned alive.*

Such were the methods employed by the Roman commission to force the abhorrent doctrines of their church back into the unwilling hearts of those who rejected them. They made use of scourges to beat them, of cords to strangle them, and of fires to roast them alive.

But the ultramontanists did not confine themselves to hawking at untitled prey. In the year 1533 they flew at a higher quarry. Margaret of Navarre, herself a queen, and sister to the king, was venomously assailed.

Margaret, sighing after the time when a pure and spiritual religion should displace the barren ceremonials of popery, had published, first at Alençon, in 1531, and then in Paris, in 1533, a poem, entitled, "*The Mirror of a Sinful Soul, in which she discovers her Faults and Sins, as also the Grace and Blessings bestowed on her by Jesus Christ her Spouse.*"†

The poem was mild, spiritual, and inoffensive; but it was written by a queen, and it made a great sensation. Many persons read it with interest, and admired Margaret's piety and genius.

But not so the Sorbonne. Beda, the fiery syn-

* Journal d'un Bourgeois, p. 291; cited in D'Aubigné, vol. 1, p. 350.

† Du Bellay, Memoires, p. 189.

dic, absolutely devoured the little book; he had never been so charmed with any reading, for at last he had proof that the king's sister was a heretic. A diabolical plot had been laid by the ultramontane party to ruin Margaret a little before, and her household were steeped to the lips in the plot.* But there was no occasion now to invoke the "Scythian ingratitude" of the queen's dependents. "Understand me well," cried the exultant syndic, holding up the volume, "this is not a dumb proof, nor a half proof, but a literal, clear, complete proof."†

The Sorbonne assembled. "Listen," said Beda. The attentive doctors fixed their eyes upon the syndic. Beda read:

"Jesus, true Fisher thou of souls,
My *only Saviour, only Advocate.*"

"Point against the accused," said Beda. He continued:

"Pain or death no more I fear,
While Jesus Christ is with me here."

"Confirmation," growled the syndic. "Listen again," said Beda:

"Not hell's black depth, nor heaven's vast height,
Nor sin, with which I wage continual fight,
Me for a single day can move,
Oh, holy Father, from thy perfect love."

The doctors were scandalized. "No one," said they, "can promise himself any thing certain as

* Miss Pardoe, Court of Francis I. D'Aubigné, vol. 2, p. 164.

† Theod. Bèze, Hist. des Eglises Reformées, 1, p. 8. Freer, Life of Marguerite d'Angoulême, 2, p. 112. See Les Marguerites de la Marguerite, 1, pp. 63, 65, etc., for the extracts quoted.

regards his own salvation unless he has learned it by special revelation from God."*

"Let us proceed," said Beda, overflowing with delight:

> "How beautiful is death,
> That brings to weary me the hour of rest.
> Oh, hear my cry, and hasten, Lord, to me,
> And put an end to all my misery."

"Deadly heresy," said Beda; "what insolence!" He made his report. "Of a truth," said his colleagues, "that is enough to bring anybody to the stake."

The Sorbonne instantly prohibited the *Mirror of a Sinful Soul,* and put it in the *Index Librorum Prohibitorum.*†

The faculty decided that the first thing to be done was, to search every bookseller's shop in the city, and seize all the copies found.‡ A priest named Leclery made the search. Accompanied by the university beadles, he went to every bookstore, seized Margaret's poem wherever the tradesmen had put it out of sight, and returned to the Sorbonne laden with the spoil.

Then the faculty deliberated upon the measures to be taken against the queen.

Meantime insinuations and accusations against the king's sister were uttered from every pulpit.§

* The Council of Trent made this precise declaration an article of faith.

† D'Aubigné, 2, p. 173.

‡ Calvini, Epp., p. 2.

§ Lettres de la Reine de Navarre, 1, p. 280. Freer's Life, 2, p. 118.

Margaret was even lampooned in a college comedy which Calvin reported.*

But still the faculty hesitated. They knew that Francis loved his sister, and they dreaded punishment. The monks were everywhere exasperated. "Let us have less ceremony," cried one of them, the superior of the Grey Friars; "put the queen of Navarre into a sack, and throw her into the Seine."†

Margaret supported these insults with admirable mildness. But when Francis heard of them, his rage knew no bounds. The constable Montmorenci, who had caballed against the queen of Navarre, was publicly snubbed.‡ The insolent prior who had proposed to sew Margaret into a bag and throw her into the river was next dealt with. "Let him suffer the punishment which he desired to inflict upon the queen," said Francis. But Margaret interceded for the wretch, and his life was spared. Stripped of his ecclesiastical dignities, he was sent to the galleys for two years.§ The collegians who had satirized the queen were imprisoned,‖ and the Sorbonne was severely rated; Beda was exiled, and the faculty were advised "not to mix themselves up in such dangerous matters, or to beware of the terrible anger of the king."¶

Thus auspiciously to Margaret and to the reform ended this tilt with the Sorbonne doctors.

* Calvini, Epp., p. 1. † Lettres de la Reine, etc., 1, p. 282.
‡ Brantome, Vie de Marguerite.
§ Castaigne, Notice sur Marguerite. Freer, Vie de Marguerite.
‖ Calvini, Epp., 1. ¶ Ibid.

But a terrible tragedy was about to be enacted, which compensated the faithful for the mortification of this defeat. The unhappy Vaudois appear once more upon the historic stage; now, as always before, agonized as martyrs.

Some of the Vaudois remained in France even after the cessation of the atrocious harries of De Montfort and St. Louis in the thirteenth century; and reference has been made to those of Cabrières and Merindole, who were protected by the noble fiat of Louis XII.* After their transitory appearance in that reign, the Vaudois had disappeared from the excited history of the succeeding ages, and wrapped in the mountain fastnesses of the French Alps, they procured the means of subsistence by pastoral industry. Thus they lived in peace with man and serving their fathers' God until the Reformation began to stir the world. Then Calvin, from his seat in Geneva, offered them his alliance.† He was familiar with the hoary tenets of their ancient faith, and he endorsed them.

Then the tranquil rest of the Vaudois mountaineers was broken. Their confession of faith was reported at Paris. Eighteen of their principal teachers were cited to appear before the Parliament.‡ But ere the summons could be obeyed, a decree of extermination was pronounced upon them without a hearing.

* See chap. 9, p. 126.
† Du Bellay, Memoires. Calvini, Opusc. Duncan, p. 9.
‡ Ibid.

William du Bellay was then governor of Provence. This gentleman was appointed by Francis to execute the sanguinary edict. With a humanity rare in those cruel times, the governor determined to see the king, and if possible to turn him from his purpose. Francis, who had previously appointed Du Bellay his envoy to the conference of Smalcald,* held him in high favor, and condescended to hear his representations.

"I have come, sire," said he, "to inform your majesty of the actual character of the Vaudois, which, in my official capacity, I have taken great pains to investigate. They do certainly differ from our communion in many respects; but they are a simple, irreproachable people, benevolent, temperate, humane, and of unshaken loyalty. Agriculture is their sole occupation; they have no legal contentions or party strife. Hospitality is one of their cardinal virtues; and they have no beggars among them. No one is tempted to steal, for his wants are freely supplied by asking."†

"But they are heretics," responded Francis sternly.

"I acknowledge, sire," said the governor, "that they rarely enter our churches; and if they do, that they pray with their eyes fixed on the ground. They pay no homage to saints and images; they do not use holy water; they do not acknowledge the benefit to be derived from pilgrimages, nor do they say mass either for the living or the dead."

* Du Bellay, Memoires. † Ibid.

"And is it for such men as these," said the king, "that you ask clemency? Go, go, Du Bellay; for your sake they shall receive pardon, if within three months they present themselves before the archbishop of Aix, renounce their heresies, and become reconciled with the mother church. If they are still rebellious, they must expect the utmost severity. Meantime the edict stands unrepealed. Think you that we burn heretics in France only that they may be nourished in the Alps?"*

The Vaudois cherished their patriarchal opinions too faithfully, they were embalmed in the tradition of too much suffering, to enable them even to think of submitting to the king's conditions. They therefore awaited their doom in frozen despair.

But it happened that the Provençal Parliament had for its president an advocate of unrivalled legal skill, M. Chassanée, and his noble heart prompted him to use every wile known to his profession to defeat the decree; and he did indeed succeed in postponing the execution of the edict until after his death.†

But Chassanée was succeeded by a fierce bigot named D'Oppede, who had no scruples to overcome. That we may not be accused of overcoloring the woful catastrophe which followed, we extract the account from the unfriendly pages of a Romish chronicler, the abbé Anquétil:

* Du Bellay, Memoires.

† Browning, Hist. Huguenots, p. 23. Abbé Anquétil, Esprit de la Ligne, vol. 1, p. 13. Maimbourg, Hist. du Calvinism, liv. 2.

"In 1545, Francis I. gave permission to employ the aid of arms against the Vaudois mountaineers. It was granted at the solicitation of the Baron d'Oppede, president of the Parliament of Aix, a violent and sanguinary man, who revived against those heretics assembled in the valleys of the Alps on the side of Provence a parliamentary decree given five years before."

"Every thing was horrible and cruel," says the historian De Thou, "in the sentence denounced against them; and every thing was still more horrible and cruel in its execution. Twenty-two villages were plundered and burned, with an inhumanity of which the history of the most barbarous people scarcely affords an example. The unfortunate inhabitants, surprised during the night, and pursued from rock to rock by the lurid light of the fires which consumed their dwellings, only avoided one ambuscade to fall into another. The piteous cries of old men, of women, and of children, far from softening the hearts of the soldiery, as mad with rage as their chiefs, only served to indicate the track of the fugitives and mark their hiding-places, to which the assassins carried their fury.

"Voluntary surrender did not exempt the men from slaughter or the women from excesses of brutality which human nature blushes to record. It was forbidden, under penalty of death, to afford them any refuge. At Cabrières, the principal town of the canton, seven hundred men were murdered in cold blood; and the women who had remained in their houses were shut up in a barn, which was filled with straw and then fired. Those who attempted to escape from the window were hacked back by swords or impaled on pikes. At the last, according to the tenor of the sentence, the houses were razed, the woods cut down, the fruit-trees plucked up by the roots, and this country, so fertile and so populous, became an uninhabited desolation."*

Such is the ghastly picture of this massacre, as painted by the reluctant pens of two inimical historians, De Thou and the abbé Anquétil.

Maimbourg, in describing the scene, says that more than three thousand persons were slain, and that nine hundred houses were plundered and then burned.†

Thus with a quivering wail passed this last remnant of the ancient Vaudois from the inhospitable and persecuting shores of time, to join their martyred ancestors in eternity.

But the Vaudois had accomplished their mission They had dropped the seed which sprang up and bore a hundred-fold. Severity, far from checking the progress of the Reformation, only inspired its professors with sublimer energy. They died, on the scaffold or amid the flames, with the steadfast devotion of martyrs.

Hitherto the reformers had only ventured to

* Abbé Anquétil, Esprit de la Ligue, vol. 1, p. 14. De Thou, tom. 1.

† Maimbourg, Hist. du Calvinisme, liv. 2.

assemble at night, and in the unknown byways and slums of France. Now they met openly in the light of day. They even erected a church in the heart of scoffing Paris, while the chief cities in the provinces hastened to imitate the example of the capital.*

Thus was fulfilled the later saying of John Calvin, that "the kingdom of Christ is strengthened and established more by the blood of martyrs than by force of arms."†

* Duncan, Religious Wars in France, p. 10.

† Calvin, Comm. sur S. Jean 17·36.

CHAPTER XV.

FRENCH POLITICS.

On the 31st of March, 1547, Francis I. died. Vacillating in his temper, arbitrary in his rule, selfish in his policy, yet generous in his private relations, he was the Don Quixote of a vicious chivalry. By his death, one more link was broken which bound France to feudalism.

Francis was succeeded by his son Henry II., a prince who inherited many of the qualities, and who adopted the essential policy of the paladin king; but he did not sway an unvexed sceptre. Schism, dangerous and ever growing, was within the temple; the court was fretted by hostile cabals; the Commons were turbulent; France bristled with rebellion; while from without, the pope had his clutch upon Henry's dominion, England fomented discord, and Spain, under Charles V.,

> "Forging the prodigal gold of either Ind
> To armèd thunderbolts,"

was a perpetual menace.

Let us glance for a moment at the politics of the court at this critical epoch, and form the acquaintance of some of the grand historic figures who were destined to sway France, and to mould her future—some by their wicked ambition, others by the healthful play of their noble aspirations.

The reign of Henry II. was emphatically an embryo period. It contained the roots of "many and tall trees of mischief," which afterwards covered France with an accursed shade.

Initiation into the vile mysteries of the temple of court intrigue—this is essential.

Four rival factions formed the substratum of the state.

Anne de Montmorenci, constable of France, the minister and favorite of Henry II., headed one clique. Montmorenci was able in the cabinet, and had won wide fame in the wars of the age; but his character was stained by bigotry and fierce rancor.*

The leader of a second party was Diana de Poitiers, duchess of Valentinois, the king's mistress, who, through her wit and beauty, possessed boundless influence with her royal paramour.†

Catharine de Medici, a daughter of the illustrious Florentine house which had given two popes to Christendom, the consort of the impetuous king Henry II., led a third faction in this scramble for power. Catharine's character had barely shown itself during the lifetime of Francis I.; but now she began to emerge from her former obscurity, and during the successive reigns of her three sons, she possessed supreme influence in the government.‡ The wily queen surpassed Machiavelli himself in tortuous statescraft. By constantly adjusting

* Davila, liv. 1. De Thou, liv. 3. Brantome, Vie de Henri II., vol. 7, p. 11.

† Ibid. Vielleville, vol. 1, p. 203, et seq. ‡ Ibid.

and readjusting the equilibrium of the contending factions, she prevented each from overwhelming the other; played one off against another; and by prolonging this contest, she extended the duration of her own power.*

The fourth faction of the court was that of the princes of Lorraine, better known in history as the Guises.† These were the greediest and most unscrupulous jackals of this courtly pack. The Guises were looked on as foreigners, and their power in France was a mushroom growth.

René de Lorraine, who fought with Charles the Bold of Burgundy, and who more than once brought the claims of his house upon Provence, Naples, and Jerusalem to remembrance, ordained in his last will that Antoine, his eldest son, should succeed him in Lorraine and Bar, and that the other, Claude, should inherit his possessions lying in France: these were estates scattered throughout Normandy, Picardy, Flanders, and the Isle of France, with the baronies of Joinville, Mayenne, Elbœuf, and the counties of Aumale and Guise,‡ all destined a little later to give names to distinguished warriors and prelates.

Among the chivalric leaders of Francis I., this Claude, who styled himself "Guise," whose domain had been raised from a county into a dukedom,§ made a brilliant figure. His bravery and miraculous preservation at the battle of Marignano, the

* Browning, p. 25.

† Davila, liv. 1.

‡ Ranke, Civil Wars and Monarchy of France, p. 168.

§ Brantome, Vie de Henri II., vol. 7.

central part which he took in preserving the peace of the kingdom during the captivity of the king after the fatal rout at Pavia, the pains he took to ingratiate himself with the masses and to cement the foundations of his power, ere long made him a great name in the realm. To crown all, he made a fortunate marriage, wedding a princess of the royal blood, Antoinette de Bourbon. From this union sprang six sons, full of vital energy, three of whom devoted themselves to the church, and three to arms, all achieving fame in their respective spheres.* These were Francis duke of Guise, sometimes called prince of Joinville, Charles archbishop of Rheims and cardinal of Lorraine, Claude duke d'Aumale, Louis cardinal of Guise, Francis grand prior, and René marquis d'Elbœuf.†

Such was the formidable house of Guise, propped by its six stalwart pillars; and even in the reign of Francis I., their rise and progress towards power had been so rapid and insidious, that the dying king bequeathed to Henry a legacy of distrust of their talents and ambition, which he thought—rightly, as the sequel proved—were of an order to endanger the peace of France.‡

Between these factions raged the utmost hate.

* Ranke, p. 168.

† Davila, liv. 1.

‡ Duncan, p. 20. This quatrain was then very common in France:

"Le roy Francois ne faillit point,
Quand il prédit que ceux de Guise
Mettroient ses enfants en pourpoint,
Et tous ses sujets en chemise."

See Memoires de Condé, and Satyre Menippée.

Usually they were at open war; but when peace reigned, it was but a hollow truce—*mars gravior sub pace latet*, war bitterer for the disguise. A coalition had been formed between Diana de Poitiers and the constable of France; so that the chief of the Montmorencis and the courtesan duchess for a time swayed the sceptre with untrammelled hands.* The duchess disliked Cardinal Tournon, and one of Henry's first acts was to dismiss this personified inquisition from the public service.† Montmorenci favored this move, and seeing that his only strength lay in Diana's smiles, he exerted himself to the utmost to flatter the king's passion for her.

Whatever was done or left undone owed its origin to no zeal for the public welfare, but was simply a manœuvre to deceive the king, whom all parties conspired to blind, and who throughout his reign was merely the empty shadow of an authority which was really vested in powers behind the throne.

Such was the political situation at the commencement of the year 1548.

The ambitious projects of the house of Lorraine were rendered doubly dangerous and difficult to foil by the masterly tactics of Francis duke of Guise, one of the most remarkable men of that age. As a soldier, he had distinguished himself by the capture of Calais from the English, who had usurped it in a preceding century, and by his defence of Metz against the Spaniards. He possessed in an eminent degree most of those external advantages which

* Browning, p. 25.

† Ibid.

captivate the multitude—a commanding presence, dignity, affability, an ingratiating address, and a certain chivalry. These rendered him the admiration of the populace, and made him the delight and ornament of the court.*

His aspiring schemes were of course powerfully supported by his influential brothers with their hosts of retainers, all as anxious as himself to share the patronage and emoluments of office.†

In pursuance of her favorite policy of an adjusted equilibrium, Catharine de Medici coalesced with the Guises, whom she both hated and feared,‡ against Montmorenci, who stood in the path of their ambition.

It was against this powerful confederacy that the constable had to struggle. Feeling his inability to resist it single-handed, he had already, as we have seen, called Diana de Poitiers to his side. He now resolved to attach the princes of the blood to his party. The next heirs to the throne after Francis and the other sons of king Henry, were Antony de Bourbon and the prince of Condé.

Antony de Bourbon, who had become king of Navarre by his marriage with Jane d'Albrét, the daughter of the good queen Margaret, was weak, indolent, vacillating, and too fond of ease to take any active part in the troubled and stirring scenes which were soon to convulse the kingdom. He was only roused from his habitual torpor by the hope of recovering that portion of his realm which had

* Duncan, p. 16. † Ibid. ‡ Vielleville, vol. 1, p. 298.

been seized and retained by Spain. As his success in this object depended entirely upon the armed assistance of France, he was easily drawn into the ranks of the ruling party by empty professions of friendship and hollow promises of material aid.*

His brother, the prince of Condé, who was connected with Montmorenci by a marriage with his niece, was a man of more determined character; and though not possessed of those high qualities which are requisite in a successful party leader, he compensated the political defect of ordinary talent by great moral courage and inflexibility of purpose.†

With many others of the higher nobility, he had espoused the reformed creed; and though he was too frank and open to shine as a diplomatist in an age when fraud and mendacity were the prime merits of a negotiator, he yet brought vast strength to the ranks of Protestantism. His finançes were scanty, but he was liberal to his followers; and when life was at stake or honor in peril, he displayed a promptitude and magnanimity of bearing which commanded universal respect.

Condé was the intimate friend of the Chatillons, an ancient family which had once exercised sovereign authority over Nantua and Moulonét, two towns in the neighborhood of Geneva.‡

The marshal de Chatillon had married Louisa de Montmorenci, the constable's sister, by whom

* Duncan, pp. 17, 18. † Ibid.

‡ Brantome, Vie de Coligny. Browning, note, p. 37.

he had three sons, two of whom achieved an immortality of fame. The eldest of these, Odét, became bishop of Beauvais and Cardinal Chatillon. He was a keen observer of the world, mild in his address, polished in his manners, an adept in the intrigues of the day, and possessed of all those winning and conciliatory arts which disarm an enemy and fix a friend.

The second son was the famous Gaspard Chatillon de Coligny, admiral of France,* one of the brightest and grandest names in history, doubly consecrated by a life of sublime fidelity to Christian duty, and by martyrdom.

The gallant Francis Chatillon d'Andelot was the youngest member of the family; he held the office of colonel-general of French infantry.†

The two younger Chatillons, better known by their seignorial appellations of Coligny and D'Andelot, were early initiated into politics by their uncle of Montmorenci, who placed great reliance upon their counsel and discretion. The fine talents of this famous family, their influential connections,

* The office of admiral of France is supposed to have been created in 1337, during the reign of Charles the Fair. Valnè, in his elaborate commentary on the French marine ordinance of 1681, gives a list of these officers, amounting in number to thirty-eight, down to 1626, at which date Henri de Montmorenci resigned the office into the hands of Louis XIII., or rather into those of Richelieu, who suppressed it by an ordinance dated January 16, 1627, together with that of constable of France. The duties of the old admiral were somewhat similar to those of an American secretary of the navy.

† Brantome, Vie de Coligny.

their high offices, rendered them most formidable to the vaulting house of Guise.

D'Andelot became very early an enthusiastic adherent of the Reformation. His open and generous nature made him scorn concealment, and he frequently startled the court by his liberal conversation.* On one occasion Henry II., upon hearing that his colonel-general had been heard to utter heretical sentiments, sent for him, on the advice of his favorite, Charles, cardinal of Lorraine, and interrogated him upon his opinions.

"How is this, sirrah?" said the king menacingly; "have you too become moon-stricken, that you utter this vile trash of Calvin, and rant like a common heretic against our holy mother church?"

Although D'Andelot had been cautioned to use prudence in his answer, he scorned to equivocate, and he replied firmly, but respectfully, "Sire, in matters of religion I can use no disguise, nor could I deceive God should I attempt it. Dispose as you please of my life, property, and appointments; but my soul, independent of every other sovereign, is only subject to my Creator, from whom I received it, and whom alone I deem it my duty to obey in matters of conscience. In a word, sire, I would rather die than go to mass."†

This calm speech roused the king to such fury, that he drew his rapier and menaced the intrepid disciple with instant death. But when his rage

* Brantome, Vie de Coligny.

† Brantome, Browning, Duncan.

cooled, he stripped D'Andelot of his honors, and threw him into the prison of Mélun.*

This punishment had no moral effect. It was well known that the court was tainted with Protestantism, and that many nobles were as heretical as D'Andelot, though few might have the Christian courage so openly to avow their faith. It seemed partial and ungenerous to incarcerate a gentleman who had shown so much honor and daring. So that this imprisonment increased the popularity of the persecuted doctrines of the Bible. The reformers, jubilant over the support of D'Andelot, and trusting that all the members of his powerful family would espouse his creed, fearlessly assembled at the Pré-aux-Cleves, situated in the modern *Faubourg St. Germain*, and at that time one of the most fashionable promenades in Paris. There they sang the Protestant psalms of Marat in the open air. It became the fashion to visit these reunions; and many an idle courtier, who had lounged down to ridicule the "fanatics," as they were called, returned with his curses turned into benedictions, and his mocking laughter choked in prayer. Antony de Bourbon, king of Navarre, and Jane d'Albrét, were *habitués* of these gatherings; and while they animated the preachers by their presence, they did not deign to disguise their attachment to the new opinions.†

Coligny was remarkable for his caution in tak-

* Vie de Coligny, p. 86. Browning, p. 37.

† Duncan, pp. 12, 13.

ing a step, but when he reached a decision he was inflexible. No one possessed greater intrepidity or more perseverance. Difficulties, instead of daunting him, only spurred him to greater activity, and served only to excite his ardor to surmount them.*

It was his brother D'Andelot who first persuaded him to inquire into the justice of the Protestant claims. Coligny paused long. He studied carefully. Meantime he used his utmost exertions to secure the liberation of his brother. With great difficulty he at length prevailed on D'Andelot to acknowledge that he had spoken to the king too roughly. This acknowledgment, backed by the influence of Montmorenci, obtained his dismissal from the Mélun dungeon.†

Pope Paul IV. was very angry when the news reached him that D'Andelot was again at liberty. He imperiously demanded that he should be burned for heresy. Easier said than done. D'Andelot's uncle was then the arbiter of France; his brother, the cardinal of Chatillon, was one of the grand-inquisitors:‡ he would doubtless hesitate long before consigning so dear a relative to the flames; so the unhappy pontiff had to content himself for a while with less distinguished victims. The Guises shared in the sadness of the holy father on this account, and they set spies upon Montmorenci while his nephew was in prison, in the foolish hope of being able to find some ground on which to base

* Vie de Coligny.

† Browning, p. 37.

‡ Ibid.

an accusation against that persecuting Saul of favoring heretics.*

Coligny, like Calvin, was of the strictest sect of the papists. In an age of almost universal license, no blot has ever been found upon his moral purity. He maintained several priests at Chatillon; he also established free schools for the education of youth. Upon joining the reformers he continued the same acts, simply substituting Protestant preachers for the former monks.† Girt with his conscience and armed with his principles, he would have braved the universe. When a little later he did, after long pause, declare his adherence to the Reformation, there was no more vacillation, no more timidity, no more doubt; not D'Andelot himself was more open and inflexible.

"Coligny and D'Andelot," says their biographer Brantome, "were both endowed with such imperturbable equanimity and coolness, that it was quite impossible to put them in a passion, and their countenances never betrayed their secret thoughts and inward emotions."‡

So admirable in their mental structure and in their moral nature were these brothers, the first political leaders of Latin Protestantism; their brilliant genius, their constancy, their unwearied zeal, their unflagging faith, made them the idols of the French reformers.

* Vie de Coligny, p. 192. † Ibid., p. 74.
‡ Brantome, C., vol. 7, p. 163.

CHAPTER XVI.

MUTATION.

In the field of persecution, Henry II. walked in the footsteps of Francis I. He regarded the extirpation of heresy and the convention of costly and knight-errant tournaments as the double mission of his kingly career.* For the accomplishment of the one, he squandered the blood, the treasure, and the honor of France; in the pursuit of the other, he lost his life, dying "as the fool dieth."

That he might secure leisure for the gratification of his bias for pageants and *autos da fé*, a hollow truce of five years' duration was patched up between France and Spain,† of which Henry could not say, as Francis I. did on the dismal day of Pavia, "All is lost, *save* honor," for in this case honor went first.

Just before the declaration of this truce, in 1556, Charles V. abdicated, after one of the most stormy, eventful, and checkered reigns in history. The self-deposed emperor retired into the monastery of St. Just, in Estremadura, where he spent his hours in vainly attempting to make a hundred clocks tick together,‡ precisely as he had endeavored to wind

* Fra Paolo, Hist. Concile de Trente, p. 280.

† Frost, Hist. of France. Robertson, Life of Charles V.

‡ Motley, Rise of the Dutch Republic, vol. 1.

up his subjects' consciences, and compel them to keep the time of the Vatican.

During the war just ended with Spain, in which Henry had been the ally of Maurice of Saxony and Albert of Brandenburg, who led the armed Protestantism of Germany, the cardinal of Lorraine had advised the temporary cessation of the religious persecution in France, in order to present the semblance of consistency.

Now the fires were once more lighted, Henry, to add dignity and importance to the executions, went in person to several of them. On one of these occasions he recognized an old domestic dying in the flames; his follower recognized him, and called out faintly from within the fire, "Save me, my king!" and the monarch was seized with such horror that, turning on his heel, he instantly quitted the scene, to hide his agitation and remorse in the depths of the Louvre.*

But the reformers were not to be deterred from following the dictates of conscience. It was in vain that funeral piles were kindled in every town in France. The danger of martyrdom, while it excited every generous feeling in the hearts of the devout, and fanned enthusiasm to a white heat, also became a preventive to desertion. It confirmed the wavering. Many who would have acknowledged themselves persuaded in a theological dispute, would avoid the disgrace of yielding through dread of so unsatisfactory a proselyter as the fire.

* D'Aubigné, Hist. Universelle, vol. 1, p. 75. Browning, p. 27.

In May, 1557, an event occurred which showed that the reformers were numerous even in Paris itself. Five hundred of them one night were assembled to celebrate the Lord's supper in a house in the Rue St. Jacques, opposite the College Plessis. The opportunity for a tumult was too good to be lost. The populace, instigated by the monks, gathered about the house, but no attempt was made to interrupt the service. When the assembly was dismissed, however, the reformers were assailed not only with threats and abuse, but with stones and rapiers. The darkness of the night would have enabled most of them to have escaped, had not lanterns been placed in the windows of the adjacent dwellings to illuminate the street.*

Many were murdered; some few who had arms cut their way through the mob; but the cld men, the women, and the children were left to massacre. In the midst of the orgie, some soldiers charged and dispersed the rioters; and while the guilty escaped, the innocent reformers, to the number of two hundred, were taken into custody.†

Proceedings were immediately commenced against these, notwithstanding the fact that among them were many persons of distinguished family connections.‡ The cardinal of Lorraine demanded that they should all be condemned to the fire; but the parliament had not so capacious a maw: they did not require a hecatomb of victims to glut their

* De Thou, liv. 19. † Pasquier, vol. 2, p. 76.

‡ Browning, p. 31. Duncan, p. 11.

appetite; and after a long process, five of the Protestants were sentenced to the flames.*

Fortunately for the others, Henry required some levies in Switzerland and Germany; the elector-palatine solicited the enlargement of these prisoners; and as it would have been inconvenient for the king to lose the friendship of that prince, he reluctantly ordered them to be treated with moderation, to the infinite regret of the pontiff Paul IV., who loudly complained in the consistory.†

While Henry was at war with Charles V., a decree, called the edict of Chateaubriand, was passed, which placed the reformers under the secular jurisdiction.‡ But now the cardinal of Lorraine was desirous of devising some method of defeating that edict, which served as a shield to the evangelicals. Accordingly he advised the appointment of an inquisitor of the faith in France, who should have the power to cite, interrogate, and punish suspected persons, and who should likewise possess, through a bureau of trained spies, mischievous and ubiquitous, the means of penetrating into the privacy of families, and of exercising an unsleeping surveillance over the whole kingdom, from the mountains to the sea.§

The pontiff greedily seized on the idea, and

* Browning, p. 31. Duncan, p. 11. Felibéru, vol. 11, p. 1060. They were burned in Sept., 1557.

† Fra Paolo, Hist. du Concile de Trente, p. 338. Soulier, Hist. du Calvinisme, vol. 2, p. 15. Browning, p. 31.

‡ De Thou. This was dated June 27, 1551.

§ Davila. Beza, Hist. Eccles.

appointed Matthew Oni, a Dominican monk, to that hateful office.* The king and his council approved this investiture of a foreigner with absolute power within the borders of his kingdom; but the parliament, somewhat leavened with the progressive ideas, and not wholly infatuated, ventured to remonstrate. "Sire," said Sequier, one of the presidents of the parliaments, "we abhor the establishment of this tribunal of blood, where secret accusation takes the place of proof, where the accused is deprived of every means of defence, and where no judicial form is respected. Begin, sire, by procuring for the nation an edict which will not cover France with funeral piles, which will not be wetted either by the tears or the blood of your loyal subjects. At a distance, sire, from your presence, bowed down under the pressure of rural labor, or absorbed in the exercise of the arts or of trade, the people are ignorant of what is preparing against them; they do not suspect that it is proposed to separate them from your throne by the intervention of an irresponsible foreign tribunal, which shall wreak its unchallengeable will upon them, and deprive them of their natural guardian. It is for them and in their name that we now present our humble remonstrances, nay, our ardent supplications.

"As for you, sirs," continued the orator, turning towards the sycophantic crowd of counsellors and ministers who surrounded the king, "you who

* Davila. Beza, Hist. Eccles.

so tranquilly hear me, and secure in the royal favor imagine that this affair does not concern you, learn that it is fit that you divest yourselves of that foolish notion. So long as you enjoy the king's friendship, you wisely make the most of your time—'t is your harvest; benefits and kindnesses are showered upon you without stint, and it enters into the mind of no one to attack you. But the more you are elevated, the nearer you are to the thunderbolt; one must be a stranger to the history of courts who does not know the trivialities which often precipitate disgrace.

"Under the present *régime,* even should that misfortune befall you, you could now retire with that fortune which would in a measure console you for your fall. But dating from the registration of this edict, your condition would cease to be the same. Mark! You will have for successors men poor and hungry, who, not knowing how long they may remain in office, will burn with a desire to enrich themselves at once and by whatever means. They will find a wonderful facility in doing so; for, certain of obtaining your confiscation of the king, it will only be necessary to bribe an inquisitor and two witnesses. Then, though you may be saints, you will burn as heretics."*

This *argumentum ad hominem* of the subtle par-

* Garnier, Hist. de France, vol. 14, p. 28. Pierre Sequier, born 1504, died 1580. His speeches, which are remarkable for their courage and boldness, have been collected and printed. The one from which this extract is taken is one of the finest of the series.

liamentary orator, produced a profound impression upon the council, and also on the king, who was so affected that he remitted the consideration of the question to another day.*

Apropos of this edict, it was just before the wily cardinal of Lorraine conceived his notable scheme for the extirpation of heresy, that the society of the Jesuits, the pests of modern Europe, commenced their machinations, under the protection of this same prelate. So early as 1550, the cardinal procured from Henry II. letters patent, by which they were permitted to build an establishment in Paris.†

The order of the Jesuits owed its origin to the efforts of a fanatic Spaniard, Ignatius Loyola, who, "poor, obscure, without a patron, without recommendations, entered that city—where now two temples, rich with paintings and many colored marbles, commemorate his great services to his church; where his form stands sculptured in massive silver; where his bones, enshrined amid jewels, are placed beneath the altar—and by his activity and zeal launched his protean *propaganda*."‡

"With what vehemence, with what unscrupulous policy, with what forgetfulness of the dearest private ties, with what intense and stubborn devotion to a single end, with what laxity and versatility in the choice of means, the Jesuits fought the battles of their church, is written on every page of the

* Browning, p. 30. † Duncan, p. 10

‡ Macauley, Essay on Ranke's Hist. of the Popes.

annals of Europe during several generations. In 'the order of Jesus' was concentrated the quintessence of the Romish spirit, and its history is the history of the papal reaction against Luther. The order possessed itself of all the strong-holds which command the public mind—of the pulpit, of the press, of the confessional, of the academies. It was into the ears of the Jesuit that the powerful, the noble, the wretched, and the beautiful breathed the secret history of their lives. It was at the feet of the Jesuit that the youth of the higher and middle and lower classes were brought up, from the first rudiments to the courses of rhetoric and philosophy."*

Such was the order which, dominant in the south of Europe, now sued for admission into France. At the first their welcome was not hearty.

When Henry's letters-patent were presented to the parliament for registry, the procureur-general strongly opposed their reception, and the act of legalization was suspended in consequence of his remonstrances. But in 1552, the Jesuits obtained new letters-patent, which contained a peremptory order for their registration. The procureur-general, however, persisted in his opposition, and for two years more the question hung undecided. Finally, on the 3d of August, 1554, the parliament decreed that, before the matter was definitely decided, the letters of the king and the papal bulls which the Jesuits had obtained, should be referred

* Macauley, Essay on Ranke's Hist. of the Popes.

to the bishop of Paris and the dean of the Sorbonne Faculty of Theology.*

The bishop, whose name was Eustace de Bellay, did not hesitate to declare "that the bulls of Paul III. and of Julius III. contained several articles which were contrary to reason, and which could not be tolerated or received in the Christian religion; that those in whose favor they were issued, by arrogating to themselves the title of 'Company of Jesus,' which could only be applied with propriety to the universal church, of which Christ was the head, appeared to desire to constitute themselves that church; moreover, as the principal object they proposed to themselves was the conversion of the Mohammedans, it would be better to give them a house on the frontier of the Ottoman empire, than in Paris, which was so distant from Constantinople."†

The answer of the Sorbonne was not more favorable. Feeling persuaded of their ability to cope singly with heresy, and

> "———— too fond to rule alone,"

able to

> "Bear, like the Turk, no brother near the throne,"‡

that body, by a unanimous vote, declared the new society "dangerous to the holy faith, calculated to disturb the peace of the church, and more fitted to destroy than to edify."§

* Duncan, p. 10. † Ibid.

‡ Pope, Epistle to Dr. Arbuthnot, Dyce's ed., vol. 3, p. 9.

§ Duncan, p. 11.

These two replies annihilated the hopes of the Jesuits during the reign of Henry II.; but they plotted in the dark, and bided their time.

Meantime the truce with Spain had been broken; both kingdoms had placed large armies in the field, and the constable, Montmorenci, after sacking the town of Sens, and pillaging Artois, came upon the Spaniards before St. Quintin,* which place, the admiral Coligny, one of the ablest captains of the age, held for France.

St. Quintin had been vigorously besieged, and though it was but indifferently strong, the gallant admiral had kept it for his king, while Montmorenci was coming to succor him.

On the 10th of August, 1557, the constable reached St. Quintin, and attacking the enemy with Quixotic indiscretion, suffered a disastrous defeat, in which he was himself captured.†

In consequence of Montmorenci's captivity, the cardinal of Lorraine became the administrator of the government, and the family of Guise employed their opportunity in securing the hand of the Dauphin for their niece Mary, queen of Scots,‡ and in promoting their adherents to all the influential offices of the court, the capital, and the provinces.§

But upon this occasion the Guises' lease of power was not of long duration. Philip II., tired of the French war, and familiar with Henry's friend-

* De Thou, liv. 18. Motley, Rise of the Dutch Ref., vol. 1.

† Ibid. ‡ Browning, p. 32. § Duncan, p. 21.

ship for Montmorenci, played upon these chords a tune of reconciliation with his "dear brother of France;" and after several ineffectual attempts, the treaty of Chateau Cambrisis was signed on the 3d of April, 1559.*

Montmorenci immediately resumed his ministerial functions, and the humiliated Guises were completely stripped of their snug stations and usurped honors. The cardinal of Lorraine, however, who had contrived to render himself necessary to the king, remained near his person, like an evil genius, ever prompting the impressible monarch to wicked and arbitrary acts.†

The cardinal's next act was atrocious. By the treaty of Chateau Cambrisis, it had been stipulated that Henry's daughter Elizabeth should marry the king of Spain.‡ The city was now crowded with illustrious Spaniards who had come to witness the marriage ceremony, and to accompany the young queen to Madrid. Henry's penchant for magnificent follies and splendid *fêtes* led him to celebrate the occasion with unusual pomp, and to prepare the lists of endless tournaments.

The bias of several prominent members of the parliament towards heresy was well known; and the independent and liberal action of the legislature on several recent occasions, had disgusted the bigoted cardinal and provoked the king.

Lorraine determined to make use of the Span-

* Vie de Cidlon, vol. 1, p. 39.

† Browning, p. 33. ‡ Ibid.

ish marriage to wreak his vengeance upon the obnoxious legislators.

One day he entered Henry's cabinet, and delivered this infamous harangue: "Sire, although it would serve for nothing more than to show the king of Spain that you are firm in the faith, and that you will not suffer any thing in your kingdom which will disparage your excellent title of most Christian king, still you ought to proceed about it boldly, and with great courage. You must gratify all these grandees of Spain, who have accompanied the duke of Alva for the solemnity and honor of their sovereign's marriage with your daughter, by ordering half a dozen councillors of the parliament to be burned in the public square as Lutheran heretics, which indeed they are. By so doing we shall preserve the bulk of the legislature; but if you do not take these measures, the whole court will be infected and contaminated with heresy, even to the clerks, attorneys, and tipstaves."*

The cardinal then, with the craft of those Jesuits whom he befriended, persuaded the king to go to the legislative chamber as if to consult his counsellors on the measures to be taken for the suppression of heresy, but really to observe the responses of the members of the parliament, and if possible to ascertain their secret sentiments, by submitting to their frank consideration and judgment some project which should draw from them an avowal of their own heresy.†

* Vielleville, liv. 7, c. 24. † Ibid. Prowning, p. 34.

Montmorenci, instead of dissuading Henry from such black treachery, approved it in open council.* Vieilleville alone, who records the incident, raised his voice against it, as degrading to the royal dignity, affirming that "he was about to take upon himself the office of an inquisitor, and that the cardinal's proposal would entirely destroy the joyous feeling of the public."†

But the cardinal's advice prevailed. Henry convoked the Parliament, and in a few well-disguised and gracious words, begged the advice of his counsellors upon the best means for the pacification of the kingdom. The more wary judges confined their remarks to general and vague expressions, believing that the use of language was to disguise one's meaning, as one of their later countrymen, the famous Talleyrand, phrased it.

Some were less cautious, or more honest. "Let us begin," said Louis Faur, "by examining who the real author of our troubles is, lest the same answer should be made to us which Elijah made to Ahab, 'It is thou that troublest Israel,'" and a look at Cardinal Lorraine directed the application to him. The celebrated Anne Du Bourg, the son of an illustrious family in Auvergne, and nephew of the chancellor of France, next spoke. He surprised his hearers by the boldness of his speech, enlarging upon the cruelties heaped upon the reformers, and remarked with emphasis, "While men

* Vieilleville, liv. 7, c. 24. Browning, p. 34. † Ibid.

are conducted to the stake for the sole crime of praying for their prince, a shameful license encourages and multiplies blasphemies, perjuries, debaucheries, and adulteries."*

The courtiers trembled, for they considered this sentence as intended for the king and the duchess de Valentinois.†

When Du Bourg resumed his seat, Henry rose in a great passion, and gave vent to a torrent of reproaches against the moderate party, and especially against those who, enamoured of the beauty of plain speech, had boldly avowed their sentiments.‡

On quitting the chamber, he made a sign to Count Montgomery, captain of his Scotch guard, who had surrounded the convent of the Augustines, where the Parliament was then sitting, with his men-at-arms. A fierce look directed towards Faur, Du Bourg, and three others, gave sufficient instructions for him. They were arrested in the midst of a parliamentary session, and immediately thrown into a dungeon—a high-handed violation of public law and official etiquette, the mere attempt at which, in the succeeding century, cost an English king his head.

Charges were instantly huddled up against the five counsellors, the trials were pushed on with indecent haste, and so hot was the anger of the king,

* D'Aubigné, vol. 1, p. 84. De Thou, liv. 22.

† Pasquier, vol. 2, p. 77.

‡ Ibid. D'Aubigné. Falibien, vol. 2, p. 1066.

that "he expressed a desire to see Du Bourg burned before his own eyes."*

But before this brutal wish could be gratified, Henry's own life was abridged by violence; and singularly enough too, he was doomed to die by the blundering lance of that same Montgomery whom he had just employed in outraging the higher majesty of the Parliament, in the very sanctuary of justice.

At a tournament held in the Faubourg St. Antoine, on the 27th of June, 1559, the last of a succession of jousts which Henry meant should give *éclat* to his daughter's marriage, the king, after contending with and vanquishing several of his politic courtiers, elated by his success, challenged Count Montgomery to enter the lists with him. The count was reluctant to comply, but Henry would not accept his refusal. Finally Montgomery entered the arena; two fresh lances were given to the champions; the trumpets sounded the charge; the knights met, with a terrific crash, in mid-career; and when the dust rolled up, Henry was seen unhorsed, and with a portion of his captain's shattered lance protruding from his visor. The shiver pierced into his brain through the left eye; and after lingering through eleven days, he expired on the 10th of July, 1559, in the forty-first year of his age, and the twelfth of his reign.†

* Hist. du Concile de Trente. Vieilleville, vol. 4, p. 158. Duncan, p. 12.

† Brantome, vol. 7, p. 46. Browning, p. 36. Duncan, p. 14.

If history has not scourged the character of this puppet king so severely as it has those of his monster brothers, Charles IX. and Henry III., it is not because he was less deserving of obloquy, but because he was fortunate enough to cheat history by a death which struck him at the very moment when he had matured a plan for the extermination of French Protestantism.* Henry II. was as weak, as deceitful, and as execrable as any scion of the Valois line. Informers were encouraged by the prospect of reward to denounce the innocent; a casual, an ambiguous phrase was a sufficient warrant for arrest; suspicion was equivalent to proof; whoever sheltered a heretic was held to be a participater in his crime; confidence between man and man was lost; members of the same family distrusted each other; the worst passions of human nature were let loose by a bribe, and France became an extended dungeon.

It was in the reign of Henry II. that the soubriquét HUGUENOTS began to be generally applied to the French reformers. Like the names "Puritan," "Methodist," and "Abolitionist," this was originally a term of reproach; but the Protestants of France, like those of England and America, were wise enough to seize an epithet hurled at them as a missile, and wear it proudly as a jewel. In a few years this designation completely superseded all others: "Protestant" and "evangelical" were swallowed up in it; and HUGUENOTS became the

* Browning, p. 36. Duncan, p. 13. Brantome, vol. 7, p. 50.

honorable and universal synonym of politico-ecclesiastical reform.*

* The etymology of the word "*Huguenot*" has been the subject of much discussion. No less than ten different opinions as to its derivation have been more or less popular.

The etymology most generally received is that which ascribes its origin to the word *Eignot*, derived from the German *Eidgenossen*, which means *Confederate*. A party thus designated existed at Geneva; and it is probable that the French Protestants would receive a name so applicable to themselves. See Browning, Hist. Huguenots, Appendix.

It is probable that the precise form *Huguenot* may be owing to the fact that an influential leader of the republican Protestants of Geneva was named *Hugues*. "In any case," says D'Aubigné, "it must be remembered that this soubriquét had a purely political meaning until after the Reformation—a meaning in no respect religious, and simply designating the friends of civil independence. Many years after, the enemies of the Protestants of France called them by this name, wishing to stigmatize them, and impute to them a foreign, republican, and heretical origin. Such is the true etymology of the word." D'Aubigné, Ref. in Calvin's Time, vol. 1, pp. 88, 89.

CHAPTER XVII.

THE CONSPIRACY.

WITH the death of Henry II. terminated a historic rivalry. Diana of Poitiers at length succumbed to the subtleties of Catharine de' Medici, who not only drove the courtesan from the court in ignominy, and confiscated her immense estates, but who actually appropriated the fair Diana's jewels.*

The politics of the Louvre were once more revolutionized. Montmorenci, whom Catharine hated because he had coalesced with Henry's mistress, and put her authority under the ban, and whom the Guises intrigued to displace because he had deposed them and himself swayed the sceptre, was one morning politely advised by the boy king to quit Paris, and take the benefit of the air at his country-seat.†

The Guises were reseated in power. The feeble hands of Francis II., who was but sixteen when he ascended the throne, on the 10th of July, 1559, and poor Mary Stuart, were not old or energetic enough to hold the reins of government. Their uncles of Guise and Lorraine were kind enough to perceive this, and to relieve their majesties of the cares and honors of the state.‡

* Davila, liv. 1.

† Vie de Coligny, p. 92.

‡ Brantome, vol. 9, pp. 469, 470.

To be sure the witty Parisians were so unkind as to frame epigrams, and to assert that this philanthropic action of the bashful and modest house of Guise, whose probity was thus slurred, *really held the king in duress.** But when did a generous action ever fail to be misconstrued?

The naughty Huguenots took this view of the case; and esteeming it to be their first duty as loyal subjects to emancipate their king, they immediately prepared to stereotype their opinion into action. The Huguenots caballed. The king's duress bred a conspiracy. But while the conspirators yet plotted in the dark with an immature programme, another *auto da fé* was kindled; which caused all France to growl ominously.

Anne du Bourg had remained in prison since the death of Henry II. The cardinal of Lorraine, securely intrenched in power, and emboldened by success, ordered that noble counsellor's trial to proceed. Du Bourg, though deserted by the craven parliament which had permitted itself to be dragooned into submission, defended himself with the utmost vigor and spirit: he challenged one of his judges, president Minard, his bitter personal enemy; despite of which Minard took his seat on the judiciary bench, and presided at the trial.†

Du Bourg could not resist the impulse to upbraid this French prototype of the English Jeffries; and he concluded a scathing philippic by prophe-

* Brantome, vol. 7, p. 82. Davila, liv. 1.

† Browning, p. 38. Mem. de Condé, vol. 1, p. 300.

sying that this base judge would soon be called to appear before a more awful bar, when he would wish to be as guiltless as his prisoner then was known to be.*

These words were quickly and strangely verified. As Minard was returning home one evening from the court, he was assassinated.† This occurred in the night of the 12th of December, 1559. On the morning of the 23d, Du Bourg, despite the herculean efforts made by the Huguenots to save him, was led out to be executed.

The counsellor's firm demeanor on reaching the fatal plaza, excited the sympathetic admiration of the hardened mob which haunted the gallows. Measures were taken to prevent his addressing them; the executioner was ordered to gag him, should he attempt to speak.

At the foot of the gibbet a crucifix was held before his lips, but he refused to kiss it; after which he was immediately pulled up and strangled, amid shouts of *Jesu Maria* from the human tigers below.‡

His last words were a prayer: "Father, abandon me not; neither will I abandon thee."

"Thus," says a historian, "perished Anne Du Bourg, in his thirty-eighth year, a man of rare tal-

* Vie de Coligny, p. 197.

† Browning, p. 38. Minard was killed by a Scotchman named Robert Stuart, a distant relative of Mary Stuart, who afterwards shot the Constable Montmorenci at the battle of St. Denis.

‡ Mem. de Condé, vol. 1, p. 300. Browning, p. 38.

ents, and yet rarer integrity, loved, wept, and honored even by many of those who did not share his faith."

After hanging for some time, the body was cut down and burned, the ashes being scattered to the four winds.*

As in the classic story of the Roman Gracchi, so the martyred counsellor, mortally smitten, flung his dust towards heaven, calling the avenging God to witness; and from that dust sprang ere long the embattled ranks of D'Andelot and De Coligny, eager to defend their faith and liberty.

While this tragedy was being enacted, the conspiracy of Ambois ripened. History has recorded few undertakings of a similar character in which the design was more extensive, the motives more just, the plan more skilful, the means more adequate, and the failure more miserable.

The Jesuits, ever watchful to obtain a foothold in France, now that their protectors of the house of Guise were the arbiters of the kingdom, ventured to emerge from their holes, and, though denounced by the parliament, the bishop of the metropolis, and the Sorbonne, to sue for legal recognition. This, through the *finesse* of the cardinal of Lorraine, was at length accorded them, and the privy council distinctly declared that "the Jesuits claimed no privileges hostile to the episcopal supremacy, the authority of curates, colleges, or universities, or to the liberties of the Gallican church."†

* Duncan, p. 24. † Ibid., p. 25.

The parliament, overawed by the execution of Du Bourg, and filled with servile counsellors, did not venture to baulk the cardinal for a third time; and after sprinkling rose-water, in the shape of explanatory articles, over the charter with dainty fingers, the Corps Legislatif and the bishops agreed to the act of incorporation,* though an additional clause, which plainly indicated the distrust of the court itself, was appended ere the registration, which provided that "if, in the course of time, any thing should result prejudicial to the prerogative of the crown or the rights of the people, the constitution of the Jesuits might be reformed."†

The legal recognition of this hateful tribunal filled the reformers with alarm, for they justly suspected that these mysterious and ubiquitous priests, who spun their webs in the dark, who invented every thing, who denied every thing, who even seized blank paper and, "*after the manner of spiders*, sucked heresy from it," would ally themselves with their patrons the princes of Lorraine, in a grand effort to annihilate the Huguenot idea.

The alarm of the reformers; the discontent of the nobility, excluded from all posts of trust, replaced in office by the upstart retainers of the house of Guise; Montmorenci, the king of Navarre, the prince of Condé, all disgusted by the haughty behavior of the cardinal of Lorraine—these circumstances seemed at once to warrant and to guarantee the success of an insurrection against the "hated

* Duncan, p. 25. † Ibid., pp. 25, 26.

foreigners" who, through their niece, ruled the king.*

The discontented nobles and the Huguenot politicians at once formed a confederacy, the former to end the political usurpations of the Guises, the latter to protect their party against the repetition of those severities which were threatened by the ugly precedent of Du Bourg.†

The conspirators held their first conversations at the castle of La Ferté, which was situated on the frontier of Picardy. The prince of Condé was unanimously elected chief; but he was not to be known as a participator in the plot until the decisive moment came.‡ Condé accepted this position, annexing this reservation: "Providing nothing be done or attempted against God, the king, my brothers, or the state."§

In the mean time a gentleman named La Renaudie, of a noble family of Perigord, a Huguenot, was selected to be the nominal head of the conspiracy.‖ La Renaudie combined every quality requisite for the elaboration and direction of such a movement. Eloquent, energetic, persevering, intelligent, brave even to rashness,¶ familiar, through a long residence at Geneva, with those multitudinous religionists who had been expatriated for their faith, no

* Vie de Coligny. † Duncan, p. 26.

‡ Vie de Coligny. Davila, liv. 1. De Thou, liv. 24.

§ Veritable Inventoire de l'Histoire des Français, par Jean de Serres, tom. 1, p. 681. Cited also in Duncan, p. 26.

‖ Brantome, vol. 7, p. 82. ¶ Davila, liv. 1.

one could be better fitted to secure the cordial co-operation of the Huguenots.

On the 1st of January, 1560, the confederates assembled in a ruined chateau in the outskirts of Nantes—attracted thither by the cloak to their movements which the vast concourse of people who then crowded the city to witness the holiday *fêtes* would be—and here the final arrangements were made.*

When night had fallen, and the conspirators had all gathered at the rendezvous, La Renaudie addressed them in a low but intensely earnest voice. In a few vivid sentences he painted the tyrannies of the house of Guise, dwelt with graphic rhetoric upon the injuries which they had entailed on France, affirmed his belief that the princes of Lorraine only waited for the death of the feeble and boyish king—who might die at any moment under their skilful nursing, as the orator darkly hinted—to usurp the sceptre of poor Francis II., and seat one of their own family upon the throne. "For my part," he continued, forgetting in his heat to observe that cautious monotone in which he had so far spoken, and rising in vehemence, "for my own part, I protest, I swear, I call God to witness, that I will never think or say or do any thing against the king, against the queen his mother, against the princes his brothers, against any of his blood; but that I will defend to my latest breath the authority of the throne, the majesty of the laws, and the liberty of

* De Thou, liv. 24. Browning, p. 40. Duncan, p. 29.

France against the hateful tyranny of foreign usurpers."*

"We swear it!" echoed the band, bathed in the swarthy light of the stars, with upraised hands and uncovered heads. The tyranny of the Guises had excited such a feeling that no intervening danger, not the dread of the block, nor the awful pangs of inquisitorial torture, could chill the ardor. All signed the oath, shook hands in unison, embraced each other weeping, and loaded with imprecations any wretch who should be perfidious enough to betray the plot. Just before the separation, the fifteenth of the following March, and Blois, were fixed on as the time and place for the execution of their programme.†

Ten minutes later and the old chateau of Nantes resumed its disturbed dreams; soon the conspirators were scattered to the four corners of France, each on his mission of mischief to tyrants.

The purpose of the confederates was to possess themselves of the royal person, to arrest the princes of Lorraine, and to vest the administration of the government in the prince of Condé.‡ There was no intention to injure the king, but simply to release him from the duress of his uncles of Guise; and the distinct avowal of this principle won the confidence of all the loyal gentlemen in France.§

Francis II. was of a fragile and sickly constitu-

* De Thou, liv. 24. † Davila, liv. 1. Browning, p. 40.
‡ Vie de Coligny. Hist. du Tumulte d'Amboise. Browning, p. 40. § Duncan, p. 27.

tion; and since, in the spring of 1560, he was a greater sufferer than usual, the court physicians prescribed a change of air and scene for the royal invalid. Accordingly the Guises transported him to the town of Blois, whose climate was mild and salubrious.

It was at Blois then, where the court was yet sojourning, that the mine was to be sprung upon the Guises.

For a time "all went merry as a marriage bell;" the confederates sailed over a placid and auspicious sea. Success seemed certain. The princes of Lorraine, charmed by the syren songs of prosperous wickedness, lay lapped in supine security, when suddenly the overconfidence of the chief conspirator withdrew the veil of secrecy, and every thing was revealed.*

La Renaudie quitted the rendezvous at Nantes for Paris, where he was to station himself and direct the plot.

He lodged in the house of an old friend, Avanelles, a lawyer, who, suspecting mischief from the vast number of persons who called upon his comparatively uninfluential guest, mentioned his suspicions to La Renaudie. That gentleman very indiscreetly acknowledged the existence of the conspiracy.†

The meddlesome and perfidious attorney professed to be well pleased with the plan and pur-

* Davila, liv 1. De Thou, liv. 24. Browning, p. 41.

† Hist. du Tumulte d'Amboise. Vie de Coligny. Davila, etc.

pose of the intrigue, and after sucking its minutiæ from his overconfiding friend, he hastened to the metropolitan residence of the Guises, and unfolded the whole plot to the cardinal's secretary, who instantly posted Avanelles off to Blois to apprize the court of the volcano upon which it trembled.*

The messenger arrived travel-stained and weary, and his interview with Francis duke of Guise speedily interrupted the frivolous festivities with which his ambitious relatives amused the attention of the king.

Francis, unaware of the existence both of Avanelles and his news, was strolling in the meadows of Blois, while the agitated Guises interrogated the volunteer attorney. He found his principal solace and amusement in the company of his beautiful and at that time innocent young queen, Mary Stuart. Her harp often soothed the painful restlessness engendered by disease; and though flattered and worshipped and caressed wherever she appeared, though walking upon roses, she really seemed devoted to her royal husband.†

The hair of the girlish queen was singularly beautiful, and curled in natural ringlets. It was then a custom to wear low skull-caps; these, as a matter of fashion, were considered regal; but Francis was so proud of his pet's head that Mary threw them off. The king delighted to hear the tones of her voice in singing, in speaking, in reading; and often,

* Esprit de la Ligue, liv. 1, p. 39. Davila, liv. 1.

† Huguenots in France and Amer. Cambridge, 1843, v. 1, p. 55.

when sleep fled from his weary pillow, Mary would patiently lean over him, and lure the truant back by low, sweet chants, or by the touching music of her own dear Scottish ballads.*

This was the queen who was, in later and more dismal years, arraigned for the murder of Darnley, her own husband.

She may have been guilty, for who can spell the riddle of corrupting circumstances? Early separated from her mother, trained at a licentious court by ambitious uncles, that firm, unyielding principle, that elevation of character which is developed and strengthened by judicious education, could hardly have been acquired. Instigated by hatred, beckoned on by passion, poor Mary may have erred most sadly in the melancholy hours of her later career; but now her generous and gentle nature still controlled her.

On the morning of Avanelles' advent, Francis and Mary, together as usual, were in the fields—pausing here on an eminence which commanded a wide prospect, there by the side of the magnificent Loire, and wiling away the hours in sweet converse. Francis, looking forward to a life of regal splendor, expressed an earnest desire for the time to come when, unfretted by his uncles, he might govern his own empire. Mary chatted of her native land, of the heath-covered mountains of Scotland, and many a quaint legend gathered from the superstitious gossip of her attendants.

* Huguenots in France and America, vol. 1, p. 56.

Suddenly the duke of Guise joined them.

"A fair morrow," said he, "for the hopes of France. What says my royal cousin, what says his consort, to a hunting gallop to-day?"

A ready acquiescence was given; and returning to the castle of Blois, where Louis XI. had been born, the court-yard was speedily filled with hounds and steeds, and ere long the merry party were flying over the country at great speed.

When the walls of Blois had been left far behind, Guise reigned up beside Francis, and informed him of the discovered plot, and told him that the hunting party was only a pretence for removing him from an unfortified town to the stronger protection of the Amboise donjon.

Francis was displeased that duplicity had been used, and turning towards his guardian he said pointedly, "It is so difficult now to distinguish friends from enemies, that perhaps it had been better for us to remain at Blois."

The duke replied that "he had acted from the truest motives of tenderness, fearing that any uncommon agitation might injure him in his present feeble and broken health."

Francis made no further objection to the journey, but contented himself with saying sadly, "What can be more injurious or painful than to see one's self an object of party hatred and contention?"*

The princes of Lorraine were now in possession of the chief features of the plot to unseat them from

* Huguenots in France and America, vol. 1, pp. 59, 60.

the government. They also knew the names of a number of the actors in the *émeute*. Beyond this all was shadowy. Suspicion began where knowledge ended. Coligny and D'Andelot were supposed to be implicated; and though Brantome distinctly declares that the admiral had no part in the conspiracy,* they were summoned to present themselves before the king at the earliest moment. Both hastened to comply with this requisition; and upon being introduced into the queen mother's chamber, Coligny spoke warmly against the bad administration of affairs, pleaded the cause of the Huguenots, and recommended that the penal statutes against them be expunged from the judicial code.†

The chancellor, Olivier, and the moderates of the council, seconded this bold appeal, which was finally embodied in an edict, and published on the 12th of March, 1560.‡ The edict appeared too late to strangle the conspiracy. The outbreak was to occur upon the sixteenth instant; the time had been changed from the fifteenth by the removal to Amboise.§

Every thing now looked as black for success as before La Renaudie's admission to the recreant Avanelles the auspices had appeared bright.

Nevertheless Condé, no whit discouraged, went boldly to Amboise, and picking out a band of reso-

* Brantome, vol. 7, p. 168. Browning, p. 40.
† D'Aubigné, Hist. Universelle, vol. 1, p. 93.
‡ Ibid. Browning, p. 41.
§ Mem. de Condé, vol. 1, p. 340.

lute men-at-arms from the body of his retainers, introduced them as his body-guard into the donjon walls.

But the Guises, aware of the plan of attack, took every precaution, filled the tower with their adherents, and posted the Chatillons and Condé in conspicuous places, and surrounded them with confidential persons who were pledged to prevent their joining the assailants.*

Forewarned was forearmed; and when the Huguenots attacked Amboise, they were repulsed with great slaughter. La Renaudie rallied the fugitives, who returned gallantly to the charge; but their chief, surrounded by a party of his foes, after slaying a number of his assailants, was struck from his saddle dead by a bullet fired from a distance. The confederates then scattered in all directions. The pursuit was pressed with vindictive fierceness, and the body of La Renaudie was placed on a gibbet with the inscription, "Chief of the Rebels."†

During the battle, the duke of Nemours recognized at the head of a Huguenot squadron a gentleman named Castelnau, for whom he entertained a warm friendship. He reined in his horse, and asked the Calvinist cavalier why he had taken arms against the king. "Our intention," was the reply, "is not to war against the king, but to expel the tyrant Guises from authority."

"If that be the case," said Nemours, "sheath

* Davila, liv. 1. Browning, p. 41.

† Ibid. De Thou, liv. 24. Browning.

your sword, and I promise you on my honor that you shall speak to the king, and I pledge myself for your safe return." Castelnau accepted these terms, and Nemours reduced his engagement to writing, and signed it; on which his late foeman followed him to Amboise.

Castelnau was seized upon his entrance into the town, put into irons, and despite Nemour's urgent remonstrances, he was sentenced to death, Guise insisting that Nemours had no authority to undertake to do what he had written and sworn to do.

On this proceeding Vieilleville makes this comment: "This caused Nemours great uneasiness and vexation *on account of his signature;* for had he only passed his word, he would have denied it, and given the lie to any man who should charge him with having plighted it, *so valiant and generous was this nobleman.*" "A remarkable instance," observes Anquétil, "of the point of honor badly understood, which fears a crime less than the proof."*

The Guises triumphed. They revoked the edict obtained by Coligny, arrested the prince of Condé, commanded that no quarter should be given the insurgents, and hung their prisoners on a gallows erected in the Amboise square. Those who escaped this death were condemned, without trial, to be tied hand and foot, and thrown into the Loire.†

Many of the confederates were racked, and especially La Bique, La Renaudie's secretary, the object

* Duncan, p. 32. Anquétil, Esprit de la Ligue.
† Davila, Duncan, Browning, Vie de Coligny, De Thou.

of the ministers being to secure some testimony which should implicate Condé, or at least justify his arrest. They failed on both points. Only one person was found who implicated the prince, and he spoke only from report, while La Bique doggedly refused to give any specific information, affirming that La Renaudie kept his own secrets, and only entrusted him with general correspondence.*

Condé, on his part, was indignant. He concluded a long speech to the king's council in these words: "If any man has the audacity to affirm that I have instigated a revolt against the sacred person of the king, I renounce the privilege of my rank, and am willing to attest my innocence by single combat."†

Then occurred a notable instance of hypocritical *finesse*. The duke of Guise, the secret author of the arrest, rose, and unmindful of the evident application of Condé's words to himself, said with apparent heat, "And I will not suffer so great a prince to be accused of so black a crime, and entreat you to accept me as your second."‡

Thus ended the conspiracy of Amboise with a liberation—Guise being as convinced of the treachery of the prince, as Condé was sensible of the duplicity of the duke.

"The prince of Condé was liberated," says an old contemporaneous historian, "in the hope that

* Browning, p. 42. Duncan, p. 32. Vie de Coligny, p. 208.

† Mem. de Condé, p. 400. Davila, liv. 1. De Thou, liv. 24.

‡ Ibid.

the apparent confidence thus placed in his loyalty might throw the king of Navarre, the Constable, D'Andelot, and the vidame* of Chartres off their guard, and thus enable the Guises to seize their persons; for they feared to put Condé to death, and leave so many of his friends alive to avenge him. Past examples had taught them that it is in vain to cut down the body of a tree, how high and lofty soever, if there be any quick roots left, which may shoot forth new sprouts.†

* A vidame was a person who held lands under a bishop, on condition of defending the temporal interests of the see. Browning, p. 37, note. Francis de Vendime, vidame of Chartres, was a noble who had recently joined the Huguenots.

† Davila, liv. 1.

CHAPTER XVIII.

ALMOST A TRAGEDY.

After their fierce suppression of the Amboise conspiracy, the Guises returned to Fontainebleau with the court in their pocket. Meantime France wailed under a grinding tyranny which could no longer be endured. Even the just choked *émeute* was not able with all its blood to stifle the agonized cry for relief. Something must be done; and it was determined to convene an assembly of the Notables, without reference to party or creed, for the investigation of the existing evils: all proved grievances were to be remedied—such was the burden of the Guises' syren song.*

The Montmorencis and the Chatillons attended; but fearful of being entrapped, they were accompanied by a long train of mailed cavaliers, the escort of the old constable alone numbering eight hundred men-at-arms.†

The sky brightened for a moment. Chancellor Olivier, a statesman of moderate views, but weak and yielding, was so affected by the brutal policy of the princes of Lorraine, that just as the conspiracy of Amboise was definitively quelled, he died‡ of

* Brantome, vol. 7, p. 103, Davila, liv. 1. De Thou, liv. 25.
† Vie de Coligny, p. 213. Duncan, p. 34.
‡ March 30, 1560.

grief at the holocaust of immolated victims. It is related of him, that when the cardinal of Lorraine called on him just before his decease, he turned his face to the wall, and refused to see him, saying, "I will look no more upon his face, for he is the accursed cardinal who is the cause of all the condemnations."*

Olivier was succeeded in the chancellorship by Michael l'Hôpital, a lawyer of distinguished fame, whom Brantome calls a second Cato,† who did his utmost to inaugurate a reign of peace, and whose memory France is bound to revere as the active, unwearied friend of tolerant politics.

The king of Navarre and Condé had been urgently summoned to attend the convention; but their wiser partisans, familiar with the wily character and deadly rancor of the Guises, advised them to absent themselves,‡ and they followed this prudent counsel.

The debates at Fontainebleau were long and animated. Coligny on his knees presented to Francis a petition from the Huguenots. The king handed it to his secretary L'Aubespine to read. He commenced: "A request of the people who address their prayers to God, according to the true rule of piety;" and when he had gotten thus far, he was interrupted by the clamors of the Guises' adherents.§ Francis commanded silence; and the sec-

* Vieilleville, vol. 4, p. 193. Browning, p. 43.
† Brantome, vol. 7, p. 91. ‡ Browning. Duncan.
§ Vie de Coligny, p. 213.

retary resumed reading the memorial, which contained a prayer that the prevalent persecutions for conscience' sake might cease; it showed also that those who were nicknamed heretics were quite ready to abide by the declarations of Scripture, asking only to be convicted of error from the Bible; that the pope was not a fit person to decide such matters, since his position as the leader of the hosts of error made him necessarily more partial than just; and the paper concluded by calling upon the king himself to arbitrate.*

When L'Aubespine had finished, the cardinal took the floor, and opening the flood-gates of his wrathful bitterness, poured forth a torrent of vituperative epithets. "The docility, the meekness," he said, "of these *perfect Christians*, these *new evangelicals*, might be judged by the flood of libels levelled at himself; that, for his own part, having collected no less than twenty-two scandalous writings against his *single self*, he carefully preserved them as badges of honor." He added, that "though he pitied the ignorant, who were misled, extreme measures ought to be adopted against those who carried arms without the permission of the king."†

Coligny, in his reply, said that "his voice was that of fifty thousand Huguenots." "Well then," retorted the duke of Guise with bitter emphasis, "I

* Vie de Coligny, p. 213. De Thou, liv. 25. Browning, p. 44.

† Davila, liv. 2. Pasquier, vol. 11, p. 80.

will break their heads with a hundred thousand papists whom I will lead against them."*

This verbal tilt is said to have been the beginning of the mortal feud between the duke of Guise and the admiral, who had heretofore been warm personal friends†—a hatred never appeased. Crimination and recrimination succeeded, mutual defiances were haughtily exchanged, and amid great confusion the conference was adjourned, and the convocation of the states-general was decided upon, to whom all the political and religious points of controversy were referred.‡

While this rude blast was rushing over France, and roaring in the antique galleries of lordly palaces, the still small voice of the Word was making its way into the homes of praying men. In private chambers, in the lecture-rooms and refectories, students, and even masters of arts, were to be seen reading the Latin Testament, Erasmus' Greek version, and even the Bible in French. Animated groups were discussing the *rationale* of the Reformation. "When Christ came on earth," said some, "he gave the word; and when he ascended up into heaven, he gave the Holy Spirit. These are the two forces which created the church, and these are the forces which must regenerate it." "No," re-

* Davila, liv. 2. Pasquier, vol. 11, p. 80. Brantome, vol. 8, p. 70.

† Browning, p. 44. Duncan, p. 18. Vie de Coligny, p. 220.

‡ D'Aubigné, Hist. Universelle, vol. 1, p. 97. Duncan, p. 34. Browning, p. 44. Mem. de Condé, vol. 1, p. 535.

plied the partisans of Rome, "it was the teaching of the apostles at first, and it is the teaching of the priests now." "The apostles," rejoined the Huguenots; "yes, 't is true, the apostles were, during their ministry, a living scripture; but their oral teaching would infallibly have been altered by passing from mouth to mouth. God willed, therefore, that these precious lessons should be preserved to us in their writings, and thus become the ever undefiled source of truth and salvation." "To set the Scriptures in the foremost place, as your pretended reformers are doing," replied the monks and their satellites, "is to propagate heresy." "And what are the reformers doing," queried their apologists, "but what Christ did before them? The sayings of the prophets existed in the time of Jesus only as *scripture,* and it was to this written word that Christ appealed when he founded his kingdom.* And now in like manner the teaching of the apostles exists only as scripture; and imitating Christ, it is to this written word that we in our turn appeal, in order to reëstablish the kingdom of our Lord in its primitive condition. The night is far spent; the day is at hand; all is in motion—in the lofty ancestral chateaus of the nobility, in the classic aisles of our universities, in the mansions of the rich, and in the lowly dwellings of the poor. If we wish to scatter the darkness, must we light the shrivelled wick of some old lamp? Or shall we not

* Matthew 22:29; 26:24, 52; Mark 14:49; Luke 18:31; 24:27, 44, 45; John 5:39, 46; 10:35; 17:12, etc.

rather open the doors and shutters, and admit freely into the house the great light which God himself has hung in the heavens?"*

But while by these and kindred conversations the Huguenots were burying the Romanists in their own nonsense, public events were marching towards a crisis.

Although the Bourbon princes had absented themselves from Fontainebleau, the Guises had strongly suspected that some of their emissaries were present, who were empowered to negotiate with the leaders of the court opposition, with Montmorenci, with the Chatillons, and the rest. From information received, they arrested a Gascon gentleman named La Saque; he was put to the torture, and the confession that Navarre and Condé were prepared to take the field as soon as the states-general were convened at Orleans, was wrung from his unwilling lips.† "Dip the wrapper of this letter in water," faltered La Saque, enfeebled by the rack, and whose quivering sinews yet anguished him. The inquisitors hastened to comply with the direction, when lo, the whole plot lay disclosed. What had before seemed blank paper, teemed with ominous meaning. The handwriting of Dordois, the constable's secretary, became visible; a letter to the vidame of Chartres was revealed, and the Guises learned that, despite the failure of the Amboise in-

* D'Aubigné, History of the Reformation in the Sixteenth Century, vol. 5, p. 162.

† Duncan, p. 34. Davila, liv. 2. De Thou, liv. [illegible].

trigue, the hostile nobles still hoped to succeed in expelling them from France.*

The Bourbons were soon apprized of the apprehension of La Saque, but they were at first uncertain whether he had made any disclosures, as his confession was kept a profound secret. But the imprisonment of the vidame of Chartres, one of their most faithful adherents, who was shut up in the Bastile and treated with great rigor,† convinced them that their projects were known. They were soon specially summoned to Orleans by Francis. But traversing Gascony at the head of a considerable number of gentlemen, both Romanists and Huguenots, pledged to support them, they bade defiance to the king's mandate.‡ However, repeated commands from the court, intimating that further disobedience would be deemed an act of overt rebellion and constructive treason, imperilling both their liberties and their lives, intimidated the feeble spirit of the king of Navarre, and he dismissed his little army, saying, "I must obey, but I will obtain your pardon of the king." "Go," said an old captain, "and ask pardon for yourself; our safety is in our good swords;" and the gentlemen who composed this nucleus force broke ranks indignantly, and separated for their homes.§

* Davila, liv. 2. D'Aubigné, Hist. Universelle, vol. 1, p. 97. De Thou, liv. 25, p. 542. Browning, p. 45.

† August 29, 1560. Journal de Brulárt, quoted in Browning, p. 43.

‡ Browning, p. 45.

§ Vallaire, Essai sur les Guerres Civiles de France, quoted in Browning, p. 45.

In the month of October, the Bourbon princes set out for Orleans. Navarre, anxious not to make a misstep, made the greatest *faux pas*. He walked straight into the net, and death touched both Condé and himself so closely, that its clammy fingers might have been felt.

The Guises were prepared for a crushing victory. They had persuaded the king, by perverting La Saque's confession, that the princes of the blood, and especially Condé, whom they most feared on account of his energy, boldness, and talents, had conspired against his life; and they urged him for his personal safety to arrest Condé as an example. To this advice the irritated monarch lent a willing ear. When Condé reached Orleans in the latter part of October, he ordered him into his presence, reproached him with his many supposed crimes, and without deigning to hear any reply, commanded his immediate imprisonment.*

The trial soon followed, before the chancellor and some commissioners chosen by the Parliament, now become a mere echo of the Guises.† The prince refused to plead, protested against the competence of this mushroom tribunal, and demanded, as a prince of the blood, to be tried by the king in person and by the peers of the realm.‡ This privilege, though perfectly legal and strictly in accordance with the letter and spirit of the Constitution,

* Brantome, vol. 10, p. 365. De Thou, liv. 25. Vie de Coligny.

† Brantome, vol. 10, p. 366.

‡ Ibid. Browning, p. 45. Duncan, p. 35.

was refused, and Condé was sentenced to be beheaded on the tenth of the following December.*

When Condé was informed of the decision, his tranquillity was unruffled. A priest was sent to him to perform mass. "What want you, reverend sir?" queried the prince. "I come to prepare you for death," was the reply. "This is a work," said Condé reverently and solemnly, "that I can safely trust with my Master; it rests between God and myself. Leave me, good father; it is time for the work to begin."†

The priest retired, shocked at this blasphemy.‡

Then a gentleman of the court, an emissary of the Guises, came to Condé's cell. The prince received him with the courtesy which distinguished him. Having expressed his deep sympathy, the courtier hinted that possibly affairs might yet be accommodated, and requested the prince to appoint him mediator.

"I ask but one *Mediator*," said Condé with an upward gesture, "and that one is interceding for me now at the throne of God. Return, my lord, to your employers, and tell them *you have failed in your mission*."§

One more trial yet awaited him. His wife was conducted to his prison. When she entered, she threw herself into her husband's arms, unable to speak.

* Mem. de Condé, vol. 1. D'Aubigne, Hist. Univ., vol. 1, p. 101. † Huguenots in France and America, vol. 1, p. 74.
‡ Ibid. § Ibid.

"Now this is kind," said Condé with rare tact. "I know your errand: it is to confirm, to support, to give new strength to your husband; to tell him that you will live to perform *his* duties and your *own;* to teach our children that their father, though dying an ignominious death, still bore a true and loyal heart. And now farewell. Let us not prolong this painful interview. Nothing can be done by your means or mine; it is hopeless. Let us not add disgrace to sorrow. All things are in the hands of God; he may yet save a life that has been sincerely devoted to his cause."

Again the princess would have spoken; but Condé said, "No more, sweet wife; write all you would say. Farewell." And the hero quitted the apartment for an inner room.*

When Condé's sentence was made public, his powerful relatives importuned the king for his pardon; but they plead in vain. His wife, Eleanora de Roye, Montmorenci's niece, accompanied by her children, threw herself before Francis, and with a woman's devotion endeavored to beat through the icy coldness of the king. "Madame," said the monarch, "your husband has assailed the crown, and conspired against my life; he must pay the penalty." In despair the poor princess implored the intercession of the Guises. "It is our duty," they said, "to strike off the head of heresy and rebellion at one blow."†

* Huguenots in France and America, vol. 1, p. 75.

† Dav., l. 2. Brown. p. 46. Dun., pp. 35, 36. Mem. de Condé

The complete destruction of the Huguenot party was to follow the execution of Condé, and every one was to be compelled to choose between death or the signature of the confession of faith drawn up in 1542 by the Sorbonne, in response to Calvin's "Institutes."*

The king of Navarre, though himself but little better than a prisoner, was for once extraordinarily active, and he made efforts constant and tireless to save his brother, even humbling himself to the cardinal of Lorraine, by whom, however, he was rudely repulsed. The duke of Guise had conceived a scheme to murder Navarre, and had even secured the king's assent to it.† It was arranged that Francis should summon Navarre to his presence, and that at a sign from him some bravos, whom Guise would station behind the arras, should pierce their victim to the heart.

Navarre was indeed summoned into the king's chamber; but having received word from some quarter that to go would be to commit suicide, the reluctant prince refused to obey the citation. At length, after being summoned three times, he yielded, saying to a confidential friend as he departed on the perilous visit, "Duty compels me to go; I will defend myself, if attacked, to the last gasp. If I fall, take my shirt, stained with my blood, carry it to my son, and may life abandon him sooner than

* Davila, liv. 2. Browning, p. 46. Duncan, pp. 35, 36. Mem. de Condé. Maimbourg, Hist. du Calvinisme, liv. 2.

† Cayét, liv. 6, p. 525. Browning, p. 46.

the purpose to avenge his murdered father."* Navarre went to the king, listened calmly to his reproofs, replied gently, and retired unharmed: Francis' courage failed him at the critical moment. "Oh the fool, the coward; what a contemptible monarch we have!"† exclaimed the incensed duke of Guise as he saw Navarre quit the royal presence unsmitten.

Disappointed in their hope of assassinating the Navarrese sovereign, the princes of Lorraine pressed with increased vehemence for Condé's early execution. The fatal day approached. Francis, unwilling to witness the ghastly spectacle, had resolved upon a tour to Chambord, when suddenly he was taken alarmingly ill. The chancellor instantly sent for Ambrose Paré, the king's physician; and upon being informed that Francis was not likely to recover, the cunning lawyer had recourse to a stratagem. He was very desirous of postponing Condé's death, and had delayed signing the order for his execution for several days by one pretext or another, using the weapons of his profession. Now the Guises hastened to him and implored him to sign; alarmed by the king's health, they feared that Condé might yet cheat the executioner. L'Hôpital pretended to be seized with a violent colic, which

* De Thou, liv. 25. Davila, liv. 2. Duncan, p. 36.

† De Thou. D'Aubigné, Hist. Universelle. Cayét. Browning. Duncan. "According to the Abbé Anquétil, Guise's expression, when he found that Francis' courage had deserted him at the last moment, was, '*O le lâche! O le poltron!*'" Esprit de la Ligue, vol. 1, p. 84; cited in Browning, p. 46, note.

prevented him from examining the body of the decree, an essential preliminary to his signature; but when Francis' danger became imminent, the keen chancellor suddenly recovered from his pain, and hurrying off to the queen mother, advised her to take advantage of the posture of affairs by uniting herself closely with the princes of the blood, as the Guises had already despoiled her of power and influence. The Machiavellian Catharine agreed with L'Hôpital, and charged Coligny, who had been summoned with the other nobles to attend the assembly of the states-general, with the negotiation.

Thus stood affairs when, on the 5th of December, 1560, the thread which attached the shattered health of Francis to life, snapped, and the young king, then but seventeen, lay dead in the midst of a court which instantly gave itself up to the mockery of woe.*

* Davila positively asserts that the execution of Condé was deferred by the Guises themselves, who hoped to entrap the old constable in the same net. Montmorenci was urgently called on, but did not appear. It was also the wish of the Guises to involve the king of Navarre in the same punishment, but sufficient evidence did not exist. Duncan, p. 37, note.

CHAPTER XIX.

THE LOST LEADER.

CHARLES IX., a fatal name, an infamous memory, succeeded in his eleventh year to the vacant throne of his dead brother. Now once more the politics of the court were completely revolutionized. The Guises had been entrenched by the influence of their niece, Mary Stuart, over Francis II. Of this support they were now of course deprived. Chaos reigned, not Charles; and the selfish struggles of the chiefs of the several factions, ambitious not for their country's honor, but for their own governmental advancement, held France a second-rate power for a quarter of a century, and made this period one of the most calamitous in its history.

Upon Charles' coronation, Catharine de' Medici assumed the position of arbiter almost without opposition. Almost the first act of the infant king, under the queen mother's direction, was to write the Parliament, on the 8th of December, 1560, a letter, in which, after announcing his brother's death, he informed that body "that, considering his youth, and confiding in the virtue and wisdom of the queen mother, he had requested her to undertake the administration of affairs, with the wise counsel and assistance of the king of Navarre, and of the gentlemen of distinction in the late king's counsel"*

This crafty move at once deposed the princes of Lorraine, but their real influence remained almost untouched, since they were the representatives of the reactionists of France, as the Bourbons were of the Huguenots.

Still, many changes occurred. The command of the army was taken from the duke of Guise, and confided to Antony of Bourbon, who was made lieutenant-general of the kingdom.†

The prince of Condé was released from prison; and while as a matter of form he retired for a little to his government of Bearn, his innocence was openly proclaimed at court.‡

The nobles who had been placed under the ban by the haughty Guises in the days of their *régime*, were recalled with honor, and the constable Montmorenci resumed his ancient functions, and regain ed his former titles.§

At the council board of the king the queen mother was now seated as regent, while upon either hand the princes of Bourbon, the princes of Lorraine, and Montmorenci were clustered.‖

Between all the members of this heterogeneous cabinet a rankling hatred still existed, which threatened at every session to inaugurate fresh convul-

* Browning, p. 47. Brantome, Davila, etc.

† Brantome, vol. 10. Mem. de Tavannes, p. 243. Davila, liv. 2. ‡ Browning, p. 47. Mem. de Condé.

§ Duncan, p. 39. Esprit de la Ligue, vol. 1, p. 93.

‖ Ibid.

sions. But Catharine, cozened by her favorite theory of an "adjusted equilibrium," foolishly hoped to be able to hold the scales evenly poised between these implacable enemies.*

The first measures of the new administration were indeed judicious. All persons were released who had been imprisoned for heresy, and their property was restored, while a general amnesty was proclaimed.†

While the reconstruction of the cabinet was being effected, the states-general continued their sittings at Orleans. L'Hôpital implored the assembly to adopt such measures as would insure domestic tranquillity, burying, in devotion to the general good, the bitter feuds of the past reign, which had so nearly kindled a civil war.‡ But this statesman-like and noble appeal of the patriotic chancellor was not much heeded.

The nobles, taught wisdom by experience, insisted, as a *sine qua non*, upon the exile of the princes of Lorraine. Condé, Navarre, and Montmorenci declared that if Catharine did not concede this measure to the safety of the state, they would march to Paris, proclaim one of themselves regent in her place, and execute their purpose. But this scheme was rendered abortive by the action of the chancellor, who prevailed upon the king to command the constable to remain at court; a command which

* Duncan, p. 39.

† Mem. de Condé, vol. 2, p. 260, et seq. Duncan, p. 40.

‡ Ibid. Browning, p. 48.

Montmorenci was too old and wily a courtier to disobey.*

But a motion made about the same time by the king of Navarre in the states-general, had a more serious result. He proposed a searching examination into the financial system of the preceding reign, and that a return of all excessive gratifications in money or lands to the late court favorites be speedily ordered.† This motion instantly made a flutter in the dove-cote, and alienated a powerful friend. Every one felt that it was a blow at the extortion of the Guises, but the blow struck beyond them. It affected the gratuities of Diana de Poitiers, the marshal Saint André, an old chum of Henry II., and the servile instrument of the duchess de Valentinois, who had battened upon the gains incident to his office of pimp,‡ and of Montmorenci himself, since one of his sons had married a daughter of Diana, and he had shared largely in the public plunder.§ A community of interest made this horde of thieves, but yesterday deadly foemen, fast friends to-day: all minor differences were buried in the unanimous desire to preserve ill-gotten wealth; and the consequence was, an infamous coalition. The Guises, Montmorenci, and Saint André united under the name of the TRIUMVIRATE.‖ These abandoned nobles swore at the altar to forget their old quarrels; and in order to give a religious flavor to

* Duncan, p. 41.

† Duncan, p. 40.

‡ Browning, Duncan, Mem. de Condé.

§ Duncan, De Thou, Pasquier.

‖ Ibid.

their avaricious league, they signed a treaty by which they pledged themselves to the extermination of heresy. It was a fitting collocation; a horde of titled plunderers, met to preserve their booty from the clutch of justice, and leagued to earn a good right to their stolen gold by filching the yet more costly jewel of life from their innocent countrymen whose creed taught them better things.

The Triumvirate had a powerful ally in the Spanish ambassador, who had a seat at the council, pretending that his master, Philip II., the most bigoted king in history, had taken France under his protection.* And such was the wretched and disgraceful condition of France, torn by the internecine factions, that this insolent foreigner was tamely permitted to dictate its policy. This Spaniard was personally and politically attached to the Guises, who sacrificed the honor of France and the dignity of the crown to secure his protection.†

The nation was now divided into two great parties, into which all the minor factions had melted: the Triumvirate, supported by the holy see and by the Romanists; the Bourbon princes, at the head of the Huguenots, and backed by those who, indifferent about religious creeds, longed for the inauguration of political reform, and for the reinstatement of France in her natural position of a commanding power in Europe.‡

Between these parties stood the queen mother,

* Duncan, p. 42. † Ibid., p. 43. Ranke, p. 208.
‡ Browning, p. 50.

muttering her shibboleth, and eternally grasping the shadow of power, but never its substance.

The Triumvirate and the Bourbons were about equally matched, and Catharine long hesitated which way to lean. Finally judging that it would be safest to favor the Huguenots for the moment, she permitted the eager chancellor to wring from the states-general a decree, published in July, 1561, and hence called the Edict of July, which relieved the Huguenots from the punishment of death without a judicial condemnation, but which still refused them their principal prayer, permission to assemble for public worship.*

This edict was the pretext for a simulated reconciliation between Condé and Francis of Guise. They met at the palace, where the king desired that the duke should declare how affairs had been managed at Orleans. Guise accused the late king of having peremptorily ordered the imprisonment of Condé; on which the prince answered, looking earnestly at the duke, "Whoever put that affront upon me, I hold him to have been a scoundrel and a villain." "And I also," replied the hypocritical duke; "but it does not regard me in the least."

They then dined together, interchanged vows of friendship,† and separated with mutual, but smothered curses,

> "And study of revenge, immortal hate,
> And courage never to submit or yield."

* Browning, p. 50. Pasquier, vol.2, p. 84. Mem. de Condé, vol. 2.

† Duncan, p. 43. Browning, p. 51.

Such was the apparently placid, yet really uneasy and abnormal political situation—a heterogeneous cabinet, a double-faced edict, a hollow reconciliation—when a remarkable event occurred, the famous colloquy of Poissy was convoked.

The chancellor L'Hôpital, eager in the pursuit of his panacea for the existing evils, a grand conference upon religious differences, in which both Romanists and Huguenots should be represented, and in which theological rights should be definitively defined and regulated, persuaded Catharine de' Medici to assent to his project, and to command the debate.*

The Roman publicists and orators were reluctant to accede to the conference; but stung by the jeers of the evangelicals, who hailed the project of a free colloquy with enthusiasm, they finally consented.†

Accordingly, after great preparations, the oratorical representatives of the two ecclesiastical parties met, in the month of August, 1561, in the little village of Poissy, a short distance from St. Germaine, where the royal family then resided.‡

The leading Roman disputant was the cardinal of Lorraine, a prelate of fine, though sadly perverted intellect, of rare scholarship, and whose discourse, sustained by a never-failing memory, flowed from him intelligibly and gracefully.§ He was as-

* Duncan, p. 43. Browning, p. 51. De Thou, liv. 25. Davila, etc. † Ibid.

‡ Esprit de la Ligue, tom. 1, p. 88. Duncan, p. 45.

§ Ranke, p. 169.

sisted by five other cardinals and by forty bishops.*

The reformers were represented by Theodore Beza, a divine of singular genius, erudition, acumen, and eloquence, the friend and biographer of Calvin, who was supported by twelve celebrated doctors of the Reformation, among whom were Marloratus and Pierre Martyr.†

On the ninth of September the session opened with great *éclat*. Never had a grander audience been convened, not even when Luther's Demosthenian eloquence sounded over Worms. The king himself attended the first sitting, accompanied by the queen mother, his elder brother Henry of Anjou, his sister Margaret de Valois, the Bourbon princes, the princes of Lorraine, the old constable, the ministers of state, the holder of the great seal, and the chief officers of the crown.‡

The debate was opened by L'Hôpital, in a conciliatory address, which breathed the spirit of a politician, not of a theologian; for, careless about matters of religious belief, he was anxious only to preserve a false peace, to tide over differences. He proposed a compromise, and urged the papists to relax upon some points, in order to win back the Calvinists.§ This conservative, Erasmian course was distasteful to both parties. It was thought,

* Duncan, Esprit de la Ligue. Browning, Vie de Coligny, etc.

† Ibid. Hist. du Cardinal Tournon, p. 369. Hist. du Calvinisme, liv. 3.

‡ Ibid.

§ Hist. du Concile de Trente, p. 435. De Thou, liv. 28.

and rightly thought, that in radical differences radical methods should be employed.

When the chancellor finished his speech, Beza, the orator of the Huguenots, was called on to state his opinions. The questions at issue were two, the authority of the church of Rome and transubstantiation.*

The Protestant orator stepped forward into the middle of the hall, knelt, and prayed God to enlighten his mind and inspire him with the luminous truth, and then commenced his address. He adduced numerous and irresistible arguments to disprove the assumption of Rome that she alone is the true church, made a profession of the reformed faith, expatiated upon the rigors, unchristian and abhorrent, which were exercised against the primitive theology, defended the different points which Rome disputed, and after an exhaustive discussion of the dogma of the real presence in the eucharist, concluded with the affirmation that Christ was as far from the sacramental elements as the highest heavens were from the earth.†

Horrified by this bold declaration, the adherents of Latin orthodoxy broke out into vociferous clamors. The cardinal of Tournon suddenly started from his seat, and after asserting that he entirely disapproved of the colloquy, and had only sanctioned it in deference to the wish of Catharine de

* De Thou liv. 28. Discours des Actes de Poissy. Browning, etc.

† Ibid. Duncan, p. 47. Browning, p. 53.

Medici, exhorted the infant king not to be led astray by the subtle and impetuous eloquence of Beza, but to suspend his judgment until he had listened to the reply of the orthodox divines.* Tournon further pointed out the impropriety of the young monarch's attendance upon the debates, as they involved questions above the capacity of his tender age: this hint was taken, for Charles did not afterwards appear.†

The cardinal of Lorraine then rose to speak, and he delivered a harangue of great astuteness and rhetorical talent. When he concluded, the cardinals and bishops formed a circle around him, and declared that he had expounded the true faith, for which they were all ready to suffer martyrdom.‡

Beza demanded to reply, but since the hour was late, the conference was adjourned to the following day.§

The debates continued through several days, and Beza astonished his opponents by his accurate learning, his acute reasoning, his evangelical fervor, and his animated, graphic eloquence.‖ Still the good results of the colloquy were scarcely perceptible; the ecclesiastics in general were convinced that no reform could take place without stripping them of their vast wealth, of their usurped power, and of

* Bossuet, Hist. des Variations, tom. 1, p. 65.

† Duncan, p. 47. Browning. Hist. du Concile de Trente.

‡ Ibid. De Thou, liv. 28. Discours des Actes de Poissy.

§ Ibid.

‖ Vie de Coligny. Hist. du Card. Tournon, p. 367. Browning, p. 53.

their impunity.* And when the conference of Poissy was dissolved, the disputed points stood just as unsettled as when the debates commenced, while both sides claimed the victory. But while in some respects the colloquy resulted unsatisfactorily, in others it was not without effect. The papists felt that they had committed a blunder in consenting to it at all—it compromised a faith which had existed for so many ages; the bare discussion of these questions was an acknowledgment that Rome might err. "The government," says a violent Jesuit who wrote at a later day, "committed a grave error, or at least idleness, in permitting the conference of Poissy, instead of sending Beza and his troop to the then sitting council of Trent."†

Besides this moral gain and recognition, several bishops were so affected by Beza's masterly arguments, that they devoted themselves to an inquiry after the truth.‡ By the conversations which they had with Catharine de' Medici, they so far wrought a change in her sentiments, that she not only invited Beza, but actually insisted upon his remaining at the court. The divine complied; and protected by the queen mother, delivered a series of powerful sermons which greatly advanced the Reformation.§

Catharine did more; she wrote an epistle to the

* "The chief part of the wealth of the church being given to have prayers said for the dead, the heritics, by destroying purgatory, would impoverish it." Mem. du Tuvannes, p. 121.

† Caveyrac, Apology for Louis XIV., p. 30; cited in Browning, p. 53.

‡ Browning, p. 54.

§ Huguenots in France and America, vol. 1, pp. 81, 82.

pontiff: "Those of the reform," she said, "are neither Anabaptists nor libertines; they believe in the twelve articles of the apostles' creed; therefore many persons think that they ought not to be cut off from communion with the mother church. What danger could there be in taking away the images from the churches, and in retrenching some useless forms in the celebration of the sacraments? It would further be very beneficial to allow to all the communion in both kinds, and to permit divine service to be performed in the vulgar tongue."*

Thus spoke Catharine de' Medici shortly after the conclusion of the colloquy of Poissy. She boldly recommended to the sovereign pontiff the adoption of a series of innovations which the most heated enthusiast, the most Utopian dreamer among the Huguenots would not have demanded. Yet this was the woman who, a little later, instigated the massacre of St. Bartholomew! Catharine is the Sphinx of history; and though many an Œdipus has assumed to solve the riddle, the wily tiger queen yet remains a mystery. Of course Beza's eloquence could not have touched her heart; she had none—only a muscle to circulate the blood. It is probable that Beza's flattering reception and retention at court, and the papal letter, were both simply parts of some scheme for preserving the balance of power in her own hands.

Be this as it may, Paul IV. was alarmed, and he

* Hist. du Concile de Trente, p. 433. Davila, liv. 2, p. 185. Browning, p. 54.

instantly instructed his legate at Paris to spare no exertions for strengthening the papal party in France.*

The most plausible plan for the achievement of this purpose seemed to be to alienate the king of Navarre from the Huguenots. It was thought that if that monarch could be won over to Rome, "heresy would be a clock without a pendulum." The legate, seconded by a score of cunning satellites, commenced the congenial work. Every wile which could affect the human mind and heart was put in active operation. Temptation after temptation was thrown into his way. The pope offered to dissolve his marriage with Jane d'Albrét, on the ground of her heresy;† the Guises offered him the hand of their niece Mary Stuart, with her prospective claims on the English throne;‡ a marriage with the king's sister Margaret de Valois was hinted at as quite possible;§ but to all of these seductions Navarre was deaf. He even refused a promise of Sardinia, as an indemnification for that portion of Navarre of which the Spanish king had deprived him.‖

Finding that Antony of Bourbon could not be bribed to desert his faith, the Jesuits changed their tactics. Then this man, proof to all the proposals of temporal advantage which had been made him, fell a victim to his own pride and vanity.

* Brantome, vol. 8, p. 269. Browning, p. 54.

† Hist. du Cardinal Granville, p. 361, et seq. Davila, liv. 2, p. 178.

‡ Pasquier, vol. 2, p. 95. De Thou, liv. 28.

§ Ibid. Strada, lib. 3.

‖ Brantome, vol. 8, p. 270. Duncan, p. 49.

Antony of Navarre was known throughout his whole life as a man amiable, but weak and vacillating; who, although he adopted his opinions with vivacity, did not hold them with firmness.* And when with insidious and tireless zeal it was insinuated that Condé was the actual chief of the Huguenot party, while he was only his brother's second, his pride and vanity revolted. He hesitated; the king's youth opened for him a long career of authority; and if he became a papist, his power and influence in Europe would be so much enhanced, that he might dictate to Philip II. of Spain the restoration of his stolen kingdom. The Spanish ambassador himself breathed this insinuation into his ear.†

Quite overcome and dazzled blind to the infamy of the action by his brilliant prospects, Navarre at length succumbed; the renegade king joined the triumvirate, and this "lost leader," in the excess of his newly acquired zeal, became one of the bitterest persecutors of his old companions.‡ Similar revulsions are the never-failing accompaniment of political and theological treason.

Navarre soon proceeded to carry his new opinions into practice. He declared that he considered the reformed preachers as charlatans, and expressed his determination to remove his son—afterwards the famous Henry IV.—from their influence, and

* Ranke, p. 209.

† Browning, p. 54. Mem. de Condé, vol. 2, p. 10.

‡ Duncan, p. 48. Hist. du Cardinal Granville, etc.

place him under Romanist governors. Jane d'Albrét, who had inherited her faith and Christian devotion from her mother Margaret of Navarre, the mother also of French reform, heard this avowal with dismay. After vain entreaties, she was compelled to yield; but passionately embracing her child, she exclaimed, "Oh, my son, if you renounce the religion of your mother, she will renounce and disinherit you. Keep to the faith in which you have hitherto been educated, and God will be your guide and support."*

"My dear madame," said Catharine, who was present, "let me advise you to suppress this violence of emotion. I have always found it best *to appear to yield.* Assume a seeming conformity to your husband's will; even attend mass, and you will the more easily get the reins into your own hands."

To this characteristic advice Jane d'Albrét replied indignantly, "Rather than deny my faith by attending mass, if I had my son in one hand, and my kingdom in the other, I would throw them both into the sea."†

Such was the difference between these two women and between their creeds.

But Jane d'Albrét was ere long relieved of her fears by her vain and vacillating husband's death.

Ere Navarre's defection startled France, the indefatigable chancellor, not discouraged by the

* Huguenots in France and America, vol. 1, p. 83. Vie de Coligny.

† Ibid. De Thou, liv. 28. Davila, etc.

failure of the colloquy of Poissy to apply a remedy to the ecclesiastical abuses, contrived to convoke another assembly of the states-general at St. Germaine.

"The object of your deliberations," said L'Hôpital in his opening address to the deputies, "is simple and clear. Is it advantageous, in the existing state of affairs, to tolerate or to forbid the meetings of the Calvinists for the exercise of their devotions? That is the single question you have to decide. To come to a right conclusion, you must keep out of view whatever relates to creed, doctrine, or religious discipline. Even let it be assumed that Calvinism is one continuous error of judgment, is that a reason to bar their assemblies, or to justify the proscription of those French subjects who have embraced it? Can a man not be a good citizen without being a good Romanist? Do not then waste your time, or entangle yourselves in fruitless controversy, in the vain attempt to decide which is the true religion. We are not here to establish a mode of faith, but a rule of government."*

It was thus that the keen and cautious chancellor exhibited his anxiety to make all vexed points of theology subservient to the vital interests of political government. By dexterously narrowing down the discussion into this limited space, and extracting the sting of theological hate, the triumph of the Huguenots was rendered certain; for had

* De Thou, liv. 29. Davila, liv. 2. Vie de Coligny. Hist. du Concile de Trente, p. 452.

the duke of Guise affirmed that none but Romanists could be good citizens, the prince of Condé would have resented it as a personal affront, and demanded satisfaction at the sword's point. The papists were thus compelled to make concessions, or raise the standard of civil war, for which they were not yet fully prepared.

The assembly of St. Germaine therefore passed a decree, called the Edict of January, 1562, by which many of the disabilities of the Huguenots were removed. The reformers might meet unarmed without the walls of cities and towns, and the local magistrates were commanded to afford them protection; though prohibited from levying money to pay their preachers, they might receive any sum voluntarily contributed.* In return for these concessions, the Huguenots were to restore all images and reliques of saints which they had seized, and to pay tithe and other ecclesiastical dues, while their preachers were commanded to abstain from all violent invectives against the mass.†

Some bloody scenes occurred in various sections after the promulgation of this edict;‡ but as a whole the winter glided quietly away. The Huguenots were grateful and satisfied; the Romanists sullen and discontented. But both parties felt conscious of an approaching rupture, convinced that this temporary calm was only the harbinger of a fearful storm.

* Vie de Coligny, p. 238. Browning, p. 55. Duncan, p. 50.
† Ibid. ‡ Browning, p. 55.

CHAPTER XX.

THE APPEAL TO ARMS.

The Huguenots were surprised and grieved by the renegadism of the king of Navarre: the queen mother was alarmed; and to restore the equilibrium, she openly allied herself with the reform party.*

Coligny, anxiously watchful for the interest of religion, was early apprized of the efforts being made to win over Antony of Bourbon; and when the illustrious deserter joined the Triumvirate, he was "sad, but not astonished;" he knew Navarre's character. He had suspected the motive of a mission to Spain in the early months of 1562, and employing persons to watch the emissary, he ordered them to arrest and search him on his return. Shortly after the messenger, in the garb of a pilgrim, endeavored to reënter France. He was seized and searched; nothing was found. Some one, however, observing that he threw away his staff, informed Coligny of the circumstance. The acute admiral ordered it to be brought to him; a countryman had picked it up and carried it to his cottage. On examination it was found that the staff was hollow, and that it contained a budget of letters from the king of Spain.† Upon examining

* De Thou, liv. 28. Davila, liv. 2. Pasquier, vol. 2, p. 90.

† Vie de Coligny, p. 238. Browning, p. 55.

these letters, they were found to be directed to the king of Navarre, to the Triumvirate, to Catharine, and to others of the leading Roman chiefs, expressing poignant grief at the concessions recently made to heresy, and exhorting them to take arms and crush the Huguenots by a single blow, to effect which Philip offered to furnish men and money.*

Catharine was absolutely frightened; Coligny was calm and resolute. The queen mother allied herself more closely than ever with the admiral. The admiral, perceiving that the foes of his faith were about to kindle the flames of civil war, worked with Titanic energy to prepare his party for the ordeal of battle. He united with Condé, and securing the appointment of that prince to the chief command of the reformers, called upon him to make a public confession of the Protestant creed.†

The gallant prince complied; and so great was the effect of his example, that many nobles did not scruple to do likewise. The number of persons who came to the Faubourgs to hear the Reformation preached in a little time numbered fifty thousand,‡ a very respectable congregation.

Navarre, witnessing Coligny's activity, and galled perhaps by the presence of his old companion in arms, urgently pressed Catharine to banish him from court. She would consent, however, on but

* Duncan, p 50, 51. Browning, p. 55. Vie de Coligny, p. 300.

† Ibid.

‡ Vie de Coligny, p. 243. The cardinal of Chatillon and the bishop of Nevers were *publicly married.*

one condition: that the duke of Guise, the cardinal of Lorraine, and the marshal St. André, the original triumvirs, should also quit the capital for their estates. Unexpectedly to Catharine, her terms were accepted; for the chiefs of the reaction, knowing that their interests might safely be intrusted to Montmorenci and the king of Navarre, who were to remain in Paris, were willing to go into temporary exile for the purpose of removing their dangerous rivals from the vicinity of St. Germaine.*

But this compromise did not long stop up the mouth of Vesuvius with its cotton. The adherents of Guise at the capital wrote him that the queen mother was every day becoming more closely connected with the Huguenots, and urged him to hasten back to Paris. Guise obeyed the summons, leaving his estate of Joinville towards the close of February, 1562. His suite, already numerous when he quitted his chateau, was augmented as he advanced, until, when he reached the little town of Vassy, he was at the head of a small army.†

At Vassy a fatal event occurred. A Huguenot congregation attending divine worship in a barn, attracted the attention of the bigoted chieftain and his fanatical retinue. Filled with hate, and armed, they rushed upon the reformers, who endeavored to shut the doors against the assailants. A collision resulted; Guise himself was slightly wounded in

* Duncan, p. 51. Vie de Coligny, p. 250.

† Davila, De Thou, Browning, Vie de Coligny. Vassy is a small town in Champagne, some sixty leagues east of Paris.

the cheek by some chance missile, and his followers, infuriated at the sight of his blood, massacred the whole helpless congregation.*

The news of this bloody foray spread with almost incredible rapidity; it reached the metropolis before its hero; and when Guise appeared, the civic mob of Paris hailed the "*butcher of Vassy*" with "frenzied shouts and tears of joy."† A sanguinary and cowardly slaughter of an unarmed assembly, convened for religious worship, was hailed as a great and heroic exploit.

In later days Guise protested that he had no hand in this wholesale assassination; but whether he intended it or not, it is enough that he did not prevent it. The deed was his; upon his head history heaps her malediction.‡

Nor was Vassy the only scene of violence. Cahors, Toulouse, Sens, Amiens, and Tours hastened to follow in Guise's bloody footsteps.§ At Tours a refinement of cruelty was displayed. Three hundred Huguenots were shut up without food for three days; then, tied together two by two, they were led to a slaughter-house and butchered like beasts.‖

At Sens also there was an exhibition of atrocious fanaticism: during three successive days the bell of the cathedral invited the citizens to murder

* Ranke, p. 211. Browning, p. 57. Duncan, p. 51. Vie de Coligny, p. 243.

† Duncan, p. 51. Ranke, p. 211, etc.

‡ Ibid.

§ Beza, Life of Calvin. D'Aubigné, Hist. Univ. De Thou, liv. 29.

‖ Browning, p. 58.

the reformers. Even the vines which embellished their dwellings were plucked up by the roots. The bodies of the victims, floating down the Seine, appeared to speak trumpet-toned to their brothers in the faith for justice.* The Huguenots did indeed bestir themselves to obtain redress. When some of the shocking incidents of the massacres were related to Navarre, the traitor cried with a sneer, "They were all factious heretics." "Sire," replied Beza, who chanced to be present, with indignant emphasis, "I speak on behalf of a religion which pardons injuries, instead of resenting them; but remember, it is an anvil which has blunted many hammers."†

But while one party demanded justice, the other clamored fiercely for the extermination of the Huguenots, and Montluc addressed a memoir showing how easily it might be effected.‡

Meantime Condé, overpowered, quitted Paris with his preachers and armed followers.§ "Cæsar has not only crossed the Rubicon," wrote he to D'Andelot and Coligny, "he has already seized Rome, and his banners will shortly be everywhere displayed."‖

Guise was aware that in a *coup d'état* audacity

* Browning, p. 58.

† Duncan, p. 52. Beza, Hist. Eccles., liv. 6.

‡ This memoir may be found at length in Mem. de Condé, vol. 3, p. 184, et seq. Browning, p. 58.

§ Vie de Coligny. Browning, p. 59. Ranke, p. 211.

‖ Duncan, pp. 52, 53. Browning, p. 59. Journal de Henri III., vol. 2, ed. Cologne.

and energy were necessary. Catharine was sojourning at Meaux with her royal son. The princes of Lorraine sped thither, seized the regent and the king, and hastening back to Paris, received another ovation.* Their captives were lodged in a building which had been used as a prison for a century.† The possession of the king's person was the grand object of their policy, and they succeeded, spite of the prayers and menaces of the queen mother.

Emboldened by their success, the triumvirs rejected all compromises, all overtures, and determined to strike a vigorous blow at once in the very commencement of their lawless campaign; they designed a revocation of the tolerant edict of January, in the chief cities first, and then throughout the kingdom.

Meantime Paris was surrendered to a carnival of fanaticism; the cardinal of Lorraine commenced preaching in the style of his predecessors, St. Dominic and Torquemada; and Montmorenci displayed his zeal on the evening of the youthful monarch's return to the metropolis, by plundering the Huguenot chapels, destroying the books, and building bonfires with the reading-desks of the preachers. The fanatical violence with which he sought after and destroyed these desks, gained the hoary old bigot the soubriquét of *Capitaine Brule-Bancs*.‡

* Ranke, p. 212. Thuanus, lib. 29. Mem. de Condé, vol. 3, p. 195

† Beza, Hist. Eccles., liv. 29.

‡ Mem. de Condé, vol. 3, p. 198. Duncan, p. 53. Brantome, vol. 7, p. 79.

While these events were occurring at the capital, Condé was not idle. He received, through a secret messenger, a letter from Catharine, in which she implored him to save the mother and the child, at the same time assuring him that all her hopes rested upon him; the liberty of the king, the prosperity of France, all was staked upon the pluck and loyalty of the Huguenots.*

Condé at once published two manifestoes, which roused France as with the blast of a trumpet. The eloquent prince implored the Huguenots to arm and attack their common enemy, and he conjured all true Frenchmen, whatever their creed, to couch their lances for the liberation of their captive sovereign.† The response was enthusiastic. Orleans was seized after a sanguinary battle, and there Condé set up his banner. This city became the Huguenot rendezvous.‡

The triumvirs, to destroy the effect of Condé's appeal, forced the irresponsible toy who at this awful moment played king, to sign and publish an official denial of the charges of the Bourbon prince, and an affirmation that both his mother and himself enjoyed perfect freedom;§ but the cheat was too transparent, and even the reluctant pen of an old

* The queen's letters are printed in Mem. de Condé, vol. 3, p. 222.

† These manifestoes were dated, the first on the 8th, the other on the 25th of April, 1562. Mem. de Condé, vol. 3, pp. 222, 319.

‡ La Noue, p. 554. Davila, liv. 3. Browning, p. 60.

§ Davila, liv. 3. Duncan, p. 53. Mem. de Condé, vol. 3, p. 320.

contemporaneous historian, devoted to that side, was forced to pen these significant words: "It is most certain that the young king was seen by many to weep that day, being persuaded that the Romanist lords had restrained his personal liberty; and that the queen mother, being discontented that her wonted arts had not prevailed, and foreseeing the mischiefs of the opening war, seemed perplexed, and spoke no word to any one; of which Guise made light, saying publicly, 'The good is always good, whether it proceeds from love or force.'"*

The enthusiasm of the Huguenots was at flood-tide. They were very soon in possession of the principal cities of the provinces—Lyons, Bourges, Vienne, Rouen, and the rest.† All the Orleanoise was subjected to them, and the whole of Normandy declared in their favor. Levies of men were everywhere made to swell their embattled ranks, and detachments flocked from every quarter, with the motto "God and liberty" emblazoned on their banners, to Condé's camp.

Brantome relates that a squadron of fifty Huguenot cavaliers set out from Metz for Orleans, and M. d'Espan, governor of Verdun, learning the circumstance, determined to cut them off on the march. When he came up with them, they had taken a position in an old windmill, where they defended themselves with stubborn valor, until night closed the combat. Before morning they made a sortie,

* Davila, liv. 3.

† Mem. de Condé, vol. 3, passim.

surprised their weary assailants, and routed them. The cavaliers then recommenced their march, and after thirty different skirmishes, they reached Orleans with the loss of but three of their number, an incident which the quaint old chronicler justly thinks illustrative of remarkable pluck and zeal.*

The leaders of the reformed host were Condé's nearest relatives: there were the three Chatillons, the cardinal, Coligny, and D'Andelot, the uncles of his consort; the Count Porcian, who was married to his niece; Francis de Rochefoucault, who was married to his sister-in-law, of whom it was said that he could bring an army into the field composed of his friends and vassals in Poitou alone. The viscount René de Rohan led the Bretons, Antony, count de Grammont, the Gascons; Montgomery—the count who had accidentally slain Henry II. in the tournament of 1559—was present from Normandy, and Hangest de Genlis from Picardy. There assembled at Orleans in a short time three thousand gentlemen, of whom Lanquét says, "If they were destroyed, the very seed of masculine virtue would have been exterminated in France."†

The triumvirs received assistance not only from the reactionary home party, they drew upon Romanist Europe. The king of Spain, the pope, Cosmo, duke of Florence, all lent jubilant levies; and soon the Guises marched towards Orleans at the

* Brantome, Discours sur les Belles Retraites; cited in Browning, p. 64.

† Ranke, p. 214. Duncan, p. 54.

head of ten thousand men-at-arms, the vanguard of the larger host to come.*

Between the hostile ranks of Condé and Guise the government of a boy and a woman disappeared.

Catharine made one last effort to regain her lost *prestige*. As usual, her weapons were hypocrisy and treason. Instigated by Guise, with whom she appears now to have allied herself,† overawed perhaps by the threat that she would be deposed even from the nominal regency, unless she lent herself to the projects of the usurpers, the queen mother attempted to entrap Condé.

A personal conference was appointed between them at Thuri.‡ Condé, unsuspicious of treachery, nearly fell into the snare. It was proposed that he and his friends should quit France for a time, while the triumvirs also retired from the court. "Offer these terms," said the wily queen in a seductive whisper; "they will certainly be refused; then you will gain the credit of having made a patriotic proposition, which will augment your strength."

The frank soldier for once attempted to play Machiavelli; he was unequal to the part. Condé assented. After some delay, the council replied, "Your terms are accepted," but no allusion was made to the retirement of the triumvirs.§ Condé was thunderstruck; his diplomatic *ruse* had recoiled upon himself; Catharine had played him false. His

* Davila, liv. 3. De Thou, liv. 29. Duncan, p. 54.

† Mem. de Condé, vol. 3, p. 508. Browning, p. 63.

‡ Ibid. Duncan, p. 55.

§ Ibid.

troops were indignant; his nobles protested against the validity of the contract; the preachers inveighed against the regent's duplicity; and Condé, declaring that he had been deceived, retracted the agreement, and mounting his horse, bade defiance to his own and his country's foes.*

This *faux pas* convinced the Huguenots that no reliance could be placed either on the friendship or the good faith of Catharine de' Medici.

Condé was anxious to strengthen his cause by alliances with the Protestant powers of Europe. In Germany, the proofs he advanced in justification of his action were regarded as satisfactory. The old landgrave, Philip of Hesse, gave Marshal Rollshausen orders to advance into France with some thousands of *lanzknechts* and arquebusiers.†

The Huguenots also dispatched a mission to England to sue Elizabeth for an alliance. The stingy queen agreed to aid them on condition that Havre de Grace was delivered to her as a compensation for Calais, whose loss still rankled.‡ This conceded, Elizabeth furnished one hundred thousand crowns, and garrisoned Havre de Grace, Dieppe, and Rouen, with six thousand English yeomen.§

Towards the close of June, 1562, the contending armies opened the campaign. Condé and Coligny left Orleans to attack Paris and deliver the king;

* Duncan, p. 56. † Ranke, p. 215.

‡ Davila, liv. 3, p. 236. Browning, pp. 61, 62. Duncan, p. 57. § Ibid. De Thou, liv. 29.

the triumvirs quitted the metropolis to besiege the Huguenots in Orleans.* The two parties were about equal, each having ten thousand men.†

To detail the various skirmishes which steeped the provinces in fraternal blood, to enumerate the villages plundered and razed, to record the deeds of cruelty committed by individual and remorseless leaders of roving bands attached to either army, would occupy volumes, and would form a narrative of crime hideously diversified in its features, from which humanity would recoil. Both sides undoubtedly committed excesses. Where the Huguenots triumphed, they destroyed altars and broke images; where the papists were successful, Bibles were burned and heretics were racked.

The picture of France rent by demoniacs is the most melancholy and pathetic that ever employed the pencil of an artist. Not Angelo nor Raphael nor Rembrandt could have originated so woful a canvas.

It is an unquestionable historic fact, that in this drama of death the papists were the most frenzied and remorseless actors. The testimony of the Abbé Anquétil will scarcely be impeached in the court of Rome. Let us see what this inimical witness has to say: "For the heretics there was no security, no asylum; the faith of treaties and the sanctity of oaths were alike set at naught. Tortures, contrived with cruel care for delaying death and increasing the duration of pain, were inflicted upon persons

* Browning, p. 62. De Thou, etc. † Ibid.

who had surrendered upon capitulation. Husbands and fathers were poignarded in the arms of their wives and daughters, who were then violated in the sight of the dying loved ones. Women and children were treated with a brutality which defies description. Aged magistrates, the victims of an unbridled rage, were insulted after death by the populace, who dragged their yet palpitating entrails through the streets, and even ate their quivering flesh."*

Beaumont, baron des Adrets, one of the Huguenot leaders, determined to meet cruelty with cruelty, forgetful of the mild tenets of the faith which he professed to serve. He killed and laid waste with a barbarity which made his own officers shudder; superstitious nurses frightened children by the simple repetition of his name: his vengeful acts drew forth an admonition from the admiral, and a severe reproof from Calvin.†

Beaumont's rival was the ferocious Blaise de Montluc, who relates in his memoirs, with the utmost *sangfroid*, the chilling cruelties which he practised upon the heretics: "I procured," he says, "two executioners, who were called my lackeys, because they were so constantly with me *in active service*."‡

* Abbé Anquétil, Esprit de la Ligue, vol. 1, pp. 161, 164; cited and summarized in Browning, p. 64.

† Beza, Hist. Eccles. D'Aubigné, Hist. Univ. De Thou, liv. 3, etc.

‡ Montluc, Memoires, liv. 5, vol. 3, p. 27. Browning, p. 64. Concerning Baron des Adrets, "Maimbourg, whose testimony on

Thus, while France wailed and heaven wept, the hideous dance of the loosened furies of death and hell went smoothly on.

this occasion is unquestionable, states that he blindly threw himself into the Huguenot party to revenge himself upon the duke of Guise, who had offended him; and the queen, wishing to injure that family, wrote to Des Adrets, exhorting him to destroy Guise's authority in Dauphiny by any means whatever, even by the aid of the Huguenots, and promising him her protection and authority.

"But it was not necessary to know his motives for making a profession of Protestantism, for his conduct showed that he had no religion whatever. We learn from the Abbé Caveyrac that 'he returned sincerely to God and his king,' but not without his resentment being again called into action; for his cruelty excited such horror, that the prince of Condé sent Soubise to supersede him in the government of Lyons, which made him renounce the Protestant religion and return to the Roman church." Browning, p. 65.

CHAPTER XXI.

DEATH'S COUP D'ETAT.

Before a fanatical conception of religion, morality, which lies at the base of civilization and of human society, vanished. A kind of fatalism reigned. A species of resignation linked with enmity, of religion mingled with hatred—this was what took place in these sad years. It was like a bloody Scottish feud, in which those who held the same principles regarded themselves as members of one clan.

Both armies were in the field, and Guise especially was viciously active.

Navarre assailed and captured Bourges. Then pausing and looking towards Paris, he asked, Where next?

The Triumvirate hungered for Orleans, the rendezvous and the dépôt of Condé and the Chatillons. Catharine said No; she thought that if the citadel of Protestantism should fall, the already over-powerful league would shoot up to a still loftier pinnacle. "Let us resnatch Rouen," said the wily queen; "these bulldog Englishmen have seized Normandy; we must shake it from their greedy maw."* The Parisians were cozened; besides, the Hugue-

* Davila, liv. 3, p. 246. De Thou, liv. 33. Mem. de Condé, vol. 3. Browning, p. 67.

not garrison of Rouen would suffer no merchandise to ascend the river from the sea. Inexorable Rouen stood guard upon the Atlantic. Trade was sulky; commerce was angered. "We will give two hundred thousand crowns to the king, if he will drive the Huguenots from Rouen,"* cried the Parisian merchants. Navarre marched into Normandy, and at the close of September, 1562, laid siege to Rouen.†

Montgomery held the town, supported by two thousand English men-at-arms, twelve hundred choice infantry from Condé's army, four squadrons of horse, and one hundred gentlemen who had volunteered their services.‡

The attack was vigorous; the defence was obstinate. A breach was no sooner made, than the indefatigable Montgomery threw up behind it a new intrenchment. "This count is a necromancer; he juggles in war," said Navarre dispiritedly, as he returned one day from a foiled assault.§

Mining and countermining succeeded. The Huguenot bombs fell within Navarre's lines with but slight effect; burying themselves in the soil softened by recent rains, they only made volcanoes of mud; the explosion was changed into a splash.

At length, an the 25th of October, Guise, who had joined the army before Rouen, led an assault, after a spirited harangue, the effect of which he heightened by a brilliant display of chivalric valor.‖

* Vie de Coligny, p. 269. † Ibid., p. 271. Browning, p. 67.
‡ Ibid. Davila, liv. 3, p. 250. § Mem. de Condé, vol. 4, p. 45.
‖ Brantome, vol. 8, p. 262. De Thou, liv. 33.

Rouen was captured by this *coup de main;* Montgomery had only time to leap into a galley which was in port. By the promise of liberty, he induced the galley-slaves to row so well, that he got to sea despite some chains swung across the river a few leagues below the city by the besiegers, to prevent the English sending any assistance from the ocean.* Shortly after, Montgomery safely touched the shores of Britain.

Rouen was pillaged through three days; many citizens were massacred; the reformed preachers especially were hunted down with vindictive cruelty; and Marloratus, who had been a central figure at the Poissy colloquy, was hung in front of the cathedral, amid the jeers of the brutal soldiery and the insults of Montmorenci and his son Montberan.†

That which characterizes other Romanic races even at this day, the habit of repaying violent deeds with violent deeds, was then the general custom of France. The Huguenots at Orleans, as a reprisal for the Rouen massacres, hung the abbé Gastines, a violent Jesuit, and Sapin, one of the hostile presidents of the Parliament of Paris.‡

The capture of Rouen cost Navarre his life. Emulating the prowess of Guise, he descended into the trenches one day to view the town; while there,

* Brantome, vol. 8, p. 262. De Thou, liv. 33. Browning, p. 67.

† D'Aubigné, Hist. Univ., vol. 1, p. 159. Mem. de Condé, vol. 2, p. 105.

‡ Beza, Eccl. Hist., liv. 8. Brantome, Davila, etc.

he was struck in the shoulder by a discharge of musketry. The surgeons at the outset laughed at the wound, and the king even desired to make a triumphal entry into the conquered city. Soon however symptoms of danger appeared. Navarre desired to be transported to the village of St. Maur, near Paris. He did not live to reach it, but died at Andelys on the 17th of November, 1562, in his forty-fourth year.*

All writers who have sketched Antony of Bourbon's character, describe him as deficient in every princely quality except personal courage. He was ambitious without foresight, vain without capacity, and intriguing without diplomatic skill. He threw away that noble part which fortune destined for him. Denying his faith, he ceased to be the head of a powerful party, to sink into the despised tool of abler rogues.

"Antony of Bourbon, father of the firmest and most intrepid of men, was the weakest and least decided," says one of the most celebrated of French critics. "He was always so wavering in his religion, that it is doubted in which faith he died.† He bore arms against the Huguenots whom he loved, and served Catharine de' Medici whom he detested, and the party of the Guises who oppressed him."‡

* Davila, liv. 3, p. 260. De Thou, liv. 33. This historian says that Navarre was forty-two years of age. Browning, p. 68.

† "Brantome states, that 'he died regretting his change of religion, being resolved to help the Protestants more than ever if he lived, and that he sent word to that effect to the prince his brother.'" Browning, p. 68. ‡ Voltaire, note to "Henriadé"

While these events were occurring in Normandy, the Huguenot leaders, Condé, Coligny, and D'Andelot, united their forces, and tempted by the absence of the main army of the Triumvirate before Rouen, marched towards Paris. The prince actually pitched his tents at Montrouge, from whence his troops pillaged the faubourgs on that side.

This movement hastened the return of the triumvirs from the ruins of Rouen, to effect the salvation of the imperilled capital.

Condé then determined to march into Normandy, and forming a junction with the English forces, secure Elizabeth's subsidy. On the 10th of December he broke camp, and commenced his march. Guise, who had meanwhile arrived in Paris, upon being apprized of the prince's intention, determined to pursue him, and force a battle.

Condé was overtaken near Dreux, and finding it impossible to avoid an action, he prepared to fight.

Here, by the banks of the sparkling Eure, the first collision between the hostile armies in the open field occurred. The sight was a singular one. It seemed as if this mass of human beings had become a monster, and had but one mind. Each squadron undulated and swelled like the ring of a polype. They could be seen through the thick smoke, as it lifted brokenly here and there. It was a pell-mell of casques, cries, sabres; a furious bounding of horses, a blare of trumpets; a terrible and

* Mem. de Tavannes, p. 267. Pasquier, vol. 2. p. 101. La Noué, p. 583.

disciplined tumult; over all the cuirasses, like the scales of a hydra.

Condé charged first. His cavalry, composed of the *élite* of the Huguenot party, cut clean through the enemy's centre, which was commanded by Montmorenci. Smitten by this resistless thunderbolt, the constable tumbled from his saddle. Rising again, he strove to redeem his position. In vain; Condé's cuirassiers would not be stayed, and Montmorenci was ere long himself made prisoner, while his son Montberan, who had so recently jeered at the martyrdom of Marloratus in the streets of Rouen, lay dead before his face.*

The battle lasted seven hours, during which time wavering success perched with capricious whim upon both banners. At the moment when victory seemed finally to have declared for the Huguenots, Guise, who had held himself carefully in reserve,† thundered down upon the conquerors, and wrested the hard-earned laurels from their grasp. By a singular reverse of fortune, Condé fell wounded, and was made a prisoner by D'Amville, Montmorenci's son.‡

The wearied and dispirited Huguenots' infantry were instantly panic-stricken. Guise pressed them fiercely, and their rout was complete.§

Coligny, perceiving that safety lay in retreat,

* Hist. des Derniers Troubles, liv. 1.

† Vie de Coligny, p. 274. Brantome, vol. 8, p. 112.

‡ Brantome, vol. 8, p. 113. Browning, p. 70.

§ Vie de Coligny, p. 274. Ranke, p. 217.

held his men well in hand, and shouting, "He who holds his troops together to the last carries off the fruit of the battle," he commenced to retire leisurely and calmly to a neighboring morass, where, entrenching his followers behind a pile of felled timber, he awaited Guise's attack with nonchalance. At the same time the admiral, divining that Orleans would be the next point assailed, directed D'Andelot to collect as many of the dispersed battalions as possible, and hasten with them to reinforce the menaced city.*

Meantime Guise pressed on, and renewed the battle with great ardor. Coligny obstinately defended his position. In vain did the fiery duke hurl squadron after squadron upon his imperturbable lines. The marshal St. André at length fell; and Guise, glancing sadly at his terribly thinned ranks, desisted from the attack, and preparing to bivouac upon the battle-field, dispatched a courier to Paris to announce a victory.†

The battle was a bloody one. Eight thousand dead strewed the plain.‡

The Huguenots were far from considering themselves defeated, though Guise remained master of Dreux, and Coligny, after the cessation of the duke's assaults, continued his retreat.

"Our infantry," wrote the admiral in a letter to Elizabeth of England, "has suffered a defeat with-

* Vie de Coligny, p. 274. Ranke, p. 217. Browning, p. 70.

† Brantome, vol. 8, p. 117. Browning, p. 70. La Noué, vol. 5, p. 7.

‡ Ibid. Davila, liv. 3.

out fighting; but our cavalry, which alone fougnt the battle, is undamaged, and wishes for nothing more ardently than to meet once more without delay the enemies of God and of this kingdom. These will deliberate whether to attack us, or to await an attack from our side.*

Guise was wonderfully elated by his success, disputed as it was. The first account of the battle which reached Paris ascribed the victory to Condé. "Well then," said Catharine coolly, "we shall have to pray to God in French."† And when she received the second report from Dreux, she was far from expressing joy at the event. The death of St. André and Montmorenci's captivity delivered Guise from all rivals; no one shared his triumphs. The duke wrote a letter, demanding the disposal of St. André's baton in so arrogant a tone, that young Charles himself was astonished.‡

Condé, in his captivity, was treated with politic kindness. Guise conducted him to his quarters; they supped together, and the prince accepted the offer of half the duke's bed.§ He was afterwards taken to court, where Catharine exerted herself to win him from the Huguenot party, a task which she did not esteem very formidable, since, removed from the counsels of the inflexible Coligny, she thought he might be easily biassed.

* Coligny's letter to queen Elizabeth, cited in Ranke, p. 218.

† Voltaire's second note to the "Henriade."

‡ Vieilleville, vol. 5, p. 7. Browning, p. 71.

§ Brantome, vol. 8, p. 248. Duncan, p. 60.

Montmorenci was taken to Orleans, where his niece, the princess of Condé, used every persuasive measure which she could devise to reconcile her uncle and her husband; all however to no purpose. The sulky veteran only growled and swore.*

Meanwhile Guise led his victorious squadrons to the Orleanoise, and laid close and resolute siege to the Huguenot citadel.

D'Andelot's defence of Orleans was as skilful as the duke's assault. While the fate of the city hung undecided, murder stepped between the combatants, and dictated a decision: Guise was assassinated.†

In the dusk of the evening the duke went to superintend the erection of some redoubts. While the party trotted pleasantly along, chatting and laughing, a shot was fired from behind a hedge, and three balls lodged in Guise's left shoulder. The shock made him stagger; but he only said, "This was to be expected; but I think it will be nothing."‡ He was carried to his tent, when the surgeons, on examining the wound, pronounced the bullets to have been steeped in poison.§

Upon his death-bed he expressed regret for many of the occurrences of his violent, ambitious, and warlike career; but this late repentance served but to inflict upon him sharper pangs of remorse.

* Browning, p. 71.

† La Noué, p. 503. Vie de Coligny, p. 282. Duncan, p. 60.

‡ Brantome, vol. 8, p. 126. Vie de Coligny, p. 287. Browning, p. 71.

§ Ibid.

The massacre of Vassy tormented his conscience, which could neither be soothed by all the pæans of the priests, nor quieted by the hymns of the Parisians.

On the 4th of March, 1563, eight days after the infliction of the fatal wound, this celebrated soldier heaved his last sigh.

This event stirred France profoundly. The animated attacks upon Orleans suddenly ceased. The famous Triumvirate crumbled to pieces. Navarre, St. André, and Guise were lost to Rome.

The duke's assassin was finally arrested and put to the torture. He was a madman named Paltrot.* What was called a "confession" was wrung from his crazy lips, which implicated several of the Huguenot chiefs in a plot to butcher Guise. Bossuét accuses Coligny and Beza of having instigated the insane zealot to commit the crime; but the eloquent Frenchman, with all his subtlety, could not twist the circumstances of the case into giving color to the charge. All impartial chroniclers have acquitted these illustrious and unspotted Christians of any participation in so odious a deed. History dismissed the accusation to contempt.†

Yet despite Coligny's published and reiterated denial at the time, Henry de Guise persisted in charging the admiral with his father's murder; and young as he was at the time, he swore against him

* Davila, liv. 3, p. 87. Brantome, vol. 8, p. 120, etc.

† Duncan, p. 60. See the very elaborate consideration of this matter in Browning, pp. 72–77.

an unrelenting hatred, which was only appeased by one of the bloodiest catastrophes in history.*

With the dissolution of the Triumvirate there came a general pause. Death's *coup de main* startled France. The genius of civil war halted for a moment before the bier of Francis Guise.

* Duncan, p. 61.

CHAPTER XXII.

THE HOLLOW TRUCE.

By the death of Guise, Catharine de' Medici regained supreme power. Her first act was to intrigue for tranquillity. Every insidious art was employed to cajole Condé into signing a treaty of peace. The Chatillons were absent in the field. Their inflexible spirit insured the continuance of the war until liberty was guaranteed, unless some disgraceful concession could be won from the prince.

The Huguenot sky never looked so bright. Hardly a cloud spotted the horizon. Two of the triumvirs were dead; the third was a prisoner. Every thing was propitious for a liberal and righteous peace. The reformers congratulated one another, and said, "The wished-for day has come."

Suddenly these hopes were dashed; a courier arrived in Coligny's camp one morning, and flung this announcement into the admiral's face like a thunderbolt: "Peace is declared; Condé orders arms grounded."* The messenger then circulated an edict which had just been ratified at Amboise. This was eagerly scanned by the surprised Huguenots. It contained a permission for the reformers to assemble for the exercise of their religion in

* Mem. de Condé. Vie de Coligny. Brantome, etc.

those towns which were in their possession on the day the edict was signed; but the general permission to preach in the country places, contained in the preceding edict of January, 1562, was considerably curtailed. The lords high justiciaries could only convene their friends and neighbors on the demesnes of their seignories. The nobles were only allowed to hear their preachers in their own chateaux, and even that indulgence was withheld if they resided in a city or territory over which a Romanist governor exercised judicial power. The decree contained neither censure nor amnesty; but declaring that Condé and his friends were good and faithful subjects, buried the past in oblivion.*

Such was the niggardly decree to which Condé, without consulting his friends, had irrevocably set his hand. The Huguenots were indignant. D'Andelot was chagrined. "Alas," said Coligny, "our prince has injured the Reformed church more by this stroke of his pen, than the Triumvirate could have done in ten years with all their armies."†

Sadly and dejectedly the admiral dismissed his old companions in arms, paying them great attention, that he might, in case of need, calculate upon their speedy aid.‡

Catharine was displeased at this precaution; but when she complained of it to Condé, he silenced her by replying, "Nay, madame, this conduct of

* Anquétil, Esprit de la Ligue, tom. 1, p. 150. Duncan, p. 62.
† Vie de Coligny, p. 291. Hist. du Concile de Trente, p. 674.
‡ Ibid.

Coligny ought to be attributed solely to a grateful desire to acquit his obligations to the nobility; sure 't is the least he could do for those who quitted home and friends to serve our cause."*

The queen mother was doubly provoked at this unexpected speech; she had done her utmost to convince Condé that Coligny's influence was prejudicial to his own. She now perceived how cautious Condé was of taking the bait; indeed she feared the prince saw into her treacherous design; she therefore referred no more to the subject, but redoubled her blandishments.†

One clause of the recent treaty bound the Huguenots to unite with the royal forces in expelling the English from Normandy.‡

Condé, conscious that nothing could justify him in admitting the hereditary foemen of France once more into the kingdom, and entrenching them within important strong-holds, proffered his services for their dislodgment.§

The prince's offer was accepted, and ere long he returned to Paris from this expedition completely successful. France was no longer dismembered; no hostile foot profaned her soil.

Elizabeth of England was very indignant at the loss of Havre de Grace, which she hoped would have compensated her for Calais. "When the

* Mem. de Condé, vol. 2, p. 163. Browning, p. 78.

† Mem. de Condé, vol. 2, p. 163.

‡ Pallavicini, lib. 20, p. 407. Browning, p 78

§ Ibid. Mem. de Condé, vol. 2, p. 175.

admiral again desires my assistance, I shall know how to act," said the maiden queen.* But when her anger subsided, she observed, "The king of France is happy in having such faithful subjects."†

Condé's star was now at its zenith. As he had distinguished himself by his bravery in the field, so now he desired to shine through his versatility, by taking part in the knightly festivities of the court, in which it was then the fashion to represent the heroic fables of the Greeks.‡ His wit and vivacity made him a great favorite. All restraint was removed by the recent death of his excellent wife Eleanora du Roye; and Condé, whose amorous disposition disposed him to fall an easy prey to the intrigues of the queen, frittered away his time and strength in dissolute and infamous orgies.§

The condition of the Huguenots now became as bad as it had ever been. Encroachments upon the edict of Amboise were of constant occurrence. The Protestants would not submit without attempting to defend their rights. The consequence was, that the uneasy kingdom fretted under the abnormal pacification—a name without a substance. The Huguenots inundated France with apologies, complaints, and remonstrances—some addressed to the king, some to the queen, but most to Condé, who

* Vie de Coligny, p. 297. † Ibid.

‡ Ranke, pp. 223, 224.

§ Browning, p. 81. Huguenots in France and America, vol 1, p. 100.

was generally held responsible for the strict fulfilment of the treaty, since he had signed it.*

But Catharine had so artfully engrossed the forgetful prince in lewd amusements, he was so surrounded with every charm and variety of pleasure, that he had neither time to think nor heart to bestir himself on behalf of imperilled liberty of conscience.†

The noblesse were ensnared in a similar manner. Catharine's maids of honor, young and beautiful, but abandoned girls, were the syrens employed to captivate the more worldly and impressible of the Huguenot leaders. Treachery was the leading feature in the queen mother's policy; her aim being bad, she naturally was not scrupulous as to her means, and the morals of her licentious court would be exposed to but little scrutiny. Those of her pimps, men or women, who were most successful in their infamous work, received the highest honor. Thus it was that those twin devils, debauchery and perfidy, were the earliest and most intimate companions of Charles IX.

Thus was the Reformation compromised by its political chiefs. While the current ran in lowlier channels, it coursed unwaveringly to the sea. The alliance of the nobles lowered the religious *morale*. The fervor of Calvin, the eloquence of Beza never injured the cause they loved; the treason of Navarre, the licentious coxcombry of Condé, wasting

* De Thou, liv. 35. Mem. de Condé, vol. 2, p. 180.

† Browning, p. 81.

precious hours lapped in the arms of Catharine's dancing syrens, melted, like a common fop, in baths and perfumes—these worked God's cause incalculable mischief.

It is a pity, some say, that the noblesse gathered under the Huguenot banner; why, query others, did Beza's pulpit stoop to preach politics?

Great moral movements necessarily and inevitably bubble over into politics. If politics invade the domain of morals, if diplomacy attempts to strangle religion, if iniquity enthrones itself in law, then it becomes the preacher's duty with one hand to appeal to the state for redress, and with the other to uncloak the cheat. This was what Luther did. This was what Calvin did. They desired to preach Christ. The state said, No. Then the reformers created a party in the state whose circumstances enabled them to obtain the required liberty to preach God's word.

In this sense, wherever statutes withhold permission to proclaim salvation, if men's thoughts influence their laws, it is the duty of the pulpit to preach politics. If it were possible to conceive of a community whose opinions had no effect upon their government, there Beza and Calvin and Luther would have no call to impeach bad laws and ungodly policies. But those worthies knew of no such community. The czar, at the head of a government whose constitution knows no check but poison and the dagger, yet pauses when he hears his subjects growl. The sultan dared to murder his janizaries only when the streets came to hate them as much as he did. Though sheltered by Roman despotism, Herod and the chief priests abstained from this and that because they "feared the people." Certainly then there can be no question that the *rationale* of the reformers was right.

At all events, the pontiffs never scrupled to bring the pressure of public opinion to bear upon governmental action. In the early years of the reign of Charles IX., Pius IV. directed the politics of the Vatican. This crafty pope perceived that the temporal authority of his see would be undermined if the Huguenots could enjoy religious liberty; his object therefore was to make them hateful to the French government.

To prevent the clergy from giving the Reformation countenance, he determined to punish those prelates who had either wholly adopted the new theology, or had at least tolerated it. He excommunicated the cardinal of Chatillon, St. Romain archbishop of Aix, Montluc bishop of Valence, Caraccioli of Troyes, Barbançon of Pomiers, and Guillart of Chartres, all of whom were summoned to appear before him and account for their conduct.*

Pope Pius' audacity saved these prelates from his wrath. He cited the queen of Navarre to give an account of her faith; and if within the space of six months she did not appear before him, he declared that she should be proscribed, convicted of

* Hist. du Concile de Trente, p. 769. Browning, p. 81.

heresy by default, and deprived of her kingdom, which should be given to the first occupant.*

This insolent assault upon a crowned head and a near relative of the king of France, caused a strong remonstrance to be filed by the French ambassador at Rome; in consequence the bull was withdrawn, and affairs remained *in statu quo*.†

Upon the heels of the pope's rescinded bull trudged a new edict; it was called a declaration, and was avowedly to explain the obscurities of that of Amboise, but in reality to curtail once more the rights of the Huguenots.‡

The month of December, 1563, was rendered remarkable by the conclusion of the Council of Trent, one of the most famous of the Roman synods. Long before the doctrines of Calvin had become popular in France, Germany, embracing Martin Luther's evangelical opinions, demanded the convocation of a general council to settle disputed points of orthodoxy. Finally Paul III., who then wore the tiara, yielded to the request, and in the year 1537 selected Mantua as the ecclesiastical rendezvous; but the sovereign duke of that city refused his consent, in consequence of which the assembly was transferred to Vicenza, and postponed to 1538. Various contingencies delayed the conference till 1542, when Paul convened the council at Trent.§

* The bull is dated Sept. 28, 1563, and is to be found *in extenso* in Mem. de Condé, vol. 4.

† Hist. du Concile de Trente, p. 796. Mem. de Condé, vol. 4, p. 680.

‡ Browning, p. 81.

§ Hist. du Concile de Trente.

From that date the sessions dragged their slow length along, amid constant and frivolous adjournments, through twenty-one tedious years, during which time the dogmatism, the bigotry, and the tergiversations of the council, wholly devoted to Rome—there was not a Lutheranist or Calvinist present—so disgusted the Protestants, that they refused to recognize its authority, or to be bound by its decrees.

Pius IV. had renewed the sessions and pressed for a decision, because he was persuaded that unless some fixed principles were adopted, to which the floating creed of the Vatican could be anchored in case of need, the most sincere adherents of the holy see might be seduced into heresy by the arguments of those who claimed the right of interpreting the holy Scriptures for themselves.*

The different discussions during the twenty-five sessions of the council, embraced the whole range of subjects which affected the purse, wealth, and supremacy of the court of Rome.† The decrees were prefaced in this style: "The holy Œcumenic Council, legitimately assembled under the guidance of the Holy Spirit, the apostolical legates presiding."‡ But as the various pontiffs had the council completely under their control, no latitude of discussion was permitted, no breath of liberality stirred the murky air. Instead of deliberating upon the spiritual interests of Christendom, for effecting

* Browning, p. 82.

† Ibid. Hist. du Concile de Trente, passim. ‡ Ibid.

an abolition of the superstitions and corruptions which were the grounds of Luther's terrible attacks, it was only proposed that one or two of the more glaring abuses should be slightly modified, while additional authority was conferred in every point in which the councils and traditions of the church were at variance with the Scriptures. Thus what was professedly intended to reform the Roman communion, served only to confirm its errors.

How could this be otherwise, when the council was packed with the creatures of the pontiff, whose number he could increase at his pleasure, while the most learned and evangelical divines of Europe at large were never invited to shed over the discussions the light of their luminous counsel, when even those papists who ventured to differ with the legates upon trivialities were speedily gagged?*

The last act of the council was to establish the absurd dogma of the pope's infallibility;† and it was observed at the time that the "Holy Spirit," of which the decrees spoke, "was sent from Rome in a portmanteau."‡

So greatly did the ultramontane interest predominate in the decrees of the Council of Trent, that even the papists of France would not submit inconsiderately to their reception.§ A celebrated law-

* Hist. du Concile de Trente, passim. Browning, p. 82. Turretin, Hist. Eccles.

† Fra Paolo, Hist. du Concile de Trente. Maimbourg, Hist. du Lutheranisme.

‡ Turretin, Hist. Eccles. Browning, p. 82.

§ Ranke, p. 225.

yer, Charles du Moulin, published a memoir, showing that the council was null and vicious, contrary to former decrees, and prejudicial alike to the prerogatives of the crown and to the liberties of the Gallican church.* He was arrested for this while upon the steps of the Palace of Justice, and that circumstance nearly caused a tumult, for the whole legal profession felt indignant that an advocate who honored the law so highly should be treated like a malefactor for a legal writing. The clerks were incited to attempt a rescue. The conciergerie, however, being close at hand, the guard hustled their victim within its walls and shut the gate, thus by a prompt flight escaping the vengeance of their pursuers.†

No sooner did this affair reach Coligny than he made the case his own, for he had encouraged De Moulin to publish the memoir; he went to the queen mother, and by a full representation of the facts and the probable result of the incarceration, soon obtained an order for the advocate's release.‡

As the king's minority had afforded the pretext for many of the attempts against the government, Catharine was desirous that he should be declared of age; that measure could not affect her influence over the boy, while it would protect her from the intrusion of meddlers. In 1563, Charles entered

* Mem. de Condé, vol. 5, p. 81, et seq. Ranke, p. 225.

† Mem. de Condé, vol. 5, pp. 86, 87. Vie de Coligny, p. 304.

‡ Matthieu, Histoire de France, vol. 1.

his fourteenth year, the age fixed by a law of Charles the Wise as marking the majority of the king.*

After some manœuvring this point was gained, and the royal party then set out upon a tour of observation through France.† As the brilliant retinue of the young monarch passed through the country, the populace crowded to salute the king with their acclamations. The court first tarried at Lorraine, where a number of fétes were given in honor of the visit. But though Catharine's policy made her countenance these lavish revels, since "thereby she caught many gudgeons," the wily queen was very far from permitting herself to be engrossed by the follies she set afoot. Availing herself of this opportunity, she negotiated with the neighboring German princes, for the purpose of persuading them to restrain their subjects from arming to aid the Huguenots in case of another civil convulsion in France;‡ her efforts, however, were not crowned with full success.

From Lorraine, Charles journeyed into the south of France. At Avignon the queen met a special legate from the pope, a Florentine, and Pius' confidant. While the besotted court was amused with pageants, this precious pair had an interview of long duration. Catharine is supposed upon this occasion to have opened her full budget of perfi-

* Matthieu, Histoire de France, vol. 1.

† Browning, p. 83.

‡ Pasquier, vol. 2, p. 309. Davila, liv 3, p. 329.

dies, for the nuncio was reported to have been "*merveilleusement satisfait.*"*

On the 10th of June, 1565, the court arrived at Bayonne. Here the king met his sister the queen of Spain, who had been dispatched by her husband Philip II. as an unconscious instrument in a hideous plot.† She was accompanied by a splendid suite led by Alvarez de Toledo, duke of Alva, celebrated for his atrocities in the Low Countries,‡ an envoy quite equal, by his talents and his sanguinary, bigoted temper, to the infamous commission confided to him.

Here, at Bayonne, it was that while the French and Spanish courts endeavored to outvie each other's pageantry—for it was a peculiarity of Catharine de' Medici, that when she plotted most infamously she hid her intrigues behind a pageant—that Alva and the queen mother hatched the massacre of St. Bartholomew.§

By a gallery which she had ordered to be constructed to connect her apartments with those of her daughter, she conversed every night with the duke of Alva.‖ Here the monster duke and the serpent-like queen discussed the best means of extirpating French heresy;¶ sitting there in the

* Maimbourg, Hist. du Calvinisme, liv. 5. Davila, liv. 3.

† Browning, p. 84.

‡ Motley, Rise of the Dutch Republic, vol. 1.

§ Browning, p. 84. Duncan, p. 66. Ranke, p. 227.

‖ De Thou, liv. 37.

¶ "Les Reynes de France et d'Espagne à Bayonne, assistiés du Duc d'Albe, resolvent la Ruine des Heretiques en France et

gloom, like two conspirators, they agreed upon the adoption of one of two plans: to expel the whole body of Huguenot preachers from the country, or else to assassinate at one stroke the four or six unhappy men who stood at the head of the party, and whose loss was supposed to be irreparable.*

"Ten thousand frogs are not worth the head of one salmon," cried Alva when speaking of the contemplated massacre. The young prince of Bearn, afterwards Henry IV., who was with the royal party on this tour, and whose penetration was far beyond his years—he was then but twelve—treasured up this expression, which he accidentally overheard, and considered applicable to Condé and Coligny. He repeated the words to his mother, Jane d'Albrét, who warned the prince and the admiral that sly mischief was afoot.†

Revolving in her mind these "mortal accidents for the ruin of the state," Catharine concluded the royal progress, and in 1566 convened an assembly of the Notables at Moulins. Her chief object now was to lull all suspicion to sleep; and then, when the Huguenots were entrapped, to give them the *coup de grace*. If the Samson of reform could be won to recline in the lap of this Delilah, she felt competent to insure that when she pronounced the words, "Samson, the Philistines be upon thee," the

Flandres." Mem. de Tavannes, p. 282. Strada's history also mentions it. Browning, p. 84, note.

* Ranke, p. 227.

† Matthieu, Hist. de France, tom. 1, p. 283. Duncan, pp. 67, 68, etc.

undone Hercules should not have the strength to rise and avert his fate.

We shall see how well Catharine succeeded.

The result of the conference at Moulins was the promulgation of an edict which settled many controverted points of jurisprudence, and which, in reference to religion, ordered that the former decrees should be solemnly confirmed.*

Had there been any sincerity in the professions of Charles, or had honesty swayed the counsels of his authoritative advisers, the privileges and disabilities of the Huguenots would have been clearly and fundamentally fixed by this edict. But though there was a general ratification of prior decrees, all of which had been distorted by unfair constructions put upon essential clauses, yet it was so loosely worded as to leave all the main principles in confusion and incertitude. Indeed the court had no wish to establish any definitive settlement of the questions at issue; on the contrary, it was their intention to leave all the mooted points in such a fluctuating and doubtful state, as to render the constant interference of the royal council necessary; by these means it was hoped gradually to fritter away all the protective securities of religious liberty.†

Through these perfidious negotiations the queen mother had great difficulty in restraining the belligerent bigotry of the young king, whose hatred of the Huguenots was only equalled by his dissimula-

* Vie de Coligny, p. 314. Davila, liv. 3. De Thou, liv. 37.

† Duncan, p. 69.

tion; for though yet a mere boy, he masked his real opinions with a wiliness and duplicity which deceived the oldest and craftiest courtiers.* Every fresh demand of the Huguenots for the extension of their privileges, or for the protection of those already conceded, roused his choler.

One day he broke out in great anger against the admiral: "It is not long since," said he, "that you were satisfied with being merely tolerated by the orthodox; now you claim to be their equals; presently you will wish to be supreme." The habitual caution of Coligny kept him silent. Charles left him abruptly, rushed into the apartment of the chancellor, and exclaimed, "The duke of Alva was right; heads held so high are dangerous to a state; tact and skill are useless, for they may be parried by the same weapons. We can only keep our ascendency by force."†

Catharine also was heard to mutter darkly that "ere long the ancient faith would have few enemies in France."‡

Below the deceitful calm which smiled above, these ominous words presaged St. Bartholomew.

* Duncan, p. 71. Mem. de Condé. Brantome, etc.

† Ibid.

‡ Browning, Vie de Coligny, Mem de Condé, etc.

CHAPTER XXIII.

RECOMMENCEMENT OF THE WAR.

THE treaty of pacification gave no satisfaction to either party. As in all compromises upon vital questions, one side esteemed that too much had been conceded; the other thought that assured triumph had been bartered to obtain a hollow and treacherous edict. Gloomy and suspicious, all France rested upon arms; while the Huguenot chiefs, fearful of Catharine's poisoner or of the steel of her bravos, quitted the dangerous vicinage of Paris for a safer residence.*

No sooner had the champions of the Reformation left the court, than the cardinal of Lorraine, plotting busy mischief, arrived at St. Germaine, and resumed his seat at the council board.† Notwithstanding his apparent moderation and the vacillation of his ordinary conduct, this consummate intriguer was ever the same—unchangeable in his views, and, despite of all reconciliation, implacable. The effects of his presence were soon visible.

The king of Spain, determined to exterminate the Protestants of the Netherlands, designed, at the commencement of 1567, to march an army, under Alva, by the route of Savoy and the mountain chain

* Ranke, p. 229. † Ibid.

of Lorraine skirting the French frontier, into the Low Countries.*

The plotters at Paris eagerly seized this pretext to augment the army. Catharine expressed great alarm lest France should be invaded by the Spaniards. Avowedly to avert the menaced danger, six thousand Swiss were taken into the pay of the government, new captains were appointed to the civic militia of Paris, and the companies of the *hommes d'armes* were raised to their full complement.†

At first the Huguenots took the bait. Condé, with Hotspur impetuosity, even tendered his services to guard the frontier.‡ But ere long their suspicions were aroused. It was perceived that all stations of trust were bestowed exclusively upon Romanist officers, and that Alva, so far from meeting with any opposition, received the warmest of welcomes and the heartiest, was supplied with abundant provisions, and trod through France amid an ovation.

The keen eye of the sleepless admiral instantly pierced into the depths of Catharine's perfidious policy. A secret council of the Huguenot chiefs was speedily convened at his residence, Chatillon-sur-Loing. It was determined to foil stratagem by stratagem. French history teaches that that party which is master of the court can alone accomplish

* Duncan, p. 72. Davila, liv. 3. Motley, Rise of the Dutch Rep., vol. 1.

† Ranke, p. 230. Davila, liv. 3. De Thou, liv. 37.

‡ Mem. de Condé, vol. 2.

its designs;* therefore, since it had been ascertained that Catharine had resolved to imprison Condé for life, put Coligny to death, distribute the Swiss to garrison Paris, Orleans, and Poitiers, and to revoke all edicts of tolerance and pacification, that the extermination of the reformers might proceed unfettered by statutes, the wary Huguenots determined to take the initiative—by a grand *coup d'etat*, to elope with the court.†

In the secrecy with which this plan was formed, and in the rapidity and precision of its execution, the learned men of the age could find nothing in history to be compared with it, without going back to the times of Mithridates king of Pontus.‡

The court was sojourning at Monceaux, near Meaux, in an open residence, quite unsuspicious of danger.§ Catharine, steeped to the lips in treachery, was now caught napping; the biter was nearly bitten. At the critical moment however, the king was warned, and he returned to Paris under the escort of his Swiss, whose steady, disciplined valor beat back the headlong charges of Condé's cavaliers.‖

But though foiled, the Huguenots were not disheartened. Condé pressed forward, and encamped before the capital. His head-quarters were at St. Dennis, from whence his troops blockaded the city,

* La Noué, Memoires, chap. 47, p. 169.

† Vie de Coligny, p. 325. La Noué, p. 609. Davila, liv. 3.

‡ Davila, liv. 3. De Thou, liv. 37. Ranke, p. 231.

§ Ibid. Duncan, p. 73.

‖ Vie de Coligny, p. 328. Browning, p. 91.

destroyed the mills, mastered the river, and fortified all the surrounding castles which commanded the main roads.*

Tedious and subtle negotiations ensued. The Huguenots demanded the general, distinct, and irrevocable guarantee of religious toleration, complete and public, as the essential basis of pacification. The court not only refused this concession, but speaking through the octogenarian lips of Montmorenci, declared that those indulgences which had been granted to the heretics were always intended to be temporary; that the king had now determined upon their revocation, since henceforth he would permit no lisp of any religion in France save that of Rome.†

The decision was then left to the arbitrament of battle. The royal army, much the more numerous and the best equipped, sallied out, and led on by the old constable in person, charged Condé upon the plain of St. Dennis. A sanguinary battle ensued; Montmorenci himself, the scarred veteran of a hundred fights, fell mortally wounded; and the Huguenots, borne back by stress of numbers, rested at a little distance from St. Dennis, with unbroken ranks and undiminished ardor. The field and the spoil remained to the royalists, but the honor of the day belonged to the vastly outnumbered Huguenots.‡ The admiral commanded; and Marshal Ta-

* Vie de Coligny, p. 328. Browning, p. 91. La Noué, p. 614.
† Davila, liv. 4. De Thou, liv. 42.
‡ Browning, p. 92. Brantome, vol. 6, p. 420.

vannes, himself an accomplished soldier, said admiringly, "*Faut confesser que l'Amiral de Coligny estoit Capittane.*"*

Montmorenci was taken to Paris, where he shortly died. "Those who speak without passion of the constable," says Davila, who knew the old soldier well and personally, "give him three principal attributes: that he was a good captain, a loving servant, but a bad friend; for in all his actions he was ever swayed by the single consideration of himself."†

Brantome bears this quaint testimony to his piety: "He never failed in his devotions; for every morning he would repeat his paternosters, whether he was in the house or on horseback among his troops; which caused the saying, '*Beware of the constable's paternosters;*' for while he was repeating them and muttering the creed, as occasion presented he would cry, 'Go hang up such a one; tie this man to a tree; run that fellow through with your pikes this instant; shoot all those fellows before me; cut in pieces those vagabonds who wish to hold yon church against the king; burn me this village:' and such sentences of justice or war he would utter without leaving off his paternosters until he had quite finished them, thinking that to defer them to another time would be to commit a great error, so conscientious was he."‡

At the solicitation of Condé, John Casimir of

* Tavannes, Memoirs, p. 88.

† Davila, liv. 4, p. 117. ‡ Brantome, vol. 7, p. 76.

the palatinate, who was zealous for his creed, and always ready to battle for it, entered France at the head of seven thousand five hundred cavalry and some thousands of infantry, to assist the Huguenots; not, as he said, to resist the French king, but to protect his coreligionists against the enemies of their persons and their faith.*

Condé and Casimir formed a junction shortly after the stricken field of St. Dennis, and directed their united march towards Paris, pausing on the way to capture Chartres.†

The Huguenots had agreed to pay their German auxiliaries one hundred thousand crowns; the military chest contained but two thousand. What was to be done? Condé's army served without pay; they had suffered severely in the retreat from St. Dennis in the most rigorous season of the year; their provisions were scanty, and regiment after regiment walked barefooted. To all these privations they cheerfully submitted for conscience' sake. It was doubtful whether this impoverished and frozen host would exert themselves to discharge the claims of the Germans. The experiment was tried; it was successful: thirty thousand crowns were raised at once by voluntary contribution, and Casimir's followers were satisfied.‡ History records no circumstance more extraordinary, or which more finely illustrates the influence of religious principle.

While the Huguenot army lay before Chartres,

* Ranke, p. 233. † Davila, liv. 4. De Thou, liv. 42. etc.

‡ Duncan, p. 79.

Catharine, alarmed by the formidable danger which menaced her government, had recourse once more to vicious diplomacy: she granted the reformers what they had demanded from the beginning, the complete restoration of the original edict of pacification.*

Both Condé and Coligny were dissatisfied. They wanted guarantees.† But the gentry, fatigued by an arduous campaign, longed for their homes; they imagined that their object was accomplished; they hoped to "honor God and serve the king in peace." Very reluctantly the Huguenot chiefs disarmed. Trusting God, they yet "kept their powder dry."

After the ratification of peace, the German troopers left France. The Huguenots insisted that the Spanish and Swiss auxiliaries of the court should also depart. Spite of this protest, they were retained. This distinction between the foreign levies sufficiently announced the hollowness and insincerity of the recent negotiations. Presently events proved that the reënacted edict was only a concession wrung from the reluctant fear of the perfidious court—a concession made only to be broken. Distrust and suspicion everywhere arose.‡ Every possible discourtesy was shown to the admiral, to D'Andelot, and even to Condé,§ while the Huguenot masses were exposed to an infinite variety of petty vexations. The papist pulpits resounded with invec-

* Davila, liv. 4. De Thou, liv. 42. Ranke, p. 234.

† Ibid. Vie de Coligny, p. 333.

‡ Duncan, p. 81. Vie de Coligny, p. 352.

§ Ibid.

tives against the heretics, with seditious reflections on the recent peace, and with clamorous exhortations to break it. The clergy had become inoculated with the *virus* of Jesuitism; and digging up from its grave of three hundred years the infamous maxim of Innocent III., they openly proclaimed that "no faith should be kept with heretics," and that their massacre was just, pious, and conducive to salvation.*

These inflammatory ravings provoked constant tumults, and occasioned frequent assassination. The ignorant and superstitious *canaille* ran frenzied and foaming through the streets, panting for murder. Huguenot writers affirm that under this "pacification," in the space of three months ten thousand of their persuasion perished by poison, by the dagger, and by the slow torture of imprisonment.†

The astute policy of Catharine aided the frantic zeal of the priests and the Jesuits. Fearing lest any of her diabolical plans might reach the ears of Coligny or Condé, she new-modelled the cabinet. De l'Hôpital, whose virtue and equity had frequently thwarted the exterminating plans of the princes of Lorraine, was ordered to deliver up the seals, and he was banished to his estate. The effective powers of government were confided to a faithful few, and shrouded in mystery. Every possible precaution was taken to render the next blow struck at the Huguenots decisively fatal.‡

* Duncan, p. 81. † Ibid. La Noué, p. 625.

‡ Ibid. Vieillemain, Vie de l'Hôpital.

In pursuance of her scheme, the queen mother determined to seize Condé and the admiral. The prince was at his castle of Noyers, in Burgundy; Coligny at Chatillon-sur-Loing.* "Their retreat," *naïvely* writes one of the admiral's biographers, "would have been extremely satisfactory to Catharine, if she had not seen that one half of the kingdom paid court to them. And indeed so great was the confluence at Chatillon and Noyers, that the Louvre was a desert in comparison. All the noblesse of the Huguenot party went in crowds to see them; and when ten gentlemen went out by one door, twenty passed in at another. This obliged the admiral especially to incur great expense; and if he had not been a careful man in every thing else, it would have ruined him. However, he was so much beloved that a thousand presents were constantly brought to him; and although he forbade his attendants accepting them, this did not prevent the same thing from occurring every day. The different reformed churches collected and sent a hundred thousand crowns to prevent the prince and himself from entirely bearing such a charge."†

The queen mother sent an engineer to reconnoitre Noyers, to familiarize himself with Condé's habits, to learn the weak points of the castle, and to see whether it would be possible to get possession of it by a *coup de main.* The spy entered Noyers without difficulty under the guise of a poulterer. He was well received; but when he began

* Browning, p. 98.

† Vie de Coligny, p. 346.

to talk, it was suspected that he was not what he pretended to be. The prince ordered him to be watched; when lo, one night he was detected sounding the moat. Condé dissembled, and dismissed him pleasantly; but when he was gone, he wrote Coligny, acquainted him with the circumstance, and advised him to be upon his guard.* The two chiefs then dispatched couriers to arouse their friends, and to request them to stand ready to grasp the sword at any moment.†

In the mean time Coligny also had a visitor. Catharine sent Castelnau, an able diplomatist, to Chatillon-sur-Loing, to penetrate the admiral's designs; but the wary Huguenot was on his guard, and the hoodwinked politician reported that he found him busily engaged in his vineyards.‡

When Castelnau left him, Coligny posted off to Noyers to confer with the prince.§ Upon being apprized of this, Catharine ordered Marshal Tavannes, who commanded in Burgundy for the king, to seize them at all hazards.‖ But though Tavannes was a bitter foe of the Reformation, he had a keen sense of military honor; and he knew besides, that if the scheme miscarried he would be sacrificed by the queen mother without a scruple, to allay the ensuing storm. He was too wary a courtier, however, to disobey openly so authoritative a mandate;

* Vie de Coligny, p. 346. Browning, p. 99. † Ibid.
‡ Duncan, p. 74.
§ Mem. de Tavannes, p. 314. Brantome, vol. 9, p. 109.
‖ Ibid.

so he set himself dexterously to save Condé and the admiral while yet appearing to perform his mission.

Approaching Noyers, he wrote Catharine, "The stag is at bay; the chase is prepared." After dispatching this laconic epistle, he sent two scouts to sound the depth of the water in front of the prince's strong-hold. They were captured, as Tavannes intended they should be, and upon being interrogated, confessed the plot.*

Condé and Coligny prepared for instant flight. They quitted Noyers with their families in August, 1568, and after enduring the severest hardships, traversing mountain paths hitherto untrodden, and crossing the Loire at a ford never before passed, reached, in September, the protecting walls of the friendly city of Rochelle.†

Nor were these the only victims of intended perfidy who baffled the subtle arts of the outwitted petticoated Machiavelli. Odet, cardinal of Chatillon, in the disguise of a common sailor, reached England from a port in Normandy, where his negotiations with queen Elizabeth subsequently proved of eminent service to his party.‡

The queen of Navarre, whose arrest had been entrusted to Montluc, retired from Bearn at the critical moment, and accompanied by her son and daughter, sought safety at Rochelle.§

* Mem. de Tavannes, p. 314. Brantome, vol. 9, p. 109. Duncan, p. 83.

† Vie de Coligny, 346. Pasquier, vol. 2, p. 127. Davila, liv. 4, p. 443.

‡ Duncan, p. 83. Ranke, p. 238.

§ Ibid.

Thus St. Bartholomew was again postponed.

Hostilities instantly recommenced.

The feeling at the court was very bitter. The edict of January, 1562, confirmed by the last peace, was again revoked; the exercise of any other form of worship than the Roman was prohibited, under penalty of death;* and the nominal command of the royal army was given to the duke of Anjou, the second brother of the king, a youth of sixteen, with the title of lieutenant-general of the kingdom.† But Marshal Tavannes commanded in reality.

A feeling of the utmost jealousy and hatred existed between Anjou and the young king; and Charles let no opportunity slip of mortifying his brother. When Anjou was nominated to the chief command of the army, Charles protested vehemently, and on one occasion an angry altercation took place at the supper-table. "Cousin," said the duke, "if you strive to obtain what belongs to me, I will make you little in the same degree as you imagine to become great."‡

In this convulsion Rochelle became the Huguenot rendezvous, as Orleans had been in the preceding war. The extreme measures of the court rallied the whole Huguenot party to fight for their common safety; nor did they on this occasion require any stimulus from the exhortations of their preachers. Their chiefs levied troops in all the provinces in which they had personal interest. So great was

* Davila, liv. 4. Castelnau, liv. 7, ch. 2. † Ibid.
‡ Ranke, p. 229.

the influence of these leaders, that James Crussal, lord of Acier, alone raised and equipped twenty-five thousand men in Languedoc and Dauphiny;* a striking proof of the comparative weakness of the royal prerogative, and of the vast power still retained by the descendants of the ancient baronial aristocracy.

Marches and counter-marches, skirmishes and manœuvres innumerable succeeded.

At length the two main armies fronted each other on the banks of the Charente, near Jarnac, a small frontier town which divided Limousin from Angoumois. The river separated the combatants, and had the Huguenots exercised common prudence, they might have avoided the calamities which soon befell them; but they neglected to keep a diligent watch through the night, and Tavannes passed the Charente unchallenged.†

Condé's army was spread over a wide tract of country, while that of the marshal advanced in a compact phalanx. The prince, surprised and beaten before the battle commenced, attempted to retreat upon his main body commanded by the admiral. In vain; Tavannes held him in a vice. Condé then wheeled and charged the royal cavalry led by the duke of Anjou. At this critical moment his leg was broken by a kick from the horse of De la Rochefoucault, who was riding by his side. Undaunted by this accident, the gallant prince held his

* Duncan, p. 84.

† Davila, liv. 4. Mem. de Tavannes. De Thou, etc.

saddle, and encouraging his feeble escort, plunged like a hero into the thickest of the fight. Surrounded on all sides, he was soon dismounted; with one knee upon the earth, he still shook his sword in fierce defiance of his enemies. He was commanded to surrender by the royalist officers who recognized him; but ere he could do so, Montesquieu, a captain of Anjou's guards, came behind him and shot him through the head.*

Such was the end of Louis de Bourbon, prince of Condé, a man of many noble and some great qualities, distinguished for his heroism, skill, and wit in an age when such a reputation necessitated corresponding ability. His licentiousness was the chief blemish upon his character. This exposed him to many snares, and impeded him in the rigid maintenance of his principles. Aside from this grievous fault, his character was free from spot; a sincere friend, an unwavering advocate for religious toleration, an ardent, unbending Huguenot in his

* La Noué, p. 659. Davila, liv. 4, p. 470. Browning, p. 102.

"Oh plaines de Jarnac! O coup trop inhumaine!
Barbare Montesquieu! moins guerrier qu' assassin!
Condé dejà mourant tombé sous ta furie,
J'ai vu porter le coup, j'ai vu trancher sa vie.
Helas! trop jeune encore, mon bras, mon foible bras,
Ne peut ni prevenir, ni venger son trépas."

HENRIADE, chant. 2.

The body of the prince was carried into Jarnac upon a pack-horse, "All the army," says Davila, "making sport of the spectacle, though while he lived they were terrified even by his name. The body was afterwards restored to his nephew, Henry prince of Bearn, by whom it was buried at Vendome, in the sepulchre of his ancestors." Davila, liv. 4, p. 484.

intellectual convictions, if not always in his practical conduct, he was mourned by his friends with poignant sorrow, while his memory was respected even by his foes.

The defeat of the Huguenots was complete. Many of their best officers were captured, among the rest the brave and talented La Noué, whose graphic pen has left a stirring picture of his age. Upon this gallant soldier the cruel and remorseless duke of Montpensier pronounced summary sentence. "My friend," said he sneeringly, "your trial is finished; yours, and that of all your comrades: look to your conscience." Martigues, a captain in the royal army, who had been an old brother in arms of La Noué, obtained his pardon, and he was exchanged.*

The Huguenot army was only saved from utter rout by the coolness and skill of Coligny.† Collecting the remnant of the dispersed and shattered squadrons, the imperturbable admiral held them firmly together, and retreated with slow and stubborn valor upon the neighboring village of Cognac.‡ Pausing here only long enough to fortify the town, he left there a strong garrison, and then resumed his retreat, resting at St. Jean d'Angely, from whence he could advance to the assistance of Cognac, should it be besieged, while he was enabled also to open a road for the duke of Deux-

* La Noué, p. 700. Davila, liv. 4. Duncan, p. 87.

† Vie de Coligny, p. 358. Mem. de Tavannes.

‡ Ibid.

Ponts, who was advancing to his assistance at the head of some German auxiliaries.*

The conduct of the royalists after the battle of Jarnac was weak, vacillating, and impolitic. The dukes D'Aumale and Nemours, relatives of the cardinal of Lorraine, commanded an army fully equal in numbers to that of the duke of Deux-Ponts; still the Bavarian general marched steadily through the heart of France. The duke of Anjou did not push on to Cognac till Coligny had strongly fortified it; and then he no sooner reached it than he hastily retreated from its walls. The solution of these mysterious tactics is to be found in the memoirs of Tavannes, who attributed the whole of these faulty operations to the jealousies and intrigues of the court.†

Meantime two inauspicious events occurred: the duke of Deux-Ponts fell a victim to the fever which then raged as a pestilence;‡ but he did not die before delegating his authority to his lieutenant, Mansfeldt, to whom his troops swore allegiance.§

The loss of the Bavarian general was immediately succeeded by another of more importance to the Huguenots. Coligny's brother, D'Andelot,

* Vie de Coligny, p. 358. "The army of the duke of Deux-Ponts, who was also called Wolfgang of Bavaria, was composed of fourteen thousand men, and among his officers were William of Nassau prince of Orange and his two brothers Louis and Henry, who quitted the Low Countries to avoid the merciless persecutions of the duke of Alva." Davila, liv. 4.

† Mem. de Tavannes. Duncan, p. 89.

‡ Davila, liv. 4. Esprit de la Ligue, vol. 1, p. 291.

§ Archives de la Maison d'Orange-Nassau, vol. 3, p. 281.

whom the admiral termed his right hand, was also stricken down by the remorseless fever. His death soon followed, and the first patrician apostle of religious liberty was lost to France. D'Andelot was a man of spotless integrity and singular hardihood of character; frank, open, generous, he was a universal favorite, while he *lived* his religion as well as *thought* it. "He was true and sincere," says the Romanist abbé Anquétil, "and of all the Calvinist chiefs, one of the most honestly persuaded of the truth of his faith. Naturally frank, candid, and generous, he attracted friendship, as his brother, more severe and reserved, conciliated esteem."*

Coligny deeply felt this bereavement; but carrying it to God, he subordinated private sorrow to his stern sense of public duty, and remained at his post.

Upon the death of Condé the leadership of the Huguenot army had devolved upon Coligny. But ere long dissatisfaction arose. There were many nobles in the ranks who were his equals in wealth and birth; these, while they readily conceded the admiral's military superiority, considered themselves degraded by accepting him as their chief.† The wise admiral accordingly wrote the queen of Navarre, who still tarried in Rochelle with her children, that the time had come when she should raise her son to the dignity which was his due.‡

* Anquétil, Esprit de la Ligue, vol. 1, p. 298.

† Browning, p. 105. Duncan, p. 88.

‡ Davila, liv. 4, p. 488.

This politic move exhibits at once Coligny's wisdom and his self-abnegation. He served God, not his own interests; he was anxious for union, not greedy for power. Nothing could more finely prove this than his appeal to Jane d'Albrét.

That illustrious woman, who inherited all her mother's fervid piety and brilliant genius, responded to the call in the same spirit. Hastening to Coligny's camp, her presence at once rallied the desponding spirits of the mutinous army, and animated them to fresh exertions. Her son Henry, prince of Bearn, and the eldest son of Louis of Bourbon, prince of Condé, who was a few years younger than her own boy, and destined also to achieve wide fame, accompanied her. Holding the two princes by the hand, she presented them to the Huguenots in these stirring words:

"My friends, we mourn the loss of a prince who, to his dying hour, sustained with equal fidelity and courage the faith which he had undertaken to defend; but our tears would be unworthy of him, unless, imitating his bright example, we too firmly resolved to sacrifice our lives rather than abandon God. The good cause has not perished with Condé; his unhappy fate ought not to fill with despair men who are devotedly attached to their religion. God watches over his own. He gave that prince companions well fitted to serve him while he lived; he leaves among us brave and experienced captains, able to repair the loss we have sustained in his death. Here I offer you my son the young prince of Bearn; I also confide to you Henry Condé, son of the captain whom we bewail. May it please heaven that they both show themselves worthy heirs of the valor of their ancestors, and may these tender pledges, committed to your guardianship, be the bond of your union, and the assurance of your future triumph."*

As the beautiful queen, blooming with excitement, concluded, shouts of acclamation made the welkin ring; the timid were reanimated, the dissatisfied were reassured, and the boldest panted for action. The enthusiasm of the army was kindled to a still higher pitch when the prince of Bearn and young Condé, with warlike vehemence of gesture, swore to defend the reformed religion, and to persevere in the "good fight" until death or victory.†

Henry of Navarre was immediately proclaimed generalissimo of the Huguenots: all dissatisfaction ceased; the scrupulous point of honor was satisfied, and Coligny became in fact what Henry was in name.‡

In the summer of 1569, active operations were resumed. The Huguenot army, forming a junction with the German auxiliaries, numbered twenty-five thousand; the royalists under Anjou were still stronger.§ Coligny met the young duke at La Roche l'Abeille, and worsted him in a severe en-

* Esprit de la Ligue, vol. 1, p. 292. Browning, p. 106.

† Davila, liv. 4, p. 490. Duncan, p. 88.

‡ Browning, p. 106.

§ Duncan, p. 92.

gagement;* he then pressed on to besiege Poitiers. Here an epidemic broke out among the Germans, who had eaten immoderately of the autumnal fruits; whole regiments were incapacitated for service; the camp became a hospital, and the admiral himself was prostrated. While the army thus lay *hors du combat*, Anjou, who had marched to the relief of Poitiers, suddenly retreated; and this afforded Coligny also a pretext to retire without compromising his honor.†

If Coligny was adored by his own party, he was admired and esteemed by all the high-minded and generous cavaliers among the royalists. No one questioned the sincerity of his faith; all praised his invincible fortitude. Some of the royalist officers sent him word from Anjou's camp of their vast numerical superiority, and urged him to avoid an engagement. To these admonitions the admiral, whose military genius was of the Fabian order, lent a willing ear. But this skilful policy was rendered impossible by the rashness of the Hotspur spirits in his ranks, and by the open mutiny of the Germans.‡

On the 3d of October, 1569, the two armies joined battle at Moncontour. The hospital army of the admiral, enfeebled and demoralized, was quickly routed. A pistol-ball shattered the lower jaw of Coligny, who still kept his saddle, and continued to display the courage of a soldier and the

* Davila, liv. 4. D'Aubigné, Hist. Univ., vol. 1, p. 285.

† Ibid. Duncan, p. 92.

‡ Ibid., p. 93.

talent of a captain. But the fortune of the field could not be retrieved. Cannon, baggage, banners, all fell into Anjou's hands; and of an army of twenty-five thousand men, but six thousand reached St. Jean d'Angely on the retreat.*

But the Huguenots were too numerous, too well organized, and too enthusiastic to be subdued by the loss of a stricken field.

Upon this occasion they were especially assisted to recover their feet by the bickerings and dissensions of the court. Tavannes, under whose skilful guidance Anjou had achieved his victories, was insulted out of the service by the cardinal of Lorraine.† "Sir cardinal," said the indignant marshal when the inflated churchman ventured to dictate military tactics to him, "each to his trade; no man can be at once a good priest and a good soldier."‡

The victory of Moncontour obtained for Anjou the loudest praises of his party; but the glory he had acquired rankled in the envious heart of Charles IX. The king departed for the army, hoping that his presence, even after the battle, would transfer to his own brow the laurels which his brother had culled in the ghastly carnage of the battle's front.§

The disunion in the royal camp enabled Coligny, indefatigable and ubiquitous, to recruit his

* Duncan, p. 93. Davila, liv. 4. Ranke, p. 241.
† Mem. de Tavannes. ‡ Ibid. Duncan, p. 94.
§ Ibid.

forces, in order to try the success of a new campaign. Early in the spring of 1570, he descended from the mountains of Upper Languedoc, and marshalled his troops on the plains of Toulouse. Thence he spread his two wings, and carried pillage and desolation to the Loire. Arrived in Burgundy, he was opposed by Marshal Cassé Gouner, at the head of thirteen thousand men. Though the admiral's army numbered but six thousand men-at-arms, he attacked boldly and with such skill that he gained a complete victory at Arnay-le-Duc.*

This defeat alarmed the court, but nothing was done. The vigor of the government was paralyzed by the intrigues of rival cliques. Catharine once more dissembled; the tragic-comedy of a reconciliation was sought to be once more enacted.

The overtures of the government were received with joy by the Huguenots. Peace on the basis of toleration was their dream. Saddened by reverses, wearied by tedious campaigns, longing for their homes, the cavaliers of the Reformation required nothing but insured liberty of conscience to make them doff their armor with enthusiasm.

This was Catharine's programme: All preceding edicts ratified; a general amnesty; the free exercise of the reformed religion; confiscated property restored; the Huguenots declared eligible to all offices of the state; the complete possession of four important cities, Rochelle, Montauban, Cognac, and La

* Browning, p. 120. Vie de Coligny, p. 381. Matthieu, vol. 1, p. 327.

Charitè, as guarantees: such were the terms demanded and conceded in order to renewed pacification.*

France hailed the peace with acclamations; but the curtain fell upon a dreary war, only to rise upon an atrocious massacre.

* Vie de Coligny, p. 383. Browning, p. 120. Duncan, p. 95. Mem. de Tavannes, p. 98. Matthieu, vol. 1, p. 335.

CHAPTER XXIV.

HOODWINKED FRANCE.

WITH the pacification of 1570 came a new *régime.* The court changed front. Foiled in the field, Catharine changed weapons. The crafty Florentine determined henceforth to use those perfidious and deadly arts which were so congenial, in which she was strongest, and which were in such fatal vogue in her native Italy. Every effort was made to lull France into a feeling of profound security.

The Huguenots especially were treated with profound and unprecedented respect. Did any one demand additional privileges? the concession was ready. Did a murmur of complaint wail through the court? vengeance was swift. This very excess of graciousness was enough to excite suspicion, especially when it was well known that Catharine and treachery were synonymous terms; that she smiled, and, like Cassius, "murdered while she smiled." Strangely enough, it did not. The party seemed infatuated. Indeed all France, save the conspirators who sat darkly hatching their hideous plot, said, "Lo, the millennium is come," and fondly believed that the present tranquillity would be permanent.

At the outset the Huguenots were wary. Upon the cessation of hostilities, the Bourbon princes,

Jane d'Albrét, and the admiral fixed their residence at Rochelle, where the queen of Navarre held her court.* It was the study of the government to allay the suspicions which this policy proved to exist, and to tempt the noblesse of the reformed party to the metropolis. Every artifice known to the queen mother's extensive *repertoire* was exercised. "As soon as the peace was signed," says Davila, "every secret spring which the king and queen held ready in their thoughts was put into action to draw into their nets the principal Huguenots, and to do by artifice that which had been so often vainly attempted by means of war."†

Never had Catharine acted her part with more consummate skill. Not a wrinkle of vexation marred her placid features. She even in appearance surrendered that authority for whose acquisition she had damned her soul; and perfectly aware that the reformers observed her closely, she made her son assume the direction of public affairs, convincing him that it was necessary to success that he should gain the confidence of the heretics, and particularly of Coligny.‡

On the 23d of October, 1570, the year of the pacification, which Charles with paternal affectation styled "my peace,"§ the king was married to Elizabeth of Austria, second daughter of the reign-

* De Thou, liv. 47. Davila, liv. 5. Vie de Coligny, p. 385.

† Davila, liv. 5, p. 578.

‡ Ibid. Browning, p. 123. De Thou, liv. 47.

§ Ranke, ch. 15. Duncan, p. 103. Memoires de Sully, tom. 1, p. 18.

ing house of Hapsburg. This princess possessed the esteem and confidence of her husband, but she exercised no influence over him, for her mild temper quailed before the assumption of the imperious Catharine.*

To commemorate the nuptials, a giddy round of *fètes* was given, and the nobility of all parties were invited, so that a superficial observer would have imagined that the words "Huguenot" and "Romanist" had been swept from the language and merged in that of Frenchmen.†

Yet still the admiral and his coterie absented themselves; the queen of Navarre, with obstinate suspicion, continued to hold her modest court within the stout walls of devoted Rochelle.

A new scheme was hatched. With the ostensible view of conciliating conflicting interests, but with the real design of masking his perfidious and sanguinary plot, and to insure the presence of the chief victims, Charles endeavored to promote various alliances among the leading families of the kingdom, and proposed his youngest sister, the beautiful but frail Margaret of Valois, as the consort of young Henry prince of Bearn.‡

Now for the first time this prince, who in after years achieved an immortal fame, begins to make a central figure in the checkered and tragic history of his epoch. It is fitting therefore that the more

* D'Aubigné, Hist. Univ., vol. 1. Duncan, p. 96.

† Ibid.

‡ Davila, liv 5. D'Aubigné, De Thou, etc.

salient features of his early life should be briefly recited.

Henry was born at Pau, in Bearn, on the 13th of December, 1553.* He was the grandson of Henry d'Albrét, the brother-in-arms of Francis I.; his grandmother was the beautiful, accomplished, and pious Margaret de Valois, the sister of the paladin king.

The young prince was reared in the castle of Courasse, in the mountains of Navarre. Here he was exercised like a Spartan boy; nourished on the coarsest diet, brown bread, beef, cheese; he was also sent to play with the children of the peasants, bareheaded and barefooted.† Thus from his cradle he was hardy, independent, and self-reliant. This harsh apprenticeship, so unlike that of most princes, prepared him for heroic destinies.

While Henry d'Albrét lived, he personally superintended his grandson's education, a task for which his fine scholarship well fitted him. Indeed Charles V. considered him one of the most accomplished men of his age.‡ Upon his death, Jane d'Albrét provided him with an excellent and learned tutor named La Gaucherie, who cultivated his illustrious pupil's mind chiefly by conversational instruction.§ He had the wisdom to abandon that trifling course of study invented in an age comparatively barbarous, which was calculated rather to disgust than to

* Matthieu, Hist. de France; Cayet, vol. 1; Mem. de Sully, etc.

† Ibid. Duncan, p. 99. ‡ Browning, p. 84, note.

§ Duncan, p. 101. James, Life of Henry IV., vol. 1.

enlighten. La Gaucherie, moreover, instilled into young Henry's mind principles of honor and of public virtue, which ever after, if we except his many and sad errors of gallantry, and these the Christian and moralist must condemn, guided his conduct.

When this able teacher died, Henry was confided to the tuition of Florent Chrétien, a Huguenot preacher of high merit.* He readily entered into the views of the queen of Navarre, and trained the prince in the reformed faith with careful assiduity.

When the young mountaineer was first presented at the court of France, his blunt frankness caused much amusement; but his biting wit, grace of manner, and *bonhomie* speedily subdued all hearts.†

"Will you be my son?" queried Henry II. on one occasion as he stood chatting with the little prince. "No," was the frank reply, "he is my father," pointing to the king of Navarre. "Well," retorted the king, "will you be my son-in-law then?" "With all my heart," said Henry; and from this early date his marriage with the princess Margaret is said to have been decided upon.‡

At Bayonne the duke of Medina, looking at him earnestly, said, "This prince either will be or ought to be an emperor."§

In the *Memoires de Nevers*, some letters written

* Duncan, p. 101. James, Life of Henry IV., vol. 1.

† Cayet, tom. 1, p. 236. Browning, p. 84.

‡ Cayet, tom. 1, p. 240. § Ibid.

in 1567, by the principal magistrates of Bordeaux, are found, which contain interesting particulars of young Henry's manners and person at that time. "We have here with us," says one of them, "the prince of Bearn. It must be confessed that he is a charming youth. At thirteen he has all the riper qualities of eighteen or nineteen. He is agreeable, polite, obliging, and behaves to every one with an air so easy and engaging that wherever he is there is sure to be a crowd. He mixes in conversation like a wise and prudent man, and speaks always to the purpose. When the court is the subject discussed, it is easy to see that he is *au fait*, for he never says more nor less than he ought. I shall all my life hate the new religion for having robbed us of so worthy a subject."*

Another describes Henry's personal appearance: "His hair is inclined to a reddish tint, yet the ladies think him none the less agreeable on that account. His face is finely shaped, his nose neither too large nor too small, his eyes full of sweetness, his skin brown, but clear, and his whole countenance animated by a striking vivacity. With all these graces, if he is not well with the ladies, it must be strange."†

Henry was early initiated into the science of war, in which he was destined to achieve so wide a celebrity. Even at the early age of fifteen, when his mother conducted him to Rochelle and presented him to the army, he criticised the military

* Mem. de Nevers, tom. 2, p. 586, et seq.

† Ibid., tom. 2, p. 590, et seq.

faults of Condé and Coligny, two of the greatest captains of the age.*

Such was the embryo king of Navarre—whose white plume at a later day led the headlong charge at Ivry—when, in his nineteenth year, he was invited to wed Margaret of Valois.

For many reasons, the proposal was extremely distasteful to Jane d'Albrét. She instinctively distrusted the tortuous politics of the court. Now, without putting a decided negative upon the plan, she yet withheld her positive sanction, for she had a dark foreboding of Catharine's sinister designs. This tacit opposition disconcerted the court. It was feared that the slightest breath of suspicion would detect the exterminating conspiracy ere it was ripe. The precautions were redoubled. Every device was adopted with renewed zeal to lull the Huguenots into false security. Any infringement of the recent treaty was severely punished.† And Charles carried his duplicity to such a length, that he insulted the Guises into apparent exile, expressed a wish that young Condé should marry Mary of Cleves, marchioness de l'Isle, who had been reared in Jane d'Albrét's court, and was an advantageous match; and to crown all, he brought about a marriage between Coligny, now a widower, and Jacqueline of Savoy, countess d'Entremont, a wealthy and noble Protestant lady who had become deeply interested in the admiral,‡ giving them a

* Duncan, p. 101. † Ibid. Davila, liv. 5; De Thou, liv. 47, etc.
‡ James, Life of Henry IV. Vie de Coligny.

nuptial present of a hundred thousand crowns, together with all the benefices enjoyed by Odét, cardinal of Chatillon, who had just died abroad.*

These generous and successive acts of kingly comity produced the desired effect; only the most cautious and penetrating of the Huguenots still held out; but unfortunately among these were Coligny and the queen of Navarre. Charles perceived this, and in the summer of 1571 he made a tour into Touraine, hoping that Jane and her suite would visit him on the route; nor was he disappointed; she came to his itinerant court, accompanied by the princes and escorted by the admiral.†

When Coligny stood in the presence of his majesty, out of habitual respect the old soldier was about to fall upon one knee. Charles saw his intention, seized him by the arm, and prevented the intended obeisance, saying, "Nay, I hold you now, admiral, nor shall you for the future quit me when you please; I cannot spare so valuable a friend."‡ Then, with great emphasis and much apparent genuineness of feeling, he added, "This is indeed the happiest day of my life." The queen mother, the duke of Anjou, and all the attendant nobles loaded Coligny with compliments and caresses, and especially the young duke of Alençon, youngest brother of the king, who, giving full play to the vivacity

* Duncan, p. 103. Vie de Coligny. De Thou, liv. 56. Odét of Chatillon died at Southampton, England, in 1571, just as he was about to embark for France. He is said to have been poisoned by his *valet*. Duncan.

† Brantome, Duncan, Mem. de Sully. ‡ Vie de Coligny.

and frankness of boyhood, expressed his esteem for the admiral in extravagant terms.* But he alone was sincere; he was not yet old enough to be steeped in dissimulation.

On this ill-fated visit it was definitely settled that Henry of Navarre should wed Margaret de Valois, and Jane d'Albrét and her suite consented to celebrate the nuptials in the spring of 1572 at Paris.† The two courts then parted, with mutual professions of eternal amity.

Catharine returned to the metropolis with sardonic satisfaction. "The cautious fish have taken the bait," said she with a leer of triumphant malice.

On her part, the queen of Navarre reëntered Rochelle sadly and thoughtfully. Reasons of state, anxiety to cement a lasting and righteous peace, had wrung from her a reluctant assent to the ill-omened marriage of her beloved boy; but not all the persuasions of apparent gain could satisfy her maternal instinct, nor quiet her apprehensions. She repeated incessantly, "This union is not, nor can it come to, good."‡

The political heavens now seemed serene; not a cloud specked the horizon. The awful lightnings which lurked behind this smiling sky yet hid their thunderbolts.

Completely cozened, the leaders of the Huguenots crowded to Paris, from which they had been

* Vie de Coligny, La Noué, Brantome, Mem. de Sully.

† Mem. de Sully, Vie de Coligny, Duncan, La Noué.

‡ Ibid.

so long debarred, anxious to share once more in the pleasures of the capital.*

In the middle of May, 1572, the queen of Navarre, accompanied by a brilliant retinue, arrived at the Louvre. On the 9th of June she was a corpse. Suspicions of foul play were at once bruited through the streets. Her death was attributed to poison, which they say was given to her in a pair of gloves by a Florentine named René, the queen mother's perfumer.†

This melancholy event of course postponed the marriage of Henry, who now assumed the title of king of Navarre.‡

Singularly enough, the fate of their great queen did not persuade the Huguenots of the doom which awaited them. Dazzled blind by Catharine's wiles, they lingered on at the court, nor made an effort to escape the impending horrors.

Coligny indeed, profoundly grieved by the death of Jane d'Albrét, which however he considered natural,§ retired to his estate of Chatillon-sur-Loing for a few weeks; but it was not long ere he was once more an habitual visitor at the Louvre.‖

The admiral's conduct at this time bordered upon infatuation, and is all the more remarkable on account of his natural caution and penetration.

* Davila, liv. 5. De Thou, liv. 50. Esprit de la Ligue.

† See the Memoires of L'Etoile, D'Aubigné, and others. Davila, liv. 5, also corroborates this account. Jane d'Albrét was forty-two years of age when she died.

‡ Mem. de Sully; De Thou; Browning, p. 129; Duncan, p 117.

§ Vie de Coligny.

‖ Davila, liv. 5, p. 179.

While at his country residence, he was flooded with letters from his friends urging him not to return to Paris, and presaging calamity. They did not indeed base their appeals upon any specific facts; their admonitions were rather the result of general inferences from current reports and peculiarities of conduct observed at Paris.*

But the admiral was deaf. One day one of the gentlemen attached to his suite requested leave of absence. "On what account?" demanded Coligny. "Because they caress you too much," was the reply, "and I would rather escape with the fools than perish with the wise."†

The chiefs of his party, relying upon the habitual wariness of Coligny, and noting his calmness, shared his confidence, and partook of his doom.

The fact is, that the admiral was attacked on his weak side. His darling project, a war against Spain for the assistance of the staggering Protestantism of the Netherlands, was held out to him as certain to be adopted.‡ Extended conversations were held between the king and himself, in which he dilated upon the advantages certain to accrue to France from such a war.§ The profound and far-reaching mind of the great admiral formed plans of the grandest character. Philip II. was destitute of money; the French forces, disciplined by innumerable internecine wars, were superior to the Span-

* Davila, liv. 5, p. 179. Duncan, p. 167.

† Davila, liv. 5, p. 179.

‡ Duncan, p. 104; Browning, Ranke, De Thou. § Ibid.

iards in military science; he had but to throw united France into the Low Countries, and reinforce the kingdom by an alliance with England and Protestant Germany, and then the Reformation might be cemented into an indestructible unit, while Roman Europe would be lassoed into quiet imbecility.*

Such, according to the best contemporaneous authorities, was the brilliant programme of this statesmanlike Huguenot.

The French court listened with courteous attention to the admiral as he unfolded his plans, and map in hand, pointed out the salient features of the grand campaign. Catharine and the king appeared to enter with his own ardor into the scheme; and then, when Coligny quitted them, retired to the secret recesses of the palace, and spent half the night in arranging the details of the slowly ripening holocaust.

* Ranke, p. 256; Mem. de Sully, Vie de Coligny, Brantome.

CHAPTER XXV.

THE MASSACRE OF ST. BARTHOLOMEW.

THE preachers in Geneva and the cardinals at Rome foresaw and predicted a catastrophe from the abnormal political situation at Paris. The radical antipathy between the rival parties who stood nudging each other's elbows at the Louvre, with reconciliation painted on their faces, but hatred still unsubdued in their hearts, could not but forebode evil.

Yet, unmindful of the petulant murmurs of the king, oblivious of the old threats which had issued from Bayonne, the Huguenot leaders still lingered at the court, while one more act was played in the dreary comedy which ushered in the awful tragedy of St. Bartholomew. On the 18th of August, prince Henry and Margaret de Valois were married.*

The young duke of Guise had cherished the hope of marrying the king's sister; he had long entertained a violent passion for her, while her affection for him was equally undisguised.† But mutual affection was compelled to succumb to vicious state policy, and the wedding was consummated.

It had been agreed that the ceremonial of the

* Brantome, vol. 8, p. 180. Davila, liv. 5, p. 609.

† Davila, liv. 5. Browning, p. 126.

marriage should not be wholly conformable to either creed: not to the Protestant, because the vows were to be received by a priest, the cardinal of Bourbon; not to the Romish, because those vows were to be received without the sacramental ceremonies of the Vatican. A great scaffold was erected in the court before the principal entrance of the cathedral of Notre Dame; and standing upon this typical structure, the inauspicious nuptials were celebrated.* It was remarked by many that when the princess was asked if she were willing to take king Henry of Navarre to be her husband, she stood obstinately silent; she had said repeatedly that Guise alone should be her husband. But the king her brother, who stood just behind her, with his own hand rudely inclined her head, and this was taken for Margaret's assent.† This done, the bridegroom retired into a neighboring Huguenot chapel, while the reluctant bride passed into the cathedral with a bitter and broken heart to listen to the mockery of the mass. In the evening the coldly indifferent husband and the sulky spouse attended the brilliant festival with which Charles crowned the dismal day.‡

From this time horrible events begin to jostle each other. Four days after the wedding, an attempt was made to assassinate the admiral as he was returning from one of his daily interviews with

* Decade de Henri Quatre, tome 2. Duncan, p. 108.

† Davila, liv. 5, p. 609. Mezeray, La Grain, etc.

‡ Ibid.

the king at the Louvre. He was fired at from a window screened by a curtain. Coligny was indebted for his life to an accidental movement made at the moment; but as it was, his left arm was broken, and the index finger of his right hand was shot off. With imperturbable *sang froid* the old soldier pointed out the house from whence the bullet sped; but ere his suite could break open the gate, the assassin had escaped.*

This assault caused a profound commotion. The hostile mob of Paris, which had only borne the presence of the Huguenots with suppressed fury, now heaved in almost open insurrection. Navarre and Condé, supported by the whole Protestant party, presented a petition for justice and protection; and the king, who was playing at tennis when the news reached him, threw down the racket in a violent rage, muttered something about immature action, and exclaimed, "Must I be perpetually troubled by broils; shall I never have quiet?"†

Active measures were then taken to allay suspicion, to quell the rising tumult, and to flatter the angered Huguenots into renewed stupefaction.

Coligny, who had been borne to his apartments by his attendants, weltering in his blood, was shortly visited by the king, the queen mother, Anjou, and many of the chief nobility. Every expres-

* Sully, liv. 1. De Thou, liv. 52. The assassin's name was Maurevel, an adherent of the Guises.

† Sully, tome 1, p. 33. Davila says that the king merely *feigned* displeasure; he was playing with the duke of Guise.

sion of condolence was uttered, signal vengeance upon the assassin was promised, the police were ordered to make domiciliary visits and arrest all suspected persons, and his majesty even carried his hypocrisy so far as openly to notify his high displeasure at the occurrence to all the public ambassadors.*

This energetic action at once disarmed the suspicion and conciliated the respect of the Huguenot chiefs. Startled Paris resumed its tranquillity, and that awful hush which precedes a storm succeeded.†

Meantime, warned by this *émeute* of the danger which lurked in procrastination, perfectly well aware that every hour lost was an opportunity for misfortune, the conspirators worked with diabolical zeal to complete the preparations for the wholesale slaughter, and the time was definitively fixed—the 23d of August, 1572, the eve of St. Bartholomew's day.‡ A pistol was to be fired in front of the Louvre as the signal for the commencement of the butchery.

A few of the Huguenots were alarmed, and boldly proposed to quit Paris with the admiral. The vidame of Chartres strongly advised this course. He even informed Coligny that the Guises, despite their ostensible disgrace at court, had been twice seen in masks at the Louvre in secret conver-

* De Serres, tome 11, p. 470. Duncan, p. 109.

† Browning, De Thou, Vie de Coligny.

‡ Davil·, liv. 5; Mem. de Sully; Duncan, etc.

sation with Catharine and the king. "We **have** been shamefully ensnared," he added.*

Coligny was averse to showing any suspicion. "If I do so," said he, "I must display either fear or distrust: my honor would be hurt by the one; the king, I hope, would be injured by the other. Besides, I should then be obliged to renew the civil war, and I would rather die than again see such ills."†

The shrewd vidame, however, was not to be persuaded, and accompanied by a number of equally wise friends, among whom were Rohan and Montgomery, he passed out of the fatal city.‡

Under pretence of protecting the admiral and his friends from any tumult which the Guises might stir among the populace, the whole Huguenot faction were lodged in one quarter of the city, and the chiefs were huddled together for the double purpose of preventing their escape and keeping them under easy surveillance. Perhaps too Charles called to mind the pithy maxim of Alaric: "Thick grass is easier mown than thin." Around this doomed quarter was drawn a cordon of the duke of Anjou's guards, professedly to protect the victims, but who shortly became their most zealous murderers.§ At the same time arms were profusely delivered to the *canaille* of the metropolis, previously crazed by the clamors of the Jesuits, and these were hidden in

* Sully, liv. 1, p. 32. De Thou, liv. 52. Browning, p. 136.

† Matthieu, Hist. de France, vol. 1, liv. 6, p. 343.

‡ Browning, p. 137.

§ D'Aubigné, Hist. Univ., vol. 2, p. 17. De Thou, liv. 52.

the slums of the capital.* Finally, couriers were dispatched to all parts of France with orders to make the massacre general and exterminating.†

France was commanded to commit suicide. The kingdom was to stagger and bleed beneath self-dealt and frenzied blows.

The awful eve arrived. At midnight the pistol shot was fired; the talismanic word was uttered. Charles cried, Havoc, and let slip the thunderbolt. The wild populace swayed through the streets, crying, "Blood, blood!" The protecting guard of the Huguenot quarter was suddenly transformed into a legion of demoniacs. "Bleed, bleed!" shouted Tavannes; "the physicians say that bleeding is as good in August as in May."‡ The dukes of Guise and Montpensier rode through the streets, crying, "It is the will of the king; slay on to the last, and let not one escape." The count of Coconnas seized thirty prisoners, put them in prison, and put them to death with his own hand by slow and lingering tortures.

The butcher Pezon, who slaughtered men, women, and children as he did cattle, boasted of having in one day killed a hundred and twenty Huguenots. René, Catharine's perfumer, frequented all the gaols in which the evangelicals were immured, and amused himself by stabbing them with daggers. He decoyed a rich jeweller into his house, under pretext of saving him; but after plundering his person, René

* Browning, p. 136. Brantome, vol. 8, p. 184.

† Ibid. Mezeray. ‡ Mem. de Tavannes.

cut his victim's throat, and threw the body into the Seine. "This arm," said Crucé, a gold-wire drawer, taking off his coat and exhibiting his naked arm, "on the day of St. Bartholomew, put to death four hundred heretics."*

At the first signal the duke of Guise sped for the residence of the admiral, pausing but to ring the great bell of the palace, which was only tolled on days of public rejoicing.† He was accompanied by his two creatures, Petrucci, an Italian, and Bérne, a German bravo; a company of men-at-arms also followed. The bravos rushed into the chamber of the helpless admiral, who, awaked by the noise, had just arisen from his bed and now stood leaning against the wall of his apartment.‡ "What means the tumult?" queried he of his attendants. "My lord," was the solemn reply, "God calls us to himself." The admiral then bade his suite to leave him. "I cannot escape; it is all over with me; I have long been prepared for death; but save yourselves, dear friends." Such were the collected and noble words of this martyr, whose spirit, armed by faith in God, no danger could quell. Coligny's attendants at once quitted him, while he composed himself in prayer.§

Unmoved by the entrance of the assassins, he continued his supplications. Awed by the gran-

* These anecdotes are found recorded in Sully's Memoirs, Tavannes' Memoirs, in Browning, Vie de Coligny, and in Duncan.

† Mezeray, Abregé Chron.

‡ De Thou, liv. 52. Vie de Coligny. Browning.

§ Ibid.

deur of the scene, the majestic figure of the calm and venerable old soldier engrossed in devotion, Petrucci instinctively paused. "Art thou Coligny?" demanded the bravo. "I am indeed," responded the admiral. "Young man, you should have respect unto my gray hairs: but work your will; you can abridge my life only by a few short days."*

A moment later, and Gaspard de Coligny, the foremost subject in France, the most distinguished man in Christendom, lay dead.

Bérne plunged his sword into Coligny's body, and his companions then gave him multitudinous stabs with their stilettos. "Your enemy is dead," cried Petrucci from the window to the duke of Guise, who awaited the dénouement impatiently in the court below. "Very well," was the answer, borne up through the midnight gloom; "but M. d'Angouléme will not believe it until he sees the body at his feet." The next instant the corpse, flung from the window, fell with a thud at the feet of the princes; the yet warm blood even spirted out on the clothes and into the faces of the disbelievers. With brutal nonchalance Guise stooped and wiped Coligny's face, then ordered his satellites to hold a torch, that he might recognize his foe. When, through the lurid and flickering gloom, he detected that it was indeed the mighty admiral who lay before him, he spurned the body with his foot, and ordered the head to be cut off.† This was sent to Catharine: what disposition

* Brantome, vol. 8, p. 185.

† De Thou, liv. 52. Browning, p. 139. Vie de Coligny.

she made of it is uncertain; Tavannes and Felibien affirm that it was dispatched to Rome;* others say that Philip II. of Spain received the ghastly present. The decapitated body was mangled and drawn through the streets during two or three days; the populace then threw it into the river, but afterwards drew it out and hung it by the heels to the gibbet of Montfauçon; a slow fire was then kindled beneath it, which disfigured it horribly.†

The body swung from this gibbet when Charles went with his court to gloat over the abused remains of that man whom he had so recently termed "his father," and assured of his affectionate veneration. The odor emitted by the decomposing body was so dreadful, that the courtiers stopped their noses with their handkerchiefs. "Fie, fie!" cried Charles, borrowing the language of the classic brute Vitellius: "'The carcass of an enemy always smells pleasantly.'"‡

Marshal Montmorenci, Coligny's cousin, had these insulted remains cut down one night, and secreted, for he feared to inter them at Chantilly, lest they should be molested. Subsequently, when the decrees against the admiral's memory were reversed, they were buried in the tomb of his ancestors at Chatillon-sur-Loing.§

While Coligny's murder was being perpetrated, the drunken pavements of bewildered Paris were

* Mem. de Tavannes, p. 419. Felibien, Histoire de Paris, vol. 2, p. 1119. † Vie de Coligny, D'Aubigné, De Thou.

‡ Brantome, P. Masson, Browning, Duncan, etc. § Ibid.

glutted in blood. The Huguenots, surprised and overmatched, could make no resistance. Escape was impossible; the city gates were shut and guarded; numerous lights, placed in the windows of the dwellings, deprived the reformers even of the normal protection of night;* and patrols traversed the streets in all directions, butchering every one they met. From the streets, as the carnival grew wilder, the frenzied multitude swept into the houses. Neither age, sex, nor condition were spared. Priests, holding a crucifix in one hand and a sword in the other, preceded the murderers, encouraging them to butcher alike relatives and friends, and promising them absolution from all crimes and heavenly happiness as the reward of these "acts of devotion."†

Even the Louvre became the scene of great carnage; the king's guards were drawn up in double line, and the Huguenots who lodged in the palace were summoned out one after another and killed with the halberds of the infuriated soldiers.‡ Most of them died without complaining; others appealed to the public faith and the sacred promise of the king. "Great God," cried they, "be the defence of the oppressed. Just Judge, avenge this perfidy."§

While these events were occurring in the court-

* Mem. de Tavannes; D'Aubigné.

† Browning, p. 140. Duncan, p. 114.

‡ Mem. de Tavannes, p. 418. Davila, liv. 5.

§ D'Aubigné, Hist. Univer., vol. 2, p. 18. Browning, p. 140.

yard, Charles, seated at a window of the Louvre, amused himself by shooting down all who came within range of his musket.*

The monarch's ferocity was contagious; even the ladies of his court were seen descending into the square of the Louvre, then filled with the dead bodies of Huguenot gentlemen, many of whom had cheerfully passed with them some hours of the preceding day. It was by their syren-like qualities that some of the victims had been enticed to their death; they now became harpies, through the addition of cruelty to fanaticism and wantonness, and trampling common decency under foot, they jested and laughed as they recognized the murdered Huguenots,† precisely as the king did from the window of the Louvre, and beneath the gibbet of Montfauçon.

Among those who fled within the precincts of the palace was a nobleman named Soubise, whose wife had recently instituted a suit of divorce against him. His mangled body underwent a careful examination from these brazen wantons, whose barbarous curiosity was worthy of such an abominable court.‡

When day dawned, Paris exhibited an appalling spectacle of slaughter: headless bodies were dangling from innumerable windows; gateways were blocked up by the dead and dying; the houses were

* Duncan, p. 124. Browning. Notes to the "Henriade."

† Browning, p. 143. Mem. de Tavannes.

‡ De Thou, liv. 52, vol. 6, p. 402. Browning, p. 144.

battered, while the doors were smeared with gore; and the streets were filled with carcasses, which were drawn, bleeding and mutilated, across the bloody pavements to the choked and reddened Seine.*

These atrocious scenes were continued through three days and nights, and the orgies only slackened from lack of victims.

Meantime the massacre spread throughout France; the reeling kingdom bled at every pore with mute heroism. The slaughter at Meaux, Angers, Bourges, Orleans, Lyons, Toulouse, Rouen, and in many of the smaller towns of the provinces, was horrible.†

But the genius of humanity had not wholly fled from France. Claude de Savoy, count of Tende, saved the lives of all the Huguenots in Dauphiny. "This missive," said he when the king's letter ordering the massacre was handed to him, "must be a forgery, and I shall so treat it."‡

Eleoner de Chabat, count of Charny, who commanded in Burgundy, acted with similar heroism; there was but one Huguenot murdered at Dijon.§

Heran de Montouvin, governor of Auvergne, positively refused to obey the mandate, unless it were supported by the personal presence of the king.‖

* D'Aubigné, Davila, Maimbourg, De Thou, Browning, etc.

† Ibid. Duncan, p. 122.

‡ Sully, tome 1, p. 45. De Thou, lib. 52, 53.

§ D'Aubigné, Hist. Univ., tome 2, lib. 1.

‖ Duncan, p. 122.

The Viscount d'Ortes, the governor of Bayonne, penned this immortal response to the royal order: "Sire, I have communicated your majesty's mandate to your faithful inhabitants in this city, and to the men-at-arms in the garrison. I find here good citizens and brave soldiers, but not one executioner. On this point, therefore, you must not expect obedience from me."*

But despite these luminous exceptions, from seventy to a hundred thousand victims were slaughtered, and the lives of two of the heroes who refused obedience to the bloody fiat of Charles IX.—the Count de Tende and the Viscount d'Ortes—were abridged by the infernal skill of the royal poisoner.†

Both the Romish and the Huguenot chroniclers of this tragedy have bequeathed to posterity many episodes of personal adventure, which are replete with thrilling interest. But after "supping full of horrors," the imagination wearies and palls. Details grow hideous. "The deep damnation of their taking off" appalls those who peruse the history of the Huguenots; readers have no appetite for *minutiæ*.

It was long a mooted question whether Condé and young Henry of Navarre should be saved or not. Upon this point the testimony is clear. "It was anxiously deliberated," says the archbishop of Paris, "whether the prince should be murdered with the others; the conspirators were for their

* Duncan, p. 122. Sully, De Thou, Davila, Browning.

† Sully, lib. 1. Péréfixe. Duncan, p. 125, note.

death; nevertheless they escaped by a miracle."* "The duke of Guise," remarks Davila, "wished that, in killing the Huguenots, Henry of Navarre and the Prince de Condé should be included; but the queen mother and others had a horror of dipping their hands in royal blood."† "Indubitably," says quaint old Brantome, "they were proscribed and down on the 'red list,' as they called it, because it was remarked that it was necessary to dig up the roots of the heretical faction, Navarre, Condé, the admiral, and other noted personages; but the young queen Margaret threw herself upon her knees before king Charles her brother, to beg her husband's life at Catharine's command. The king granted it to her after much urging, since she was his good sister."‡

Margaret, in the account she gave of the horrors of the night which ushered in the massacre, relates that "on retiring to rest, Henry's bed was surrounded by thirty or forty Huguenots, who talked all night of the accident to the admiral, and resolved the next morning to demand justice upon the Guises. No sleep was had; and before day the king of Navarre rose, with the intention of playing at tennis until king Charles was up."§

Margaret then narrates that she fell asleep after the retirement of Henry and his suite, but that in less than an hour she was awakened by loud shouts in the palace corridors, and by a man striking with

* Péréfixe, Hist. de Henri le Grande.

† Davila, liv. 5, p. 616. ‡ Brantome, vol. 1, p. 261.

§ Mem. de la Reine Marguerite, p. 181, et seq.

hands and feet against the door of her room, and crying, "Navarre, Navarre!" Thinking it might be her husband, she opened the door, when lo, a man besmeared with gore rushed in, and clasping her by the feet, conjured her to save him. This cavalier was quickly pursued by four soldiers, from whose greedy swords the young queen with difficulty saved her strange client. At length his life was spared to her prayers, and she was conducted to the chamber of her sister the duchess of Lorraine, where, at the very moment of her entrance, a gentleman was killed just at her side.

Margaret fainted: upon her recovery she inquired for her husband, and was told that both Henry and Condé were then in the presence of the king.*

When the princes were summoned to the king, Catharine, in order to affright them into submission, ordered them to be conducted under the palace vaults, and to be made to pass through the royal guards drawn up in files on either side, and poised in menacing attitudes.†

"Charles received them," says Sully, "with a fierce countenance and a volley of blasphemies. He avowed that the admiral and the other heretics had been slaughtered by his mandate; affirmed that he would no longer be thwarted or questioned by his subjects; declared that all should revere him as the likeness of God, and be no longer the enemies

* Mem. de la Reine Marguerite, p. 181, et seq.

† Péréfixe, Hist. de Henri le Grande.

of his mother's images; and ended by calling on the princes to recant."*

"Sire," replied Condé with noble candor, "I am accountable to God alone for my religion; my possessions, my life, these are in your majesty's power; dispose of them as you please; but no menaces, nor even death, shall make me renounce the truth."†

"And you, sir," said Charles with bitter emphasis, turning to prince Henry, "what say you?"

Henry expressed the same determination, though less frankly.‡ "Well, sirs," said the king, "I give you three days in which to consider; then the mass, death, or the Bastile; take your choice."§

Charles then gave way to sardonic glee. "Have I not played my part well?" asked he of Catharine de' Medici. "*He who cannot dissemble is not fit to reign*," said Louis XI. "Have not I known how to dissemble?" queried Charles, quoting this precept; "have not I well learned the lesson and the Latin of my ancestor, king Louis XI.?"‖

Thus the hideous *fête* of St. Bartholomew closed with a laugh and a sarcasm.

The slaughter was complete. The heads of the most distinguished Huguenot families in France were the victims of the holocaust. Coligny, Rochefoucault and his son Teligny, the admiral's son-in-law Briquemont and his sons, Plauviant, Bemy,

* Sully, liv. 1.

† D'Aubigné, Hist. Universelle, vol. 2, p. 19.

‡ Duncan, p. 121. § Ibid. **Sully.**

‖ Brantome, vol. 9, p. 424.

Clermont, Lavardin, Caumont de la Force, and many thousand more gallant gentlemen and Christian soldiers, formed the trophies of the fanatics. The zealous reformer of the University, La Rameé, hunted out in his hiding-place by one of his colleagues whose ignorance he had frequently exposed, was surrendered up to a gang of hired assassins.*

Nor did fanaticism alone sharpen the sword and direct the dagger. Defendants in actions at law assassinated the plaintiffs, debtors slaughtered their creditors, jealous lovers butchered their rivals.† It was a combination of religious frenzy, private vengeance, and public condemnation such as the world has never seen since the days of Sulla's proscriptions.

When the ghastly *saturnalia* had continued through a week, Pibrac, the king's advocate, waited upon his majesty to inquire whether he would be pleased to have the "joyous" event registered in Parliament, to perpetuate its memory.‡ The lawyer also begged that the "revels" might be discontinued. To both these propositions Charles acceded, and orders were given by sound of trumpet forbidding further murder.§

Shortly after proclamations were issued in which the king assumed the responsibility of the massacre, which he declared that he had ordered;‖ affirm-

* Ranke, p. 277. † Duncan, p. 114.
‡ Le Pape Derniére, liv. 29, p. 66. Browning, p. 145.
§ Anquétil, Esprit de la Ligue, vol. 2, p. 50.
‖ Ibid. Browning, p. 146.

ing that Coligny and his associates had plotted regicide; branding the admiral's memory as infamous, confiscating his property, degrading his family to plebeian rank, ordering his body—and if that could not be found, his effigy—to be drawn on a hurdle, hung up at the Place de Grève, and then fixed on the gibbet of Montfauçon. Coligny's portraits and arms were commanded to be destroyed wherever they could be seized, by the public executioner; and his residence at Chatillon-sur-Loing was to be razed, and the trees cut down to within four feet of the earth. The decree concluded by declaring that in future the anniversary of St. Bartholomew should be celebrated by public processions and *feus de joie*.*

It was perhaps honestly believed that these spiteful and abortive insults would affect the posthumous fame of the illustrious admiral, thrice honored by the stigmatization of such a king.

In the conduct of Charles IX. it is difficult to decide whether his atrocity or his dissimulation is most detestable. His own edicts, which closely followed one another, were ridiculously contradictory; and it is asserted by a Romish partisan that the day after the publication of the edict commanding tranquillity, he dispatched courtiers of note to the larger provincial cities with verbal orders to continue the *fête* despite the proclamation.†

These orders were quite unnecessary; the un-

* Browning, p. 146.

† Abbé Anquétil, Esprit de la Ligue, vol. 2, p. 52. Davila, liv. 5. De Thou, liv. 52.

slaked rage of the fanaticized multitude was not to be suppressed by a parchment fiat. From time to time the "Paris matins," as the massacre was called—a name suggested by the "Sicilian vespers"—were renewed; the tocsin sounded everywhere, and the *sans-culottes* stormed the houses of the Huguenots with undiminished ardor, robbing, murdering, and ravishing with the talismanic cry, "The king desires and commands it."*

The minds of men were filled with wild fantasies, which made them fear even themselves, and caused the very elements to appear fraught with terror. In after years, Henry IV. used openly to relate, that during the seven nights which immediately succeeded the slaughter, flocks of ravens perched upon the eaves of the Louvre, and croaked loudly and lugubriously, always commencing as the palace clock tolled twelve.†

Henry mentions another prodigy still more extraordinary: "For several days before the massacre commenced, I noticed, while playing at dice with the dukes of Alençon and Guise, that drops of blood clotted upon the table: twice I tried to wipe them off, when they reappeared; upon which, seized with horror, I quitted the game."‡

About eight days after the slaughter, Charles IX. summoned his Huguenot brother-in-law to his bedside at midnight in great haste. Henry found him as he had sprung from his couch, filled with

* Ranke, p. 277.

† Notes to the "Henriade." Duncan, p. 124. ‡ Ibid.

terror at a wild tumult of confused voices which resounded through the chamber. Henry himself imagined that he heard these sounds; they appeared like distant shrieks and howlings, mingled with the indistinguishable raging of a furious multitude, with wails and groans and smothered curses, as on the day of the massacre. Messengers were dispatched into the city to ascertain whether any new tumult had broken out, but these returned with the assurance that Paris was quiet, and that the commotion was in the air. Henry could never recall this scene—the affrighted courtiers huddled in the middle of the room, the half-distracted king, and the agonized wail of the phantom voices—without a horror that made his hair stand on end.*

Thus, for his share in the awful "pageant" of St. Bartholomew, the weak and too late affrighted king was tortured by the reproachful visions of his distempered imagination, compelled

> "To groan and sweat under a weary life,"

while conscience gradually stung him into an untimely grave.

* Ranke, p. 278.

CHAPTER XXVI.

THE TRIUMPH OF ROCHELLE.

THE massacre of St. Bartholomew created an unprecedented sensation throughout Christendom. Affrighted Europe, frozen with horror, stood on tiptoe gazing towards France, and asking with white lips, "What next?"

This was regarded as the signal for a general crusade against Protestantism.

Even the maiden queen of England was far from esteeming her insulated position to be a guarantee of safety. She was familiar with the tortuous morality of the Vatican. She had already experienced the character of Romish intrigues in the different manœuvres made to unseat her and install Mary queen of Scots in her throne. The pretended rupture between France and Spain, which had cozened the profound penetration of Coligny, vanished as soon as its object was accomplished. Elizabeth feared either an immediate attack from Philip II., or a general revolt of the papists in Great Britain.*

Fénélon was then the French ambassador at the court of St. James. Upon being summoned into Elizabeth's presence to present the dispatches of

* Hume, Hist. of England; Lingard, Hist. of Eng.; Browning, p. 152.

his king, which represented this monstrous act of treason against his subjects as the offspring of necessity, Fénélon blushed at being a Frenchman.* When he attended the hall of audience, he found the whole court arrayed in deep mourning; a gloomy silence was preserved; no friendly eye was turned towards him; every countenance was mournful and downcast. He approached the queen, who neither rose from her throne nor extended her hand, as was the courtesy of the times. Elizabeth read the documents with marked displeasure, and broke the stillness only to express her astonishment and indignation.†

A cry of horror rang through Germany and the Low Countries. Many writings were published, all denouncing the massacre, which was justly characterized as a compound of trickery, perfidy, and atrocity, exceeding in turpitude all that had ever been perpetrated in the annals of tyranny.‡

The court of France was the more sensitive to these animadversions, as negotiations were then pending to secure the crown of Poland for the duke of Anjou. It was feared that the prejudices and antipathies of the neighboring Germans might frustrate these expectations. Accordingly a deputation was sent to the Protestant princes to disarm their resentment.§

The pleas of justification were as various as they were absurd. Sometimes the whole transac-

* Condillac, tom. 13, p. 184. † Ibid. ‡ Duncan, p. 127.
§ Ibid. Davila, De Thou, Esprit de la Ligue, etc.

tion was defended by citing the odious maxim of Innocent III., more recently decreed by the Council of Constance and adopted by the Jesuits, that *no faith need be kept with heretics.** Some condemned in part, and extenuated in part; while others regretted the event, but denounced what they were pleased to term Coligny's regicidal intentions, borrowing the "buncombe" of their king. But these lame explanations, these limping apologies, were not able to stand on their own feet. Such absurdities produced but little effect in the outraged Netherlands and in angered Germany, where the assassins of the Huguenots were always held in undisguised abhorrence.†

There were two courts which received the news from Paris with acclamations. At Rome diabolical joy was manifested. Cannon were fired, bonfires blazed, the city was illuminated as if to celebrate a glorious achievement, and a solemn mass was intoned, at which pope Gregory XIII. personally officiated, with all the imposing ceremony of the papal church.‡ The cardinal of Lorraine, who was resident minister of France at the Vatican, questioned the messenger like a person informed beforehand;§ and a medal was struck, bearing on one side the head of Gregory XIII., and on the other the exterminating angel smiting the Huguenots, with the legend, "*Huguenotorum Strages,* 1572."‖

* Abbé Caveyrac. † Duncan, p. 127.

‡ Esprit de la Ligue, vol. 2, p. 65. Browning, p. 153.

§ Ibid. ‖ Ibid. Duncan, p. 128, note.

Thus Rome embalmed the massacre in barbarous Latin.

Yet despite his processions, his high masses celebrated in St. Peter's, and his honorary medals, it is said that the pontiff shed tears when he listened to the private recital of the excesses which smeared France with fraternal gore. "I cannot but weep," said Gregory, "when I think how many of the innocent must have suffered with the guilty."* The abbé Anquétil cites these words, and observes, "A sentiment of compassion not incompatible with those public demonstrations which policy required."† But it has been justly said that this is a dangerous morality which permits a jubilant exultation in public over a crime which is condemned in privacy, which distinguishes between the natural and the artificial man, and throws the mantle of hypocrisy over the spotless form of shrinking virtue.

It was at Madrid that the horrible crime was welcomed with the loudest plaudits. Philip II., the dark and gloomy bigot whose habitual demeanor was as frigid as the outside of a sepulchre, then showed for the first time that he could be sensible to joy. The sombre gravity which had been proof against Alva's cruelty, which had given no outward sign of pleasure when the great naval victory of Lepanto crippled the Ottoman, now quite forsook him, and his black heart gloated over the streams of blood which had reddened the streets of Paris. He made

* Brantome, vol. 8. † Esprit de la Ligue, tom. 1, p. 312.

magnificent presents to the courier who brought him the thrice-welcome news, wrote an autograph letter of congratulation to Charles IX., caroused with his courtiers, rejoiced in public, ordered *Te Deum* to be chanted, and summoned all the functionaries of the state to wait on him and tender their felicitations.*

The admiral of Castile read the French dispatches at table, thinking to increase the festivity of the occasion. "Prythee, good admiral, were Coligny and his friends Christians?" queried the young duke del Infantado, who was seated among the guests. "Undoubtedly," replied the admiral. "Why then," rejoined the young prince, "since they were Christians, were they butchered like wild beasts?" "Gently, gently, my prince," said the admiral; "know you not that war in France means peace in Spain?"†

But while agitated Europe was commenting thus variously upon the massacre of St. Bartholomew, France, plagued once again by those ills which Coligny so pathetically deprecated,‡ was plunged in civil war. The pacificatory results which the court crazily imagined would ensue, failed to appear; it was divinely fixed that the sowers of the wind should reap the whirlwind.

To slaughter the representatives of an idea even in hecatombs does not extinguish the principle,

* Brantome, vol. 8, p. 189; cited in Browning, p. 153, and in Duncan, pp. 128, 129. † Brantome, vol. 8, p. 189.

‡ Chap. 25, p. 350.

does not settle controverted points, does not weaken the right of private judgment. Moreover, the massacre of the Huguenots, extensive as it was, was very far from an extermination. Thousands survived the bloody deluge; and seeking asylums in the Netherlands, in the German duchies, and in England, they still had faith in God, and bided his good time.

Others, making no effort to quit France, fortified themselves in Montauban, in Nîmes, in Rochelle; and these three towns, forming themselves into a confederation, declared their union an independent republic—*imperium in imperio.**

"The court," says the abbé Crillon, "thought to have drowned Calvinism in the blood of its chief defenders; but that *hydra* soon regained its vigor."† The Huguenots were indeed so far from being crushed, that they speedily put eighteen thousand well equipped and devoted men-at-arms in the field, and became masters of a hundred towns.‡

The court made strenuous exertions to throttle the infant confederation. Three armies were levied. One, under La Chastre, was employed to reduce Sancerre; D'Amville Montmorenci, with another, undertook to choke the *émeute* in Languedoc, while the third, commanded by Villars, the new admiral of France, was sent into Guyeure. Besides

* Matthieu; Maimbourg, Hist. du Calvinisme; Duncan, p. 133.

† Vie de Crillon; cited in Browning, p. 150.

‡ Duncan, p. 133; Davila; De Thou.

these, there were the forces under Strozzy and Montluc's army.*

It was determined that Rochelle, now, as always before, the Huguenot citadel, should be conquered at all hazards. After various intrigues to foist upon the Rochelloise a Romanist governor, all of which were foiled by the keen inhabitants, the city was besieged by an immense army, officered by Strozzy and Bovin, accompanied by the duke of Anjou.†

Rochelle had long been one of the first maritime cities in France. It was well known to the early English merchants under the name of the "White Town," as they called it, from its appearance when the sun shone and was reflected from its rocky coasts. It was also much frequented by the Netherlanders. There were merchants among the Rochelloise who had each as many as ten ships at sea at one time.‡

Ever since the period of the English wars for the French succession, Rochelle had enjoyed extraordinary municipal franchises. It had by its own unaided power revolted from the English dominion; and for this heroism Charles V., in his customary manner, conferred upon the burghers valuable privileges; among others, that of independent jurisdiction in the city.§

Rochelle exhibited Protestant sympathies at an

* Mezeray; Browning; D'Aubigné, Hist. Univ.

† Davila, liv. 5. Browning, p. 163.

‡ Arcére, Histoire de Rochelle, vol. 1, p. 302. From the contemporary narrative of Barbot, advocate, and mayor in 1610.

§ Hist. de Rochelle, vol. 1, p. 208.

early period. Habituated to civil liberty, intelligent and self-reliant, the citizens were excellently well prepared to accept the Reformation; and when a Genevese preacher arrived there in 1556, on his return from an unsuccessful missionary enterprise to Brazil, he found no difficulty in building up a prosperous church among the Rochelloise. With the rough and hardy population, habituated to the sea, a teacher like this, who had boldly performed his voyage across the ocean to serve God, was sure of a generous reception. In all the reactionary changes and alternations of party through the civil wars, the faithful Rochelloise clung to the tenets of the Reformation, to Christ and their open Bibles, with unshaken firmness.*

The town had a fine harbor, and was naturally well fortified, while nature had been carefully reinforced by art. The garrison now consisted of fifteen hundred regular troops and about two thousand of the burghers, who belonged to the trainbands of the city.† These had been well disciplined in the frequent wars, and their ardor was at this time raised to fever heat by the enthusiasm of the women, who at once emulated and animated their husbands, fathers, and lovers.‡

The influence of the preachers was also very marked. Two among them, La Place and Denard, were remarkable for their ability, energy, and devotion. Their discourses marvellously strengthened

* Hist. de Rochelle, p. 208. Ranke, p. 242.

† Arcére, p. 419. Davila, liv. 5. ‡ Browning, p. 162.

the determination of the populace, whose humanity was appealed to by descriptions of the sufferings endured by their brothers in the faith; but they chiefly dwelt upon the paramount claims of religion to their utmost devotion. Denord was very eloquent; and he possessed such influence by his persuasive style, that he was called the pope of Rochelle.*

Although the town was not completely invested before the close of January, 1573, there were several assaults in December, 1572; one especially was upon a mill near the counter-scarp. As it could not easily be fortified, it served as a barbican or post of observation in the daytime, and at night it was left under guard of a single sentinel. Strozzy, considering that the position would be valuable to the Rochelloise, advanced by moonlight to attack it. The solitary sentinel, with a hardihood rarely equalled, resolved to defend the mill, although two culverines were pointed against it. He briskly fired on the assailants; and in order to deceive them, he called out to an imaginary troop of followers, as if encouraging them or giving orders, while an officer hallooed from the nearest bastion that he would soon be reinforced. The contest was too unequal to allow time for the arrival of the promised assistance, and to avoid the consequences of an assault, the sentinel demanded quarter for himself and men. It was granted; when lo, he walked out alone. Strozzy was so enraged at his presumption in pre-

* Browning, p 162. Arcére, p. 421.

tending to hold out, that he ordered his heroic prisoner to be hung for his insolence; but Biron interfered, and saved his life, at the same time condemning him to the galleys. Happily the courageous fellow managed to escape. His name has not been preserved, but Barbet says that he was a brazier of the isle of Rhé.*

The conduct of the court in the prosecution of the war was enigmatical. La Noué, a fearless soldier, a skilful captain, and a zealous Huguenot, had been absent in Hainault, whither he had been sent by Coligny to collect such intelligence as might be useful in that Netherland campaign which was never to occur, at the time of the "Paris matins;" thus he had escaped the massacre.† On his return to France, Charles received him with open arms. He gave La Noué the confiscated estate of his brother-in-law Teligny, and then entreated him to use his influence with the Rochelloise, whose commander he had been in the preceding war, to induce them to accept terms of peace.‡

At first La Noué peremptorily refused; but after a long struggle he yielded to the importunities of the king, and influenced both by anxiety for peace and the hope of serving his party, he accepted the delicate commission.§

Upon approaching Rochelle, La Noué halted in

* Arcére, p. 436; cited in Browning, pp. 162, 163.

† Brantome; Vie de Noué.

‡ Duncan, p. 135.

§ Browning, p. 161.

an adjacent village, and sent to the town announcing his errand and arrival.

The Rochelloise at once dispatched deputies to meet the distinguished soldier. Familiar with the character of the court, they feared that some treachery lurked beneath La Noué's overtures. "We have been invited," said they, "to confer with La Noué; but where is he? It is nothing that the gentleman to whom we speak resembles him in person, when in character he differs so widely from him." The soldier pointed proudly to his artificial arm, which had procured for him the *sobriquet* of *Bras de fer*, thus mutely to remind them of the limb which he had lost in their service.* But the deputies persisted that they remembered with gratitude their valued friend, but that they did not now recognize him.

Finding it impossible to treat with them, La Noué asked permission to enter Rochelle. The citizens received him joyfully, but would not listen to his proposals for peace. They left him to choose one of three alternatives, a safe passage to England, a residence in their city as a private individual, or the governorship of Rochelle. After some hesitation, he accepted the command.†

Strange to say, this step did not destroy the good opinion which Charles and the whole court party entertained of him; and it is a case almost

* "At the siege of Fontenay, in 1569, his left arm was so severely fractured by a musket-ball that amputation was necessary." Browning, p. 162, note.

† De Thou, liv. 53. D'Aubigné, Hist. Univ., vol. 2, p. 34.

unparallelled that, being commissioned by two contending parties, he preserved the confidence of both. In action, none more bravely joined in repelling the assailants; and at quiet intervals he never omitted to exhort the townspeople to listen to the king's offers—liberty of conscience, and full security for themselves. But the gallant Rochelloise were not satisfied with simple liberty to worship God for themselves: while their coreligionists went with shackled lips, they knew no peace. They insisted on treating for all the Huguenots; a demand to which the king would not accede.*

After a time La Noué, dissatisfied with his equivocal position, requested and obtained permission to quit Rochelle for an honorable retirement.†

The Rochelloise could not but regret the loss of their skilful chieftain, but they "bated no jot of heart or hope." The siege dragged through six bloody months, and still the Huguenot bastions remained impregnable. There was no order among the royalists, no unity, no combination of plans; jealousy and bickering poisoned their counsels;

> "And enterprises of great pith and moment,
> With this regard, their currents turned awry,
> And lost the name of action."

Anjou was wounded; Aumale was killed in the trenches; many others of rank also perished; an

* Browning, p. 162.

† Davila, liv. 5; De Thou, liv. 53; Arcére, etc.

epidemic broke out in the camp, and fifty thousand men died either by the sword or by disease.*

Anjou began to weary of a siege in which his reputation was frittered away; and as the negotiations for the crown of Poland wore an auspicious aspect, the elated prince forgot his duty to France, and passed his time with his favorites in planning schemes of pleasure and magnificence on his installation at Warsaw.†

The royal arms were as unsuccessful in other sections as before Rochelle;‡ and in July, 1573, the exhausted state of the court exchequer compelled the cessation of hostilities.§

On the 6th of July a treaty of peace was signed, which guaranteed to the confederated cities, Rochelle, Montauban, and Nîmes, the free exercise of their religion and their civic independence.‖ Thus the self-sacrificing efforts of the gallant Rochelloise to secure the enfranchisement, not only of themselves, but of their brothers in Christ, were crowned, through God's favor, with success.

In November, 1573, the duke of Anjou quitted France for his new kingdom of Poland, for that crown had at length been tendered him.¶ His departure was followed by the birth of a new conspiracy, which originated with the duke of Alençon, the

* Davila, liv. 5; De Thou, liv. 53; Arcére, etc. Duncan says forty thousand; Browning's estimate is twenty thousand.

† Davila, liv. 5.

‡ Brantome; D'Aubigné.

§ Duncan, p. 137.

‖ Ibid.; Arcére, p. 424; Brantome; Vie de Crillon, by his son.

¶ De Thou, and others.

Montmorencis, Biron, and Cossé, to which Navarre and Condé, both of whom had finally succumbed to the king's threats, and apparently united with the Roman church, also adhered.* But a variety of circumstances united to strangle this infant cabal in its cradle; and though its aim had been to effect certain needed reforms in the state, without any consideration for religion, it exploded in a laugh.

Charles IX., meanwhile, was every day drawing nearer to his grave. His last hours were embittered by that remorse which agonizes the conscience of the dying sinner. From the fatal eve of St. Bartholomew, he was observed to be always gloomy and wretched; he would groan involuntarily when the horrors which he had perpetrated were recalled. The king's physician, Ambrose Paré, though an outspoken Huguenot, possessed a greater share of his confidence than any other person; and to him he frequently unbosomed the tortures of his soul. "Ambrose," said Charles, "I know not what has happened to me these two or three past days; but I feel my mind and body to be terribly at enmity with each other. Sleeping or waking, the murdered Huguenots seem ever present to my eyes, with ghastly faces and weltering in their blood. I wish the innocent and the guiltless had been spared."†

It is pleasing to record these expressions of repentance, says an eminent historian, for they

* Mem. de Bouillon, p. 24; Vie de Mornay, liv. 1, p. 25; and others.

† Sully, tom. 1, p. 43.

show that humanity can never be wholly despoiled of her rights, and that outraged conscience will sting the most callous soul.

Henry of Navarre was present at the death of Charles IX. The expiring monarch called him to his side, and recommended his wife and infant daughter to his protection. At this solemn hour he appreciated this manly prince whom he had so bitterly outraged. He drew Henry to his pillow, and cautioned him to distrust ——; but he whispered the name so faintly, that none heard it but his kinsman into whose ear it went. Catharine however, who stood near by, guessed his meaning, for she said, "My son, you should not speak thus." "Why not?" queried the king; "it is perfectly true."*

On the 30th of May, 1574, Charles IX. expired, bathed in a bloody sweat, which oozed from every pore.†

* Duncan, Davila, and others. In the notes to the "Henriáde," it is said that Charles alluded to the duke of Anjou. Caget makes Catharine the object of the remark.

† Caget, Brantome, Duncan, De Thou.

The reason assigned for Charles' death by his physician was, his passion for hunting, when he incessantly blew the horn. "However," says Brantome, "it could not be driven out of some people's ideas that he was poisoned when his brother set out for Poland; and it was said, with the powder of some marine animal which makes the victim languish a long time, and then dwindle away till he becomes extinct like a candle." Brantome, vol. 15 p. 440.

"Marshal Bassompierre relates in his memoirs that, having cautioned Louis XIII. not to blow a horn too much, as it killed Charles IX., the king answered, 'You mistake: blowing the horn did not cause his death; but he quarrelled with the queen Catharine his mother, at Montceaux, and left her and went to Meaux.

Standing beside this awful death-bed, the solemn words of the apostle may be discerned written across the livid lineaments of the atrocious king: "THE WAGES OF SIN IS DEATH."

If he had not yielded to the persuasions of Marshal de Retz, who conducted him back to Montceaux, to join the queen his mother, he would not have died so soon.'" Mem. de Bassompierre, vol. 2, p. 21; cited in Browning, pp. 168, 169.

CHAPTER XXVII.

VICISSITUDES.

Upon the death of Charles IX., Catharine de' Medici, grown old and hag-like, but as energetic and unscrupulous as in her prime, dispatched a courier to Poland to inform Anjou that the vacant throne of France awaited him;* she then assumed the regency during the interregnum.†

In these troubled times, the slightest change at court was the signal for a cabal; so important an event as the demise of a monarch was certain to precipitate a revolution. France soon heaved in insurrection, and even private gentlemen made forays upon the royal strong-holds in the southern provinces.‡

This outbreak had no special religious significance, but was rather one of those periodical upheavals which occur at stated intervals in countries where justice and law are recklessly overridden by selfish, licentious, and abandoned despots. France through all this dismal epoch was emancipated from judicial forms; a strong hand and an unsheathed sword—these were the synonyms of government. The arbiter of all disputes, public or private, was the dagger, the bullet, or the poison-

* Mezeray, Abrégé Chron. Journal de Henri III.

† Brantome; Vie de Charles IX. ‡ Davila, liv. 5, p. 667.

er's bowl. To such a desperate strait had the Italian morality of Catharine de' Medici—the morality which looks upon all means as lawful by which power is obtained and preserved, which stands muttering the favorite Jesuitical shibboleth of the Vatican, "The end sanctifies the means"—reduced unhappy France. Catharine's ancestor, Cosmo de' Medici, had maintained his authority at Florence by severity, guile, and vengeance; should she scruple to use the weapons of so consummate a politician?

She now used all three. Her severity and ven geance were shown by the execution of La Malle and Coconnas;* by the arrest of Montgomery in Normandy, shortly followed by his beheadal, ostensibly for killing Henry II. in the tournament of 1559, but really because he was one of the most indefatigable and uncompromising of the Huguenots;† by the imprisonment of marshals Montmorenci and Cossé in the Bastile, and by the confinement of Alençon and Henry of Navarre in a grated chamber of the Louvre under careful surveillance.‡

Her guile was exhibited by the attempts which she made to wheedle those chiefs who wisely absented themselves from her dangerous vicinage, and especially by her efforts to cajole D'Amville Montmorenci, who, dissatisfied by the imprisonment of his brother the marshal, by the insult offered his

* Matthieu, Brantome, De Thou.

† Journal de Henri III. D'Aubigné.

‡ Brantome, vol. 1, p. 171. James, Life of Henry IV.

family in the assassination of Coligny, and by the exile of his house from court, aided, *sub rosa*, the insurgents in his government of Languedoc, while professing to quell the *émeute*.*

Such was the political situation when Henry III. returned to France.

Henry received intelligence of his brother's death within fourteen days after his arrival in Poland. The austere behavior of his new subjects made him regret, even in that brief period, the unchecked profligacy of Paris; and his companions, young libertines from twenty to twenty-five years of age, disgusted by the restraints of decency and virtue, longed to lap themselves once more in the licentious arms of Catharine's court beauties. In this desire the dandy king, who wore earrings,† and perfumed his person so that he smelled like a walking Cologne-bottle, fully shared. Fearing lest the Poles might remonstrate against his departure, one dark tempestuous night he quitted his palace at Cracow by stealth, thus abandoning as a fugitive a crown which he had gained by bribery and intrigue, and in two days he reached the frontiers of the German empire.‡

A little later Henry joined Catharine at Lyons.§ On arriving at his capital, he found the seeds of civil war again sown; and amid the hireling shouts of gratulation which hailed his presence, he heard

* Davila, liv. 5, p. 671. † Ranke, p. 307.
‡ Matthieu, liv. 7. De Thou, liv. 58.
§ Duncan, p. 143. Browning, p. 171.

the ill-suppressed murmurs of seditious discontent.

But discord was Catharine's element, she revelled in it: "I prefer to fish in troubled waters," said she.* She told Henry that it became the hero of Jarnac and Moncontour to crush sedition sword in hand; and the weak monarch succumbed to this subtle flattery, and adopted Catharine's pernicious counsel. Siege was at once laid to one of the insurgent towns—Livron.†

At this juncture died the cardinal of Lorraine,‡ whose infamous policy and vaulting ambition had bathed France in blood. He possessed great talents, which he devoted to the aggrandizement of his family, careless of the honor or advantage of his country. He was the centre of a circle, and his relatives bounded its circumference; no thoughts of national utility ever, even transiently, entered into his conceptions of state policy. He made use of religion as the ladder of his ambition;§ he embroiled the various members of the royal family with each other, while he directed their concentrated fury against the best subjects in the kingdom. He was a priest without piety, a statesman without honor, a libertine by practice, a hypocrite by habit, avaricious, unfeeling, treacherous; concealing, under an engaging air of simulated candor, a black heart, malignant and revengeful.‖

* Brantome. † Sully, liv. 1.

‡ Brantome, vol. 8, p. 148.

§ "He availed himself of piety for purposes of grandeur." Brantome, vol. 8, p. 149. ‖ Duncan, p. 148.

Ere the court recovered from the sensation produced by the cardinal's death, the chiefs of the insurrection met at Millaud and bound themselves by oath to two distinct articles: the political malcontents covenanted never to lay down arms until the Huguenots were secured in the complete and free exercise of their religion; the Huguenots pledged themselves neither to sign a peace, nor to consent to a truce, till the liberation of the captive marshals Montmorenci and Cossé.*

Meantime the feeble garrison of Livron defied the utmost exertions of the royal army, and Henry himself went to the camp, accompanied by the queen mother and the court, expecting that his presence would insure the speedy fall of the stubborn town. He was mistaken; when the besieged learned of his arrival before their walls, they crowded to the ramparts and hurled the bitterest insults into his ears. "Cowards," they cried, "assassins, what are you come for? Do you think to surprise us in our beds, and to murder us, as you did the admiral? Show yourselves, minions. Come, prove to your cost that you are unable to stand even against our women."† Thus Henry was literally hooted from the walls of Livron; he lost his heroic laurels, and raising the siege in a great passion, retired ignominiously to Paris.‡

The court had scarcely settled itself in the Louvre, ere it was startled by the news that Alen-

* Davila, liv. 5. Brantome, liv. 9. † De Thou, liv. 60.
‡ Mezeray, Abrégé Chron.

çon, the king's brother and heir apparent to the throne, had escaped his mother's surveillance and joined the insurgents.* Alençon, whose only importance consisted in his position, for he was utterly destitute of talent and honesty, had been angered by the king's refusal to bestow upon him the lieutenant-generalship of the kingdom, which Henry withheld because he knew his brother's turbulent incompetence.

Still, Alençon was a prince of the blood, and his accession to the opposition gave them increased strength. The confederates had nominated Condé, who had quitted Paris some time before, and was now in Germany recruiting an army for the Huguenots, as their leader, in the absence of Navarre, still held at court; but with rare good sense, when Condé heard that Alençon had joined his party, he conferred the nominal leadership upon that prince, satisfied with retaining its essence.†

Soon the confederates had a large army in the field; Condé was rapidly advancing at the head of his German mercenaries; and Thoré Montmorenci, who commanded the advance guard of the main body, met the dukes of Guise and Mayence, brothers, and two of the ablest captains of the age, at the village of Dormans. The forces at once joined battle, and after a sanguinary contest, Thoré was routed.‡ It was here that Guise obtained the wound in

* Davila, liv. 6. Mem. de Nevers, vol. 1, p. 97.

† Ibid. Mezeray, Browning.

‡ Mem. de Bouillon, p. 137. Browning, p. 177.

the face which gained for him the surname of *Le Balafré*.*

Alençon was soon surrounded by a number of distinguished gentlemen, among whom were Turenne† and La Noué. Ere long the party was still further reinforced by the arrival of Henry of Navarre, who escaped from Paris by a stratagem, to the chagrin of Catharine and the rage of Henry III.‡ At Tours, Navarre renounced popery, protested against his abjuration of Calvinism, in 1572, as wrung from him in duress, and announced his determination to battle for his faith.

The Huguenots were jubilant, and they speedily put fifty thousand men-at-arms in the field.§

Suddenly Alençon, true to his weak and perfidious nature, wavered, then went over to the court. Soured by the superior influence of Navarre and Condé in the confederate camp, he fell an easy victim to his mother's wiles.‖

Shortly after Alençon's defection, both parties wearied of the war, and a treaty of pacification was signed.¶ The Huguenots again wrung from the reluctant court those concessions so often granted and so invariably infringed. But the terms now won were more favorable than any heretofore ob-

* Davila, liv. 6.

† Henry de la Tour, Viscount Turenne, afterwards the duke of Bouillon, nephew of the constable Montmorenci, a young man of rare talent. Browning.

‡ D'Aubigné, Hist. Univ., vol. 2, p. 188. Sully, liv. 1. Matthieu, liv. 7.

§ Browning, p. 179.

‖ Davila, liv. 6.

¶ This was dated May 14, 1576.

tained: amnesty for the past; full liberty of conscience; the free exercise of religion, without exceptions of time or place; the power of erecting schools and colleges, of convening synods, of performing marriage, of administering the sacraments according to the reformed creed; the eligibility of Huguenots to office; the liberation of all prisoners of state; a promise to establish a court of justice in each parliament, composed jointly and equally of Huguenots and Romanists: these were among the chief clauses of the treaty, a treaty which was characterized at the time as "not a pacification, but a surrender at discretion of the court."*

Yet despite Brantome's epigram, the Huguenots committed a gross blunder in signing the pacification. With their experience of the hollowness and treachery of Catharine and the king, it seems strange that they should not have known that concessions so ample would never be executed. Catharine's well-known maxim was, "Divide and govern." When the wily queen was hard pressed, she negotiated a peace, and then went deliberately to work to break its most solemn ratifications.

Concerning this treaty, Davila openly confesses that the court never intended to fulfil their engagements; that all they aimed at was the withdrawal of Alençon from the coalition, and the return of the mercenaries to Germany.† And Sully, referring to the queen mother, says, "She offered more than we thought that we could demand; promises cost that

* Brantome, vol. 8. † Davila, liv. 6, p. 672.

artful princess nothing. Thus all things fell out as she wished; for in making this peace she had nothing in view but the disunion of her enemies."*

Sully and Davila were right: the treaty of pacification was scarcely ratified before it was pronounced null and void; not one of its articles was ever executed.† It produced an armistice, rather than a peace; both parties rested upon their arms. But the apparent "surrender of the court at discretion" was in fact another trophy won by the vicious statesmanship of Catharine de' Medici.

* Sully, liv. 1.

† Ibid. Duncan, p. 155.

CHAPTER XXVIII.

THE LEAGUE.

THE rose-water sprinkled upon the glowing embers of the late civil strife was so far from quenching the fire, that the flame threatened at every moment to blaze again with increased fury.

All parties were dissatisfied: the Huguenots, because they saw that they had bartered success for a worthless parcel of parchment promises, which the government had no intention of enforcing; the Romanists, because they thought that their creed had been compromised by even the empty assent to tolerant concessions, whether made in good faith or from hypocrisy; the people at large, because their taxes were vastly increased, while the court spent their substance in riot and debauchery.*

But two years had elapsed since Henry's accession, yet he was clothed in dishonor. The Polish diet had expelled him from their throne with the most degrading marks of infamy; and he now lounged in the court of France, occupied in seductions, in inventing new forms of etiquette, and in weighty consultations with his tailor upon the cut of a coat or the tie of a cravat,† while his government was crumbling into dust. He was hated by

* Sully, liv. 1. Mem. de Nevers, vol. 1.

† Ranke, p. 307. Browning, p. 182.

the reformers on account of his vices and his breaches of faith; he was despised by the Romanists for his foppish imbecility.* Thus the substance of royalty had departed from him, only the shadow remained. Openly bearded by the Huguenots, while the reactionists, led by the house of Guise, secretly conspired against his nominal authority, this miserable representative of the august Valois dynasty saw none but enemies abroad and rebels at home. His only friends, if that sacred name can be applied to such characters, were young libertines, the companions of his profligacies, whose extravagance and license put the seal to his unpopularity.

Not the slightest dependence was placed upon the unsteady royal popinjay. On behalf of his party, Condé wrote to prince Cassimir requesting him to remain near the frontier with his *lanzknechts*, as great apprehension was felt that the pacification would not be observed by the court.†

On their part, the ultramontanists, incited by the gold of the Spanish king, and filled with the venom of religious hate, longed and watched and plotted for the dismal tocsin to ring in once more the "Paris matins." They petitioned the king to revoke the recent edict; they conjured him to exterminate the heretics.

Henry's will to comply with this congenial requisition was as good as that of the fiercest fanatic in

* Duncan, p. 155.

† Hist. des Derniers Troubles, vol. 1, p. 6.

his kingdom; nothing would have pleased him better than to figure as the hero of another St. Bartholomew. But he lacked *stamina;* when weighty obstacles were to be surmounted, his unstable and weak nature succumbed. Wary and dissembling as he was, he made use of an expression which showed the wish of his heart, immediately after signing the obnoxious treaty. The Huguenots of Rouen had just resumed the exercise of their worship, and the cardinal of Bourbon, accompanied by several counsellors, went to their rendezvous to prevent the service. He entered without difficulty, but when he mounted the pulpit and began to speak, the evangelicals quitted the building and left him to address empty benches. Some one told the king that the cardinal had dispersed the Huguenots of Rouen by a flourish of his cross and banner. "Is 't so?" cried Henry; "would to God they could be as easily driven from the other towns, were it even necessary to add the holy-water basin."*

But the ultramontanists distrusted Henry's pluck, and they despised his lack of vigor. Therefore they determined to choose a fitter leader, and to league themselves together by an oath to extirpate heresy, and to exclude the Huguenots from participation in the government.†

Such, in its inception, was the famous League; such was its abhorrent and fanatic object. Later as we shall see, it assumed an additional phase.

* Amirault, Vie de la Noué, p. 191; cited by Browning, p. 181.

† Anquétil, Esprit de la Ligue. Cayét, Brant., Brown. etc.

There is a little cabinet in the castle of Joinville which has long been pointed out as the chamber in which the league was formed. There, in 1576, there were assembled Tassis and Moreo, two delegates of the king of Spain, the dukes of Guise and Mayenne, who also represented the cardinal of Guise and the dukes D'Aumale and Elbœuf; and besides these, a delegate of the cardinal of Bourbon. A covenant was drawn up and signed, Henry duke of Guise was appointed chief of the association,* and under the pretext of religion, a terrible, secret, and atrocious society was launched which, like the Jesuits who reinforced it, plotted in the dark, used all weapons of deceit and fraud and force, and ere long drenched Europe in blood.†

* Anquétil, Esprit de la Ligue. Cayét, Brantome, Browning, etc. Ranke, p. 340.

† The *ipsissima verba* of the League, translated, were as follows:

"In the name of the most holy Trinity, Father, Son, and Holy Ghost, our only true God, to whom be glory and honor. The covenant of the princes, lords, and gentlemen of the Romish religion ought to be made, and hereby is made, to establish the law of God in its purity, and to restore and settle his holy service according to the form and manner of the apostolic Roman church, abjuring and renouncing all errors contrary to it.

"Secondly, it is made to preserve king Henry, the third of that name, and his successors the most Christian kings, the state, honor, authority, duty, service, and obedience owed by his and their subjects, as the same are contained in the articles which shall be presented to him in the assembly of states, and which he swore and promised to observe at the time of his consecration and coronation, with a solemn protestation not to do any act against what shall be ordained and settled by the state.

"Thirdly, to restore unto the provinces of this kingdom, and to those other states which are under it, those ancient rights, pre-eminences, liberties, and privileges, which existed in the time of

As in antiquity Athens cannot be thought of without Sparta, Rome without Carthage, so in the sixteenth and seventeenth centuries France can

Clovis, the first most Christian king, or others better and more profitable—if any such can be found—under the same protection.

"In case there be any impediment, opposition, or rebellion against what has been premised, *be it from whom it will, or proceed from whencesoever it may,* those who enter into this covenant shall be bound and obliged to employ their lives and fortunes to punish, chastise, and prosecute those who may attempt to disturb it or prevent its execution, and shall never cease their endeavors till the aforesaid things be done and perfected.

"In case any of the confederates, their friends, vassals, or dependents, be oppressed, molested, or questioned for this cause, *be it by whom it will,* they shall be bound to employ their goods, estates, and persons, to take vengeance upon those who shall have so molested them, either by way of justice or force, without any exceptions of persons whatsoever.

"If it shall come to pass that any man, after uniting himself by oath to this confederacy, shall desire to depart from it, or separate himself on any pretence or excuse—which God forbid—such violators of their own consciences shall be punished both in their bodies and goods, by all means that can be thought of, as enemies of God and rebels and disturbers of the public peace; nor shall the aforesaid associates be liable to be questioned for any punishment they may inflict, either in public or private.

"The said associates shall likewise swear to yield ready obedience and faithful service unto that HEAD who shall be appointed; to follow and obey him, and to lend all help, counsel, and assistance, as well for the entire conservation and maintenance of this league, as for the ruin of all who may oppose it, without partiality or exception of persons; and those who fail or depart from it shall be punished by the authority of the HEAD, and according to his orders, to which every confederate shall be obliged to submit himself.

"All Romanists of the several towns, villages, and cities shall be secretly advertised and warned by the particular governors of places to enter into this league, and concur in the finding of men, arms, and other necessaries, every one according to his adjudged

neither be comprehended nor understood without the counterpart of the Spanish monarchy.

What was it that Francis I. and Charles V. contended for in their time? The emperor sought to realize that universal supremacy which was connected in theory with his title; Francis maintained the idea of France. There was now no danger to be apprehended from the Capuchin emperor; but his son and successor, powerful in the possession of extensive territories and the gold of the Indies, renewed the claim to Spanish predominance, and stepped forth himself as the champion of the ancient faith against its assailants. In the adherents of the Vatican he met with warm supporters, by whose assent he assumed the position and authority of head of the reactionists generally throughout Europe.

The League then was largely his idea, and

condition and ability. All the confederates shall be prohibited from stirring up any discord, or entering into any dispute among themselves, without leave of the HEAD, to whose arbitrament all discussions shall be referred, as also the settlement of all differences, as well in matters of goods as of good name; and all of them shall be obliged to swear in the manner and form following: 'I swear by God the Creator—laying my hand upon the holy gospel—and under pain of excommunication and eternal damnation, that I enter into this holy Roman league according to the form of that writing which has now been read to me, and that I do faithfully and sincerely enter into it either to command or obey, as I shall be directed; and I promise on my life and honor to continue in it to the last drop of my blood, and not to depart from it or transgress it for any command, pretence, excuse, or occasion which by any means whatsoever may be represented to me.'" Davila, liv. 6, p. 223, et seq.

Guise became merely the lieutenant of Philip II. when he assumed the nominal leadership.*

The emissaries of the new society circulated the forms of the covenant with equal celerity and secrecy: at first no proselytes were made; only papists of known zeal and discretion signed the rolls and took the oath, for the association did not mean to strike a hasty blow; they intended rather to perfect their organization at leisure, and to await an auspicious moment for the manifestation of their prodigious power.†

Thus the League lay coiled and torpid, like a huge serpent, ready to spring upon the victim when events should warm it into vicious life.

Meantime, towards the close of the year 1576, the states-general were convened at Blois;‡ France was agitated; Henry had just learned by accident§ of the formation of the League; the Huguenots were clamorous for the enforcement of the edict of pacification; the papists were mutinous; chaos seemed come again. The king was alarmed. The League boldly demanded war; he felt himself too weak to resent their insolence; yet to yield was in effect an abdication. In an unhappy moment Henry determined himself to head the League,‖ to become the chief of a faction, instead of the sovereign of a nation.

* Ranke, p. 305.

† Anquétil, Esprit de la Ligue. Maimbourg, Hist. de la Ligue

‡ Cayét, liv. 1, p. 10. De Thou, liv. 63.

§ Browning, p. 183. Maimbourg, Hist. de la Ligue, vol. 1.

‖ De Thou, Péréfixe, La Grain.

This manœuvre disconcerted the confederates; but instantly recovering their equanimity, they dispatched the duke of Guise to visit the king, and enjoin him as a member of the holy union to annul the last edict and proclaim war.* It was however desirable that, before the sword was unsheathed, Navarre, Condé, and D'Amville should be summoned to obey the king, in order that on their refusal to recant, the responsibility of the ensuing strife might appear to rest on their heads.†

This was done. Navarre declared that "if God opened his eyes that he might see his error, not only would he immediately abjure it, but he would contribute his utmost efforts to abolish heresy altogether,"‡ a speech which has been well said to be characteristic of the epoch. Navarre was at the time in arms for liberty of conscience, and yet declared his readiness to become a persecutor if a change took place in his opinions, a remark which actually justified the leaguers in their course, and which cried Amen to the tortuous diplomacy of Catharine de' Medici.

The deputies to Condé and D'Amville received this answer: "We ask only for peace; let the promises given us be fulfilled, and all will be well; besides, we do not acknowledge your states-general, and we protest against every resolution there made to our prejudice."§

* De Thou, Péréfixe, La Grain.

† Mem. de Nevers, vol. 1, p. 451. ‡ Ibid.

§ De Thou, liv. 63.

Towards the close of March, 1577, the war recommenced; the campaign, however, was a tedious one; little was accomplished on either side; it was a war of skirmishes. The League, persuaded that their policy dictated patient preparation, and convinced that they were not yet fit to take the field, dissembled; and Henry, true to his weak nature, speedily tired of the contest when no longer hounded on by bolder rogues. The consequence was the conclusion of a new treaty at Bergerac, in September, 1577,* which was immediately followed by the edict of Poictiers,† confirming, in all essential respects, the tolerant enactments of the past.‡

Peace—if a society torn by feuds and cursed by incessant *émeutes,* can be said ever to enjoy that blessing—now reigned through three years.

In 1580, a wanton insult offered by king Henry to the queen of Navarre, by a brother to a sister, again kindled war. Henry, impelled by his love of mischief or by his dislike of Navarre, wrote that prince that Turenne was criminally intimate with Margaret.§

Both Turenne and the queen were naturally indignant at this insult, with which Navarre acquainted them by showing the royal letter, and they spared no pains to precipitate another revolution.

This contest had no religious basis; yet such was the peculiarity of the times, that in any trouble

* Davila, liv. 6.
† Ibid. Mem. de Nevers.
‡ Browning, p. 188.
§ D'Aubigné, vol. 2, p. 345.

the chiefs of either party could depend upon the support of their partisans, who took it for granted that the object for which they battled was just.

After raging fiercely for some months, the "Lover's war," as it was called on account of its origin, was concluded by another pacification, and weary France again rested for a moment from internecine butchery.*

But the kingdom had undergone so many and such violent convulsions, had become so habituated to martial strife, that a parchment treaty had no power to tranquillize it. The civil wars had created a distaste for the ordinary occupations of life; a large portion of the population, demoralized by the camp, hated whatever made for peace; the country swarmed with *banditti;* bravos, ready to assassinate or to plunder, awaited employment in the open market-place.† Such was France under the imbecile sceptre of Henry III.; but while the papists, in the excess of their fanatic zeal, did not scruple to charge these crying evils to the prevalence of heresy, the Huguenots, with better philosophy, attributed them to the wickedness of France, abandoned to licentious despots and the whims of fanaticism; no text was more frequent upon their lips than this: "Righteousness exalteth a nation; but sin is a reproach to any people."

* Browning, p. 193.

† Mezeray, De Borg, Life of Henry IV., Vie de Henri III., etc.

CHAPTER XXIX.

THE WAR OF THE THREE HENRIES.

IN June, 1584, the duke of Alençon died at Château-Thierry, a castle on his *apanage*, and his demise opened a vast field to those intriguers who were fomenting civil war.*

Instantly the torpid League sprang to its feet, full of Satanic energy, and prepared for action. In the reigning monarch the house of Valois became extinct. Henry had been married ten years, but he was childless; by the death of Alençon, Navarre of the line of Bourbon became next heir to the throne. This the Salic law decreed; this abstract right not the fiercest bigot questioned.† But the Navarrese prince was a Huguenot; and the champions of the Vatican in France appealed through the League to the intolerant passions of the people, affirming that the accession of a Calvinist monarch would necessitate the overthrow of Latin orthodoxy.‡

The chiefs of the League were again convened at Guise's castle of Joinville, and to this rendezvous Philip of Spain also sent his delegates. A pronunciamento was agreed on, and shortly published.§ Proceeding from the fundamental princi-

* Brantome, Duncan, Mem. de Nevers.

† Pasquier; Browning, p. 196. ‡ Ibid. Duncan, p. 174.

§ Mem. de Nevers, Davila, Hist. de la Ligue.

ple that a heretic could not be king of France, this paper declared the League to be of one mind, that the sceptre should not pass to the king of Navarre, but to his uncle the cardinal of Bourbon, a younger brother of that renegade Antony, who married Jane d'Albrét, and from whom these claims were derived.* The cardinal, by his plenipotentiary, joined the union and adopted the shibboleth. Further, the League was announced to be intended to effect the extirpation of the Huguenots not only in France, but also in the Netherlands.† The king of Spain promised for the first year a subsidy of one million scudi.‡ The French princes, on their part, regarding themselves as already clothed in the royal purple, bound themselves to renounce the alliance with the Ottoman Porte; to give up the system of piracy carried on in the West Indian waters; to restore Cambray, wrung from Philip by the valor of the Protestants; and to assist Spain in the subjugation of the Netherlands.§

Such, in its main features, was the extraordinary treaty concluded between the traitorous subjects of Henry III. and the Spanish government, without the consent, nay, without the knowledge of the king of France.‖

When Henry learned of the mischief which was brewing, he was prodigiously startled. One of his favorites, Epernon, was hastily dispatched to Henry

* Ranke, p. 340. † Davila, liv. 6. Duncan, p. 176.
‡ Hist. de la Ligue. § Ibid. Maimbourg.
‖ De Thou, liv. 81. Villeroy, vol. 3.

of Navarre, to offer him the undisputed succession, provided he would return to the court, renounce his creed, and reconcile himself to Rome.*

The League, in its turn, was now startled. Matthieu, a Jesuit, who was nicknamed the *courier of the League*, was sent to Rome to procure the pontiff's dispensation for the action of the confederation, a move which looked to the murder of the king.† But Gregory XIII. steadily refused to sign any document, while his verbal answers were always expressed with non-committal craft.‡

In the mean time Epernon had been received by Henry of Navarre with courtesy. The Navarrese prince hesitated. By renouncing Calvinism he smoothed his path to the throne, but he distrusted the sincerity of the court: he feared to exchange his present independence for a gorgeous imprisonment; nay, more, should the Guises regain the ascendency, his assassination was certain. He was also much influenced by the recent conduct of his wife, who was separated from him, and who led a licentious life in Auvergne. He felt that he would be obliged to receive her back to secure the sincere friendship of the queen mother and the king, if any such quality as sincerity could be expected from Henry III., whose other name was duplicity, and from Catharine, whose synonym was treachery.

These considerations made him finally resolve neither to embrace Romanism nor to return to the

* Duncan, p. 179.
† Duncan, Davila, D'Aubigné.
‡ Ibid.

court; but he offered to assist the king against the League, and declared himself open to conviction in religion.*

Just as Henry III. received this answer, and stood deeply lamenting the failure of the negotiation, the leaguers, who had assembled at Gaillon, in the neighborhood of Rouen, published a manifesto declaring war without awaiting the king's assent, artfully blending together the interests of religion, the privileges of the nobles, and the oppressions of the poor; demanding the definitive revocation of all tolerant edicts, and dictating the expulsion of the Huguenots from France.†

The emissaries of the League then seized every strong-hold which they could surprise;‡ while Guise, at the head of an insignificant army, rendezvoused at Chalons, and anxiously awaited reinforcement.§

The king published a counter-declaration, in which he appeared rather to justify his imbecile government than to condemn the rebellion. "Forgetting the arms which nature and necessity presented to him, he had recourse to pen and paper," says a satirical contemporary; "but so tamely that you would say he did not dare to name his enemy, and that he resembled a man who complains without saying who has beaten him."‖

* Duncan, p. 181; Hist. de la Ligue; Vie de Henri III., etc.

† De Thou, liv. 81. Davila, liv. 7. This paper was dated March 13, 1585.

‡ Maimbourg, Hist. de la Ligue.

§ Ibid. Browning, p. 201.

‖ Hist. des Derniers Troubles, liv. 1, p. 20.

The king's appeal produced no effect; not a sword was drawn.

Had Henry possessed either courage or energy, he might have easily dispersed Guise's nucleus force. Indeed Guise himself said to Nangis, when that gentleman asked him what he should do if the king assailed him, "Retire as quickly as possible to Germany, and await a more favorable opportunity."*

But when fear chills the heart and paralyzes the arm of a sovereign, all is lost; the audacity of revolt increases with impunity. Could Henry have exhibited the conqueror of Jarnac, he would have insured tranquillity. But anxious to appease the insurgents, not to quell them, he entreated the queen mother to meet Guise, assure him of his friendship, and accede to the terms of the League, rather than disturb the peace of France.†

Lyons, Bourges, Orleans, Angers, had succumbed to his feeble army, and Guise, emboldened by success, met Catharine with an air of bravado, and with rare insolence actually dictated a peace to his king. A request, signed by himself and the cardinal of Bourbon, was presented, demanding an edict for the extirpation of heresy, the forcible expulsion of the Huguenots from the kingdom, a pledge from Henry to adhere to the League, and to renounce the protection of Geneva.‡

* Mem. de Beauvais Nangis.

† Hist. des Derniers Troubles; Mezeray.

‡ Davila, De Thou.

This "request" was at once adopted, and the royal imbecile signed the ignominious treaty at Nemours on the 7th of July, 1585.* From this hour Henry III. ceased to be *de facto* king of France; he was merely the nominal chief of a religious faction. He himself felt this, and he once said with a touch of pathos, "'T is true that I wear the crown, but Guise is the king of hearts."† The king now came to hate Guise with the peculiar virulence of a weak and treacherous nature, and he determined to avail himself of the first opportunity to avenge his humbled honor by the stiletto of a bravo. "This overpowerful subject," muttered he, "must be swept from my path."

The Huguenots received the intelligence of this fatal treaty with grief and consternation. The king of Navarre was astounded. Condé's troops had been largely disbanded; the party were unprepared for war; the fiercest harry yet organized, sanctioned by the king, was about to swoop upon them. So terrible was Navarre's agony, says the historian Matthieu, that "his mustachios became white in a night."‡

But unlike the king, his energy and fertility of resource were not to be paralyzed by danger, either menaced or present. With Titanic zeal he labored to save imperilled Christianity. Negotiations with Protestant powers abroad were opened; the home partisans of reform were summoned to assemble;

* Matthieu. † Ranke, p. 366.

‡ Matthieu, Hist. de France, liv. 8, p. 501.

Condé went into Germany to recruit his *lanzknechts;* Navarre published an appeal to Christendom, in which he complained of being stigmatized as a relapsed heretic, a persecutor of the church, a disturber of the state, false and malicious libels on his character invented to deprive him of the royal succession; declared that he had been compelled to appear to abjure his faith on the St. Bartholomew to save his life; that he was open to conviction, but that efforts had always been made to destroy rather than convert him: he repudiated the accusation of persecuting the papists, showing that many of that creed held high offices in his hereditary domains, and that others were constantly in attendance upon his person: he averred that he had never molested the persons nor touched the revenues of the Romish priests; offered to place all his fortresses in the king's hands if the Guises and their adherents would imitate his example; denounced the ambition of the house of Lorraine; and concluded by giving the lie to his enemies, and offering to decide the quarrel with the duke of Guise according to the chivalric habit of the times, by combat, either singly, or with two, ten, or twenty on a side.*

This manifesto produced a profound sensation.† Liberal Europe cried, Amen. His friends displayed increased devotion; the indifferent joined him, partly from admiration for his fortitude, partly because

* Cayet, liv. 1, p. 8. Browning, p. 202. Mem. de Duplessis.
† Ibid.

they were clear-sighted enough to perceive that he was the victim of a base and unprincipled faction, who, to compass their ambitious views, would hazard laying France prostrate at the feet of Spain.

Small detachments of cavaliers reached Navarre from time to time, the precursors of more formidable levies; and this prince, who was supposed by many to be preparing for flight, was soon strong enough to attack the overconfident League.*

Thus Navarre was supported by his own indomitable heroism, by the enthusiasm of his party, by the prayers of the righteous, and by God's all-powerful hand.

The contest at once commenced. It was called, *The War of the three Henries*†—Henry III. at the head of the royalists, Henry of Guise at the head of the leaguers, and Henry of Navarre at the head of the Huguenots.

At this critical juncture pope Gregory XIII. died. He had steadily refused to identify himself with the League, or to put the Bourbon princes out of the pale of the church: "I will leave the door open for their conversion," said he.‡ He was succeeded by Felici Paretti, a fanatical friar of the Franciscan order, who assumed the tiara under the title of Sextus V.§ This pontiff had no scruples; he excommunicated Navarre and Condé, stigmatizing them as relapsed heretics; as such he declared them incapable of the royal succession; he de-

* Duncan, p. 191. † Ibid. ‡ Ibid., p. 196.

§ Ranke, Hist. of the Popes. Hist. des Derniers Troubles.

prived them of their estates, absolved their subjects and vassals from allegiance, and menaced with anathema all who should thenceforth serve them either in a civil or military capacity.*

Unawed by this *brutum fulmen*, the Bourbon princes preserved their serenity, and even posted on the walls of the Vatican a protest against the anathema.†

But this authoritative voice from the "holy of holies" at Rome consolidated the League, confirmed many doubting consciences, and gave Guise *prestige*. Even Catharine was awed into the cessation of her machinations. Croaking, "Divide and govern," she had ventured to negotiate with Navarre, and to give him covert aid; for she feared lest Guise might be too successful, and thereby destroy the political balance. Guise discovered this move, and shaking his finger menacingly, bade the withered old diplomat beware of approaching the abyss of excommunication; and the queen mother shrank back affrighted.‡

The League was jubilant; the sanction of the pontiff was the text of every Jesuit sermon. The fanatics declared that victory was sure to follow a banner blessed by the vicegerent of God; and the zealots already in imagination celebrated the extirpation of heresy.

Still, on the whole, the moral effect of this insolent interference was favorable to the Huguenots.

* Browning, p. 204. † Duncan, pp. 196, 197.

‡ Ranke, Civil Wars and Monarchy in France.

The calmer and more reflecting members of the body politic deprecated the pope's presumption. They perceived that it struck at the civil franchises of the kingdom, and might be twisted into a precedent dangerous to the privileges of the Gallican church.*

The pontiff's fiat did indeed detach numerous partisans from the Huguenot banner, but these were of the lowest and most ignorant class. As a compensation, many gentlemen of rank openly adhered to Navarre; while others who did not choose publicly to join him, stood neutral, or favored him in secret. The gauntlet he had flung down to Guise and which the chief of the League had not ventured to take up, his defiance of the pope, the severe misfortunes which he had incurred, all combined to make Navarre an object of interest, of admiration, of pity; they gained him the active sympathy of the good, the generous, and the heroic.

The Swiss cantons sent deputies to Henry to intercede for the Huguenots.† The Germans, animated by the eloquence of the famous Theodore Beza, who had pleaded the cause of the Reformation before Charles IX. in happier years, armed in defence of their coreligionists, and enthusiasm gave to their movements the character of a Protestant crusade.‡

Henry of Navarre took the field: under such a leader, small bodies equalled armies. He marched

* Duncan, p. 197. † Maimbourg, Hist. du Calvinisme.
‡ Davila, Péréfixe, Duncan.

from victory to victory. Fired by his spirit, his troops captured fortresses, subjugated provinces, and baffled the most subtle tactics of Mayenne.*

On the 20th of October, 1587, the battle of Coutras was fought. The royalists, commanded by the duke of Joyeuse, were confident, well equipped, and ten thousand strong.†

The Huguenot army was composed of four thousand infantry and two thousand five hundred cavalry; but the disparity of numbers was balanced by discipline. Joyeuse was a courtier; Navarre was a soldier. The duke's officers were dressed in richly ornamented costume, and their helmets were adorned by brilliant plumes; the Huguenots displayed naught but iron, and arms rusty with rain. It was the army of Darius against that of Alexander.

Navarre drew up his men-at-arms in the form of a crescent; Condé and the count of Soisson were on his right, Turenne was upon his left. "My friends," cried the king, "behold a prey much more considerable than any of your former booties; this is a bridegroom who has still the nuptial present in his pocket, and all the chief courtiers with him."‡ Then turning to Condé and Soisson, he said, "All that I shall observe to you is, that you are of the house of Bourbon, and, please God, I will show you that I am your elder brother."§

Just as Navarre concluded, one of his principal supporters, Duplessis-Mornay, stepped forward, and

* Davila, Péréfixe, Duncan.
† Matthieu, De Thou.
‡ Ibid. Péréfixe.
§ Ibid.

in a solemn manner reminded Henry of the great injury which he had done the reformed religion by his incontinence, and particularly by the recent and notorious seduction of a young lady of Rochelle. "Sire," said this reproving Nathan, "make public reparation for your misconduct, lest God send defeat as a judgment upon your so many sins."*

Henry, influenced either by religious feeling, or considering that the ardor of his soldiers would be heightened by the freedom of their cause from so foul a stigma, consented publicly to avow his fault in the church of Pau, and also to confess it on his first visit to Rochelle. He then knelt, together with the whole army, while prayer was offered to the God of battle.

This spectacle, instead of awakening respect in Joyeuse's mind, only confirmed his vain confidence. "See," cried he with a chuckle, "they kneel, they tremble; the day is ours." Laverdin, an old soldier, who was familiar with the habits of the Huguenots, replied, "Nay, my lord, you mistake. 'T is their custom; they always pray when they mean either to conquer or die."†

The battle was decided in half an hour. The courtiers were no match for the soldiers of Christ. The royalists routed; five thousand dead; five hundred prisoners; Joyeuse slain: such were the fruits of this brilliant victory.‡

* Vie de Duplessis-Mornay, liv. 1, p. 108.

† Journal de Henri III.

‡ Davila, liv. 8. Cayet, vol. 1, p. 38.

The Bourbon princes performed prodigies of valor on that day, but Navarre eclipsed them all. He fought like the paladin of a fairy tale. A white plume fastened in his helmet made him conspicuous. When some of his friends, esteeming him menaced, threw themselves in front of him to shield his person, he cried, "Give me room, I beseech you; you stifle me: I would be seen."*

Henry did not press his victory; indeed he is charged with having frittered it away. Quitting the army, which he left under the charge of Turenne, he repaired to Bearn and laid at the feet of the duchess de Guiche, of whom he was enamoured, the colors captured at Coutras.† He dwarfed the heroic Henry of the battle-plain to the dandy carpet-knight of a courtesan's boudoir—a sad metamorphosis, shameful to the prince, and insulting to his God.

To say nothing of his duty as a professed Christian, he ought not, as an able captain, to have bartered success for a lady's smile; he ought not to have muddled the future by leaving it to the chapter of accidents, when, by energetic action, he might have anchored God's cause and his country's.

* La Grani, Decade de Henri Quatre, tome 4.

† Vie de Duplessis-Mornay, p. 111. D'Aubigné, Hist. Univ., vol. 3, p. 58.

CHAPTER XXX.

THE DOUBLE ASSASSINATION.

Tedious negotiations, which had no effect, followed the battle of Coutras.* In the meanwhile Guise was winning laurels at the head waters of the Loire. His name was on every papist's lips. Henry III., jealous of this renown, himself departed for the army; but he arrived only in time to see the hated Guise entwine the laurel about his brow; so that when the king returned to Paris, armed cap-à-pie, with the port of a warrior, the witty citizens only lampooned his vanity and satirized his assumption of stolen honors.†

But Guise was the popular idol. The metropolis especially resounded with pæans in his praise. The "new David," the "second Moses," the "modern Gideon," "the prop and pillar of holy church," such were the titles showered upon him. Every *café* in Paris hymned his virtues.

This adulation turned Guise's head. Hurried away by the madness of ambition, he summoned his family to assemble at Nancy; and here the house of Lorraine matured a scheme for deposing the king, immuring him in a cloister, and crowning Henry of Guise.‡

* Duncan; Vie de Henri III. † Ibid.; Brantome.

‡ Ibid.; Davila; De Thou; Mem. de Nevers; James, Life of Henry IV.

This shows how little interest the princes of Lorraine really took in religion; they only used it as a vehicle in which to ride to empire. Their simple, sole object in every manœuvre, from the very inception of these troubles in the reign of Francis I., through forty years of internecine strife, was the aggrandizement of their mushroom house.* To that every thing was made to bend—the public weal, religious honor, the good faith of the state: the weightiest interests were transmuted into battledoors.

The convocation at Nancy masked its real design, the usurpation of the throne by Guise; and committing to writing a series of insolent demands, forwarded them to the king. This precious document was not a petition; it was a command. Signed by the Guises, the cardinal of Bourbon, and other principal chiefs of the League, it imperiously demanded that the king should banish from his court all persons who were from any cause obnoxious to the "holy union;" that he should publish and enforce the decrees of the Council of Trent, place in the hands of the confederates such towns and fortresses as they might see fit, the crown paying the garrisons and all costs of fortification, and confiscate

* The cardinal of Guise used frequently to say that he should never die happy until he held the king's head between his knees, to fit on a monk's cowl. Madame de Montpensier, sister to the Guises, wished to use her own scissors to make the cowl. The device of Henry III. was three crowns, with the motto, *Manet ultima Cœlo*. The leaguers travestied it into *Manet ultima Claustro*. Notes to the "Henriade."

the Huguenot estates to defray the expenses of the war of extermination.*

Henry III. was quite broken by this daring insolence. As was usual with him when perplexed, he applied to the queen mother for assistance.† Discord reigned in the privy council. One set of the king's minions favored the League; another urged the monarch to identify himself with Navarre, and strangle that presumptuous union, the pest of France.‡ In accordance with the weak vacillation of his character, he took neither counsel, but contenting himself with half measures, which in stormy crises always disgust both parties, he sent the conspirators at Nancy word that he would consider their petition.§

Guise, emboldened by the king's timidity, now resolved to strike a decisive blow. His friends were ready; he was sure of the capital; the omens were auspicious; he determined to proceed to Paris, and seize Henry during the celebration of the carnival.‖

Despite the written and reiterated orders of his sovereign not to quit the camp, he entered Paris on the 9th of May, 1588,¶ at high noon. Ere he had passed half through the city, he was recognized and thronged by the admiring mob. Thirty thousand people formed his retinue.** "The shouts of the people," says an eye-witness, "sounded to the skies;

* De Thou, liv. 90. Cayet, liv. 1, p. 44. † Ibid.

‡ Duncan, p. 214.

§ Mem. de la Ligue, vol. 2, p. 269, et seq. Duncan, p. 215.

‖ Esprit de la Ligue, tom. 2, p. 144.

¶ Vie de Henri III.; Duncan, etc. ** Davila, liv. 8.

nor did they ever cry, VIVE LE ROY, as energetically as they now shouted, VIVE GUISE. Some saluted him, some gave him thanks, some bowed to him, others kissed the hem of his garment. Those who could not get near him manifested their joy by gestures · some were seen who, adoring him as a saint, and touching him with their beads, either kissed them or pressed them against their eyes and foreheads. Even the women, throwing green leaves and blooming flowers from their windows, honored and blessed his coming.

"Guise, with a smiling countenance and gracious air, showed himself affable to some in words, to some by courteously returning their salutations; others he requited with kind looks. Passing through the throng with his hat off, he omitted nothing that was calculated to win and rivet the affection and applause of the people."*

Such was the reception awarded to the "king of Paris." Guise, intoxicated by this adulation, had the hardihood to visit the Louvre. Catharine was aghast. She received him pale, trembling, and dismayed. Henry's consternation may not be described. The impudent duke stood with easy nonchalance, enjoying the astonishment which his presence caused, and smiling as the shouts of the populace, who now crowded the court of the Louvre and the adjacent streets, came borne to his ears on the exultant wind.†

* Davila, liv. 8, p. 337. † Maimbourg, Hist. de la Ligue, vol. 2, p. 323.

Henry reproached Guise for his disobedience in visiting the capital, and the stern look which greeted him at length made the champion of the League and the idol of the Parisians turn pale. After a stormy interview, the duke feigned fatigue, and took his leave amid the acclamations of the multitude.*

In the evening Guise fortified his house and stored it with ammunition. Equal vigilance was observed at the Louvre. The Swiss were under arms, and every man-at-arms whom Henry could press into service was put on guard.†

The next morning Guise again visited the Louvre; but fearful of treachery, he was accompanied by four hundred armed friends. Nothing was accomplished; and in the evening further consultations were held.‡

In the mean time every wile was employed to lash the excitable populace into a frenzy. The report was spread that a hundred and twenty of the chief leaguers were marked out for death. A counterfeit list was framed and circulated. Guise headed the victims. The people, incited by the priests, raged madly. Then commenced the famous *barricades*.

Paris, in the reign of Henry III., was not protected by the vigilant police of modern times. Now the constabulary force receives instructions from the crown minister; then it was wholly under the control of the municipal authorities. The city was then girt with walls, flanked by lofty towers; the

* Maimbourg, Hist. de la Ligue, vol. 2, p. 323. Davila, liv 9.
† Cayet, liv. 1, p. 58. ‡ Ibid.

gates were shut exactly at the fixed hour, and the sheriffs held the keys. The burgesses were formed into a militia, chose their own officers, and were frequently drilled. At the corners of the streets weighty chains were attached to rivets in the houses; these were stretched out at the least alarm, and thus all communication of one quarter of the city with another was impeded.*

The people had banners, fixed places of meeting, rallying words; and no more than a drum-tap or the sound of a bell was required to collect a mass of soldiers under arms, imperfectly disciplined, but formidable from their number.† Paris was divided into sixteen districts: in each of these a council was formed in the interest of the League; these appointed sixteen demagogue delegates, who made another council, called the "Council of Sixteen,"‡ which was so famous in the religious wars of France.

Now the SIXTEEN were in their element. The tocsin sounded; the streets were unpaved; the chains extended from corner to corner; the Swiss guard of the king, shut up in the square before the church of the INNOCENTS and isolated, were soon forced to surrender; and Guise saw himself master of Paris by an almost bloodless *coup d'état.*§

While these scenes were being enacted in the streets of his turbulent and traitorous capital, Hen-

* Duncan, p. 214. † Ibid.

‡ Esprit de la Ligue, tom. 2, p. 140.

§ Hist. des Derniers Troubles; Cayet; Davila.

ry, palsied by fear, gave up all hope. He had been informed of the object of Guise's visit by one of the repentant conspirators,* and he could not believe that his foe would let slip this opportunity: he stood disarmed and friendless; what could save him?

The craft of Catharine de' Medici extricated her inefficient son from Guise's net.

The queen mother had already visited Guise, when he had named such hard terms as amounted to the abdication of the king.† Now, returning to the duke, she held him in protracted conversation, that he might have no opportunity to invest the Louvre, while the king prepared for instant flight.‡

Proceeding into the garden of the Tuilleries on pretence of taking a promenade, Henry repaired to the royal stables, equipped himself for his journey, and immediately set off on horseback, accompanied by a suite of fifteen or twenty gentlemen, for Chartres, where he arrived safely the next day, receiving every mark of affection and respect.§

In the mean while Memville, one of Guise's attendants, having ascertained that Henry had quitted Paris, burst unceremoniously into the duke's cabinet, interrupted the queen mother's empty harangue, which meant only time, and flung into his

* Nicholas Paulain, one of the conspirators, revealed every thing to the chancellor, named his accomplices, and offered to remain in prison till the truth of his report was ascertained. The court at first doubted; but the appearance of Guise convinced the king. Duncan, p. 216.

† Matthieu, liv. 8, p. 549.

‡ Hist. des Derniers Troubles.

§ Hist. de la Ligue.

master's ears the announcement, "The king has fled from Paris." The duke started up in dismay, and said to Catharine, "Ah, madame, I am undone; while your majesty has been detaining me, the king has departed to plot my ruin."*

Catharine, versed in all the arts of dissimulation, replied, "I credit not this news," and took her leave.†

Although bitterly disappointed that the grand prize had escaped him, Guise was not inactive, but took every precaution to secure the advantages which he had gained. He secured the Bastile, took St. Cloud, Vincennes, Lagry, and thus commanded the free navigation of the Seine and the Marne to the gates of Paris, and revolutionized the municipal administration, filling all offices with his satellites.‡

Notwithstanding these usurpations, Henry, from his retreat at Chartres, had the despicable weakness to open negotiations with the triumphant Parisian leaguers; and eventually a treaty was signed, which ratified demands very similar to those drawn up at Nancy.§

In this edict a clause was inserted which guaranteed the convocation of the states-general at Blois on the 16th of October, 1588, to confirm the

* Hist. de la Ligue. † Ibid.

‡ Ibid. Mem. de la Ligue. Duncan.

§ De Thou, liv. 90. Hist. des Derniers Troubles, vol. 3, p. 86. This edict was agreed to on the fifteenth, signed by the king on the sixteenth, and registered by Parliament on the twenty-first of July, 1588.

treaty.* Victors thus far, the princes of Lorraine now used every effort to subsidize the members of the states-general; religious zeal, ambition, avarice, all were appealed to; they were again successful, and Guise was master of the assembly ere its opening session was held.†

At the appointed time, the states-general were convened, and the pomp was unprecedented. The king, who, despite his reconciliation with the League, had resolutely refused to enter Paris since his ignominious flight, sojourning meantime at Rouen, made the inaugural address. Then business commenced; manœuvre succeeded manœuvre. Guise was confirmed as commander of the *gend'armerie;* a prior decree, declaring the cardinal of Bourbon first prince of the blood and next heir to the throne, was assented to; and Guise, blinded by success, moved that the decrees of the Council of Trent be registered, an act which would have barred the house of Bourbon from the crown.‡ Even the lackey *states* paused here. They were not prepared to go to such a length. The clergy feared to jeopard the rights of the Gallican church; the nobles dreaded any extension of the papal power over their temporalities; the states secured a practical veto by postponement.§

Guise, no whit discouraged, then moved that Navarre be declared incapable of the succession; this was voted with alacrity. In spite of Henry's

* Maimbourg, Hist. de la Ligue. † Duncan, p. 225.
‡ Pasquier, vol. 2, p. 360. Cayet, liv. 1, p. 97. § Ibid.

intrigues, notwithstanding his manifest reluctance to accede to this fiat, against the protest of Navarre, who denounced the states-general as a packed and exclusive convention of his enemies, the king, finding that he could neither conquer the inflexible resolution of the League nor evade their demands, finally assented to the general vote, and said that he would issue an edict giving it validity.*

The political situation was still further confused by the seizure of the marquisate of Saluzzo by the duke of Vassy, an adherent of the League. This aggression touched the national pride, and the voice of patriotism was heard amid the din of religious discord. Henry charged that Guise had instigated the act; the duke asserted that the king himself incited it. Murmurs arose, and both *Guisards* and royalists hated each other with increased venom.†

It was now, while affairs were thus tangled, while nothing was settled, save that the Huguenots were outlawed, declared incapable of holding office, and tabooed, that Henry, driven to desperation, definitively decided to assassinate his subtle and triumphant persecutor.‡

He had recourse to Marshal D'Aumont, a brave soldier, and to Nicolas D'Augenay, an able publicist: informing them of his purpose, he asked their opinion. "Strike," advised the cavalier in a monosyllable; but the lawyer, with the instinct of his profession, counselled the duke's imprisonment and

* Davila, liv. 9. Duncan, p. 229.

† Journal de Henri III. Mem. de Nevers, vol. 2. ‡ Ibid.

trial before the regular tribunals for high treason.*

The soldier's advice was the most congenial, and the king resolved to adopt it. It was some time ere he obtained a willing instrument of revenge. At length Loignac, a partisan of Epernon, and a bitter foe of Guise, undertook the work.

On the 22d of December, 1588, Henry sent word to Guise that, as he proposed going to Notre Dame de Clery to pass the festival of Christmas, he should hold his daily council early the next morning.†

Loignac then received his last instructions. Thirteen assassins were introduced into the council-chamber and hidden behind a tapestry; and Henry himself gave each of them a poniard, saying, "Guise is the greatest criminal in my kingdom; the laws, both human and divine, permit me to punish him. Not being able to do so by the ordinary tribunals, I authorize you by my royal prerogative to do so."

In the mean time the wretched victim received Henry's treacherous note, and unmindful of the manifold warnings which he had received to beware of the king, he at once repaired to the palace, where he arrived in the grey, bleak winter dawn. Once in the trap, every thing conspired to alarm the duke. The gates were clanged to after him with ominous precaution; he passed though a long lane of soldiers stretching away to the court-yard; he met

* De Thou, liv. 93.

† D'Aubigné, vol. 3, p. 150. Davila, liv. 9.

the archbishop of Lyons, a confidential friend, who said to him in presence of Larchant, one of the captains of the guard, alluding to the light dress he wore, "That coat is too light for this season and *place*. You should have put on one stiff with fur." These words, pronounced in accents of suspicion, heightened Guise's alarm.*

In one of the anterooms he nearly fainted; recovering, he proceeded to the fatal council-chamber. The door had been walled up. Ignorant of this, Guise was in the act of raising the tapestry which screened the apartment, when the bravos sprang upon him, and ere he could draw his sword, gave him countless stabs, and flung him to the floor quite dead.†

The false door of the council-chamber was then thrown down, and Henry, followed by his suite, emerged into the anteroom where lay his late redoubted foe. The courtiers jested; and the king himself, in imitation of Guise's brutality to the dead body of Coligny, kicked the duke's remains.‡

Having gloated his eyes with this ghastly spectacle, Henry hastened to the queen mother, and cried exultingly, "Madame, the king of Paris is dead; I am now king of France."§

"I fear," replied the astute Catharine, "that you will soon be king of nothing." But she exhorted him to wait at once upon the papal nuncio,

* Hist. des Derniers Troubles, liv. 4; Davila, D'Aubigné, Cayet, and others. † Ibid. ‡ Browning, p. 230.

§ Davila, liv. 9.

and avert his displeasure, and to use diligence and resolution.*

The murder of Guise caused a profound sensation. Never was man less fit to die. He had quitted the chamber of one of the titled harlots of the court, the marchioness of Noirmontier, with whom he had passed the night, on the very morning of his death. He was stained by vices and crimes whose name was legion, and was one of the chief butchers of St. Bartholomew—a fearful record with which to face his God.

Guise possessed many of the qualities of a political leader. He was sagacious, affable, prepossessing in his physique, and possessed the keen, penetrating talent of a Machiavelli. He united in his single person the diplomatic acumen of his equally unscrupulous uncle the cardinal of Lorraine, and the military genius of his father.

Henry III. for once acted with vigor. He ordered the arrest and instant execution of the cardinal of Guise. Then the bodies of the unhappy princes were consumed in quicklime, and buried secretly.† Mayence also was upon the red list, but he escaped from Lyons to Dijon, whence he repaired to Paris;‡ but the archbishop of Lyons, the old cardinal of Bourbon, the prince de Joinville, and the duke of Elbœuf were seized. "Henceforth," cried the aroused king, "I wish my subjects to know that I will be obeyed. I will punish the

* Davila, liv. 9. † Ibid., p. 373.
‡ Ibid. Duncan, p. 234.

leaders of insurrection, and those who abet them. I will be king not merely in words, but in deeds; and it will be no difficult matter for me to wield the sword again as I did in my youth."*

News of the tragedy at Blois reached Paris on the day succeeding the assassination of the duke of Guise. Popular indignation vented itself in the bitterest and fiercest execrations. Sermons were preached on the martyrdom of the "king of Paris," and Henry was compared to Herod. Intelligence of the death of the cardinal of Guise soon followed, and the outcries of fury grew louder and deeper. The king was denounced as a favorer of heresy, as an enemy to holy church, who had dyed his hands in the blood of an ecclesiastic. Priest and layman panted for revenge. Councils of war were held in shops and cloisters. The statues of the king were broken, the royal arms were defaced; he was called simply, Henry of Valois. The Sorbonne declared that he had forfeited the crown, and that his subjects not only might, but ought to cast off their allegiance; and this resolution was forwarded to Rome for the sanction of the pope.†

In the midst of this excitement, Catharine de' Medici died. She breathed her last on the 5th of January, 1589, in the seventieth year of her active and intriguing life.‡

Catharine possessed a strong intellect, persua-

* Davila, liv. 9, p. 373. Duncan, p. 234.

† Duncan, p. 236. Davila, liv. 9, p. 378. Notes to the "Henriade."

‡ Cayet, liv. 2, p. 72. Péréfixe.

sive eloquence, and an invention so ready that it never halted for an expedient. She believed with the Vatican, that "the end justifies the means;" and in the pursuit of her purpose, she availed herself without a scruple of the most abhorrent arts, and especially of the licentiousness of her court. She was always accompanied by a bevy of fair but frail beauties; and by her encouragement of vice, she raised it to an unparalleled height of dissoluteness and infamy.

In the exercise of her cruelty and perfidy, she eventually became equally detested by the papists and the Huguenots, both of whom she had often betrayed. Fighting with such poisoned weapons, she could not fail to be despised in each camp when she became known in each.

In her stony heart maternal affection had no sway. She encouraged her children in habits of licentiousness, in order to make them subservient to her will. She is even accused of murdering two of her sons when they stood in her path; and it is not questioned that she employed the poisoner's bowl and the stiletto of the bravo to abridge the lives of several rivals. The good she did France was imperceptible; the evil she inflicted, the curses she entailed, the atrocious *régime* of deceit and perfidy and selfish despotism which she inaugurated, two centuries later crazed France—drove it to blow its own brains out in the revolution of 1793.

The death of the queen mother completed the king's embarrassment. He had leaned upon her counsel; now that prop was gone. The whole country heaved in insurrection. City was opposed to city, castle to castle. In vain did Henry strive to appease the indignation of the League by proving the treason of the duke of Guise. The correspondence with Spain and Savoy, the terms of the alliance, the monies raised to arm the traitors against the throne, all went for nothing. The country was in no mood to listen to evidence; the people were the slaves of unbridled passion; they wanted not truth, but vengeance.*

Nor was the monarch more successful in his efforts to placate the pope. When Sixtus V. learned through the French ambassador of the death of the Guises, and the imprisonment of the cardinal of Bourbon and the archbishop of Lyons, his rage knew no bounds. "Your master," said he, "thinks to deceive me, and treats me as if I were no more than a poor monk; but he shall find that he deceives *himself*, not *me;* and that he has to deal with a pontiff who is ready to shed plenty of blood when the interest of his see requires it." "But, holy father," retorted the keen ambassador, "shall not the king my master be at liberty to kill the cardinal of Guise, his mortal enemy, after pope Pius IV. has authorized the murder of cardinal Caraffe, who had been one of his friends?" Sixtus was too much enraged to reply to this home-thrust, so he dismissed the minister from his presence.†

This rebuff at the Vatican isolated the king

* Duncan, p. 238.

† Browning, p. 235.

He held a sceptre which he could not wield. On one side of the Loire the exasperated League ruled undisputed; on the other, the king of Navarre governed. Henry stood alone in the centre of his kingdom, without money, without friends, without an army.*

He attempted to negotiate with the League; but that confederacy, under the able management of Mayenne, who had been appointed head, had regained stability, and the offended brother of the murdered princes haughtily refused all overtures.†

In despair, the wretched monarch recalled the dying advice of the queen mother. He turned to Navarre, and besought his forgiveness and assistance.‡ When this was known, the papal legate and the Spanish ambassador quitted him, and proceeding to Paris, recognized the lords of the League as the legitimate government of France.§

But the Huguenot sky was propitious. Navarre acceded to Henry's request for an armistice; and on the 30th of April, 1589, clasping hands at Plessis-les-Tours, the two monarchs pledged themselves to bury the past, to unite for the future; and they entered Tours amid the acclamations of the soldiers and the inhabitants. Huguenots and royalists fraternized, and vowed to devote their consolidated strength to the subjugation of the League and the inauguration of a tolerant *régime*.‖

* Journal de Henri III. † Maimbourg, Hist. de la Ligue.

‡ Ibid. § Duncan, pp. 241, 242.

‖ La Grani, liv. 4. Péréfixe, liv. 1. Sully, liv. 1. It was

Deeply chagrined by this unexpected phase of affairs, Mayenne collected his squadrons and dashed towards Tours, hoping to surprise the kings in the midst of the reconciliatory *fêtes*. He nearly succeeded. Swooping upon Vendôme, he captured it, and then pressed into the suburbs of Tours.* After a severe contest, Mayenne was forced back; and retreating across France slowly and sullenly, he passed through St. Cloud into the friendly and sheltering walls of Paris.†

The jubilant royalists crossed the Loire close on Mayenne's heels. When they reached Poissy, they were joined by some foreign auxiliaries, ten thousand Swiss and four thousand Germans, whom the king had enlisted under his banner. These, added to the detachments of Longueville, Montpensier, De Givry, and Navarre, swelled Henry's army to forty-two thousand fighting men.‡

with reluctance that Navarre went to this interview. He feared treachery. Many of his counsellors thought that the king would take Navarre's life to purchase the pope's absolution. Navarre wrote to his confidential friend Duplessis-Mornay in these terms: "The ice is broken, not without many warnings that if I went I should be a dead man. I passed the water recommending myself to God." Mornay answered, "Sire, you have done what you ought, but what none of your friends would have advised."

Such was the apprehension of Navarre, that he halted two leagues from Tours, and took the opinion of his retinue whether to proceed or return. Sully claims the honor of having persuaded Bourbon to trust the good faith of Valois. Duncan, p. 243, note.

* Matthieu, liv. 8, p. 375, et seq. Maimbourg, Hist. de la Ligue, vol. 2, p. 161.

† Ibid.

‡ Davila, De Thou, Mem. de Duplessis-Mornay, Vie de Henry III.

The terror excited by this array reduced those towns which environed the capital to speedy submission. Consternation reigned in Paris. Mayenne could only muster eight thousand infantry and eighteen hundred cavalry. Despite his exertions, all the passages of the Seine were wrung from his control, and the approaches to the bridges fell into the hands of the king.*

Paris was almost strangled by the besiegers, so closely did they clasp the throat of the rebellious capital. Henry in person begirt the Faubourg St. Honoré, and all that side of the Louvre which borders on the river. Navarre besieged the line from the faubourg of St. Martin to that of St. Germain.†

The fate of Mayenne seemed certain; when fanaticism extricated the League from the impending danger, and once more unsettled France.

Fanatical opinions exercise their power oftener over individuals than on great corporations. From the midst of the common fermentation there now arose a monk who resolved to perpetrate a fresh deed of horror. This was Jacques Clément, a Dominican whose passions were strong, whose principles were libertine, and whose frenzy was unequalled. He had recently been ordained a priest. To persons of his own age and to his friends, he was an object of ridicule. He was weak in body and simple of mind. Such are the natures on which

* Davila, De Thou, Mem. de Duplessis-Mornay, Vie de Henry III.

† Villeroi, vol. 5. Cayet, liv. 1. Mem. de Duplessis-Mornay

fanaticism makes the most profound impression. Clément was persuaded that it was lawful to kill a tyrant, and he laid before his superiors the question whether it would be a mortal sin for a priest to assassinate a despot. He was told that it would be an irregularity, but no mortal sin.* Meantime every art was employed to heat his brain and nerve his hand for the atrocious deed.

When the fanatic communicated his project to Mayenne and D'Aumale, they approved it.† The demagogue Council of Sixteen applauded it.‡ He was promised a cardinal's hat if he did the deed and escaped; if taken and executed, he was assured of canonization;§ and on the night that his resolution was confirmed, the duchess of Montpensier sacrificed all that a woman holds most dear to the young libertine regicide.‖

Thus doubly crazed by passion and by fanaticism, Clément provided himself with forged credentials to the king; then bidding his friends adieu, he passed outside the lines of the League, loosened his frock, and walked with rapid strides towards Henry's camp. After some delay, he spent the night within the king's lines. Clément succeeded in securing an audience. Henry approached him. Pretending to draw a paper from his sleeve, he drew instead a knife, which he plunged with deadly effect into the monarch's abdomen. "Wretch," cried the

* Ranke, p. 396. † Matthieu, liv. 8, p. 772.
‡ Esprit de la Ligue. Davila, liv. 10. § Ibid.
‖ Duncan, p. 245. Browning. De Thou, liv. 96, passim.

king, "what have I done, that you should assassinate me?" and as he spoke, he drew the fatal blade from the wound, and struck it into the forehead of the miscreant friar. La Guesle, one of the attendant courtiers, ran him through. His body was hurled from the window, where it was hacked to pieces by the soldiers, burned, and the ashes thrown into the Seine.*

Henry lingered eighteen hours, counselled forbearance, deplored the unhappy state in which he left France, exhorted the nobility to remain united, and declared Navarre to be his legitimate successor.† Then turning to the anxious followers who crowded about his couch, he said, "Adieu, my friends; turn your tears into prayers, and pray for me." Shortly after this, in the thirty-eighth year of his age and the fifteenth of his reign, the last of the house of Valois died without a struggle, while repeating the *miserere*.‡

Henry's death was finer than his life. Imbecile, vacillating, vicious, even to name his vices would outrage decency. Never did monarch mount the throne under brighter auspices; never had a king more shamefully squandered his time in low debauchery, lost golden opportunities, and frittered away his reputation. His feebleness alienated the League; his treachery disgusted the Huguenots.

* Davila, liv. 10. Cayet, liv. 1, p. 223. Maimbourg, Hist. de la Ligue, liv. 3.

† De Thou, liv. 96.

‡ Ibid. Hist. des Derniers Troubles, vol. 2, p. 7. Davila, liv. 10.

His religion was hypocrisy, his prudence was craft, his liberality was licentious prodigality, his private life was a continuous round of enervating and *roué* pleasure. His death was received by the factions and by bigots with exultation, and France at large rashly attributed it to a stroke of divine justice.

CHAPTER XXXI.

THE WHITE PLUME OF NAVARRE.

THE monk who murdered Henry III. because he was not Romanist enough, by his fatal blow enthroned a Huguenot.

When apprized of the assassination, ultramontane France ran mad with ferocious joy. The Dominicans of the capital chanted a *Te Deum*.* Portraits of Clément were exposed to the veneration of the populace.† The statue of the murderer was placed in the cathedral, with the inscription, "St. James Clément, pray for us."‡ Bonfires blazed; rockets shot up to kiss the heavens. The abandoned duchess of Montpensier, in whose arms the assassin had had his purpose confirmed, traversed the Paris streets with dishevelled dress, crying, "Good news, my friends, good news! The tyrant is dead; we shall have no more of Henry Valois."§ Pope Sixtus V., in full consistory, pronounced a studied panegyric upon Clément, beginning his atrocious harangue with a quotation from the Psalms: "This is the Lord's doing; and it is marvellous in our eyes." Then, with frightful blasphemy, this pastor of the faithful declared the cow-

* Davila, liv. 10.

† Mem. du Duc d'Angoulême, p. 22. Journal de Henri IV.

‡ Hist. des Derniers Troubles, vol. 2, p. 6.

§ Ibid. Duncan, pp. 255, 256.

ardly regicidal act comparable, for heroism, to the actions of Judith and Eleazar, and for usefulness, to the incarnation and resurrection of the Saviour.*

But while the League was exulting, Navarre, aware that boldness is the mother of opinion, and that from this springs power, from power victory, and thence security, hastened to have himself proclaimed king of France under the title of Henry Quatre; then, leaning with one hand upon the Swiss auxiliaries, and with the other upon the united Huguenot and conservative parties, he calmly turned to Europe and demanded recognition.

This, however, was not readily conceded. Most of the foreign states were hostile to his claim; France itself was divided: the League, dominant in half of the kingdom, cried Veto to the new monarch's accession; many of the royalist cavaliers deserted Henry's standard at this critical moment; and the king, with his army thinned by desertion to half its original size—forty-two thousand men—raised the siege of Paris, divided his squadrons into three divisions, and retired into Normandy.†

Nor was the League a unit at this crisis. Dissension, bitter and open, ate out the heart of action. Mayenne himself, chief of the "holy union," backed by the formidable house of Guise, aspired to the throne.‡ Mendoza, the Spanish ambassa-

* Hist. des Derniers Troubles, vol. 2, p. 6. Duncan, pp. 255, 256. Browning, p. 251.

† Davila. Vie de Henri IV. James, Life of Henry Quatre.

‡ Duncan, p. 256. Rohan, Mem., liv. 4.

dor, opposed his election in favor of Philip II., who also had designs upon the crown; and Sixtus V. was urged to espouse the cause of the "most Christian king." But the pope did not enter into the views of Spain with any cordiality. He foresaw that if Philip, who was already too strong for the Vatican, should become arbiter of France and master of the Netherlands, he could reduce the pontiff to the position of mere head chaplain to the court of Madrid. Accordingly Sixtus threw the weight of his influence into the scale against Philip, whom he all the time cozened into imagining that he was assisting. This tortuous policy finally effected the election of the old cardinal of Bourbon, whom the Huguenots still held in duress, and who received the empty honor of the ultramontane allegiance, under the *sobriquet* of Charles X.* In the absence of their nominal king, the Council of Sixteen ruled Paris, and Mayenne controlled the Romanist provinces.†

In the mean time Henry Quatre, by dint of his superior military genius, beat down all opposition, and marched from victory to victory. He convened a parliament at Tours, where his authority was acknowledged, and where justice was administered in his name;‡ he overran Normandy; he gained the celebrated battle of Argens, in 1588, and subdued a multitude of rebellious towns.

After exhaustive but abortive diplomatic *ruses*,

* Sully, liv. 3. Davila, liv. 2. Matthieu, liv. 1, vol. 2. Browning, p. 260. † Ibid. ‡ Mem. de Duplessis-Mornay.

succeeded by much military manœuvring, the army of the League, commanded by Mayenne, and the Huguenots, led by Henry IV., met, in March, 1590, on the famous plain of Ivry.*

Two writers† who were with the king mention that, during a terrific thunder-storm which preceded the battle, two armies were descried in the heavens fighting furiously. "This," says Davila, "discouraged the royal army, who for the most part looked on the heavenly display as a presage of defeat, and coupled it with the unhappy rout at the fight of Dreux, fought on that very spot at the commencement of the civil wars."‡

At a time when the aurora borealis was but little known, this phantom fight in the clouds could not fail of producing consternation.

The force of the two armies was very unequal: the king had eight thousand infantry, and but two thousand cavalry. The League mustered twelve thousand men-at-arms and four thousand horsemen.§

In the king's camp much time was given by both Romanists and Protestants to devotion. The churches of the neighboring hamlet of Nanancourt were crowded by gentlemen who went to mass; while the Huguenot ministers performed divine service with their adherents.‖

When all was prepared, Henry advanced to the

* Maimbourg, Hist. de la Ligue; Matthieu; Péréfixe, etc.
† Sully and Davila. ‡ Davila, liv. 2.
§ Matthieu, Hist. des Guerres, etc., p. 29.
‖ Hist. des Derniers Troubles, vol. 2, p. 16.

head of his army, in complete armor, but bare-headed, and prayed aloud to the Almighty for his favor and protection. When he finished his supplication, a shout of "*Vive le roi*" ran through his lines. Henry then exhorted his followers to keep their ranks, and assured them that he was determined to conquer or die with them. "Gentlemen," cried he, with animated voice and sparkling eye, "if the standard fail you, keep my plume in your eyes; you will always find it in the path of honor and duty."* So saying, he put on his helmet adorned with three white plumes; then perceiving that the wind blew in the faces of his soldiers, and that in consequence the smoke would blind them, he ordered a position to be taken more to the left. Mayenne, perceiving this manœuvre, at once sounded a charge, and battle was joined.†

The field was stubbornly and skilfully contested, and the victory long hung in doubt. At length Henry in person plunged with his reserve upon Mayenne's array headlong and resistless; for a space he was swallowed up in the dreadful *mêlée:* then came the clang of sabres, the fierce shouts of infuriated combatants, the agonized wail of the death-smitten; while above all sounded the hoarse roar of musketry and the sullen boom of cannon. The suspense was awful; but when the smoke rolled up, the army of the League was descried decimated, broken, dispersed, scattered in wild rout across the

* D'Aubigné, Hist. Universelle, vol. 3, p. 231.

† Maimbourg, Hist. de la Ligue, vol. 2, p. 268.

ghastly plain, shouting madly, "*Sauve qui peut;*" while over all loomed the white plume of Navarre, and echoed the frenzied cry of, "Victory, victory!"

"Gentlemen," said the exultant monarch, "you have served God well this day; receive his benediction and your king's."*

In this famous battle six thousand leaguers perished, among whom were the count of Egmont, who commanded the Spaniards, and the duke of Brunswick, who led the Germans. Sixteen French and twenty Swiss colors, eight pieces of cannon, all the baggage and ammunition of Mayenne—these were the trophies which graced the triumph of the king.†

Henry lost five hundred killed, and two hundred wounded.‡

Mayenne retreated with his battered battalions upon the dismayed capital, at the same time dispatching a courier to the duke of Parma, the Spanish governor of the Netherlands, whom he implored to hasten to the rescue of the imperilled League.§

The victory of Ivry gave Henry IV. a *prestige* which consolidated his party and insured his eventual success. Upon this occasion he did not fritter away his triumph by misspent hours at the feet of a courtesan, as he had his prior victory of Coutras; but pressing closely upon Mayenne, he environed the discomfited legions of the League, and laid close siege to his rebellious capital.‖

* Cayet, liv. 2. Davila, liv. 2. Villeroy, vol. 1.

† Amirault, p. 357. Péréfixe, liv. 2. ‡ Ibid.

§ Villeroy, vol. 1. Davila, liv. 2. Matthieu.

‖ Jour. de Henri IV. Hist. des Derniers Troubles, v. 2, p. 20.

So skilfully did Henry invest Paris, that ere long gaunt famine stalked through its streets. The hunger of the isolated city was terrible and unprecedented. The Parisians not only ate human flesh, after consuming dogs, cats, leather, every thing masticable, but they actually ground the bones of human beings and mixed this awful powder with chaff and bran, of which, at the papal nuncio's suggestion, they made bread.*

Yet though Henry choked them with hunger, the leaguers, steeled by desperation and heated by the Jesuits, still held out. The king might have easily taken Paris by assault, but he was anxious to save it from the horrors of pillage; so he resolved to starve it into submission.†

Meantime Alexander Farnese, duke of Parma, was apprized of the desperate condition of the League. This celebrated soldier and consummate tactician at once set out to relieve Mayenne and Nemours.‡

Farnese did indeed compel Henry to raise the siege of Paris, but avoiding a battle by a series of those cunning military manœuvres which had gained him his reputation, he contented himself with this, and soon retired into the Netherlands.§

Mortified by Farnese's tactics, Henry attempted to take Paris by escalade. But the obstinate fortitude of the citizens, led by a regiment of fanatic

* Hist. de la Sorbonne, vol. 2, p. 45; cited in Browning, p. 266.

† Péréfixe, Mem. de Nevers, vol. 2, p. 601.

‡ Ibid. Duncan, p. 273.

§ Matthieu, Cayet, Sully.

monks grotesquely armed above their frocks, foiled the assault, and the king retired balked and sulky from the city walls.*

But while these scenes were being enacted, several other important events occurred. Charles X., the phantom monarch of the League, died at Fontenoy, after publicly acknowledging the right of his nephew to the throne.† About the same time the prince de Joinville, now duke of Guise, who had been imprisoned by Henry III. when he seized the cardinal of Bourbon, made his escape from duress, not without some suspicion of the connivance of Henry Quatre, who was accused of desiring to make use of the young duke to foment dissension in the ranks of the League.‡

These events were chiefly of consequence because they revived with increased earnestness the question of the succession, to which the demise of pope Sixtus V., in 1591, and the election, after a stormy conclave, of Gregory XIV., a creature of the Spanish king, gave added venom. There were several rival claimants of the French crown within the ranks of the League. Some favored Philip II.; some were for Guise; others preferred the duke of Savoy.§ After a rancorous contest, during which Henry marched from one success to another almost unopposed, the settlement of the mooted claims

* Cayet, liv. 2. Davila, liv. 11.

† Sully. D'Aubigné.

‡ Journal de Henry IV. Maimbourg, Hist. de la Ligue. Péréfixe. Duncan, p. 261.

and the election of a king was referred to the states-general.*

This decision alarmed Henry. The formal nomination of a monarch by the states-general would greatly embarrass him, if it did not ultimately baulk him of the throne. His heroism had melted all Europe into admiration. Many of the inimical nobles did not scruple to declare that, were it not for his heresy, they would serve him and die for him. His Huguenot tenets seemed the only obstacle to the almost undisputed succession. God seemed to put before Henry these two alternatives: a throne bought with a denial of his truth; a divided sceptre accompanied by loyalty to the heavenly King.

The struggle in Henry's soul was fearful. Ambition imperiously beckoned one way; religion sternly pointed the other.

At length ambition triumphed; Henry determined to recant. Many things combined to make the king desert his mother's God. He had no true faith in his soul. His Protestantism was not a saving grace in the heart; it was a cold intellectual conviction, nothing more. He was a Huguenot because Romanism was so ridiculous: "It is unreasonable," cried he, "this mummery of the Vatican." Devoted to pleasure, nay, to gallantry, what sympathy could this licentious monarch, who seduced young girls, debauched the wives of his highest subjects, and kept a dozen mistresses, have with

* Péréfixe. Duncan, p. 264. Browning, p. 268, et seq.

the pure morality, the chastened piety, the holy ardor of the children of God?

Therefore, since Henry was always a Romanist in practice, since his Protestantism was of the head, not of the heart, his apostasy was not so difficult, the abyss across which he leaped was not so yawning as some have painted it.

Henry had long thought that unless he became reconciled to Rome, he would have to pass his life in warfare, "a monarch without a kingdom," in his phrase.* He had not raised himself to the Christian height of daring to TRUST GOD. Like Simon Peter, he doubted. His favorite mistress, Gabrielle d'Estrés, constantly urged him to recant and pacify the country. When the alarmed Huguenots entreated him not to abandon them, he said, "*Ventre St. Gris!* Paris is well worth a mass."†

On the 25th of July, 1593, Henry publicly abjured Protestantism at St. Denis, and envoys were instantly dispatched to Rome to obtain the papal absolution; but the reluctant pontiff would not publish a decree of admission into the bosom of Rome until two years later. In 1595 he was absolved from all censure, upon certain prescribed conditions, with all of which he complied.‡

* Browning, p. 287.

† Cayet, liv. 5. Jour. de Henri IV. James, Life of Henry IV.

‡ The conditions were as follows: that the Roman church should be introduced into Bearn as the established religion; that four monasteries of friars and nuns should be established there, and that the decrees of the Council of Trent should be received into France, except in those articles which might injure the inde-

This event broke the back of the League; Mayenne only held out to obtain better terms; ere long he succumbed. The nobles and the commons hastened to swear allegiance to the renegade monarch,* and ere many months had passed, rebellious Paris itself opened its obstinate gates with a shout of welcome.†

But if Henry's abjuration killed the League, it also wounded the Huguenots. From the day of his mock reconciliation with Rome, Henry treated his old friends, Turenne, Duplessis-Mornay, D'Aubigné, and the rest, with shabby neglect. Happily Condé was dead, poisoned some years before, so he could not be tabooed. The whole reform party was

pendence of the Gallican church; that within one year the young prince of Condé should be delivered into the hands of Romish instructors to be educated by them; that all lands and goods taken from the church should be restored; that none should be elected to the magistracy who were heretics; that the king should give an account of his conversion and abjuration to all Christian princes. The spiritual penances imposed were, that on every Sunday and holy day he should hear a conventual mass; that he should hear mass every day; and that on some set days of the week he should say certain prayers; that he should fast on Fridays and Sundays, and receive the communion publicly four times a year. Davila, liv. 2, p. 675.

When these terms were accepted by the king's representatives, they knelt down at the gate of St. Peter's church, and abjured the heresies contained in a written document; they were then touched on the head by the cardinal Santa Seremia, and received absolution for their master. The church was opened, and immediately resounded with music, while the castle of St. Angelo fired salvos of artillery. Cardinal Alessandro de Medici was appointed legate to France, to report the papal decision, and to cause it to be published in every church. Duncan, p 332.

* Péréfixe; Cayet; D'Aubigné, etc.

† Ibid.

sad and apprehensive. "In taking the king's abjuration," wrote the wise and good Duplessis-Mornay to the duke of Bouillon, "it was proposed that he should swear to make war upon the Huguenots, which he refused to do. This is a great boldness to dare to make such a demand when he was barely on the threshold of their door."* "I expect," wrote he further on, alluding to the embassy to Rome, "that Henry will obtain absolution on condition of the revocation of his edict against the bull of excommunication; and for penance, he will be secretly enjoined to make war upon the Huguenots. The king of Spain will then remain to be satisfied: he can marry his daughter to our king, by which the two interests will be blended, and then the Philistines must be sacrificed as a dowry."†

Such is the force of pernicious example, that within a few years after the farce at St. Denis, nearly every family of distinction in France had returned to Rome,‡ like dogs to their vomit.

The loss of their protectors rendered the humbler Huguenots an easy prey to their Jesuitical foes, and the slender recompense which they obtained for their services to Henry Quatre was only an added spur to the oppressions of his successors.

The monarch now lapped himself in the caresses of his late opponents; upon them his favors were almost exclusively bestowed.§ But he did not feel strong enough to dispense with the support of his

* Mem. de Duplessis-Mornay, vol. 2, p. 367. † Ibid.

‡ Browning, p. 287. § Ibid., p. 288.

ancient comrades; so that when a Huguenot synod, convened at St. Maixent, sent deputies to petition Henry to inform them how their affairs were to be conducted, and to entreat him to convoke a general assembly of the Protestant church, he answered suavely but equivocally that his conversion had not changed his affection for them, and promising to take their petition into speedy consideration.*

All France now seemed desirous of acquiescing honestly in the new *régime*, all save the Jesuits, those pests of modern Europe. These obstinately refused to recognize or obey the king, notwithstanding his recantation and absolution. Filled with hatred, they hissed and spat their venom at the throne. They did more; they openly counselled regicide. One of these wretches named Commolet preached a sermon, in which he enlarged upon the death of Eglon king of Moab; he applauded the assassination of Henry III., and described Clément as seated among the angels of heaven. Having thus applied the text, he exclaimed, "We too require an Ehud; we must have an Ehud; be he monk, soldier, or shepherd, does not matter; but we need an Ehud; and this blow is all we want to give us a halcyon sky."†

Similar regicidal doctrines were proclaimed in Lyons and at Rouen, indeed wherever the Jesuits were influential. These madmen soon heated a

* Cayet, liv. 5, p. 259.

† Journal de Henri IV. Plaidoyer de M. Arnauld, in 1594, p. 50.

fanatic, Pierre Barriére, an ignorant and superstitious waterman of Orleans, so that he resolved to attempt the assassination of the king. He asked the advice of the grand prior of the Carmelites at Lyons, who praised his courage and eulogized his piety. A Capuchin, of whom he made a confidant, told him decidedly that his enterprise was meritorious. Happily for Henry, the embryo assassin held a similar consultation with a Dominican named Serapin Bianchi, who was attached to the royalist party. He notified the king, through a gentleman of the royal retinue, of the impending danger; and eventually, after a variety of adventures, Barriére was seized. In his ample confession he implicated all the instigators of the horrid crime in contemplation, after which he was tortured to death.*

The connection of the Jesuits with Barriére, together with their impolitic resistance to the pacification, increased the storm gathering above their heads. They had shown themselves so persistently and implacably the enemies of the king and of the state, that it was resolved to cite them before the courts of justice, as a preliminary to their total expulsion from France.†

The University of Paris led the prosecution.‡ A petition was presented to the Parliament, which narrated in detail all their crimes from their admis-

* Journal de Henri IV. Plaidoyer de M. Arnauld, in 1594, p. 50. Browning, p. 289. † Ibid. Duncan, p. 313.

‡ Cayet.

sion into the kingdom, and urged their banishment; "the Jesuits having been the tools of the Spanish faction all through the late troubles, aiming at the disseverment of the state, conspiring against the life of the king, and violating all order, political and hierarchical."*

The cause was pleaded at Paris in July, 1594. Antony Arnauld, one of the most famous advocates in the jurisprudential history of France, appeared for the prosecution.†

Since, in our day, the Jesuits are as active, as ubiquitous, and as malicious as in the epoch of the League, it becomes of interest to know what the foremost lawyers of mediæval France thought of these dangerous enemies of civilization and of God.

"Was it not among the Jesuits," exclaimed Arnauld, after a brilliant exordium, "that the ambassadors and secret agents of the Spanish king held their traitorous meetings? Was it not among them that Louchard, Ameline, Crucé-Crome, and other murderers, hatched their diabolical conspiracies? Was it not among them that, in 1590, it was resolved that nine tenths of the population of Paris should starve, rather than the city should be surrendered to its lawful king? Who was president of the Council of Sixteen, but the Jesuit Pigenot, the most ferocious tiger in the capital, who was so heart-broken at the bad success of the League, that he became insane through vexation.

"Was it not in the Jesuit colleges of Paris and

* Duncan, p. 314. † Ibid.

Lyons, in the month of August, 1593, that the last resolution to assassinate the king was formed? Does not the deposition of Barriére, executed at Mélun, prove it? Was it not the Jesuit Vorade who assured the would-be murderer that he could not perform a more meritorious act, and to confirm him in his purpose, had him confessed and absolved by another Jesuit whose name is not known? Did not these impious and execrable assassins employ the most holy, the most solemn, the most awful mysteries of the Christian religion to confirm the wavering resolution of a fanatic to massacre the first king in Christendom?

"I confess that a righteous indignation transports me beyond the bounds of forensic calmness when I see that these traitors, murderers, confessors, and absolvers of regicide walk still among us, that they live in France and breathe its air. What do I say? Not only do they live among us, but they enter our palaces; they are countenanced, they are caressed, they form cabals, leagues, and alliances.

"The humiliation of these pests in the affair of Cardinal Borromeo is quite recent. Their order was extinguished, and they were expelled from Italy by pope Pius V. And yet the Jesuits, who have attempted to murder the king of France, and who daily preach regicide, are not banished from our country! Is the life of a cardinal, then, more precious than that of the eldest son of the church? If the tribunal before which I plead does not deliver us from these monsters, they will perpetrate even more evil than they have yet accomplished.

"If the day of conservation is not less delightful than the day of birth, certainly the day on which the Jesuits shall be expelled from France will be no less memorable than that on which the University of Paris was founded; and as Charlemagne, after having delivered Italy from the Lombards, Germany from the Hungarians, passed twice into Spain, subdued the Saxons, and founded our university, which during eight hundred years has served as a refuge to men of letters banished from Italy, and persecuted in Greece, Egypt, and Africa, in the same manner Henry Quatre la Grand, having expelled the Spaniards by force of arms, and banished the Jesuits by your decree, will restore to our university, to the city, to France, the ancient splendor, the primitive glory."*

Louis Dollé, advocate of the curates of Paris, followed Arnauld, and he spoke against the Jesuits with equal force and eloquence. He said that they were not members of the ecclesiastical hierarchy, either as secular or regular priests; that they had only been received in France in the character of a collegiate society, and on the express condition that they should plot no mischief, nor undertake any thing to the prejudice of the bishops or curates; that, far from observing these conditions, they had meddled in politics, assumed to be the censors of the clergy, pretending to be universal pastors and

* Plaidoyer de M. Arnauld, in 1594, p. 30, et seq.

guardians of the church; that by virtue of the privileges too prodigally granted them by the pope, they had not only exalted themselves above the curates, but even above the bishops, and had disturbed the whole hierarchical discipline. Dollé painted in the blackest colors the furious zeal displayed by the Jesuits during the siege of Paris. "Dare you deny," cried he, apostrophizing them, "dare you deny that when Henry III. was at St. Cloud, in 1589, you went daily to the trenches distributing money to the soldiers, and exhorting them to persist in their rebellion? Have you not been compelled to acknowledge that a priest of your company was chief of the Sixteen, and presided at the meetings of those villains?"*

The relentless advocate next dwelt upon the evils caused by the Jesuits through the system of confession. "It is not necessary," said he, "to cite examples; there is not a family in France which cannot adduce several. I shall content myself with noticing one quite recent, and of public notoriety. The Jesuits of Fribourg wished to persuade the small Romanist cantons to separate themselves from the small Protestant cantons, and break their union, which is the *palladium* of Switzerland; but finding the men too firm and wise, they imitated the serpent who tempted Eve. They cozened the women; urged them to refuse all conjugal privileges to their husbands till they had consented to dissolve the alliance. They obeyed these directions;

* Cited in Duncan, pp. 319, 320.

and the men, having learned from them by whom they were seduced, punished the Jesuit seducers as they deserved."

The lawyer also denounced their infamous doctrines, that "to the pure all things are pure," and that "the *end* justifies the *means*;" he then concluded in these words:

"We have been told that the Jesuits wished to assassinate the king: not only have we evidence of the fact, but the traitor has confessed that he counselled the deed. Can we doubt after this what ought to be done to those who would cut all our throats if they had the opportunity? If you do not now banish them from the kingdom, you will positively establish them. Our first movements are full of vigor, but all efforts, national or individual, slacken with the lapse of time; of this we have too much proof, for during the thirty years that this question has been agitated, we have slumbered, and have not thought of the evil, till we have been made to feel its pressure. Behold, *now* is the appointed time. The Jesuits, who know our weak point, wish to protract your sentence by delaying the trial; thus they gain time, which in France gains every thing. Those for whom I speak know that their sacred calling prevents them from demanding vengeance upon the atrocities of this most pernicious society. But, gentlemen, as in ancient times the augurs of Rome were obliged to advise the senate concerning all prodigies that appeared, that the evils they presaged might be averted by expiations, so the plaintiffs, who have charge of things holy and sacred, as the augurs formerly had, apprize you now that there is an ominous prodigy in this city and in other towns of France; it is this, *that men who call themselves religious, teach their blind pupils the lawfulness of murdering kings.* Avert then the evils of this prodigy by timely and energetic action."*

So intense was the feeling excited by these masterly pleas, that the Jesuits did not venture to respond, but availing themselves of legal technicalities, they artfully postponed the sentence,† aware, as Dollé said, that in France to gain time is to gain every thing.

Then they renewed their intrigues, and formed new plots to assassinate the king. A miscreant named Chatél, who had studied in a Jesuit college, was now selected as their instrument of vengeance.

On the 27th of December, 1594, as Henry was surrounded by a cordon of gentlemen who had called to congratulate him upon his auspicious prospects—he had just returned from Picardy, and stood booted and spurred—Chatél stole up stealthily behind him and aimed a blow at his throat. An accidental movement saved him, and the treacherous knife merely cut his lip. The foiled assassin endeavored to escape; but he was seized, and when interrogated, confessed that the Jesuits had incited him to attempt the murder.‡

* Duncan, pp. 322, 323.

† Cayet, Mem. de Nevers, D'Aubigné.

‡ Hist. des Derniers Troubles ; Jouvenci, Hist. Soc. Jesu. Henry was not much alarmed, even at the very moment of the

The cry of indignation which reverberated over France brought down the slumbering avalanche. Proceedings against the Jesuits were hastily resumed in Parliament; and the same decree which condemned Chatél to a frightful death, choked the Society of Jesus, and flung it, banished and dishonored, from the kingdom.*

This consummation caused wide-spread gratulation; the Huguenots especially rejoiced. D'Aubigné hastened to Paris to felicitate the king. This brave soldier and unspotted Christian had expressed himself freely since Henry's abjuration; in the synodical conventions of the Protestants he had not hesitated to denounce the king's hypocrisy. Henry had in consequence been alienated from this old, tried friend, whose honest rebukes rankled. But he now received D'Aubigné kindly. On one occasion Chatél's attempt upon his life became the theme of conversation. "Ah, sire," said the frank soldier, "as you have as yet renounced God with your lips alone, they only have been pierced; whenever your heart renounces him also, that will receive the blow."†

This was at once a warning and a prophecy.

blow. With his usual readiness and wit, he said to the crowd of anxious friends who surrounded him, pointing to his wound, "I have heard from the lips of others how little the reverend Society of Jesus loved me; now I have learned it from my own."

* Jouvenci, Hist. Soc. Jesu. Cayet, liv. 6, p. 436

† D'Aubigné, Mem., p. 136.

CHAPTER XXXII.

THE EDICT OF NANTES.

FRANCE was now nominally at peace with itself, and Henry's only open enemies were the Spaniards upon the frontier of Flanders; yet the condition of the country was deplorable. Distress, the exhaustion consequent upon protracted civil war, the unsatiated ambition of many chieftains anxious to re-establish the feudal sovereignties of the middle ages, the uneasiness of the people at large, habituated to the restless vicissitudes of partisan warfare—these materially retarded returning prosperity, and sadly checked a healthy pacification.

Henry devoted the larger portion of his time to the amelioration of internal affairs; in many respects his statesmanship was wise and judicious, and every effort was made to obliterate the scars of war.*

On the 30th of April, 1598, the Edict of Nantes was signed. From its provisions it appears to have been modelled upon the old edict of pacification ratified at Poitiers. Its essence was, limited toleration. The Huguenots were permitted the most ample liberty of conscience, but they might not publicly exercise their religion except in certain specified parts of France. They were compelled to submit to the external police of the Romish church.

* Sully, liv. 9.

es, by keeping festivals, by paying tithes; but as some compensation, they were declared eligible to office; their poor were admitted into the hospitals; while, for their protection, mixed chambers were to be established in all the parliaments.*

Such, in its scope and purpose, was the famous Edict of Nantes. Upon several occasions the Huguenots had wrung more liberal terms from the mailed hands of the League, and from the reluctant diplomacy of king Henry III. The only gain now was, that the Edict of Nantes was honestly granted; the others had been mere make-shifts, intended to tide over a shallow spot—made to be broken.

Yet comparatively niggardly as were these concessions, the papists considered them super-liberal; many of the parliaments refused for some time to register the decree;† while the fanatics protested so loudly that their voices echoed to the Vatican. Still Henry would not be baulked; when the Romanists murmured, he stormed. "The edict must be registered," said he to a delegation appointed to wait on him and acquaint him with the reluctance of the parliament to ratify it; then he added in his pithy, picturesque style, "I have climbed the walls, and can easily get over the barricades."‡

As usual, firmness triumphed; the edict was

* Browning, p. 312. D'Aubigné, Hist. Univer., vol. 3, p. 459. Soulier, Hist. du Calvinisme, p. 323.

† Journal de Henri IV. Life of Henry IV., by G. P. R. James.

‡ D'Aubigné, ut antea.

registered; indeed a year did not elapse between its signature by the king and its ratification by the provincial assemblies.*

The complaisant king next turned to Spain, and opened negotiations with his ancient foe, Philip II., now grown old and worn. Both monarchs desired peace; and on the 2d of May, 1598, the French plenipotentiaries signed an advantageous treaty at Vervin, which Henry a little later ratified at Paris.†

"Thus," says Sully, Henry's Huguenot minister of state, with justifiable exultation, "in spite of so powerful a league, comprising the pope, the emperor, the king of Spain, the duke of Savoy, the great French feudatories, and all the ecclesiastics in Christendom, our king effected his designs, and crowned them with a glorious peace."‡

At this time measures were taken to annul Henry's marriage with the profligate Margaret, with whom he had not lived for many years. When the divorce was obtained, he felt considerable repugnance to contracting any new alliance. In a conversation with Sully, after enumerating the qualities which he considered essential to a happy marriage, he said with a sigh, "But I fear no such person can be found."§

Subsequently, however, he yielded to reasons of state, and in 1600 he conferred his hand upon Mary de' Medici,‖ one of the boldest, haughtiest, and most

* Sully, liv. 9. † Matthieu, Hist. des Guerres, etc.
‡ Sully, Mem., liv. 9, at the end. § Browning, p. 307.
‖ Life of Henry IV., by G. P. R. James.

revengeful queens who ever bore the name of that unscrupulous and intriguing house.

The year 1594 witnessed the revocation of the decree which banished the Jesuits.* Singularly enough, Henry himself was the most strenuous advocate of this policy, against the remonstrance of the Sorbonne, against the counsel of the politicians, against the urgent advice of the sagacious Sully. Whether the king wished to conciliate this horde of fanatics from dread of their ceaseless intrigues, or to convince Europe that he acted upon genuine and impartial principles of liberality, is simply matter of speculation. Whatever influenced his action, it is certain that the "Society of Jesus" never forgave Henry for decreeing their expulsion, that his generosity did not placate their vengeful animosity, and that the regicidal blow of Ravaillac, so shortly to be dealt, was echoed by a deep Amen from every Jesuit heart.

During the remainder of Henry's reign, the affairs of the Huguenots present no event of marked importance. Sheltered beneath the Edict of Nantes, they pursued the even tenor of their way, held their periodical synods, elected their deputies to the provincial parliaments, and were a recognized body of the state. Henry consulted the sympathies, and deferred to the wishes of the Romanist majority,† and in this sadly grieved his ancient adherents; but his place in their affections was in some degree filled by his sister Catharine of Bourbon, whom

* Sully, liv. 17.

† Browning, p. 317.

Sully pronounces "noble and generous,"* who inherited Jane d'Albrét's zealous faith, who adhered to the primitive creed with enthusiastic devotion, and whose influence in obtaining the edict of toleration, by her tears, her entreaties, her prayers, was fully recognized by her coreligionists.†

"To you, madame," wrote Duplessis-Mornay from the synod of Montauban, "we now look for our sole *illustrious* patronage. Continue firm, we entreat you, in the true faith; let not the persuasions of the king nor the arts of the Romanists prevail. Write to us, we beseech you; give us comfort and assurance."‡

Catharine at once answered this epistle, assuring the Huguenots of her unshaken fidelity. "All I see, all I feel, but the more confirms me in my convictions," she said. "You know well the pain my brother's abjuration has given me. But I have a strong hope that, when this unsettled state of affairs has passed away, he may, through God's grace, repair the breach which, for the seeming good of his people, he has now suffered to be made in his conscience. Of me personally, believe no slanders. If reports say I go to mass, receive my denial in a word: I do not, either in act or thought. Nor does the king request it; he leaves me free in the exercise of my faith; depend on it, I will not go to mass till you are pope in very deed."§

* Sully, liv. 23.

† Huguenots in France and America, vol. 1, p. 289.

‡ Ibid., p. 282.

§ Ibid., ut antea. Duplessis' influence with the Huguenots

Catharine's influence over Henry was very great;[*] and this, coupled with her lively faith and vigilant protection of all menaced privileges, was of incalculable advantage to the Huguenots, themselves exiled from familiar access to the throne. One of the clauses of the Edict of Nantes forbade the exercise of the reformed faith within the corporate limits of Paris; and even Sully, the chief minister of state, was obliged to repair to Allon, on the banks of the Seine, four leagues distant—the nearest spot where the primitive worship was held—when he listened to the Huguenot preachers.[†]

But Catharine, who usually resided at Fontainebleau, when she visited the king at the Louvre, always had divine service performed in her chapel by her own chaplain, and to these precious reunions all members of the reformed church crowded, without distinction of rank, for Catharine recognized the essential democracy of Christianity. Once the cardinal of Goudé waited upon Henry at the head of a formal ecclesiastical delegation, to protest against this "strange desecration" of the palace. "Gentlemen," said the king angrily, "I think it more strange that such language should be held to me, in my own palace, and of my own sister. I am king, not you, sir cardinal. Adieu."[‡]

The snubbed delegates withdrew, nor did they venture to renew their complaints.

was so great, that he was called the "pope of the reformed religion."

* Sully, Mem., liv. 9. † Ibid. Browning, p. 310.

‡ Huguenots in France, etc., vol. 1.

Several attempts were made at this time to reconcile the differences between the two hostile creeds.* Discussions were held; one even took place before Catharine;† but nothing was effected: Rome and Geneva could not embrace; their respective doctrines differed too radically to kiss each other.

In 1604, the death of Catharine of Bourbon occurred.‡ She had been married to Charles, duke of Bar, who loved her with romantic devotion, and with whom, despite their opposite religious opinions, she enjoyed the utmost felicity. Bar made numberless kind efforts to detach her from her faith, but in vain. One of her last acts was to visit Angers, where she received communion with three thousand devoted Huguenots. When married, the nuptial benediction was pronounced by a Protestant minister;§ and constant to the last, she died, finding "joy and peace in believing." The fervent and uncompromising princess was buried at Vendôme, in the tomb of her ancestors, beside queen Margaret and Jane d'Albrét, a noble trinity of illustrious and beneficent women.

Henry was deeply afflicted by this event. "All, all; mother and sister!" cried he with anguish. How many painful reflections must have thronged upon him. *They* slept together in a common faith; he, the hope, the pride of both, had deserted their

* Journal de Henri IV., 1609.

† Sully, Mem., supplement.

‡ D'Aubigné, Hist. Univ., vol. 3.

§ Ibid., p. 601.

God. Bitter regret for a moment wrung his heart; and when, among the letters of condolence received from every crowned head in Europe, there came one from the pope, "expressing his holiness' fears for the salvation of the princess who had died out of the bosom of the church," he exclaimed with warmth, "I have not that bitter pang added to what I now feel; not a doubt with regard to my sweet sister's salvation exists in my mind."*

To divert the king's mind, he was persuaded to visit different cities in various portions of the kingdom. Wherever he arrived, tedious addresses were delivered, of which he heartily tired. One of these municipal orators repeated very often the words, "Oh, very benign, very merciful, very great king." "Add too," cried Henry, "*very weary.*" Another began his speech with, "Agesilaus, king of Lacedæmon—" "*Ventre St. Gris,*" interrupted the monarch impatiently; "I have heard that people spoke often to this Agesilaus, but it was always when he had dined; I have not." To another, who had addressed him for some time, and who showed no signs of desisting, Henry said, "Pray, reserve the next to another time;" but the orator was not to be cheated of the full delivery of his florid prose, and he persisted in speaking. "Well," said the king, "I am going, and you must say the rest to Master William." This was the court fool; and the orator, not liking the audience, concluded his harangue.†

* Huguenots in France, etc., vol. 1, p. 306.
† Ibid., p. 298.

With few interruptions the Huguenots now enjoyed unprecedented repose. At a synod held at Gap, in Dauphiny, D'Aubigné was appointed historiographer to the reformed church, a position which his eloquence, learning, and piety enabled him to fill with great success, as his strangely vivid portraits of his epoch testify.*

In 1609, it was reported that the Huguenots were secretly plotting an insurrection—that this was what their unwonted repose really meant. This device of the Jesuits to reinaugurate commotion—for in tranquillity they stifled—cozened Henry for a moment. Duplessis-Mornay, the king's old Mentor of the day of Coutras, was the reported chief of the conspiracy.† But after much crimination and recrimination, the report was proved to be a Jesuit bubble, and Duplessis retired to his chateau of La Forest, in Poitou. There, surrounded by true friends, amid the venerable groves of his ancestors, he carried his long and useful life far into the reign of Louis XIII. Duplessis-Mornay died in 1623, after having witnessed all that the world has to exhibit of vicissitude in human opinion.‡

The last years of Henry's momentous reign were spent partly in licentious intrigue,§ partly in exten-

* This D'Aubigné is an ancestor of Merle d'Aubigné, the historian of the Reformation, a worthy descendant of a noble ancestor.

† Cayet; De Serres, Hist. de France; D'Aubigné, Hist. Univ.

‡ Huguenots, etc., vol. 1, p. 313.

§ Matthieu; D'Aubigné; Mem. de Duplessis, etc.

sive preparations for some grand expedition whose object is shrouded in mystery. Into the chapter of gallantry it is not necessary to go. To speculate upon Henry's design in the giant preparations which Sully mentions, but cannot explain, is equally futile. It is supposed that he had conceived a scheme for the consolidation of Europe into a *République Chrêtienne,* which should promote the happiness of man, and insure perpetual peace.* "Rumor, with her thousand tongues," bruited through Europe misty reports of the projected movement. The din of preparation resounded from Paris to the Pyrenees.

The execution of the scheme would necessitate the lengthened absence of the king from France. Mary de' Medici insisted upon the regency *ad interim.* In vain did Sully and even Henry himself combat this demand; the queen would not be put off; indeed she increased her request, and asked to be crowned, in order to give additional sacredness to her government and person. With much reluctance Henry made these concessions; on the 13th of May, 1610, nine years after her marriage, the grasping Florentine's coronation occurred.† The king assisted at the pageant as a private spectator, and though fifty-six years of age, inspired general admiration by his grace of carriage and charm of manner. Throughout his life he possessed a remarkable power of captivation; on this occasion his frank, social, and yet dignified demeanor,

* Sully, Mem., supplement.

† Ibid.

caused Mary to turn towards her suite of Italian parasites, and say to Leonora Concini, her chief *confidante*, in Tuscan, "Ah, if he were mine alone."*

On the following day, the fatal 14th of May, the queen was to make her public, ceremonial entry into Paris. The capital was gay with flags, with legendary banners, with *fleurs-de-lis*. Opening with a laugh, the day closed with a cry of horror.

Henry was early astir. His buoyancy at the coronation pageant had given way to icy gloom. He was haunted by terrible apprehensions. A premonition of disaster, vivid and awful, chilled his blood. The morning he spent in his own apartments. In the afternoon he rode out with several friends, gentlemen of his suite. The curtains of the king's carriage were drawn up, not only on account of the beauty and warmth of the weather, but to enable him to witness the joyous aspect of the city, dressed in its gala garb to welcome Mary de' Medici.

The streets through which they passed were narrow; in one of them two carts were met, one laden with wine, the other with hay; the greater number of attendants passed beyond the carts to give more room to the royal coach, which meantime halted; two footmen only were near, one occupied in clearing the road, one stooping to adjust some portion of his dress.

At this moment, while Henry's guards were thus scattered, an assassin, who afterwards proved to be

* Huguenots in France, etc., vol. 1, p. 319.

a wretch called Ravaillac, stepping on one spoke of the stationary vehicle, leaned forward and struck Henry on the left breast with a dagger; it glanced on one of the ribs, and the king cried faintly, "I am wounded:" determined not to be baffled, the resolute miscreant repeated the blow; this time it went to the monarch's heart; the blood rushed up impetuously, and in an instant he was suffocated; he had no time to speak another word.*

The assassin was at once seized; and the gentlemen present, alighting from the blood-smeared carriage, caused the curtains to be closely drawn, and marched back to the Louvre benumbed with horror."†

In order to avoid a tumult, the king's death was concealed; a cloak was thrown over the yet warm body, and a surgeon and restoratives were ordered.‡

The queen was in her closet when the news was broken to her; rushing out wild with terror, she cried, "Great God, the king is dead!" "Madame," responded the chancellor, who was present, "the kings of France never die. We must take care that our tears do not undo the state; we have need of remedies, not of grief."§

"When I heard the fatal news," writes Bassompierre, afterwards the famous marshal, "I ran to the

* Huguenots in France, etc., vol. 1, p. 320. Sully, Journal de Henri IV., etc. † Ibid.

‡ Ibid.; D'Aubigné, and others.

§ Sully; D'Aubigné; Journal de Henri IV.; G. P. R. James, Life of Henry IV.

king's closet, and saw him extended on the bed. M. de Vie, counsellor of state, was seated upon the same couch, and had laid the cross of his order upon Henry's mouth. Milan, his head physician, was sitting by the bedside weeping bitterly, and a corps of surgeons stood near to dress the gaping wound. The windows stood open, and once we mistook the low sighing of the wind for his voice; but in a moment the physician said, 'Ah, it is over; he is gone.' M. Le Grand, as soon as he entered, knelt beside the bed, took the king's lifeless hands and kissed them. As for me, I threw myself at his feet, which I held, embracing again and again, and bathing them with my tears. There he lay, still and motionless—he who, but a few short hours before, was the life of every circle. It seemed as if all waited for him to break the silence; not a sound was uttered. The children of the king were brought into the chamber, but no one else was suffered to approach. Every measure was taken to deceive the people till the queen's regency was declared, lest there should be a popular commotion. About nine in the evening a number of nobles rode through the streets, and as they passed, cried, 'Make way for the king.' It being dark, the people thought Henry was among the horsemen, and shouted back, '*Vive le Roi!*' It was only in the quarter of the Louvre that the dismal truth was known. Through the night the dreadful farce was continued; the king was dressed and washed with the same ceremony as if he were alive: one gave him a shirt; another held the *serviette*, or napkin, and a third stood ready with his *robe-de-chambre*."*

Thus fell Henry Quatre, and his frightfully sudden transition from life to death is at once a lesson and an admonition. His story is strikingly romantic. He spent more than half a century in active collision with turbulent events, and in unremitting efforts to direct and mould them to the advantage of his country. Sully has pronounced his eulogy: "He was candid, sincere, grateful, compassionate, generous, wise, penetrating, and loved his subjects as a father."† It is a glowing record. But if we pursue Henry to the retreats of private life, witness his unbridled license, the impure devotion of his truant heart to the frail Gabrielles and Henriette d'Entragues of his seraglio, and recall his sad apostasy, caused by mistaken state policy, and his ostentatious *lip*-service to virtue and his *heart*-service to vice, no pleas of the faithlessness of his wedded wife, of apparent statescraft, of the profligacy of the age, of the pernicious examples of the Louvre, can shield the hero king from the censure of good men; no sophistry can avert, no swelling pæans can drown the mournful verdict of the sober muse of history:

"He knew the right, and yet the wrong pursued."

When Henry's assassin was interrogated, it was found that his name was François Ravaillac, and that he was a native of Angoumais, of low birth,

* Bassompierre, vol. 1. Nouv. Mem., p. 222.

† Sully, Mem., liv. 9.

who had passed through his novitiate in a monastery, but had never taken the final vows.* Filled with wild and superstitious notions, he had listened greedily to the laudations of Clément, and the virulent attacks upon the king daily uttered by the Jesuits drove him to frenzy—he determined to murder the king. He was put to the most frightful tortures, he suffered the most horrible death, yet he would implicate no accomplices in the murder of the monarch.†

Still, "the deep damnation of his taking off" weighed heavily against the Jesuits, not from historic proof, for it could not be had, but in a great degree from the prevalence of certain opinions which the society was well known to cherish, and which not only led Ravaillac to commit the crime, but caused others to envy the wretched notoriety he thus acquired, and to avow their readiness to perpetrate a similar atrocity. At the time, public feeling was unequivocally against the Jesuits. Even the Romanist clergy, both regular and parochial, impugned them in their sermons; and these accusations found an echo in lay publications. In the courts of law, and at meetings in the market-place, the "Society of Jesus" was alike believed to have prompted the assassin.‡

Strange to say, in the investigation of the regicide, the effort was rather to suppress than to elicit the facts. France seemed afraid to know the truth.

* James, Life of Henry IV., vol. 3, p. 403.

† Ibid., p. 404.

‡ Browning, p. 317, et seq.

"It would seem," remarks L'Etoile, the journalist of the age, "to hear the matter spoken of, that we are afraid of showing ourselves too exact and severe in inquiring into this crime, the most wicked and barbarous, and the most important to our state, of any perpetrated for a thousand years."*

Sad as is the misfortune for a nation to produce such wretches as Clément and Ravaillac, it is a still more serious calamity to have a servile magistracy. Sequier was chief president of the Parliament: his reply to the queen's inquiry respecting his opinion of the question, proves the importance of the real criminals,† yet the investigation was smothered. "If I am asked who were the demons who inspired this damnable murder," says Péréfixe, archbishop of Paris, "history answers that she knows nothing; even the judges who interrogated Ravaillac did not dare to open their mouths upon the subject, and never spoke of him otherwise than by shrugging their shoulders."‡

* L'Etoile. See also Lettres de N. Pasquier.
† Journal de Henri IV., February, 1611.
‡ Péréfixe, Hist. de Henri le Grande.

CHAPTER XXXIII.

RICHELIEU.

THE murdered king left three children by Mary de' Medici. The eldest succeeded to the throne in his ninth year, under the title of Louis XIII. The younger, the dukes of Orleans and Anjou, were infants. On the day following the assassination, the Parliament, browbeaten by the duke d'Epernon,* confirmed the queen as regent. France, remembering the regency of Catharine de' Medici, beheld with grief and terror the sceptre pass from the vigorous grasp of Henry Quatre ostensibly into the feeble hands of an infant, really into the grasping talons of an Italian interloper, who was herself ruled by foreign parasites.†

While the public *salons* of the Louvre were covered with "the trappings and the suits of woe," the private apartments of the new-made regent resounded with songs of gladness and bursts of laughter. 'T was here that the Florentine held her giddy court, smiling before the open grave of her murdered husband, gay amid her cordon of favorites who served luxurious viands and emptied sparkling goblets in her honor.

* Girard, Vie du Duc d'Epernon, p. 246.

† Wyatt, Hist. Kings of France, p. 220.

The government of Mary de' Medici was really the government of her confidants, Concini, who rose to be Marshal d'Ancre, and his wife Leonora Galigni. The pernicious art of this subtle pair cozened the queen into the adoption of their measures, while she believed them to be her own. Under their influence, the court was new-modelled. Epernon was slighted, Condé was snubbed, Sully was insulted out of office.*

An inimical contemporary bears witness to the quiet deportment of the Huguenots at this crisis: "Instructed by experience, they then displayed great moderation, and made no pretensions to innovation; *feigning* to have no wish to undertake any unfriendly action, provided they were permitted to live under the untouched edicts."†

Ere long, however, uneasiness was felt. The regent, not satisfied with remodelling the court and promoting her lackey favorites to the highest seats of honor at the council-board, and to the noblest titles of the state, revolutionized the politics of Henry Quatre. His idea was, Germany protected from the encroachments of Austria, the insidious advances of Spain sternly repulsed. Now efforts were made to placate Austria, and an alliance with Spain was eagerly sought. Despite the ominous growls of discontent provoked by this new policy of the queen regent's mushroom council, it was pressed; and with so much success, that the boy-

* Sully, Mem., last liv.

† Bernard, Hist. de Louis XIII., p. 12.

ish king was soon married to Anne of Austria, the Spanish infanta.*

The Huguenots read in these events melancholy auguries for their cause. Secret conferences were held; chiefs were chosen to maintain their menaced rights.† The Jesuits, in their sermons, openly announced the object of the royal marriage to be the extermination of heresy.‡ Threats soon passed into acts. Ancient and well-defined privileges were invaded and annulled. Slumbering animosities were rekindled.

The heads of the Huguenot party at this time were Rohan, Soubise, La Tremouille, and Bouillon. Condé and the count de Soisson had been educated as Romanists, but their turbulent ambition impelled them frequently to negotiate with the reformers. Duplessis-Mornay, broken by age, rested in honorable retirement. D'Aubigné was still an active agent of his coreligionists.§ "Rohan," says the Jesuit d'Avrigny, "was a sincere Huguenot, and aimed at the good of his party. Sully was not very devout, but felt sore at his exclusion from public affairs. Bouillon was politic, using his religion to forward his interests."‖

Bigotry and court cabal kept the country in feverish excitement. The crowd of reckless foreigners who surrounded the queen regent fomented

* Bassompierre. Pardoe, Court of Louis XIV. Bernard. Rohan, Mem.

† D'Aubigné, Hist. Univ.

‡ Arcana Gallica, pp. 74, 75.

§ Mem. Rohan, liv. 1.

‖ D'Avrigny, Mem. Chronologiques, vol. 1, p. 68.

discord; for they saw in it an opportunity to achieve wealth and fame. Their efforts were seconded by a horde of warlike nobles, whose idea of life was drawn swords and pointed cannon. Added to all, the Jesuits constantly inflamed their penitents against the toleration of heresy. Local *émeutes* were of frequent occurrence. These were sometimes terminated by mutual apologies, sometimes by negotiation.

On the 24th of April, 1617, the regency was ended, as it began, with a tragedy. The marshal D'Ancre was assassinated. This adventurer had in reality swayed the sceptre under cover of the queen. His insolence and cruelty made him feared and hated. The young king especially disliked him; and it was at the instigation of De Luines, Louis' favorite, that the former obscure notary of Florence, and later gentleman-usher of the Louvre, who had clutched a marshal's baton, was slain.*

Now the king himself assumed to reign; but his rule, like his mother's, was only nominal. De Luines succeeded d'Ancre; a satyr followed a satyr.

On the fall of her government, Mary de' Medici was "permitted to retire to Blois,"† the velvet phrase in which the court wrapped the iron reality, *imprisonment*.

Through these troubles at the court, the Huguenots did their utmost to remain quiet. Synods were frequently held, assemblies were often convoked, but their discussions were entirely devoted to questions

* Hist. de la Mére et du Fils, vol. 2, p. 185. † Ibid.

of divinity and discipline.* Ambitious nobles did their best to inveigle the reformers into adopting their quarrels and avenging their supposititious wrongs. Bouillon was active in his endeavors to enlist the party in his selfish schemes.† Condé also, relying upon his historic name and the traditional affection of the Huguenots for his house, attempted to win them to support his tortuous conspiracies to aggrandize himself.‡ But except in isolated instances, these insidious arts did not succeed; while their peaceful behavior and loyal tone gave the anxious court no pretext for persecution.

At length De Luines, supported by the ready clergy, determined to create war.

The principality of Bearn had been for many years preponderately Protestant. It was there that Margaret de Valois had taught and prayed; it was there that her daughter, Jane d'Albrét, had lived and labored in God's service; it was there that Catharine of Bourbon had garnered many souls as trophies; there Henry Quartre had been reared: it was the "holy of holies" among French provinces.

Influenced by the reiterated clamors of the Romish clergy, one of whom did not scruple to declare that "Christians were worse treated in Bearn than in Mohammedan countries," and that "the property of the church was applied to the support of its enemies,§ Louis XIII. determined not only to

* Browning, p. 334.

† Ibid., p. 320, et seq, passim.

‡ Ibid.

§ This was the bishop of Maçon.

restore the Romish religion, but to crown that pious work by the annexation of the principality to France.*

An *arrêt* was soon after given to this effect in open council; and since the resolute Huguenots, unwilling to surrender their ancient privileges without a struggle, declined to yield, the king assembled an army, and in 1620 marched to enforce his usurpation by the unsheathed sword.†

The ill-armed and unorganized partisan bands of the Huguenots could not impede the triumphal advance of the king's mailed cohorts. In October, 1620, Louis entered Pau, and the Romish worship was at once celebrated in those cathedrals which for sixty years had echoed the purer praises of the primitive ritual.

The abolition of the provincial independence of Bearn was denounced by the whole Huguenot party as an infraction of the edict of Nantes. An assembly was convened at Rochelle. Here the excited delegates, regardless of the advice of their most judicious leaders, abjured all allegiance to the king, and published a decree dividing Protestant France into military and civil districts, on the model of the United Netherlands.‡ The command of one circle was given to Soubise, the command of another to La Force, while a third was entrusted to the duc

* Bernard, Vie de Louis XIII., p. 149.

† Rohan, Mem. D'Aubigné, Mem.

‡ Arcere, vol. 2, p. 4[illegible]9, et seq ; Rohan ; Discours sur les Derniers Troubles, p. [illegible]

de Rohan, the most enlightened, virtuous, and talented soldier of his age.*

These bold proceedings instantly precipitated active hostilities. The royal army marched into Southern France, the old, familiar haunt of the twin demons of civil war and bigotry. Montpellier was entered. Montauban was besieged; but it was so skilfully defended that De Luines, now constable of France, quitted the obstinate walls with a malediction.†

During this contest, the affairs of the Huguenots became so extensively diversified that it is scarcely possible to give a connected view of the events which occurred among the many divisions comprised in their loose-jointed confederation; for the interest is no longer arrested by one body, around whose history the episodes of its satellites can be successively unfolded; but events of equal importance claim and fix attention in opposite directions.

In some respects the struggle was a gallant one; but there was a prevailing readiness on the part of many of the Huguenot strong-holds to surrender upon the king's approach, in strong contrast to their unvarying practice in the preceding civil wars. Indeed Rohan observes, "From Saumur to Montauban there was a general submission, with no resistance except at St. Jean d'Angely, which my brother Soubise defended as long as he could. And the

* Arcére, vol. 2, p. 259, et seq.; Rohan; Discours sur les Derniers Troubles, p. 101.

† Rohan, Mem., p. 130.

peace of Montpellier comprised no chiefs of provinces except my brother and myself, all the others having made treaties separately, and on advantageous terms."*

At length all parties tired of the war. Louis announced his intention to adhere strictly to the Edict of Nantes, and the divided and crippled Huguenots willingly laid down their arms on this assurance.† Amnesty was granted in October, 1622. The pacification was signed, and tranquillity once more reigned in France.

Two years later a new *régime* was inaugurated. Richelieu‡ entered the council of state. From the

* Rohan. Discours sur les Derniers Troubles, p. 101.

† Bassompierre, Mem. Arcére, vol. 2.

‡ Armand Jean Duplessis, cardinal duke of Richelieu, was born in Paris on the 5th of September, 1585. Five years after the birth of the future statesman, his father, who held several important posts at the court of Henry IV., died, leaving three sons, of whom Armand was the youngest, and two daughters, both of whom were early married to nobles of the French court. The church and the camp were the usual resources in those days of the younger sons of noble houses; and since the bishopric of Laçon, which the family of Plessis could command for one of the sons, was destined for Alphonse, the second, Armand was dedicated from infancy to the profession of arms. Ere long Alphonse resigned his see, and entered a Carthusian community; whereupon Richelieu quitted the camp, and applying himself to the study of theology, assumed the mitre of the Laçan bishopric. He was a studious and diligent scholar, and completed his course with considerable applause. In 1607 he departed for Rome, to receive from the hands of the pope, Paul V., the consecration of his new dignity. He was asked whether he had attained the age required by the canonical law, twenty-five years. The embryo prelate replied at once in the affirmative; but immediately after the completion of the ceremony, he requested the holy father to receive his confession; in which, with imper-

very outset his soaring intellect, sagacious diplomacy, and consummate tact gave him the leadership; and ere long, basing his authority upon these qualities, he governed France as absolutely as he could had he been born to the royal purple and inherited the crown.

To elevate the regal authority by destroying the festering remains of feudal *caste;* to raise the importance of France by humiliating the overbearing arrogance of Austria and Spain; to terminate all domestic differences by suppressing the few liberties still enjoyed by the Huguenots—this was the triple policy of the famous statesman;* and he

turbable composure, he admitted the falsehood of which he had just been guilty. The pontiff absolved him from the sin; but in the course of the same evening, he pointed him out to the French ambassador, with the remark that he would one day become a clever politician. The prophecy proved true; and the unscrupulous use of means which, at the age of twenty-one, he displayed in hastening his elevation, affords no bad specimen of the shifts to which he resorted through life to maintain his authority.

On his return to France, he formed a friendship with the advocate Boutheiller, who was intimate with Barbin, the confidential agent of Mary de' Medici. Through Barbin, Richelieu was presented to the all-powerful Concinis, who brought him to the notice of the queen regent. His remarkable talents soon won him the confidence of Mary, who employed him in a variety of missions, always with success. Upon the downfall of the regency, Richelieu went into exile with the queen; but returning with her to the court, he soon quitted his old protectress, and gaining the notice of the king, rose step by step to a seat in the council of state. He received a cardinal's hat in 1622; and from the date of his admission into the holy conclave, assumed the name and title of Cardinal duke of Richelieu. James, Life of Richelieu; Pardoe, Louis XIV. and his Court, vol. 1, p. 19, et seq.

* Léclerc, Vie de Richelieu; James, Life of Richelieu, etc.

steadily pursued it through the mazy intrigues essential to success. Pretexts of every kind were unscrupulously employed to veil these designs. As circumstances required, he would vary the apparent programme; but whatever hue the diplomatic chameleon reflected, the real purpose was unchanged and unchangeable.

Richelieu accomplished his first object by choking the *émeutes* of the turbulent nobility with an iron hand. He achieved the second by a system of crafty manœuvres at once protean and astounding. As a prince of the church of Rome, he naturally devoted himself to the third; yet reasons of state were his chief motive and guide. There was nothing of the fanatic in his constitution. Richelieu never persecuted merely from the love of it. Torquemada was not his model, nor was St. Dominic a congenial soul.

In 1626 England, like France, had a vizier: the duke of Buckingham, famous for his singular elevation and untimely end, swayed the councils of the British king without a rival. Recently Charles I. had espoused a daughter of the house of Bourbon. Buckingham was dispatched to receive her. While tarrying in Paris, the foppish courtier became enamoured of the queen of France: the daring libertine even had the audacity to declare his passion;* and undismayed by the frowns of the outraged wife of Louis XIII., on the conclusion of his mission,

* Some historians affirm that the queen encouraged Buckingham. See Browning, p. 346, note.

he returned to Paris to renew his advances.* But his dream of illicit happiness was shortly dissipated by a peremptory command to quit the country.†

Humiliated and enraged, Buckingham rëentered England, anxious to wipe out this "insult" of his expulsion from France, by war. He negotiated with the duke of Savoy, Richelieu's enemy. He fomented discord in the sister kingdom; and an envoy was dispatched to inveigle Rohan, who—since the death of Duplessis and the self exile of D'Aubigné domesticated at Geneva—had been the leader of the Huguenots, into arming against the incessant, though insidious encroachments of the court upon the tolerant decree of Henry Quatre.‡

Meantime a powerful armament was equipped, and in the summer of 1627 Buckingham in person appeared off Rochelle.§ After much hesitation, and through his instrumentality, the whole Huguenot party armed, really to support the projects of the duke of Buckingham, but as they thought, to wring from the greedy clutch of Richelieu the stolen and denied clauses of the Edict of Nantes.‖

This afforded the wily cardinal a desired opportunity; and acting with his accustomed energy, he speedily conjured an army into existence, at the

* Rohan, Mem. Hist., p. 279. Also Lord Clarendon and Bishop Burnet. † Ibid.

‡ Rohan, Mem., p. 212. Violart, vol. 1, p. 683.

§ Bassompierre, vol. 3, p. 64.

‖ Rohan, Mem., vol. 3, p. 61. Léclerc, vol. 1, p. 332.

head of which he in person pressed forward to besiege the Huguenot citadel.*

Richelieu's skill met and conquered all difficulties; and comprehending all the weak points in the political situation, as well as in the character of his adversaries, with the keen glance of genius, he prepared to assail both where they were most vulnerable.

He held out to the Rochelloise the prospect of renewed religious enfranchisement, and thus deceived the mayor and the city council, and secured a vacillation of purpose which gave him time—the *desideratum*. He dispatched the prince de Condé into Languedoc, to hold the reformers quiet by the mailed hand; and then, piecing out the lion's skin with the fox's, he sent Gallaud, an eloquent Huguenot whom he had secretly suborned, to persuade his coreligionists to remain in tranquillity.†

While these crafty measures were being set afoot, large garrisons were thrown into all menaced towns; quantities of ammunition were collected; provisions abounded in his camps; and fleets of boats were floated to convenient points, where they were serviceable in the transportation of supplies in the attack and defence of cities.

In the mean time the Rochelloise acted precisely as Richelieu anticipated—began with a solemn fast, and instead of admitting their English allies at once, hesitated, disputed, and inquired.‡

* Rohan, Mem., vol 3, p. 61. Léclerc, vol. 1, p. 332. James, Life of Richelieu, vol. 1, p. 82, et seq.

† Ibid.

‡ Mem. de Rohan, lib. 4.

The Huguenots of the south followed this pernicious example; but they were even more besotted. Some armed under the appeal of Rohan; some positively supported the court; but the great majority remained in hesitating inactivity, complaining of those who had taken arms before danger had grown into adversity.

Richelieu laid close siege to Rochelle. The defence was one of the most heroic on record. The operations dragged through fifteen months. At length famine began to gnaw; various attempts were made by Rohan and by the English to succor the succumbing city, but the cunning of the cardinal foiled these; and the assassination of Buckingham on the very eve of a new expedition,* rang the death-knell to all hopes of aid. Then craving nature had her way; and in October, 1628,† hitherto unconquerable Rochelle opened its maiden gates to the triumphant legions of Richelieu. So terrible had been the suffering endured during the siege, that the inhabitants were reduced from twenty-seven thousand to five thousand‡—ghastly proof of the heroism of their fight.

Richelieu completed the humiliation of this "city of refuge" by celebrating mass with great pomp on the festival of All Saints, which occurred shortly after its conquest, and by stripping it of its boasted franchises,§ a desecration over which the Rochelloise shed proud tears.

* Hume, Hist. of Eng. Reign of Charles I. Arcére, vol. 2, p. 291.

† Arcére, vol. 2, p. 323. Browning, p. 354. ‡ Ibid. § Ibid.

In other sections the Huguenots, led by the gallant De Rohan, achieved success; but when the sad news from Rochelle reached their scattered camps, quite disconcerted and heart-broken, they desired peace. Rohan convened a Huguenot assembly at Anduze in 1628. The deputies opened negotiations with Richelieu; and on the 27th of June, 1629, a treaty was concluded and signed at Alais, which guaranteed liberty of conscience and of worship on the essential basis of the often-infringed Edict of Nantes.*

No sooner was the civil war terminated, than all France resounded with pæans to Richelieu. The cardinal-duke was now firmly seated in his vizierate; but his time was largely occupied in foiling the intrigues of his foes. The court soon became the scene of rivalry and cabal; and Louis, one of the most inefficient and timid of monarchs, was so harassed by the quarrels of his family, that he acquired a habit of leaning upon the iron arm of his great minister, whom he soon came to consider indispensable to his happiness and comfort and to the government of France.

Engrossed by these events, the court paid little attention to the despised Huguenots. Stripped al-

* Menard, Histoire de Nîmes, vol. 5, p. 586. Rohan, Mem., lib. 4. Soon after the signature of this peace, Rohan went abroad, and achieved a brilliant fame in foreign service. He was, by general admission, one of the greatest men and one of the best of his age. He never abandoned his religious principles. And when, in 1638, he was killed, his body was carried to Geneva, and buried with great honor.

ready, by insidious assaults, of their political importance, the time was hastening on with giant strides when they were to be deprived of the rights of conscience. But now for a space they rested in quiet security. Protestantism was armed and triumphant on the Continent. All Europe knew the resolution of Gustavus Adolphus to make common cause with all reformers who suffered persecution. France was the secret ally of the great Scandinavian; a position into which Richelieu had drifted through his desire to humble the house of Austria. This made him cautious not to alienate the continental Protestants by the oppression of their brothers in France. Besides, the Puritan party in England was rising into influence; the *entente cordiale* between the Puritans and the Huguenots had never been disturbed; this too conspired to guard the French Protestants from unfriendly legislative action.

"The government," says Bernard, the jesuitical biographer of Louis XIV., "was engrossed by the disputes between the king, his mother, and his brother, and by the exciting foreign events; so that, deeming this a favorable opportunity for an insurrection of the Huguenots, efforts were made to hold them tranquil by granting the most reasonable of their demands."*

Emboldened by the liberal temper of the cardinal, the Huguenots held a synod at Charenton in September, 1631;† and two ministers, Amivault and De Villars, were deputed to present a statement of

* **Bernard,** Vie de Louis XIV., p. 280. † **Browning, p. 358.**

their grievances to the king, then sojourning at Compiégne. The assembly petitioned for the reacknowledgment of the right of their clergy to preach in any Protestant temple, a recent governmental decision having forbidden them to abandon their individual charges. They also requested a cessation of proceedings instituted against some Languedocian ministers for inculcating the avowed doctrines of the Reformation, and the liberation of some of their friends chained in the galleys for their opinions.*

From this modest list of their demands an idea may be formed of the condition of the Huguenots at this epoch.

* Browning, p. 358.

CHAPTER XXXIV.

THE DRAGONNADES.

From the pacification of 1629 until 1661, the general history of the Huguenots presents few important incidents. There were from time to time individual causes of complaint and isolated instances of hostility, for the spirit of the League was not extinct, and the more zealous partisans of Rome were only restrained from urging their favorite measures by the imperious genius of the celebrated cardinals who successively administered the government of France, and by the preoccupation of the court. Popular prejudice would frequently burst forth in an excess of animosity, under the garb of religion; and whenever, through some technicality, the protecting clauses of the Edict of Nantes could be invaded or infringed, the circumstance was considered as a victory over heresy.*

In December, 1642, Richelieu died; and five months later, consistent even in death, the lackey monarch Louis XIII. *followed* the famous statesman to the tomb; he could not even die till Richelieu showed him how. In the following year, Louis XIV., a boy of five, succeeded to the throne. From 1643 till 1651 the history of France is the history of the regency of Anne of Austria and the faction

* Browning, p. 361.

of the Fronde, when the "grand monarch" was merely the puppet of the queen mother and her minister; from Louis' majority until the death of Mazarin, in 1661, it is the history of that subtle and intriguing cardinal.

Not Richelieu himself had ruled France more absolutely than did Mazarin. Like his predecessor, he was a great secular statesman rather than an ardent churchman; as such he never permitted the interests of the Vatican to lure him from the path of national policy. He was enabled to maintain this position because France was now strong and consolidated. Spain had already commenced her descent into the tier of second-rate states; the peace of Westphalia had changed the tactics of several of the European cabinets; and the rise of the Commonwealth had altered the aspect of French diplomacy with England.*

Mazarin prized Cromwell's alliance; he was aware of the jealous care with which the mighty Protector guarded the interests of menaced Protestantism. The duke of Savoy had ventured to persecute the feeble remnant of the primitive Waldenses, who lived obscurely in the Lombard vallies, and all Europe saw Cromwell's powerful arm stretch across the Channel and across the Alps to snatch the Vaudois from the greedy maw of the Savoyard, while England's statesman-poet chanted pæans, and the fast-anchored island shouted glad Amen.†

* Burnet, History of his Own Times, vol. 1, p. 38.
† Ibid. Life of John Milton, published by Am. Tr. Soc., 1866.

Mazarin had no disposition to provoke Cromwell's intervention in French affairs; he knew the chord of sympathy which united the Puritans and the Huguenots; this made him cautious of overtly assailing the privileges of the reformed church in France.*

Besides, pretexts were wanting. The Huguenot party, after the capture of Rochelle, definitively disbanded its political organization; Henri de Rohan was their last armed chieftain. Weary of war, and perhaps persuaded that it corresponded not with the peaceful tenets of their creed, they sought in seclusion the simple liberty of praising God. What the sword had been unable to effect, they thought that civilization and open Bibles would accomplish.

Of their loyalty and quietude at this epoch, hostile writers bear ready and ample witness. "I have no complaint to make of the little flock," said Mazarin; "if they graze on noxious herbs, at least they do not stray."†

Through the *émeutes* of the Fronde, they furnished devoted soldiers to the menaced government. Mazarin recognized their important services; he never spoke of the pastors of Montauban without calling them his "good friends;" and Count d'Harcourt said to the deputies of that city, "The crown was tottering on the king's head, but you have steadied it."‡

* James, Life of Mazarin.

† Felice, Hist. of Prot. of France, vol. 1, p. 341. ‡ Ibid.

Louis XIV. expressed his gratitude more than once. In a declaration published in May, 1652, he said, "Forasmuch as our subjects of the pretended reformed religion have given us reiterated proofs of their affection and fidelity, with which we are well pleased, be it hereby known, that for these causes they be maintained and secured, and we do now maintain and secure them, in the full and entire enjoyment of the Edict of Nantes."*

This is the monarch who soon after inflicted long, odious, and Satanic persecutions upon these faithful subjects who had "steadied the crown upon his brow."

In comparative repose the years of Mazarin's vizierate passed away. The Huguenots, industrious, intelligent, and docile, were the pattern subjects in the kingdom.†

But in 1661 the death of the great cardinal occurred, and at once ebbing persecution began to rise towards its flood-tide.

Louis XIV. assumed the direction of affairs. In the heyday of his youth, the royal libertine, trampling with equal readiness upon the laws of God and man, was comparatively careless in religious matters. This circumstance, together with the fierce dispute between the Jesuit and the Jansenist parties, which menaced Rome with another schism,‡ restrained for a space the reactive tendency. But

* Soulier, Hist. du Calvinisme, p. 552.

† Acére, vol. 2, p. 345.

‡ Duclos, Mem. de Louis XIV., vol. 1, p. 102.

with the subjugation of Port Royal, the relapse occurred. At the outset the assault was insidious. Every five years the secular clergy held ecclesiastical assemblies, and these never adjourned without tearing away some new shred from the laws of toleration.*

Money in immense sums was supplied from the exchequer of the state to suborne heresy.† The king judged men in general by the conduct of those who breathed the atmosphere of his court. As he beheld continual sacrifices of honor and principle in the halls of the Louvre, souls bartered for gold or titles, he came to think that the Huguenots held out to obtain good terms; he thought that they could be seduced by rendering their interests subservient to their abjuration.

Among the nobles the eloquence of corruption made many proselytes; men of high birth were dazzled by the proffer of honors and rank. But to the lasting honor of the middle and lower classes, let it be recorded that they could not be bribed by such inducements to shut their Bibles and deny their God. The peaceable manufacturers, the tradesmen, the cunning artificers, continued steadfast in the faith.‡

Every device which wit could suggest to enforce proselytism was eagerly adopted; favors of every kind were lavished upon those whom fear or avarice had converted to Romanism; they were ex-

* Felice, Hist. Protestants, etc., vol. 1, p. 342.

† Soulier, Hist du Calvinisme.

‡ Ibid.

empted from taxation, from guardianship, from local contributions; were excused the payment of their debts, delivered from the coercion of parental authority, and advanced in the several professions to which they devoted their talents.*

Far different was the fate of those who clung to their persecuted creed for conscience' sake. They were constantly made the victims of new hardships and indignities; their colleges were closed; their youth barred out from every avenue of profit and honor; their churches were interdicted; their inheritances were wrested from them through technicalities; and their dead were not permitted to rest in their ancestral sepulchres.†

The infinite hard fights which God's suffering children now waged with self-interest, with abounding temptation, satanically devised and spread about them, may not be recorded. But fast anchored, through all vicissitudes they clung to the heavenly throne; they refused to dwell in Sodom, and they would not tarry in Gomorrah.

The reformers now had implacable and tireless enemies in the men who swayed the councils of the state. In the foremost rank figured the Jesuits, created expressly to extirpate heresy, the born foes of the Huguenots, monks doubly formidable as the confessors of kings, and because their system of morality authorized the use of any means. Falsehood, trickery, injustice, traffic in consciences,

* Pardoe, Louis XIV., and the Court of France, vol. 2, p. 339.

† Ibid. Anquétil, Hist. de France.

brute force, spoliation, banishment, nay, even murder—all were good in their eyes, if they tended to accomplish their end.*

Under the direction of the Jesuits, the government marched steadily from one tyranny to another. Ere long the judiciary system was tampered with. In rare instances the courts of law had given impartial decisions. By a legal trick this hope of justice was destroyed.†

In despair, many of the Huguenots began to emigrate: England, Germany, the Hague, all stretched forth welcoming hands.

But soon the exodus was stopped; a decree, issued in 1669, forbade emigration. The Huguenots not only might not enjoy in France the equal protection of the laws, they could not hope to find an asylum abroad.‡ Edict followed edict in rapid succession: a peculiar dress was prescribed for the Protestants; they were shut out from many species of employment other than political; and the penalties which awaited an unsuccessful effort to escape proceeded in an awful gradation from fine to imprisonment, and from the galleys to death.§

Yet still the Huguenots persisted in their worship and clung to their creed. The king, now become the complete slave, in civil matters, of his mistress, Madame de Maintenon, herself a renegade Protestant,‖ and the tool of the Jesuits in

* Felice, vol. 1, p. 342.

† Benoit, vol. 3, p. 453.

‡ Ibid.

§ Browning, p. 365.

‖ Ibid. Pardoe, Louis XIV., etc.

religion, dissatisfied with the slow progress made in the subornation of heresy, determined to *force* conversion. *Booted missionaries* were dispatched into the Huguenot provinces to harry the reformers into adherence to Rome.

The *dragonades* commenced.

The persecution which raged for several years subsequent to 1681, surpassed in cold-blooded malignity that of the sixteenth century; for the undisguised hostility of the last kings of the house of Valois, although barbarous, was frank; their object was avowed; the Huguenots themselves were militant, and the conflict was undisguised. But now all pretext had ceased; the Jesuits were crafty; insidious enactments rendered it almost impossible to avoid contravention; and liberty of worship was destroyed even while the Edict of Nantes remained the formal law,* so powerless are naked statutes.

The Jesuit La Chaise was the king's confessor. Like Milton's Belial, this monk

> "Seemed
> For dignity composed and high exploit;
> But all was false and hollow, though his tongue
> Dropt manna, and could make the worse appear
> The better reason, to perplex and dash
> Maturest counsels; for his thoughts were low,
> To vice industrious, but to nobler deeds
> Timorous and slothful."†

La Chaise reminded Louis that the Roman year of jubilee occurred in 1676, and he urged the monarch to signalize his piety by extirpating heresy, since

* Browning, p. 370. † Paradise Lost, book 2, p. 30.

the days of pilgrimages were gone, and he could no longer acquire fame by heading a crusade, or by travelling on foot with staff and scrip to the Holy Land. "Sire," said he, "a new Christian hero is to arise; perhaps he may find another Tasso to immortalize his name;" and the royal voluptuary, bloated with license, gouty with excess, quitted the side of his mistress for a moment to beg his ghostly confessor to inform him how he might acquire the reputation of a Christian hero.

La Chaise, Louvois the king's minister, and Madame de Maintenon, a congenial trinity, united their efforts to exterminate the Huguenots.

A brutal soldiery were quartered on the "heretics;" devastation, pillage, torture—there was nothing that they recoiled at; indeed they gave such loose rein to their passions, that their frightful excesses would have shamed a horde of brigands.*

Benoît has filled many pages of his *Histoire de l'Edit de Nantes* with hideous details of these atrocities. "The soldiers," he says, "tied crucifixes to the end of their carbines, and these they compelled the Huguenots to kiss; if any offered resistance, they thrust the crucifix in the face or stomach of the victim. Neither children nor persons of advanced age were spared; they fell on all without compassion: some were cudgelled to death; some were beaten to a jelly with the flat side of a sword; others were stabbed with the bayonet-crucifix fixed

* Narrative of the Sufferings of a French Protestant Family, by John Migault. London, 1824, p. 182, et seq.

at the end of their carbines. These wretches inflicted similar cruelties on women. They whipped them; struck them with rattans across the face to disfigure them; dragged them by the hair of the head through mire and over stones. Sometimes, finding the laborers at their ploughs, the soldiers hurried them off to the Romish church, pricking them along like bullocks with their own goads to quicken their reluctant pace."*

Behind the dragonaders were a legion of friars, Capuchins, Franciscans, Carmelites, an ignorant and restless soldiery, who worked on the fanaticism of the mob, and marched, whenever an opportunity occurred, to make an assault upon heresy.

Emigration, which had been interdicted by the edict of 1669, now began again on a still vaster scale, and thousands of families quitted France. The Protestant countries, England, Switzerland, Holland, and Denmark, offered them a shelter in official declarations.† But the ordinances prohibiting emigration were reënacted with increased severity.

The law against emigration, and that against relapsed heretics, put a two-edged sword in the hands of the persecutors. The condition of the

* Hist. de l'Edit de Nantes, tome 4, pp. 479, 480. Those who desire to know the situation of the Huguenots in detail at this epoch, should consult this work. The author has filled five quarto volumes with his narrative of the hideous cruelties inflicted on his coreligionists, from the reign of Henry IV. to the revocation of the Edict of Nantes.

† Felice, vol. 2, p. 45.

Huguenots was pitiable. In France they would not recognize them as any thing but Romanists; on reaching the frontiers they were seized as heretics. Rulhiéres, the panegyrist of Louis XIV., says that the misfortunes of the Reformed were chiefly owing to the combined operation of these two laws, which formed the boast of Father La Chaise as masterpieces of genius.*

Such were the means employed by Louis XIV. to convert France to Latin orthodoxy. "Concerning this monarch," says Macauley, "the world seems at last to have formed a correct judgment. He was not a great general; he was not a great statesman; but he was in one sense a great king. Never was there so consummate a master of what James I. called *kingcraft*—of all those arts which most advantageously display the merits of a prince, and most completely hide his defects. Though his internal administration was bad; though the military triumphs which gave splendor to the early part of his reign were not achieved by himself; though his later years were crowded with defeats and humiliations; though he was so ignorant that he scarcely understood the Latin of his mass-book; though he fell under the control of a cunning Jesuit and of a still more cunning old woman, he succeeded in passing himself off upon the people as a being above humanity.

"Death and time have exposed the deception. The body of the 'grand monarch' has been meas-

* Rulhiéres, Eclaircissements Historiques, vol. 1.

ured more justly than it was measured by the courtiers who were afraid to look above his shoetie. His public character has been scrutinized by men free from the hopes and fears of Boileau and Molière. In the grave, the most majestic of princes is only five feet eight. In history the hero and politician dwindles into a vain and feeble tyrant, the slave of priests and women, little in war, little in government, little in every thing but the art of simulating greatness."*

* Macauley, Essays, Louis XIV.

CHAPTER XXXV.

REVOCATION OF THE EDICT OF NANTES.

UNTIL the year 1685, the efforts of the *booted missionaries* were confined to one or two provinces; but now they were extended into other sections. Bearn was harried; Languedoc was bled; the Vivarias was changed into a Golgotha. The most sinister acts of the dark ages are white when set against the blackness of this modern infamy. France, to borrow the striking language of the Hebrew poet, was "a land of darkness, as darkness itself, and where the light was as darkness."

Every engine which a satanic wit could invent was put in motion to cajole, to overawe, and to torture steadfast martyrs into a denial of their faith. Pellisson, the administrator of the corruption fund, regularly handed the king lists of six, eight, ten hundred converts, vouched for by fraudulent certificates; and his miracles were daily chronicled in the Gazette. He avoided publishing that the few proselytes he did make were exclusively from the dregs of the people; either knaves who periodically made a trade of their consciences, or starving beggars who took the money to get a piece of bread.* Venial and licentious scribblers lauded the triumph. The court at Versailles, dripping with wine, drunk-

* Felice, vol. 2, p. 33.

en with blasphemy, bloated with gluttony, and reeling in obscene dances, paused a moment in its frightful orgy, to cross itself and hiccough a *viva.* The king was astonished at the number of his "converts;" the prelates applauded; Bossuet harangued, and Boileau dogmatized; while the Jesuits stood by with a cunning leer. But reasonable people did not credit Pellisson's Munchausenisms. Even Madame de Maintenon wrote, "I think that all these conversions are not sincere; but at least the children will be Romanists."*

The jubilant court was soon undeceived. Sixteen Huguenot deputies from Languedoc, Corennes, Vivarias, and Dauphiny assembled at Toulouse, and decided to recommence worship in all interdicted places simultaneously, without ostentation, but without secrecy; either with open doors, or on the ruins of their demolished temples. At the same time union, repentance, prayer, and faith, "mighty to the pulling down of strong-holds," were recommended.†

In hundreds of thousands the Huguenots assembled. "The roses and the myrtles of devotion bloomed unchilled on the verge of the avalanche."

The king was enraged; the satyrs of the court sputtered vengeance; the Jesuits spat fresh venom. "It was believed," says the abbé Soulier, "that the Calvinists, being reduced to have few public exercises, would more willingly listen to the instructions which the prelates gave in their dioceses to draw

* Letter to the Countess de St. Geran. † Felice, vol. 2, p. 49.

them from error; and that the money which the king distributed to assist the new converts would induce the religionists to enter almost voluntarily into the bosom of the church: but as these measures had not all the effect which was anticipated, and as it appeared, on the contrary, that the Calvinists, far from listening to the missionaries, became more obstinate, his majesty deemed it necessary to use stronger measures to draw them from that lethargy into which their birth had unfortunately thrown them. The king's troops were employed to coöperate with the missionaries, that thus what had been effected in Poitiers, where forty thousand of the Huguenots had been subjugated, might be done in the other infected provinces."*

As to the means employed, the testimony of another papist, Rulhiére, may be cited: "Whatever can be imagined of military licentiousness was exercised against the Calvinists. It is attributed to Foucault, intendant of Bearn, that he improved upon the most exquisite refinements of torture. Invention was employed to discover torments which should be painful without being mortal, and cause the unhappy victims to undergo the utmost which the human body can sustain without expiring."†

Thus tabooed in society, outlawed from trade, and battered and racked by the dragoons, the Huguenots had nothing to do but die or recant. The firmest suffered martyrdom; those whose spirit was

* Soulier, Hist. du Calvinisme, pp. 598, 599.

† Rulhiére, vol. 1, p. 291.

willing, but whose flesh was weak, pretended to abjure.

"That which struck men in general more than any thing else, was the material injury inflicted by the dragonades. The spiritual mischief of a forced participation in the sacrament weighed much more heavily with men of reflection and piety. To open the mouth of a heretic with the point of the bayonet, and thrust into it the host—that consecrated host which the Roman church professes to esteem it a most heinous offence to take unworthily—this offence was prescribed by those very men who decided that it was a crime of the most flagrant nature. The Spanish Inquisition had at least sufficient sense of shame to prevent its prisoners from receiving the communion and attending mass. There were a few noble protestations against it in the age of Louis XIV., especially from the abbey of Port Royal and among the Jansenists; but the majority of the clergy, hurried on by the Jesuits, forced their unhappy converts to receive the host while their very paleness and shuddering horror, as Basnage tells us, showed how their whole heart revolted at the ceremony."*

But the dragonaders did not care for sincerity; they looked only for the *éclât* of an immense army of proselytes.

The king's council, which only regarded outward acts, was as much astonished as delighted at the countless abjurations. "Sixty thousand conver-

* Felice, vol. 2, p. 60.

sions have been made in the generality of Bordeaux," wrote Louvois to his fathêr the chancellor, early in September, 1685; "twenty thousand have been won in Montauban. The rapidity with which it all takes place is such, that by the end of the month there will not be ten thousand of the heretics alive where thirty days back there were a hundred and fifty thousand."*

The duke de Noailles announced to Louvois at the same time multitudes of forced conversions at Nîmes, Uzés, Alais, Villeneuvre. "The rack is a famous proselyter," said he with a jeer. "The leading people of Nîmes," he continues, "made their abjuration in the church on the day of my arrival. There was then a chill; but things were put in a good train by quartering the military on the obstinate. The number of heretics in this province is about two hundred and forty thousand. I expect soon that I shall see all these hounds leashed to the car of Rome."†.

The hour was now considered ripe for the abolition of the nominal law of toleration. Frittered away as the statute had been until it was little more than the shadow of a law, it was still an accusing phantom in the statute book; and the government now undertook to lay this ghost: unfortunately the perturbed spirit of reform would not "down" at the king's bidding.

Louis XIV., overreached and persuaded by his confessor, his chancellor, his minister of war, and

* Felice, vol. 2, p. 60. † Ibid., p. 61.

his mistress, ill-informed perhaps as to the real condition of the kingdom, rejoicing over fictitious conversions, and duped because he lived surrounded by flatterers, like an Asiatic sultan in the recesses of his palace—Louis XIV, to whom Louvois and La Chaise had promised that "not a drop of blood should be shed,"* having consulted Harlai and Bossuet, signed the Revocation of the Edict of Nantes on the 18th of October, 1685,† and enshrined his name for ever as a monument of execration. It was at this time that he added to his other mottoes that of *Lex una sub uno*.‡ There was no need to write it in blood at Versailles; the hand of death had already engraved it on the frontlet of the monarchy. God left this king, broken by age, soured by disappointment, humiliated, his early glories turned to ashes on his shrivelled lips, to occupy the throne for thirty disgraceful years after this unhappy event, to bear the load of the crime he had committed.

The preamble of the Act of Revocation contains a brazen falsehood; what then can be expected of the body of a paper which opens with a lie? "We behold now," says the king, "with just gratitude to God, that our cares have attained the end which we proposed; the greater and better part of our subjects of the pretended reformed religion have embraced the Roman faith, and the execution of the

* Œuvres Complétes de Louis de St. Lucien, vol. 2, p. 53.

† Felice, Browning, Rulhiére, Soubier, Noailles, and others.

‡ Louis XIV., et son Siécle.

Edict of Nantes is therefore unnecessary." This is an abstract of the act: All further exercise of the reformed worship in the kingdom illegal. The Huguenot pastors ordered to quit the realm within a fortnight; and meantime to perform no clerical function, on pain of being sent to the galleys. A promise to all ministers who should become converts, of a stipend greater by one third than that which they had hitherto enjoyed, with the reversion of a moiety to their widows. A dispensation from academical studies to those which wished to practice at the bar. Parents forbidden to instruct their children in the reformed religion, and commanded to have them christened in the Romish churches, on pain of five hundred livres fine. All refugees ordered to return to France within four months, or forfeit their property. All religionists forbidden to emigrate, under penalty of the galleys if men, or seclusion for life if women. And all laws against relapsed heretics confirmed.*

Such were the main enactments of this atrocious act. "It gave," says M. Felice, "a fatal blow to the traditional policy of France—to the policy of Henry IV., Richelieu, Mazarin, and even to that of Louis XIV. himself. It was no longer possible to retain the natural allies of France in Protestant Europe, when Christendom resounded with the lamentations of the Huguenots. Protestantism rose *en masse* against the "grand monarch." Its chief was William of Orange, and the parliamentary resolu-

* Felice, vol. 2, p. 62.

tion of 1688 was the response to the royal crime of 1685."*

Meantime the act was put in force. "We have reached the end,"† said the old chancellor Letellier as he affixed the seal of state to the nascent edict, and chanted the *Nunc dimittis* of the holy Simeon with blasphemous triumph. Letellier, of whom the count de Grammont once said, on seeing him emerge from the king's closet, "I picture to myself a polecat who has just killed some fowls, and is licking his jaws, yet stained with their blood"‡—Letellier was mistaken; for the sequel proved this: that it is easier to make martyrs than apostates, and that the power of conviction is stronger than material forces.

The Act of Revocation was carried out with special rigor against the pastors; even the letter of the edict was exceeded: that granted them a fortnight's delay; but Claude,§ the famous pastor of the Parisian Huguenots, whose learning and acumen had worsted the brilliant Bossuet, received orders to quit the capital within twenty-four hours after the signature of the paper; and this *seditious fellow*, as Madame de Maintenon termed him,‖ was

* Felice, vol. 2, p. 63.

† Burnet, vol. 1, p. 402. Benoit, vol. 4.

‡ Vallaire La Beaumelle; also cited by Browning, p. 381.

§ Jean Claude was born at La Sabretat, in Rouerque, in 1619. ‖ Letter to the countess de St. Grau, dated 25th October, 1685. He was a man of piety, a learned theologian, a skilful orator, a wise and moderate writer, endowed with judgment and a readiness of mind which never deserted him. He was singularly well qualified to withstand the champions of the Roman church; and

accompanied by one of the king's footmen, who did not lose sight of him for a moment till he crossed the frontier. The other preachers of the larger towns were given two days in which to prepare for departure. Those living in the provinces had a

while his genius did not equal that of Bossuet, with whom he contended publicly, he was that great orator's superior in the solidity of his learning and the force of his argumentation. Félice, vol. 2, p. 9.

Pierre Dubose was another celebrated pastor of the Huguenots. He was born at Bayeux, in 1623, and was esteemed one of the greatest preachers in the reformed church of his century. "It may be said of him without flattery," says his contemporary Eli Benoît, "that he possessed all the qualifications of a Christian orator. His mind was enlightened by an acquaintance with *belles-lettres*. He was a good philosopher, a sound theologian, and a judicious critic. His figure was good, his voice at once sweet and powerful, and his action well regulated. The church at Charenton, in 1658, sent him the most urgent invitation to come to Paris. Marshal Turenne, the marquis de la Force, and other persons of rank added their solicitations; but Dubose refused to leave his charge at Caen, because he held that a pastor cannot with a good conscience leave his flock without first obtaining their express consent. When this invitation was repeated in 1670, the archbishop of Paris went thrice in the week to beg the king not to confirm the appointment. Was it that he thought the eloquence of Bourdaloue and Bossuet inadequate to the task of maintaining the Romanist cause against his assault? Let an anecdote answer. Dubose, who was often sent by the oppressed churches to plead their cause, was commissioned in 1688 to ask the king to enforce the Edict of Nantes. When Dubose began to speak, Louis appeared listless; but gradually he began to listen, and at last gave evident marks of great attention. The bearing, the voice, the serious and natural manner, the eloquent words of the orator completely triumphed over the repugnance which he had been taught to feel towards the heretical ministers. "Madame," said he to the queen, who stood by, "I have just heard the best speaker in my kingdom." Then turning to the courtiers, he added, "I certainly never heard any one speak so well." Benoît, Hist. de l'Edit de Nantes.

little longer space; but in open defiance of all the rights of nature, they were all deprived of those of their children who were more than seven years old. Some were even forced to abandon infants at the breast, and others supported broken-hearted wives who accompanied them on the road to banishment.

Abjurations had been counted on; few were made. Nearly all those preachers who, in a moment of stupefaction and terror, had denied their faith, returned to it again, and accepted serenely the penalty of their relapse.* Old men of ninety might be seen summoning up their remaining strength to set out on distant travel, and more than one perished ere he reached the asylum where he had hoped to rest his faltering steps and weary head.†

So long as the Huguenots had any thing to lose, though but the shadow of their ancient liberties, the empty name of Henry Quatre's great edict, the majority confined themselves to presenting petitions and praying for a redress of grievances. They cherished a hope that the sanctity of law, justice, and humanity would be reawakened in the breast of their monarch; and so far did they carry their endurance, as to give rise to the proverbial expression, *a Huguenot's patience.*‡ But when they lost all, absolutely all, they consulted only what was due to conscience and to their outraged faith; and by continuing to brave the most barbarous of edicts,

* Benoît, Hist. de l'Edit de Nantes.

† Felice, vol. 2, p. 69.

‡ Ibid.

in the face of exile, the galleys, and death, they wore out the ferocity of their tormentors.

Emigration now attained gigantic proportions. In spite of cunning preventive measures—in spite of constantly reiterated decrees, denouncing death upon all who should venture to pass the French frontier—in spite of cordons of soldiers stationed to dragoon back all refugees, the tide of emigration set resolutely, irresistibly towards Protestant Europe. England, Switzerland, Holland, Prussia, Denmark, and Sweden generously relieved their first necessities.

The depopulation of the kingdom was frightful. The best authorities estimate that France lost five hundred thousand of her best, most intelligent, moral, and industrious citizens.* She lost besides sixty millions of francs in specie, and her most flourishing manufactures;† while four hundred thousand lives paid the forfeit of the reign of terror.‡

This was what it cost to suppress the truth in France.

Thousands of emigrants perished of fatigue, cold, and hunger, besides those lost by shipwreck, and those shot by the soldiers while attempting to escape. Thousands more were taken, chained to assassins and other desperate criminals, then marched across the kingdom, that the sight of them might strike their coreligionists with terror; then they were condemned to row with the convict crews. The gal-

* Sismondi, Mem. de St. Simon. Félice, vol. 2, p. pp. 73, 74, etc. † Ibid. ‡ Felice.

leys at Marseilles were crowded with these Christians; and among them were magistrates, officers, gentlemen, and octogenarians.* The convents and the town of Constance at Aigue-Mortes were crowded with devoted women. But neither threats, barbarities, nor brutal and unheard of punishments could conquer the patience, the firmness, the energy, the sublime faithfulness of these oppressed consciences.

Of the moral results of this wholesale and most infamous proscription it is needless to speak. They are palpable. The revocation of the Edict of Nantes was the *avant courier* of the Revolution of 1789. The religion of reason was the inevitable outgrowth of the religion of bestiality. Robespierre was the counterpart of Letellier. The act of 1685 exiled Christ and struck the people; the frenzy of 1789 was the return blow of the people ignorant of Christ: the Revolution was France smiting the tyranny which Louis XIV. inaugurated; it was the explosion of ten centuries of wickedness, of bigotry, of oppression, of perfidy, in an awful crash. It was GOD raining his vengeance upon the Sodom of the monarchy and on the Gomorrah of the papacy.

Multitudes of writers bear ample witness to the economic ruin which the revocation caused. "Trade," says St. Simon, "was ruined; a quarter of the kingdom was perceptibly depopulated."† "Whole villages were deserted," says Sismondi; "many of the larger towns lost half their denizens;

* Felice.

† Mem. de St. Simon.

hundreds of factories were closed; some branches of industry became altogether extinct; and vast districts absolutely ached for hands to cultivate them."* "The Huguenots," remarks Lamartine, "repaid the generous hospitality of those peoples with whom they found a home, by contributing the riches of their cunning labor, by the example of their faith, by their lives of integrity; and while they thus enriched their adopted countries, France was impoverished."† Lemontey says, "The French Protestants carried into England the secret of those valuable machines which have laid the foundations of her vast wealth, while the complaints of these proscribed exiles cemented an avenging league at Augsburg."‡

Thus it should seem that the revocation of the Edict of Nantes was economic suicide as well as religious death. That fatal act not only filled the *salons* of modern France with infidel philosophers, it also brought pecuniary ruin. France colonized her hands away from her mouth.

Only one other nation has been guilty of so barbarous an act. In the sixteenth century, Philip II. expelled the Moors from his kingdom. Bankrupt and despicable, largely in consequence of that edict, Spain stands to-day "wicked but in will, of means bereft," serving, like the drunken helot, to show how disgusting and ruinous mean vice is.

* Sismondi, Hist. de France. † Lamartine.

‡ Essai sur l'Etablissement Monarchique de Louis XIV, p. 413.

But the exile of the Huguenots, though it could not be more ruinous than the Spanish perfidy, touched a meaner depth. The Moors were pagans, and in one sense interlopers; the Huguenots were Christians and Frenchmen. When France drove them into exile, she banished her manufacturers, her traders, her artisans; and in consequence, industry languished for three generations. Indeed, France has never regained the vantage-ground which she lost, and which the wiser policy of Great Britain won, at that epoch. The cunning of England lassoed Lyons and Marseilles and Paris to the feet of London and Manchester and Liverpool, and she has ever since kept them there. Holland, in a material sense, gained more by this act than she had lost by the victorious invasions of Louis XIV.; while the Huguenot colonies planted on the Cape of Good Hope, on the snowy steppes of the Cordilleras, and, beside the sounding Atlantic, gained the New World for God, and compensated for the mischief worked his cause by the iniquitous politics of the elder continent.

CHAPTER XXXVI.

A RÉSUMÉ.

It is estimated by authoritative historians that, despite the enormous exodus of the proscribed reformers after the suppression of Henry Quatre's edict, there still remained a million Huguenots in France, living under the ban and at the peril of the law.*

Meted and peeled, they clung to their faith with stubborn devotion. Their unwearied appeals for justice reached Paris borne on every breeze. But steeled and unmoved, the king only shrugged his shoulders, and muttered, "Persecute," while the servile magistracy echoed, "So stands the law."

But the conscience of a generous people may not always be fettered by cruel parchments. Live growths rive dead matter. Pulse-beats smite down the strongest tyrannies. Give it time, and a spear of grass will topple over the Pyramids. Gradually France, educated by the suffering of three centuries, grew broader than her statute-book. Iniquity was indeed enacted into law; bigotry was the incorporated, fundamental, avowed policy of the state. Yet the last years of the reign of Louis XIV. were gilded by the dawn of a larger charity. Religion was milder when it breathed through Fénélon. Phi-

* Sismondi, Hist. de France; Felice, Mem. de Nevers, and others.

losophy was gentler when it spoke through the lips of Pascal.* Harsh statutes were construed intó impotence wher D'Aguesseau pronounced judgment. Letters were humaner; the collectors of lewd anecdotes, the gatherers of the broken crumbs of history, recor.lers of the gossip of *cafés* and the whispers of the back-stairs of the Louvre, no longer monopolized literature; and soon, through the tragedy of "ESTHER," Racine raised his voice against intolerance.†

This was the insurrection of civilization. "It was the human mind which, constantly persecuted, opposed, headed off, has disappeared only to appear again; and passing from one labor to another, has taken successively, from age to age, the figure of all the great reformers. It was the human mind which was called John Huss, and which did not die on the funeral-pile of Constance; which was named Luther, and shook Romanism to its centre; which was called Calvin, and organized the Reformation; which, since history began, has transformed societies according to a law progressively acceptable to

* Flaise Pascal, a famous French mathematician and philosopher, born 1623, died 1662. He figured in the controversy between the Jesuits and the Port Royal school; and his "Provincial Letters" are said to have been the origin of the hostile feeling against the "Society of Jesus" which, a century later, drove them out of France for the second time.

† Racine depicted Louvois in the blackest colors; and to avoid all chance of misconstruction, he put into Haman's mouth the precise words of Louvois, which escaped him in the delirium of his pride. Nor did the poet scruple to refer to Louis:

"Et le roi trop crédule a signé ct edit."

reason; which has been theocracy, aristocracy, monarchy, and which is to-day religious democracy; which has been Babylon, Tyre, Jerusalem, Athens, Rome; which has been by turns error, illusion, schism, protestation, truth; but which has always groped towards the Just, the Beautiful, the True, enlightening multitudes, ennobling life, raising more and more the head of the people towards the Right, and the head of the individual towards God."*

The government of France might slaughter individuals, might annihilate Paris to the last pavement, and the kingdom to the last hamlet, still it would have done nothing. "There would yet remain to be destroyed something always paramount, above the generations, between man and his Maker; something which has written the books, invented the arts, discovered the worlds, founded the civilizations; something which will always grasp, under the form of revolution, what is not yielded under the form of progress; something which is unseizable as the light, unapproachable as the sun, and which God calls the human mind."†

But while the premonitory phases of a revolution were beginning to appear, the law stood long unchanged, pitiless. The war of the Camisards stained the seventeenth century; it was a frightful tragedy enacted by the Huguenot peasants of the Vivavais, frenzied by that "oppression" which, as

* Victor Hugo, Speech in the National Assembly, 1851.

† Ibid.

Solomon says, "makes the wise man mad." After the employment of fiend-like cruelties, in which the demoniacal ingenuity of Indian torture was combined with the scientific inventions of semi-civilization, the Camisards were subjugated—the throats of a whole population were cut.*

Thus passed away the age of Louis XIV.; the penal code unsoftened, but public opinion liberalized.

The first years of the reign of Louis XV. were barren of good fruit. Spasmodic acts of bigotry occurred, but the lawyers lingered more and more in the execution of the prescribed barbarities; and when a nation shudders at its laws, they are already half abolished. There were even instances of judgments pronounced by judges directly against the obnoxious statutes;† they preferred to see their decisions reversed by appeal, rather than suffer the humiliation of having them confirmed—obeying justice in disobeying the law.

Disgusted by the mummeries of the Vatican, France began at this period to imbibe the poison of infidelity; but the scholars of the philosophical school did not bestow one good word upon the Huguenots. This was happy; the benediction of infidel *savans* would not have been appropriate. Mon-

* Pardoe, Louis XIV. and the Court of France, vol. 2, p. 341. Bruey's Hist. du Fanaticisme, vol. 1, p. 183. Browning, p. 385, et seq.

† Witness the judicial records of France in this age. Some of these decisions may be found in Felice; they are referred to in "Huguenots in France and America," vol. 2.

tesquieu did not mention these oppressed children of God's right hand; Rousseau, the child of Calvin's own city, attacked Romanism more than he defended the Protestant idea. Between this bastard philosophy and Christianity there was little in common, no *point d'appui.*

In 1744, a Huguenot synod was convened at Nîsmes. Denied baptism, burial, and the marriage ceremony, deprived of a legal *status,* they determined to hold their services in the open air. "This," said one, "is better than the catacombs of the earliest Christians; since God gives us the field, let us praise him there."* These meetings were called "*Assemblées du desert.*" To avoid awakening the suspicion of the government, the Huguenots repaired unarmed to their forest *rendezvous.* There,

> "In the darkling wood,
> Amid the cool and silence they knelt down,
> And offered to the Mightiest solemn thanks
> And supplications; for their simple hearts
> Might not resist the sacred influences
> Which, from the stilly twilight of the place,
> And from the gray old trunks, that high in heaven
> Mingled their mossy boughs, and from the sound
> Of the invisible breath, that swayed at once
> All their green tops, stole over them, and bowed
> Their spirits with the thought of boundless power
> And inaccessible majesty."

And here, under the canopy of heaven, the sacraments were celebrated, the rites of sepulture were performed, and the union of affection was sanctified by religion. Yet the *marriages of the desert,* as they

* Lemontey, Essai sur l'Établissement Monarchique de Louis Quatorze.

were called, were afterwards termed *concubinage*, and the hereditary estates of the posterity of persons so united were forfeited.*

But though a crushing yoke rested upon the necks of the Huguenots, each year brought some alleviation. Four generations of persecutors and of victims passed away. *Le bien aimé*, as the most indolent and sensual of kings was ironically nicknamed, was huddled into the tomb of Hugh Capét. Louis XVI. commenced his inauspicious reign; and Marie Antoinette, beautiful as Burke described her, shared the fatal throne. Then, in 1787, the statute of toleration glittered on the horizon. It was the offspring of patience and persistence, of faith and prayer. The Huguenots wearied out the Inquisition.

The edict of toleration, clutched from the unwilling grip of the government by the impetuous statesmanship of the impending Revolution one hundred and two years after the revocation of the Edict of Nantes, was narrow and niggardly in its main features; but it granted to the non-conformists four things: the right to live in France, and to practise a profession or carry on a trade without molestation on account of religion; permission to marry legally; an authorization to certify births before the judge of their place of residence; regulations as to the burial of those who could not be interred according to the Roman ritual.†

* Lemontey, Essai sur l'Établissement, etc.

† Répertoire Ecclesiast., pp. 6, 7.

So ran the text; but the practice was not so narrow as the precept. The Huguenots had gained a legal *status*, and although they were forbidden to assemble for public worship, yet no penalty enforced the prohibition. They had not been deterred from the exercise of their religion by the fiercest prohibitory legislation; should they now desist when there was no punishment?

The heroic congregations of the wilderness held grateful jubilee; their forty years seemed well-nigh ended, and Canaan loomed up before their glistening eyes. "At length," cried Lafayette, himself one of the most strenuous advocates of every species of equality on either continent, great in the beneficence of goodness, "at length Protestants are permitted to become husbands and fathers."*

But the frail breakwater of this decree was not of sufficient importance to arrest the surging tide which now began to gurgle round the throat of France. One by one the liberties of the kingdom had been entrapped and bound. Socialist manifestoes terminated in a Jesuitical policy. An immense intrigue was baptized with the name of government.

Then intervened the Revolution. Into that yawning abyss tumbled every thing—law, order, religion. The heads of Romanist and Protestant alike fell under the indiscriminating revolutionary hatchet.† The frenzied insurgents propped up the corpse of martyred liberty upon its gory tomb;

* Huguenots in France, etc., vol. 2. † Félice, vol. 2.

then hastening to the market-place, they crowned the goddess of a spurious reason with garlands of flowers. Thus the ecclesiasticism of the Vatican, which had been rampant in France for a thousand years, inciting every crime, lauding every infamy, gloating over every outrage upon human nature, "stealing the livery of heaven to serve the devil in"—this monstrosity called Romanism ended fitly in a scoff and a blasphemy.

'T is a history full of blood and full of tears. "Never," says Lamartine, "did weaknesses more quickly engender faults; faults, crimes; crimes, punishment. That retributive justice which God has implanted in our very acts, as a conscience more sacred than the fatalism of the ancients, never manifested itself more unequivocally; never was the law of morality illustrated by more ample testimony, or avenged more mercilessly. Blood spilled like water not only shrieks in accents of terror and of pity, but gives a lesson and an example to mankind."*

At length the phantom of this bastard liberty was laid; "*Cà ira*" and the "*Marseillaise*" lost their fierceness; the tamed insurrectionary choruses died out in a plaintive wail; the revolution sobbed itself to sleep in curses. The frightful days of 1793 passed into history; above the subsiding waves reappeared the turrets and towers of old institutions. Even before the overthrow of the Republic, the "Goddess of Reason" was depos-

* Lamartine, History of the Girondists, vol. 1, introduction.

ed;* and the dismal inscription, "Death is an eternal sleep," ceased to insult God and the human heart.† Once awakened from their awful trance, men came to feel that "there would be no dignity in life, that it would not be worth the holding, if in death we wholly perish. All that lightens labor and sanctifies toil; all that renders man brave, good, wise, noble, patient, benevolent, just, humble, and at the same time great, worthy of intelligence, worthy of liberty, worthy of God, is to have perpetually before him the vision of a better world darting its rays of celestial splendor through the dark shadows of this present life. No one shall unjustly or needlessly suffer in the hereafter. Death is restitution. By limiting man's end and aim to this terrestrial and material existence, we aggravate all his miseries by the terrible negation at its close. No; there is an ulterior life. In that, mercy reigns through Christ; hope is its beacon, and the 'perfect liberty of the sons of God' is its fruition. The law of the material world is gravitation; of the moral world, equity. At the end of all reappears God, 'Judge of the quick and the dead.'"‡

When Napoleon usurped the government, one of his first acts was to reëstablish religion. In 1795, a decree was issued authorizing the free exercise of religious worship. But anxious to win the benediction of the pope, Bonaparte leaned in

* Thiers. Consulate and Empire. † Ibid.

‡ Victor Hugo, Speech in the National Assembly, 1851.

his policy towards the Vatican, and Protestantism was shackled by mild conditions.*

Under the restoration, Bonaparte's edict remained substantially unaltered. Charles X. left the law untouched, and on his flight bequeathed it to Louis Philippe. When the government of the citizen king went down before an after-dinner speech and an epigram, when a cab carried the new royalty into exile, toleration did not follow it. Firm through the days of the second Republic, it likewise survived the *coup d'état* of Louis Bonaparte in 1852, and soon received the *imprimatur* of the Empire.

Napoleon, anxious, like his uncle, to reëstablish the principle of *authority*, which in France is based on the ancient traditions of the papacy, has placated the Vatican by a succession of complaisant acts which have given Romanism the *éclat* of the national religion, and whose tendency is to suppress the growth of the dissenters. Napoleon perceives that the natural, inevitable gravitation of Protestantism is towards democracy. He remembers De Tocqueville's prophecy that all Europe is gradually marching to that goal.† Hence the emperor, at the head of an abnormal government, cannot but look with suspicion upon the non-conformists.

Still, despite the open unfriendliness of the state and the sinister efforts of the Romanist party, the descendants of the Huguenots maintain their

* Thiers, Consulate and Empire.

† De Tocqueville, Democracy in America.

ground. The Revolution robbed the ultramontanists of great *prestige* by the confiscation of the immense church property; it also made the people suspicious of their ascendency in the *état civile.* This gives the reformers a fulcrum upon which to rest their lever. They have several colleges, one at Montauban, one at Nîsmes, one at Paris.* The south of France, the ancient strong-hold of the Reformation, is yet the *rendezvous* of Protestantism.† The Lutheran, the Wesleyan, the Calvinist denominations are militant;‡ and they can afford to be patient, sure that, since their essential principles are in conformity with the fundamental tenets of the New Testament, the future is theirs, and that they will eventually subdue the conscience of the human race beneath their sway.

"Wrong," says Victor Hugo, "is but a hideous flash in the darkness; right is an eternal ray."

The object of the Huguenots was the demolition of idols, the purification of the sanctuary, the reinauguration of primitive Christianity; to bring man to God through the divine Redeemer, the "one Mediator," by the abolition of an impious, mediatorial priest-caste, and the promulgation of the golden truth which Luther reaffirmed, and which Calvin echoed, "justification by faith" in Christ, the invocation of His sole intercession at the heavenly bar.

Standing in the sunlight of the nineteenth cen-

* Felice, Hist. of French Protestantism. Browning.

† Ibid.

‡ Browning, p. 439.

tury, the age of unfettered lips, of myriad churches, of open Bibles, whose great heart throbs with that love of God which is "perfect liberty," who shall say that the Huguenots have not grandly performed their work?

Let each of us reverently thank God for the light of their example; let us determine to be worthy of the past, and the apostles of a sublimer future.